NETWARE TO WINDOWS NT COMPLETE

NetWare to Windows NT Complete

Arnold Villeneuve
Wayne McKinnon

McGraw-Hill
New York • San Francisco • Washington, D.C. • Auckland
Bogotá • Caracas • Lisbon • London • Madrid • Mexico City
Milan • Montreal • New Delhi • San Juan • Singapore
Sydney • Tokyo • Toronto

Library of Congress Cataloging-in-Publication Data

Villeneuve, Arnold
    Netware to Windows NT Complete / Arnold Villeneuve, Wayne McKinnon.
        p.   cm.
    Includes index.
    ISBN 0-07-913171-9
    1. Microsoft Windows NT.   2. NetWare (Computer file)
I. McKinnon, Wayne.   II. Title.
QA76.76.063V4515   1997
005.4'476—dc21   97-44419
                                                                CIP

McGraw-Hill

A Division of The McGraw-Hill Companies

Copyright © 1998 by The McGraw-Hill Companies, Inc. Printed in the United States of America. Except as permitted under the United States Copyright Act of 1976, no part of this publication may be reproduced or distributed in any form or by any means, or stored in a data base or retrieval system, without the prior written permission of the publisher.

1 2 3 4 5 6 7 8 9 0   DOC/DOC   9 0 2 1 0 9 8 7

P/N 067477-9
PART OF
ISBN 0-07-913171-9

The sponsoring editor for this book was Judy Brief and the production supervisor was Pamela Pelton. It was set in Century Schoolbook by Douglas & Gayle, Limited.

Printed and bound by R. R. Donnelley & Sons Company.

McGraw-Hill books are available at special quantity discounts to use as premiums and sales promotions, or for use in corporate training programs. For more information, please write to Director of Special Sales, McGraw-Hill, 11 West 19th Street, New York, NY 10011. Or contact your local bookstore.

Information contained in this work has been obtained by The McGraw-Hill Companies, Inc. ("McGraw-Hill") from sources believed to be reliable. However, neither McGraw-Hill nor its authors guarantees the accuracy or completeness of any information published herein and neither McGraw-Hill nor its authors shall be responsible for any errors, omissions, or damages arising out of use of this information. This work is published with the understanding that McGraw-Hill and its authors are supplying information but are not attempting to render engineering or other professional services. If such services are required, the assistance of an appropriate professional should be sought.

 This book is printed on recycled, acid-free paper containing a minimum of 50% recycled de-inked fiber.

This book is dedicated to my two children:
Samantha Hope and Sabrina Heather

—Arnold Villeneuve

This book is dedicated to my Uncle Jim Warren

—Wayne McKinnon

ACKNOWLEDGMENTS

First and foremost, I would like to thank my partner and soul mate Jeannette Larabie. I strive to be worthy of your goodness to me.

Second, I would like to thank Wayne McKinnon for being my coauthor. His work on Chapters 1, 5, and 6 has enhanced the book significantly. Also, he is to be credited with producing the CD-ROM single-handedly. I am fortunate to have him as a friend.

I would also like to thank the people at Learning Tree International for their support in the publication of this book. Finally, my thanks go to two important people at McGraw-Hill: Jenniffer Digiovani, who started this project, and Judy Brief, who helped us finish it.

Also due for a thank you are Ray Robinson and the folks at Douglas & Gayle, Ltd., for their great prepress work. And, I would like to personally thank Kirk Metcalf and Judith Montagano for their continued support—thanks, people. Kirk in particular must be commended for helping me set up the software I used for capturing screenshots in this book—thanks, Kirk.

Finally, I would like to thank Drew Birkett for being my friend. None better shall ye find!

—Arnold Villeneuve

Special thanks to my wife Heather, and my children Shelby and Ryan for being there for me and for understanding about the times I couldn't be there for them. Our times together keep me going when we are apart. Thanks to my parents Russ and Irene for creating the ambition and desire to succeed.

Thanks to our many clients and students for their never-ending quest for knowledge and know how. You have helped us dig deep to find the answers and remind us that you can always learn more.

I would like to personally thank Arnold Villeneuve for sharing this opportunity with me. His tenacity is what made this book a reality. I would also like to thank Jennifer Holt-Digiovani for seeing the potential in this project, as well as Judy Brief and her assistant Alice Tung for their determination to make this the best book possible. My thanks go out to all involved in this project including the hard-working production staff.

Additionally, I would like to thank Tom Kingsbury and Carlos Dwarka for being my sounding boards and Jim Malone, Jack Vos, Carlo Petrocco, Kalman

Fejes, Bob Uline, Fredrick Ranger, and Nagwa Korressa for inviting me into their challenging environments to hone my skills by solving their complex problems. This list would not be complete without mentioning Gurdon E. Merchant, Jr. for contributing to the book and my closest collegues Jeff Cockwell, Angus Ma, Randy Evans, Carlo, Michel Labarre, and Jim Logan.

The Mentors in my life, who shared their knowledge, gave me opportunities, and had high expectations include Jim Lougheed, Doug Wong, Attilla Peters, John Platts, Gary Fox, David Songco, and most importantly my Uncle Jim Warren to whom I dedicate this book.

Finally, I would like to thank all of the System Engineers at Novell, Microsoft, and other companies whose dedication to their clients and their products' success has enabled these two operating systems to coexist so well.

—Wayne McKinnon

CONTENTS

Contents

Contents

Contents

INTRODUCTION

Introduction to NetWare and Windows NT: A Practical Guide to Integration and Migration

Today's corporate and government networks are seldom singular in nature. Rarely will you find an enterprise network with just one network operating system. This book tackles the issues you will face integrating and migrating between the two most popular network operating systems on the planet: Novell NetWare and Microsoft Windows NT. This practical guide will show you all the aspects of integrating the most common desktop operating systems such as MS-DOS, Windows for Workgroups, Windows 95, and Windows NT Workstation with both NetWare and Windows NT. The goal of the book is to help you achieve a single user name space to facilitate easy access to multiplatform resources by your user community. Ultimately, you may decide to migrate fully to one platform or the other; either way, this book covers the issues you will face heading in either direction. A CD-ROM with many helpful resources and Internet links is also included.

Chapter 1, "NetWare and Windows NT Platforms," is an introduction to the two operating systems, NetWare and Windows NT. This chapter will help you understand how the operating systems differ, and also understand their strengths and their weaknesses. It provides a comparison of the management used by NetWare and Windows NT Server and what influence the differing approaches may have on your overall operating system choice. This chapter identifies issues important to consider for migrating to a single network operating system or for organizations choosing a network operating system for the first time. Finally, you will also gain a historical perspective of how the two operating systems evolved and some of the market forces that have given each operating system its place in the market.

Chapter 2, "Integration and Migration Issues: Planning, Management, and Tools," covers the major areas of concern for integrating NetWare and Windows NT. This chapter will set the stage for much of the rest of the book, as it will provide an overview of all the possible ways to integrate clients and servers in a multi NetWare and Windows NT network environment. Particular emphasis will be made on the project management and support issues involved. We will cover the migration processes and how to support a single network user login/logon in a multi NetWare and Windows NT network environment (although this issue is discussed more completely in Chapter 6, "Directory Services Manager for NetWare"). Finally, during any information systems integration and migration project, several basic steps or procedures should be followed. We will highlight these procedures and take you through actual case study examples.

In Chapter 3, "Protocol Integration," we identify all the network communication protocols used in NetWare and Windows NT network environments. Considering that organizations will potentially need to support multiple network communication protocols, we will discuss the challenges associated with multiprotocol network environments and provide heterogeneous solutions that will create efficient use of the underlying network infrastructure. Given that people can communicate from several directions over the network, we will review procedures to configure multiprotocol support on NetWare and Windows NT client workstations and servers. You will see that both systems support a range of networking transport and service protocols. We will focus particular attention on what each protocol can do because, although both network operating systems will support the same lower level transport protocol for internetworking, such support does not imply the ability to access services (file and print) running on both of the same systems. Whereas Chapter 3 covers the detail about network protocols, Chapter 4 will go into the details of implementing the many protocol variations. We cannot stress enough that a good understanding of the Open System Interconnection (OSI) Reference Model and the functions it describes is critical to later understanding the protocol solutions that vendors such as Novell and Microsoft provide.

Chapter 4, "Client Connectivity," covers NetWare and Windows NT client workstation connectivity options. Particular emphasis will be placed on highlighting connectivity from any side of the network: NetWare clients to Windows NT server, and Windows clients to NetWare server. Access to the NetWare server will be reviewed through two possible methods: directly through NetWare client software or indirectly through the Windows NT Server Gateway. After we are connected, we will demonstrate how NetWare command utilities function differently depending on which of the two connection methods are used and why the differences exists. From the Windows NT perspective, we will cover how the Performance Monitor can be used to monitor the client driver throughput to assist you in determining which client connection method best addresses your requirements. Finally, we will look at some of the alternative methods that can be used to connect network clients to either

NetWare or Windows NT such as Network File System (NFS), Macintosh Appellate, and File Transfer Protocol.

Chapter 5, "Server Integration," will help you plan your installation of the gateway services for NetWare that allow Windows NT server clients to access a NetWare server. We will also look at the installation of file and print services for NetWare; these services allow NetWare clients to access Windows NT.

For most computer systems, the expense of initial purchase and installation is not nearly as significant as the cost of ongoing maintenance and support. You should not be surprised, then, that two technologies are more costly to support than one because the level or amount of expertise and labor could be double.

Having multiple network operating systems does not magically make work simpler. In essence, many of the same tasks must now be performed twice—for example, system backups, user account maintenance, and so on. If you are to introduce Windows NT into a NetWare environment, the best solution to user management is to find a common utility that will allow you to manage both systems.

Chapter 6, "Directory Services Manager for NetWare," will tackle the task of managing two network directory systems in a multiple network operating system environment. In particular, we will focus on how to manage Windows NT and NetWare user names from one central management utility—Microsoft or Novell.

Chapter 7, "Migration," focuses on the issues of migrating between network operating platforms. Microsoft's Directory Services for NetWare allows NetWare servers to be managed as if they were resources in a Windows NT domain. Novell is also introducing its own strategy, code-named TOBASCO, to manage Windows NT servers. TOBASCO allows Windows NT to use Novell's Directory services by loading an NDS service on Windows NT. We will look at a similar third-party solution called Synchronicity for Windows NT from NetVision. Synchronicity allows Windows NT domains to become part of the NetWare 4.x Directory Services. Windows NT domain management is still used; however, Synchronicity synchronizes changes with the NetWare NDS. In this chapter, then, we will examine single management strategies based on Microsoft's Directory Services for NetWare (DSNW) and Synchronicity.

The main focus of Chapter 8, "Migration Project Planning Overview," will be an overview of some of the issues associated with project management. You can find many good books written on project management, so we won't try to make you an expert in one chapter. Many technical people are simply not good planners. We are great doers and carry out technology implementation at breakneck speeds. Projects of this type, though, take serious thought, consideration, and need to be well planned if they are to be implemented successfully. Therefore, the goal of this chapter is to introduce you to some of the project planning issues you may want to examine further.

Finally, in the appendix, a dictionary of terms will help you grasp the terminology used in both networking environments.

If you have now or are planning to have a mixed NetWare and Windows NT network, this book will assist you during and long after your integration and migration stages.

CHAPTER 1

NetWare and Windows NT Platforms

This chapter introduces the two operating systems, Net-Ware and Windows NT. It will help you understand how the operating systems differ, and understand their strengths and their weaknesses. This chapter provides a comparison of the management used by NetWare and Windows NT Server and what influence the differing approaches may have on your overall operating system choice. This chapter also identifies issues important to consider for migrating to a single network operating system or for organizations choosing a network operating system for the first time. Finally, you will also gain a historical perspective of how the two operating systems evolved and learn about some of the market forces that have given each operating system its place in the market.

Chapter Objectives

- Identifying the differences between NetWare and Windows NT
- The history of NetWare and Windows NT
- The NOS market share
- Network management models
- NOS processing methodologies
- Windows NT multiprocessing
- NetWare multiprocessing
- NT system fault tolerance

Network Operating Systems: A Historical Perspective

The trend toward networking PCs as we know it today began shortly after the PC hit the desktop. "Sneakernet" became a very popular method of transferring data from one PC to another. In this process, information was copied to a floppy disk and walked over to another PC, but this process was not very efficient. Early PC network operating systems were simply extensions to the DOS operating system used by most PCs. Because DOS became the most popular operating system for personal computers, a network operating system that could extend the power of DOS was sure to be a hit. In ideal terms, this meant any PC running DOS could talk to any other PC assuming that they had the same *network operating system* (NOS) and the correct network hardware. IBM led the way initially by leveraging the corporate accounts that put a lot of faith in IBM as the trend setter of the day; after all, the PC was its idea.

Soon other vendors took to the market with network operating systems from not only IBM, but 3Com, Novell, and Microsoft; they were later followed by Banyan as well as a slew of others. Due to a lack of standards, PCs that were clients of one network operating system could not talk to servers from another vendor. If this communication was required, the common solution was to create two boot disks, one for each operating system. If users in sales who had a 3Com network, for example, wanted to access files from the IBM network in accounting, they simply had to shut down their PCs, insert the proper boot disks for the IBM network, and reboot the PCs. They had to repeat the same process to return to the 3Com network. Interoperability was at an all-time low.

At this point, PC hard disks were usually formatted using the DOS FAT file system. FAT, which stands for File Allocation Table, is essentially an index of places files can be found on a hard disk. Although better, more efficient methods exist for storing files, the FAT file system is still the number one file system used on PCs today. Most network operating systems of the day relied on the FAT file system as a means of organizing files on the file server, a dedicated PC where users could store their files for others to access.

Peer-to-peer networking was also popular with some vendors whose operating systems allowed one user to access files on another user's PC. Because file servers were essentially just DOS workstations anyway, why spend the extra money on a file server? Of course, this setup meant that if many people were accessing one user's hard disk, the extra work load would slow down work considerably for that user. Dedicated file servers are definitely the way to go if you want performance.

Novell took a slightly different approach from the rest and initially did not even allow peer-to-peer networking. Instead, it developed an operating system that ran on a dedicated file server and called it *client server networking*, a term that has taken on a slightly different meaning today. It provided an operating system that was developed with the sole intention of storing and sharing files as well as providing printing services to the PC network. Novell's NetWare did not rely on the less-than-robust FAT file system used by DOS. Instead, Novell developed a proprietary file system with built-in fault tolerance and a more efficient file structure. The performance advantage this dedicated operating system approach provided over DOS-based alternatives ensured Novell immediate success. Novell has continued to hold this advantage well into the 1990s.

Jump ahead almost 10 years from the day when NetWare was introduced, and you will find many of the same names although the products have changed. Novell continues to market a much-improved version of NetWare. Microsoft developed a network operating system that it named LanManager; it was based on IBM's new OS/2 desktop operating system. Microsoft then licensed LanManager to many other vendors. It became IBM Lanserver, 3Com 3+ Open, and DEC Pathworks among others. IBM has taken Lanserver off in its own direction, and 3Com has since retreated to the hardware-only side of networking, thus leaving Microsoft to market the product on its own as Microsoft LanManager.

With a high-performance operating system like the new OS/2 as the underlying operating system, Microsoft now had made a considerable step forward. Among OS/2's features was the new *High Performance File System* (HPFS) it supported. HPFS supported larger hard disks and provided faster access to files when compared to FAT. One way this support was achieved was by placing the file index at the midway point between the center of the hard disk and the outside edge of the disk. At worst case, the hard disk head that read the data would have to travel only halfway across the disk to access the file index. FAT stored the index near the outside edge of the disk, which meant it may have to be moved across the whole disk. Given that the weak link in hard disk performance is the mechanical movement of the head, HPFS was significantly faster. To further speed up file access, OS/2 was capable of using the server's memory (RAM) as a file cache, or temporary storage. Files in the process of being saved could wait in cache until the operating system was less busy, at which time they could then be moved to the hard disk. HPFS was also more robust, being able to analyze the disk and prevent loss of data, something that FAT was not very well known for. Finally, there was a basis for a new network operating system Microsoft would name LanManager. It was a rival for NetWare because Novell had been using some of these tricks with great success for many years with its proprietary operating system and file system.

LanManager provided the necessary Network extensions that would allow OS/2 server resources to be shared to the network, including hard drives and printers. LanManager also provided network security, which allowed network administrators to allow or restrict access to these resources based on groups or individual users defined on the server. LanManager was a significant performance improvement over MS Net and its DOS-based counterparts, although it was no match for NetWare.

An important improvement that LanManager introduced to PC networking was the ability to group multiple servers into a *domain*. The domain concept involves taking a number of servers and managing them as a single network. Resources could be located on many different servers, yet only a single logon is required to access many servers. Users no longer need to log in to multiple servers individually, so adding a new server—when planned correctly—could be transparent to the user. LAN administrators could relocate files and resources on other servers without the users even knowing that the server had been moved and they were now accessing a new server. Of course, this situation assumes that the LAN administrators set up the users' environment correctly to point to the new location of the files.

Adding new user accounts is also easier in a domain because a single set of accounts exists for the entire domain. The accounts are created on the primary domain controller and accessed by all servers in the domain.

While LanManager was becoming easier to manage, Novell continued to have a performance edge.

Although other network operating systems were coming and going, Novell continued to gain market share. It was the first to recognize the importance of an operating system designed specifically for use as a file server. NetWare's roots run deep in PC networking. The first version was released in 1982, with many updates along the way. NetWare has traditionally required a fair amount of expertise to implement; however, implementing has become easier over the years. Up until 1988 when NetWare 3.x was released, the operating system had to be compiled by the installer before it could be installed. An installation program took the installer through a number of pages of questions regarding the file server's configuration including hardware settings and network addressing. All this information was then compiled and placed on a series of floppy disks from which the operating system would be installed. Even a simple change to hardware settings after the operating system was installed meant that the whole process must be repeated, which could take many hours at best; having many sleepless nights was more typical.

What was gained by this arduous process was a strong performing server with a relatively high degree of fault tolerance. By designing an operating system specifically for the task of file and print sharing on a PC LAN, and then expanding support to include Macintosh and UNIX clients, Novell gained a significant market share early on and had the largest installed base of any NOS.

Novell NetWare servers cannot be used as workstations; resources are therefore designed to provide the fastest access to stored information. Server memory provides *disk caching*, the ability to read information from the hard disk and store it in memory should it be needed a second time.

Novell servers were among the first to offer *disk mirroring* or *duplexing*, the ability to write information to a primary drive and then to a backup drive on the fly. If the server's hard drive failed, the backup drive would take over. Users were often not even aware a problem had occurred and could continue to work. Mirroring and duplexing functionality is now typical of any NOS, and Microsoft has responded by including this feature in Windows NT Server.

For all of NetWare's attributes, it had some faults as well. NetWare servers support *NetWare Loadable Modules* (NLM). These NLMs are NetWare server applications that are provided by Novell or third-party developers to extend the server's functionality. Server-based backup utilities are one example. An NLM runs on the server and performs a given task such as backing up all the server's files to a tape backup system installed on the file server. The NLM must share the processor time with the operating system itself, and rules must be followed to prevent the NLM from hogging all the processor time, which would prevent the server from operating. To maintain high performance, Novell has chosen to allow NLMs to have the same access to the CPU as the NetWare kernel. Installing an NLM only to begin having intermittent, unexplainable, difficult-to-troubleshoot problems with the server is not uncommon. Mature products usually have the bugs worked out, but you should be cautious when installing any new NLM-based product that lacks a proven track record. The good news is that after the problem is detected, and Novell or the third-party developer supplies the appropriate fixes or patches, the server can be made bulletproof. However, adding new services is always best left until after hours when problems will not affect a production environment. Microsoft has taken advantage of NetWare's Achilles heel in much of its marketing literature for Windows NT.

Figure 1-1 shows the history of network operating systems.

The Birth of Windows NT

Today Microsoft has replaced OS/2 with a brand new operating system with the look and feel of its highly successful Windows operating system. This "new technology" has been dubbed Windows NT. Windows NT Server takes the strengths of LanManager and combines them with a more up-

Figure 1-1
History of network operating systems. (Courtesy of Learning Tree International)

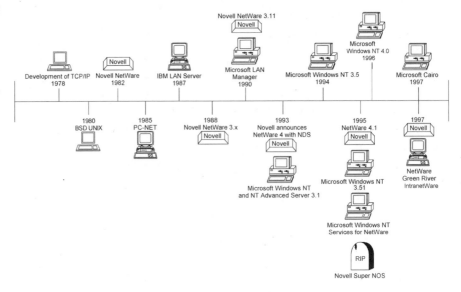

to-date core operating system. No longer is there a 16M limit to the amount of memory a server can support as was the case with LAN Manager, or more specifically version 1.3 of OS/2. Performance, although initially disappointing, improves with each new release as do functionality and features. Many people consider Windows NT to be Microsoft's first serious attempt to dominate the network operating system arena, and its presence has caused many to sit up and take notice.

Windows NT has built-in networking capabilities and boasts better performance and security over the LanManager product it replaces. Microsoft also improved the domain architecture over that of LanManager by allowing one domain to *trust* users from another NT domain. This trust means that users can easily access resources in their own domain as well as those managed by other branches of their organization who would grant them rights.

Windows NT was a vision of Microsoft founder Bill Gates who wanted to develop the next great operating system that would combine the strengths of OS/2 with the now popular Windows interface. Windows was quickly becoming *the* desktop operating system for PCs and had garnered the support of the application community who chose to write Windows applications rather than support OS/2. Providing backward compatibility with Windows and DOS applications was therefore very important. And, just to be safe, Microsoft decided to throw in limited support for OS/2 and UNIX applications while it was at it. (See Figure 2.)

To ensure Windows NT met his expectations, Gates hired Dave Cutler away from DEC. Cutler is considered the father of VMS, the highly successful operating system used on Digital Equipment Corporation's VAX

Figure 1-2
Windows NT
versions. (Courtesy
of Learning Tree
International)

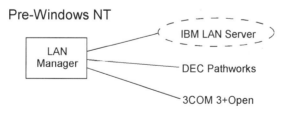

Pre-Windows NT

LAN Manager — IBM LAN Server
— DEC Pathworks
— 3COM 3+Open

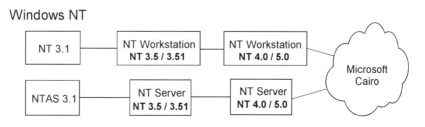

Windows NT

NT 3.1 — NT Workstation NT 3.5 / 3.51 — NT Workstation NT 4.0 / 5.0

NTAS 3.1 — NT Server NT 3.5 / 3.51 — NT Server NT 4.0 / 5.0

Microsoft Cairo

minicomputers. VMS is known for its high performance scaleability and robustness. Besides, Dave had already been working on his own within DEC to build his vision of the next operating system. When Cutler moved to Microsoft, it is rumored that he took much of his work with him, and he did, in fact, hire many of his development team directly from DEC. He assembled a team to design and build Windows NT in the late 1980s, and for much of its development time, it lacked a graphical user interface and was incredibly large.

NT was to have the familiar Windows 3.x graphical user interface, a robust crash-proof kernel, low-memory overhead (which it has not lived up to but is steadily being improved upon), and high performance. The first version of Windows NT released in 1993 sold as two separate products, Windows NT 3.1 and Windows *NT Advanced Server* (NTAS) version 3.1. Both products were based on the same architecture and could function as file servers or workstations, but NTAS was better suited for the role as a dedicated file server with more features. Poor performance was the main complaint with this version.

The next version, Windows NT 3.5, provided much better performance and had been further optimized to provide either workstation functionality (NT 3.5 workstation) or server functionality (NT 3.5 server). Windows NT 3.5, released in 1994, generated a huge amount of interest with organizations evaluating it as a replacement for Windows 3.x as a desktop operating system or as a replacement for their aging file server operating systems. Many NetWare shops began to take a closer look, with many actually making a full-scale conversion to Windows NT.

Windows NT 3.51 was released in the summer of 1995 just before the release of Windows 95. The main addition to version 3.51 was the Windows 95 application interface, which allowed applications written for Windows 95 to run on NT. Several minor improvements and bug fixes were made as well; however, speculation has been that the release of Windows 95 was actually delayed until NT was compatible with Windows 95 applications. Organizations could roll out Windows 95 today and later migrate to Windows NT workstations. Any investment in 32-bit applications purchased for Windows 95 would be preserved because these same applications could be installed on Windows NT.

By the late summer of 1996, Windows NT 4.0 was released. Among other advantages over previous versions was a more optimized use of memory as well as the adoption of the Windows 95 user interface, complete with shortcuts and right-click capabilities. These changes now made the look and feel of all new versions of Windows the same. Improvements to the user interface were more of an advantage at the desktop although the server received the updates as well.

Windows NT has done an admirable job of being all things to all people, and this use has resulted in the perception that the product is the best. If each function were compared individually, NT may not score as high; for example, although Windows NT server offers file and print services that are quite good, NetWare has a slight performance advantage. Also, although Windows NT can be used in place of UNIX for many requirements such as supporting a large database engine, it has been viewed as a low-end solution in the past. The gap is narrowing as Microsoft further optimizes the operating system and hardware manufacturers beef up their multiprocessor servers. The advantage many organizations see in Windows NT is that it is a replacement for many of their existing operating systems, not just NetWare, which leaves just one single operating system to support. The notion that Windows NT is a single operating system that can support all your needs is probably the biggest driving force behind the use of Windows NT (or perhaps a close second to the Microsoft Marketing Machine).

When you pick your method of accessing Windows NT Server, will you pick door number one? Figure 1-3 indicates the different access methods available on Windows NT either natively or from third parties. Note these abbreviations:

SMB, or Server Message Blocks: Native NT access

NCP, or NetWare Core Protocol: Native NetWare access

NFS, or Network File System: One method of UNIX file sharing

FTP, or File Transfer Protocol: Internet TCP/IP standard protocol for file transfer

http, or HyperText Transport Protocol: The standard protocol for transferring hypertext documents (Web pages)

The future for Windows NT includes plug-and-play support, even better performance, and improved server management as well as a range of Internet tools and features. To find out more about Windows NT, you can visit the Microsoft Internet Web site at **http://www.microsoft.com/**. The NT 4.0 feature list in Table 1-1 is an example of the information available at this site. Microsoft has long had plans for a new version of Windows NT code-named Cairo. Windows NT 4.0 implements some of the features expected in Cairo, and soon Windows NT 5.0 will be released, implementing even more features. Microsoft is expected to continue releasing new versions of Windows NT until all the promised functionality of Cairo is achieved.

Figure 1-3
Windows NT ser-
vices. (Courtesy of
www.ITcoach.com)

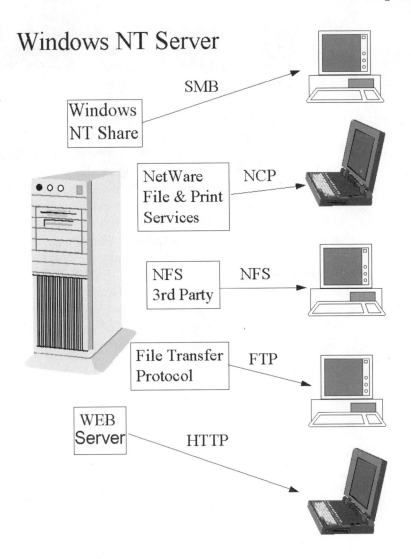

Windows NT Server

The NetWare 4.x Story

Just prior to the release of Windows NT, Novell introduced a new version of NetWare, version 4.0. Local area networks (LANs) had crept in through the back door of most organizations, with the central IS group being among the last to jump on the bandwagon in all but the most progressive companies. Now that LANs were so pervasive, it was time for some sort of central management of network resources. Branch LANs relied on central infrastructure such as network backbones and wide area network

Table 1-1

Windows NT
Server 4.0 features
list. (Source:
Microsoft
Corporation)

New Features	Description
Ease of Use and Management Windows 95 Interface	The Microsoft Windows 95 user interface has been integrated into Microsoft Windows NT Server 4.0, making the server interface easier to use and consistent with Windows 95 and Windows NT Workstation 4.0.
Administrative Wizards	Administrative wizards group the common server management tools into a single place and walk you through the steps required for each task. Windows NT Server 4.0 includes the following wizards: **Add User Accounts Wizard:** Makes adding new users to a Windows NT Server network easy. **Group Management Wizard:** Allows you to easily create and manage groups of users. **Managing File and Folder Access Wizard:** Enables you to share drives and folders for Macintosh, Microsoft, and Novell network clients in one step, including security settings. **Add Printer Wizard:** Allows you to set up printers that are connected to your computer or are on a network and share them. Installs printer drivers on the server for "point and print" installation on clients. **Add/Remove Programs Wizard:** Allows you to install or remove programs from your computer. **Install New Modem Wizard:** Allows you to set up and detect modems that are connected to your computer. **Network Client Administration Wizard:** Allows you to install or update network client workstations. **License Wizard:** Enables administrators to easily keep track of the software licenses they use for servers and clients.
Network Monitor	This powerful network diagnostic tool allows you to examine network traffic to and from the server at the packet-level. It allows you to capture network traffic for later analysis, making troubleshooting network problems easier.

Continues

Table 1-1

Continued.

New Features	Description
Ease of Use and Management System Policy Editor and User Profiles	These two features allow system administrators to manage and maintain users' desktops in a consistent manner. System policies are used for the standardization of desktop configurations and to enforce behavior and control the user work environment and actions. User profiles contain all user-definable settings for the work environment of a computer running Windows NT. Both policies and profiles can be stored on a network server; as users move computers, they always receive the same desktop, wherever their locations.
Task Manager	This integrated tool monitors applications and tasks, and reports key performance metrics of the Windows NT system. Task Manager provides detailed information on each application and process running on the workstation, as well as memory and CPU usage. Task Manager allows for the easy termination of applications and processes that are not responding, thereby improving system reliability.
Printing Enhancements	Printing performance is improved through server-based rendering of non-PostScript print jobs. This results in a quicker return-to-application time and quicker return of control to the user after the print job is initiated. Printer drivers for shared printers are located on the server for "point and print" automatic client driver installation. Remote printer folders allow easier browsing of shared printers.
Improved Windows NT Diagnostics Tool	Windows NT Server 4.0 includes an improved Windows NT diagnostics program that allows for easy examination of the system. The new version contains information on device drivers, network usage, and system resources such as IRQ, DMA, and IO addresses. This information is presented in an easy-to-view graphical tool that can also be run on a remote Windows NT system.
Performance Improvements File and Printer Sharing	Higher network throughput is achieved, with up to 66 percent better performance on Fast Ethernet (100Mbyte/sec) LANs. (Test results from NSTL.)

Table 1-1

New Features	Description
Performance Improvements Improved Scaleability	Improvements in Windows NT Server 4.0 deliver better performance scaleability on multiprocessor systems—especially those with more than four processors. New application programming interfaces for server application developers and better server performance deliver improved throughput and scaleability for server applications such as Microsoft SQL Server.
Faster Internet Server	The combination of Windows NT Server 4.0 and Microsoft Internet Information Server 2.0 delivers up to 40 percent better Web server performance (Microsoft test results).
Intranet/Internet Services Internet Information Server 2.0	Improvements in Internet Information Server (IIS) version 2.0 include the following: **Easier setup and administration:** ▪ Installation integrated into Windows NT 4.0 setup allowing installation of IIS while installing Windows NT Server ▪ Server administration of IIS from any Web browser ▪ Support for logging server traffic to NCSA Common Log File format, as well as any ODBC database ▪ Easier setup for SSL security using new Key Manager Tool **Higher Performance:** ▪ Fastest Web server available for Windows NT Server; over 40 percent faster than IIS 1.0, with better scaling on multiprocessor systems ▪ Index Server, which allows for content indexing and search capabilities of HTML and Office documents ▪ Support for HTTP byte-range enabling browsers to begin receiving data from any part of a file for enhanced performance **Improved platform for building Internet applications:** ▪ Improved programmability using ISAPI; for example, several server variables are now exposed, and nested **if** statements are supported, providing greater programming capabilities

Continues

Table 1-1

Continued.

New Features	Description
Intranet/Internet Services	▪ Improved database programmability with the Internet Database Connector (IDC); multiple database queries can be grouped together for improved performance
Microsoft Index Server (free downloadable component)	Microsoft Index Server automatically indexes the full text and properties of files, including HTML, on your server—whether it's an intranet, an Internet, or simply a file-and-print server.
	Indexes All Documents: Index Server allows you to query indexes and entire documents on intranet or Internet sites that are stored on an IIS server. The search engine has a unique ability to find documents in a wide variety of formats, such as text in a Word document, statistics on a Microsoft Excel spreadsheet, or the contents of an HTML page.
	Customizable Query Form: The Index Server allows the network administrator to create a customized query form enabling end users to choose parameters of their search. This form modification allows users to search either by contents or other document properties, such as author and subject.
	Automatic Maintenance: The Microsoft Index Server was designed for a "zero maintenance" environment in which a server must be running 24 hours a day, 7 days a week. After setup, all the operations are automatic. This includes automatic updates, index creation, optimization, and crash recovery in case of a power failure.
	Administrative Tools: Several built-in tools help administrators optimize their query service. The performance monitoring capability gives administrators key information to gauge site performance, including the number of queries processed and the response time.
	Multiple Languages: Index Server provides built-in language support allowing end users to query documents in seven different languages. Documents written in Dutch, English (U.S. and International), French, German, Italian, Spanish, and Swedish can be searched.

Table 1-1

New Features	Description
Intranet/Internet Services Microsoft FrontPage	Designed for nonprogrammers yet robust enough even for experienced Web site developers, Microsoft FrontPage version 1.1 is the fast, easy way to create and manage professional-quality Web sites. With functionality such as WYSIWYG editing and wizards to step you through the creation of your Web site, publishing on the Web has never been easier. Microsoft FrontPage also enables large teams to work together easily to create and manage sites. Its combination of flexible client/server architecture, passwords, user authentication, and other security features enables contributors in different locations to securely update different pages simultaneously on the same site.
Communication Features RAS Multilink Channel Aggregation	With PPP-compliant channel aggregation, RAS enables clients dialing into Windows NT Server 4.0 to combine all available dial-up lines to achieve higher transfer speeds. For example, users can combine two or more ISDN B channels to achieve speeds of 128K or greater, or combine two or more standard modem lines. This capability provides for overall increased bandwidth and even allows users to combine ISDN lines with analog modem lines for increased performance.
Point-to-Point Tunneling Protocol (PPTP)	PPTP provides a way to use public data networks such as the Internet to create a virtual private network connecting client PCs with a server. PPTP offers protocol encapsulation to support multiple protocols via TCP/IP connections and encryption of data for privacy, making it safer to send information over nonsecure networks. This technology extends the capacity of RAS to enable remote access and securely extend private networks across the Internet, without the need to change the client software.
Multi-Protocol Router (MPR)	This service enables small- and medium-sized sites to deploy Windows NT Server as a low-cost LAN-LAN routing solution, eliminating the need for a dedicated router. It provides LAN-LAN routing for IPX/SPX, TCP/IP, and AppleTalk.

Continues

Table 1-1

Continued.

New Features	Description
Communication Features Telephony API 2.0	The Telephony API (TAPI) enables development of integrated computer-telephony applications.
Cryptography API	This set of encryption APIs enables developers to develop applications that work securely over nonsecure networks, such as the Internet.
Network Integration Services Distributed Component Object Model (DCOM)	The Component Object Model (COM) allows software developers to create component applications. Windows NT Server and Workstation 4.0 include Distributed COM (DCOM), which extends COM to allow components to communicate across networks. An example of a DCOM application would be a stock quote server object running on Windows NT Server, distributing quotes to multiple Windows NT Workstation clients. DCOM provides the infrastructure for connecting the objects on the two workstations and supports communication between the objects so that users can receive the stock quotes. DCOM uses the same tools and technologies as COM, thereby preserving investments in training and software.
DNS Server	This version of DNS service is completely new. Features include a graphical administration utility and integration with WINS services for dynamic updates of host names and addresses. Through the WINS/DNS integration, end users can use DNS "compound" names to access network resources. For example, using the Windows NT Explorer, users can access a share via a DNS name such as `\\srv1.myco.com\public`.
Update Novell NetWare interoperability services	Client and Gateway Services for NetWare have been extended to support NetWare Directory Services (NDS). Added functionality includes browsing of NDS resources, NDS authentication, and NDS printing. This service supports authentication to multiple NDS trees. Support for processing login scripts has also been added.
Windows 95 Remote Program Load (RPL)	This service allows diskless Windows 95 clients to be booted from a Windows NT Server.

capabilities. Hardware manufacturers were also beginning to release "super servers" that were capable of supporting hundreds or even thousands of users at once. Economies of scale suggest that consolidating client departments file server requirements and offering them centrally may make financial sense. Information owned by individual branches of the organization could be placed in containers and managed by the branch LAN administrators, if they wanted. For the remaining servers, they should fit within a management model in which control could be given centrally or distributed. Users should be able to easily locate services anywhere in the organization without having to log in to each server individually.

To answer the need, Novell's NetWare 4.0 offered a hierarchical directory model based on the ISO X.500 standard, which better suits large organizations requirements. The concept behind NetWare 4.0 is a good one: the capability to design and implement a corporate directory structure made up of servers and resources and based on the x.500 addressing scheme. Another competitor, Banyan Vines, had gained the majority of its market based on successful Street Talk addressing, allowing users to connect from anywhere to anywhere. Novell could finally put to rest any criticisms for not having such a solution. NetWare 4.0 was a slow starter, and it wasn't until 1995, two years after the release of NetWare 4.0, that NetWare 4.1 finally surpassed the sales of NetWare 3.x, which was still being sold. (See Figure 1-4.)

During the early 1990s, Novell acquired a number of products in an effort to become King of the Hill. Novell purchased UNIX Laboratories and began developing what was termed *Novell Super NOS,* which was to be a best-of-both-worlds approach combining the strengths of NetWare with those of UNIX. It also purchased Word Perfect Corporation, and it looked like Novell was set to challenge Microsoft for the desktop as well as the LAN. NetWare had the largest NOS installed base, whereas WordPerfect dominated the word processing market. What Novell lacked was a good desktop operating system, and although it did have DR DOS to challenge Microsoft DOS, Windows was the future.

Eventually, the Super NOS idea fizzled. Novell was now sending out mixed signals to its customers as it was left wondering what Novell was. Clearly, Novell now had an identity crisis, and Microsoft continued to gain market share on all fronts. By the end of 1995, Novell sold off its UNIX interests, and by 1996 it had also rid themselves of its other albatross, WordPerfect. In an attempt to refocus on networking, Novell provided its customers with a series of small additions to NetWare 4.0 that would not necessarily give the product any significant new features but would

Figure 1-4
NDS tree. (Courtesy
of Learning Tree
International)

- A combination of the common name and the context of the object

- Also referred to as complete name in earlier version of NetWare 4.x

- Always starts with a leading period: ".CN"

- All NDS objects have a property called common name

- User object JLARABIE

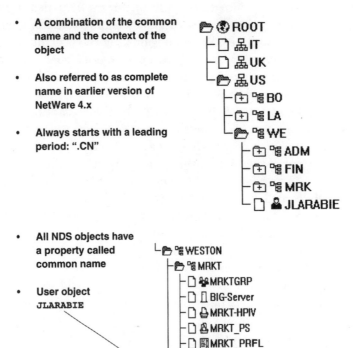

remove any criticisms for which the market, and Microsoft specifically, had been criticizing Novell. Performance enhancements were made to the *NetWare Directory Service* (NDS) to improve directory synchronization to further reduce the load on wide area networks connecting servers. Better TCP/IP connectivity was added in the form of a new product named *NetWare IP*. This capability would allow PC clients to access NetWare servers using TCP/IP, the same protocol used for Internet connectivity. NT had provided this capability two years earlier. For some time, Novell had the edge over Microsoft by providing support for UNIX workstations using TCP/IP; however, NetWare clients could not use TCP/IP to connect to a NetWare server. Instead, they continued to rely on the IPX protocol. (Protocol support is discussed further in Chapter 3.)

Throughout 1996, Novell continued to focus on PC networking. This time, the twist was that along with support for non-PC platforms, Novell caught the Internet bug and released NetWare 4.11 as IntranetWare. IntranetWare allowed Novell to jump on the Internet bandwagon by offering a Web server component, better TCP/IP support, and a trendy name. For those organizations in which the Internet was something to be feared or in which contractual obligations required that Novell follow through on its commitment to deliver NetWare 4.11, both products where released at the same time with the same price. IntranetWare was NetWare 4.11 with more components bundled with it so that it was clearly the better value. Table 1-2 lists these features.

Table 1-2

IntranetWare features comparison. (Source: Novell, Inc.)

IntranetWare Feature Comparison				
Feature	**NetWare 3.12**	**NetWare 4.1**	**NetWare 4.11**	**IntranetWare**
Intranet/Internet platform				
Web server	–	–	Yes	Yes
NetBasic tool for creating intranet applications	–	–	Yes	Yes
TCP/IP	add-on	add-on	Yes	Yes
Dynamic Host Control Protocol (DHCP)	add-on	add-on	Yes	Yes
IP/IPX gateway	–	–	–	Yes
Multiprotocol routing	add-on	add-on	add-on	integrated Supports: PPP ISDN Frame Relay ATM X.25
Internet Service Provider connectivity	–	–	–	leased line, Frame Relay, ISDN
Netscape Browser	–	–	Yes	Yes
Novell's Java Platform	–	–	–	Yes
Symmetric Multiprocessing (SMP)	–	From OEMs	Yes	Yes

Continues

Feature	NetWare 3.12	NetWare 4.1	NetWare 4.11	IntranetWare
Installation				
Hardware autodetection	–	–	Yes	Yes
Automated choice and configuration of protocols	–	–	Yes	Yes
Migration				
NDS modeling with DS Migrate utility	–	–	Yes	Yes
NetWare File Migration utility	–	–	Yes	Yes
Licensing Services	–	–	Yes	Yes
Abend Recovery	–	–	Yes	Yes
Directory Services	–	Yes	Improved	Improved
NDS Manager	–	–	Yes	Yes
Graphical Administrator	–	Yes	Improved	Improved
Security				
Network C2	–	–	Yes	Yes
RSA public key/ private key	–	Yes	Yes	Yes
Security Auditing	–	Yes	Yes	Yes
Netware Application Launcher (NAL)	–	Yes	Yes	Yes
Single Login to Network	–	Yes	Yes	Yes
Printing				
Print Management	bindery based	directory based	directory based	directory based
Printer Support	up to 16 printers	up to 256 printers	up to 256 printers	up to 256 printers

Table 1-2

Feature	NetWare 3.12	NetWare 4.1	NetWare 4.11	IntranetWare
File services				
Automatic file compression	–	Yes	Yes	Yes
Block suballocation	–	Yes	Yes	Yes
NetWare Peripheral Architecture	–	Yes	Yes	Yes
High-Capacity Storage System	–	Yes	Yes	Yes
Additive Licensing	–	Yes	Yes	Yes
Connectivity services				
Protocol management	limited support	Yes	Yes	Yes
Load and bind multiple protocols at installation	–	TCP/IP Appletalk IPX/SPX	TCP/IP Appletalk IPX/SPX	TCP/IP Appletalk IPX/SPX
WAN Support				
NetWare Link Services Protocol (NLSP)	add-on	Yes	Yes	Yes
Large Internet Protocol (LIP)	add-on	Yes	Yes	Yes
Packet Burst	add-on	Yes	Yes	Yes
Storage management services				
SBACKUP	limited functions	Yes	Yes	Yes
TSAs	limited support	Yes	Yes	Yes
End-User GUI Tools	–	Yes	Yes	Yes
Language support				
Embedded international language support	–	Yes	Yes	Yes

From a marketing prospective, Novell was once again perceived to be on a level playing field with Microsoft in the operating system arena. Novell could offer the same access to services that Microsoft could; however, by this time Microsoft had such momentum that it would take a great deal of effort to convince the public of this situation. Figure 1-5 indicates the different access methods available on NetWare either natively or from third parties. Note the following abbreviations:

SMB, or Server Message Blocks: Native NT access

NCP, or NetWare Core Protocol: Native NetWare access

Figure 1-5
NetWare supported services. (Courtesy of www.ITcoach.com)

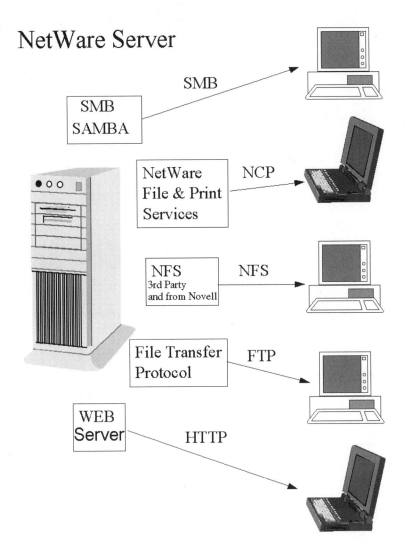

NFS, or Network File System: One method of UNIX file sharing

FTP, or File Transfer Protocol: Internet TCP/IP standard protocol for file transfer

http, or HyperText Transport Protocol: The standard protocol for transferring hypertext documents (Web pages)

Target Market and Market Share

Today de facto standards play an important part in promoting the success of one product over another. When deciding on technology, organizations can take several different approaches. Probably due to the safety-in-numbers factor, market share is used by many decision makers to establish a short list of competitors to chose from. Both Novell and Microsoft have played heavily on the market share tactics by commissioning reports, selective views of statistics, and general creative interpretations of what the market is really doing. From a marketing standpoint, saying "We have only 1 percent of the market, but we are the best" may not be very popular. Instead, a more creative approach might be to say "85 percent of all existing customers are choosing our product over our competitors."

To compare NetWare and Windows NT properly, we need to make sure that we are comparing apples to apples, or oranges to oranges, to make this analogy less confusing. Many people are confused about which operating system is truly the best. Both Novell and Microsoft have contributed to the confusion by releasing marketing material in a point-counterpoint fashion, responding to each other's criticisms by attempting to turn the competitor's strengths into weaknesses while creatively promoting its own strengths.

Our task, then, is to wade through the marketing hype to determine what we should compare. Some third-party reports can help in selecting a winner, but first we must determine who commissioned the reports. Are they unbiased?

The following are offered as examples of who said what:

EXAMPLE 1:

Microsoft says that NetWare is unstable because *NetWare Loadable Modules* (NLM) are allowed to run at ring 0, thus allowing them to have direct control over the processor, which can crash the operating system if they misbehave. This report is absolutely true, and we have had to deal with many crashed servers as a result.

Microsoft's solution is to run processes at ring 3 and the operating system kernel only at ring 0. The problem is that if a process hangs, although the operating system will not hang, it may be forced to wait indefinitely for the crashed process. In NT version 4.0, Microsoft has backed down from this stand as more processes will be moved to ring 0 for the same reason Novell has chosen this route: speed.

Novell now gives the option of running selected NLMs at ring 3 until their stability is proven, but just like Microsoft found, this setup can cause the operating system to wait indefinitely.

EXAMPLE 2:

Novell faults Microsoft for NT's capability to provide virtual memory, moving information from memory to hard disk temporarily to free up additional memory. Novell claims a real network operating system should do the opposite—provide faster disk access by reading ahead and storing data in memory. When data is required, it has already been retrieved from disk.

The real story is that servers should not rely on virtual memory to run more processes. Adequate memory must be available to handle all tasks; otherwise, performance can suffer. In the case of Windows NT, virtual memory is a good safety net for the server and a very efficient use of memory if NT is used as a workstation. Installers must plan how memory will be used depending on Windows NT's role. On the other hand, a NetWare server can crash if not enough memory is available. (Both will crash when they run out of disk space, and both do provide disk caching.)

See Figure 1-6 for further details.

NOVELL'S MARKET Novell continues to hold the largest market share for any single vendor's NOS. Its primary strengths have been in providing file and print services to a wide range of clients including DOS/Windows, OS/2, and Macintosh. UNIX connectivity has been a strength that Novell has demonstrated and is only recently being challenged by Microsoft. In general, Novell's approach has been to interoperate with a variety of technologies while providing the secure, fault tolerant storage of data.

NetWare 3.x provided mainly file and print services. NetWare 4.x takes networking to the enterprise level by introducing an x.500-based scaleable management model.

Figure 1-6
PC NOS market
share. (Courtesy of
Learning Tree Inter-
national and
Dataquest, Inc.)

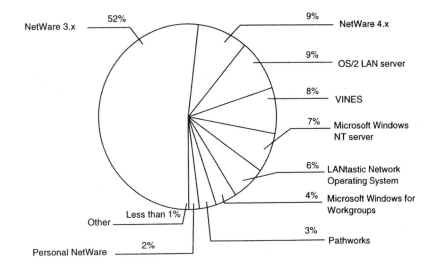

Source: Dataquest Inc. 1996

Novell's theme for 1995 was "Pervasive Computing." Computers every-
where included support for the mobile work force and home offices. In
1996, Novell introduced an improved TCP/IP client. Novell is now touting
the Global Internet as the wide area extension to corporate networks.
Clients can dial their Internet services provided and access their NetWare
servers anywhere in the world using the NetWare IP client and the PPP
or SLIP protocol.

Novell has responded to Windows NT by stating that although Net-
Ware can be used as an application server as well, NT can also be used
as an application server for client/server databases and the like and can
be incorporated into a NetWare environment for this purpose, whereas
NetWare really should be used as the file server.

A visit to Novell's home page on its Web server at **http://www.novell.com**
will yield a number of comparative reports and strategic papers indicating where Novell intends to go with IntranetWare. As a rebuttal to Microsoft's claim that IntranetWare is not a reliable applications platform,
Novell includes the following quote from *Computerworld* (March 11, 1996):

> "There is no denying that 3-year-old Windows NT Server has far fewer third-
> party applications than its more mature rival NetWare. There are fewer

than a dozen third-party packages shipping for Microsoft Corp.'s Windows NT Server, compared with thousands for Novell, Inc.'s NetWare."

MICROSOFT'S MARKET   During the 1980s and into the 1990s, the old adage "no one was ever fired for buying IBM" held true. More recently, the new twist on this old theme seems to substitute *Microsoft* for *IBM*. An interesting note is that over the last year, we have seen a significant number of organizations dump their existing NOSs for Windows NT. Organizations now using NetWare 3.x or older were faced with a relatively major planning exercise to implement NetWare 4.x. For the level of effort, many organizations justify taking the opportunity to look at an alternative —Windows NT. For lack of a definitive answer on which is best, many organizations have taken the safe decision to buy Windows NT because everyone else is buying it.

For organizations using other operating systems such as Banyan, the decision to go to Windows NT is particularly confusing. Here is one explanation that is worth considering and shows the market appeal that Windows NT has. In the case of Banyan Vines, many organizations have been fighting off Novell proponents internally by touting Street Talk, the superior Directory Services that the Banyan Vines NOS has had for many years. Now that Banyan's future is uncertain, rather than give in to the Novell forces, many organizations are choosing Windows NT as what appears to be a way out without admitting defeat. An interesting point to make note of is that NetWare 4.x has a substantially better Directory Services architecture than Windows NT's domain structure. Microsoft has promised it will deliver a solution on par with NDS in the future. For now, though, it seems that what was once a reason to choose Banyan over Novell is no longer important to many organizations; otherwise, the choice would be NetWare.

While Microsoft has been taking on Novell, it has also made significant inroads into the UNIX arena. UNIX offers a number of open standards unlike the proprietary nature of products such as Windows NT and NetWare. Support for TCP/IP services and applications such as FTP and particularly Internet Web services as well as third-party support for NFS and Telnet have allowed Microsoft to become a common ground for many groups in the corporate MIS structure. With Windows NT's platform independence, Windows NT provides a single operating system that runs on RISC platforms as well as Intel machines.

Most people would agree that although Windows NT is a substantial improvement over LAN Manager, the real reason it has generated so much interest is the WOW factor that Microsoft has been able to unleash at a time when its competitors were indecisive. Microsoft has kept its momentum by announcing new software releases and new versions of existing software on a regular basis. It has also changed direction mid-stream by embracing the Internet as the next major battleground that it needs to dominate. Product releases that have kept Microsoft in the spotlight include NT3.5, Windows 95, SQL Server 6.0, SMS, Windows NT 3.51, Microsoft Exchange, Microsoft Internet Explorer, and Microsoft's Internet Information Server. As well, Microsoft is currently marketing its Internet Assistant products for Word, Excel, and PowerPoint as low-end Web authoring tools, and FrontPage as a full-featured point-and-click Web authoring tool. Windows NT 4.0 will be followed by the next major revision, code-named Cairo. All this excitement is occurring during a time when very little is being heard from Novell. Novell has been caught in a deadly downward spiral, whereas Microsoft is spiraling upward in a whirlwind of excitement and hype. Only recently has Novell reentered the spotlight with IntranetWare.

Network Management Models

How network file servers have been deployed and managed over the last decade has changed considerably. In the beginning, file servers were deployed in pockets of technology within an organization. In most cases, no connection was made between LANs. If the marketing department wanted to share files between users, it might install a file server independent of any corporate initiatives because the corporate IS group had become too slow to respond to its needs. The engineering department might have a similar requirement to implement its own LAN, again independent of other initiatives within the organization. Each department then would develop its own technical expertise to support its own IS needs.

This trend continued through the early 1990s; today many companies have drastically cut back their requirements for mainframe-based computing. The challenge now faced by most corporations is how to manage this new distributed computing environment efficiently. In the past, each file server was managed independently. Each server had user accounts and lists of shared resources. If a user from the accounting department required access to files on the sales department's server, usually this meant an account had to be created on the sales server as well as the account that already existed on the user's home server in accounting. As employees came and went, their accounts had to be managed in two places, twice the work for the LAN administrator. (See Figure 1-7.)

The accounts on the additional servers that users may need to connect to must have user names and passwords synchronized so that this con-

Figure 1-7
Example of NetWare
3 management.
(Courtesy of Learning
Tree International)

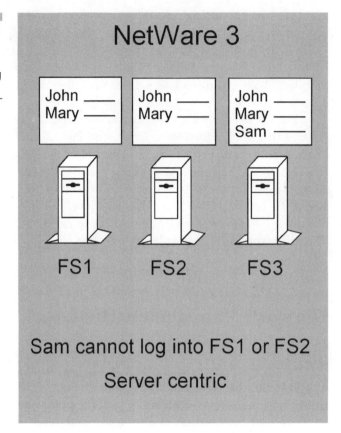

nection can occur somewhat transparently to the users. This situation is
not ideal because often users change their passwords on one server and
forget to change them on another. Any resulting problems accessing resources often require the help of the LAN administrator. Novell attempted
to provide a solution for this problem a few years earlier with an add-on
product to NetWare 3.x. Called *NetWare Name Service* (NNS), this solution did not work very well and tended to be more work than it was worth.

NETWARE 3.X MANAGEMENT MODEL   Objects in a NetWare 3.x
environment have rights and attributes associated with each object. This
information is stored in the file server's bindery, which is made up of three
files. (See Figure 1-8.) Each server's bindery is unique to that server, and
there is no mechanism for replication. If a NetWare 3.x server happens to
crash, a good backup of the data file had better be available, but also the
bindery files so that permission can be restored. In most typical cases in
which we have been called in to repair a failed server, reentering this se-

curity information from scratch is quite typical; however, this situation can be prevented. One critical network component sits between the server's keyboard and the chair back. It is commonly called the *network administrator,* and its role is to ensure that the bindery and data files get backed up. Sometimes this component is faulty! We suspect that the reason we have found this to be the case in the majority of sites we have been called to is that sites where things have been backed up properly do not need our services as often.

Figure 1-8
Components of the NetWare bindery. (Courtesy of Learning Tree International)

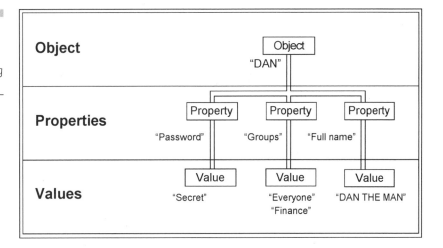

Many services and third-party network devices such as print servers have been designed to interact with NetWare bindery services. They understand how to talk to NetWare's bindery to determine who can access the resources. NetWare 4.x has a different model but can run in bindery emulation mode to maintain backward compatibility.

The NetWare bindery is a collection of files that make up the server's user accounts database on pre-NetWare 4.x servers. Bindery files are not shared between servers, so multiple servers must be managed individually. (See Figure 1-9.)

WINDOWS NT DOMAINS Microsoft recognized the weakness of NetWare 3's server management model and has improved upon it by designing its management model based on groups of servers. The domain concept began with Microsoft LanManager, and we used to joke that it didn't buy you much because it took four or five LanManager servers to do the work of one NetWare server anyway. Now that LanManager has been replaced by Windows NT—which is a much better performer—we are left looking for new material.

Figure 1-9
NetWare 4 bindery
emulation. (Courtesy
of Learning Tree In-
ternational)

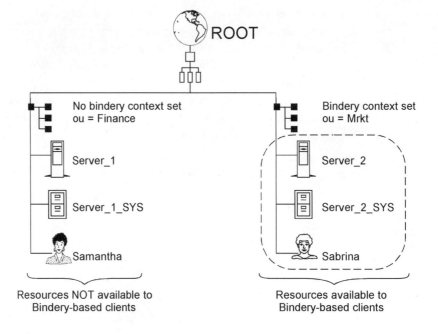

Figure 1-9
NetWare 4 bindery
emulation. (Courtesy
of Learning Tree In-
ternational)

A *domain* is a group of servers sharing a single user account database. A domain user can be granted access to one or many servers in the domain through a single network logon. Therefore, there is only one account to administer for each user and only one password to remember, regardless of how many servers are in the domain. When users log on to a domain workstation, they are given network access and the workstation is registered on the network. If the users are validated by the domain controller, then their user names and passwords are verified, allowing access to any server resources to which the LAN administrator has given them rights.

The three types of servers in an NT domain are the *Primary Domain Controller* (PDC), *Backup Domain Controller* (BDC), and just plain old servers. (See Figure 1-10.) An NT domain has only one set of user accounts, and the Primary Domain Controller contains a database of these users. Only BDCs and PDCs can manage domain user accounts and keep a copy of the user account database for the domain, whereas all types of servers including PDCs and BDCs can provide file and print services.

To create a Windows NT domain, the first server must be installed as a Primary Domain Controller. Selecting the role of when the server is installed PDC is very important because a server cannot be changed to a PDC after installation. Surely, every person who has installed Windows

Figure 1-10

Windows NT domain
users. (Courtesy of
Learning Tree Inter-
national)

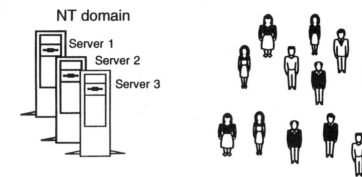

NT domain

Server 1
Server 2
Server 3

NT Server has made this mistake at least once, especially if coming from a LanManager environment in which promoting a server to the role of domain controller was possible.

When users are added to the domain, they must be added to the Primary Domain Controller's accounts database. From there, they can then be replicated to all other Backup Domain Controllers in the domain. The actual function of adding new users can be performed from any PC running Windows, including Windows 3.11, Windows 95, and Windows NT, as long as they have connectivity to the NT server, the proper NT administration tools installed, and are logged in as members of the Administrator group.

As a safeguard, installing a second server as a BDC is a good idea in case the primary fails. The role of a BDC is to keep a duplicate copy of the domain user account database, authenticate users on behalf of the PDC when the PDC is busy, and provide file and print services to the network. A BDC can be promoted to PDC at any time, which will in turn force the existing PDC to the role of BDC because only one PDC can exist at a time in each domain.

If the PDC crashes, the BDC can continue to validate user logons without being promoted; however, this will mean that no new users can be created until the BDC is promoted or the existing PDC is placed back in service. If the PDC is out of service for an extended period, the BDC must be promoted manually using the Windows NT server manager utility before you can add any new users. You must be very careful when reintroducing the old PDC to the domain because it will contain an out-of-date version of the user account database. Fortunately, when the PDC is reconnected, it can detect that another PDC already exists and does not attempt to validate any users. Only if a new PDC is already in place can the old PDC be demoted to BDC status. At this point, it can synchronize with the new PDC to receive any updates that occur while it was away. After synchronization has taken place, you can then chose to promote the old PDC from its BDC status, which will in turn cause its replacement to be demoted. The whole key to understanding this process is that you can have only one PDC per domain, and only Backup Domain Controllers can receive duplicate copies of the user account database.

Microsoft has improved the domain architecture significantly from that which LanManager supported. Windows NT domains can permit users from one domain to access resources in another domain if a trust relationship has been established between the two domains.

A domain trust relationship is very similar to a trust relationship you may develop with your friends. If you trust them, they can use your stuff. But just because you trust them does not necessarily mean they trust you.

Recently, I installed a swimming pool in my backyard. My house is my domain, just like a Windows NT domain, and any members of my family can be denied or granted permission to use the pool. My wife and children, who are members of the Administrators group in this "domain," have given me permission to use the pool.

We get along well with our relatives and have given my brother-in-law's family (anyone who lives in his domain) permission to use the pool as well. Because we have a trust relationship with them, they let us know if there are any additions to their family that we are not aware of, so we have access to their list of domain members. From this list, we can decide who can use the pool and who cannot. We have decided to allow all members of his domain except his dog Herbie to use the pool.

Trust relationships are not always two way. (See Figure 1-11.) My brother-in-law has a fast motorcycle. I, on the other hand, road-race motorcycles and have been known to fall off on occasion. Just because I trust him to use my pool does not mean he trusts me to use his motorcycle.

Two-way trust relationships do exist between my domain and some other domains. (See Figure 1-12.) My father-in-law's domain is another example. Because we have a two-way trust relationship between our domains, I let him use my pool, and he lets me use his truck.

Trust relationships are not passed on to other trusted domains. (See Figure 1-13.) For example, just because I am trusted by my father-in-law's domain and can use his truck does not mean that friends of mine from another domain I trust can use his truck.

A trust relationship, then, is simply a condition that exists between two domains in which one domain is given access to a list of users who are defined in another domain. LAN administrators can then not only grant

Figure 1-11
Trust relationships between two domains. (Courtesy of www.IT-coach.com)

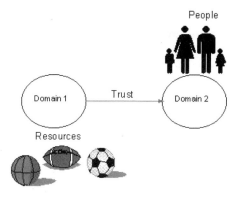

Figure 1-12
Reciprocal, or two-way, trust. (Courtesy of www.IT-coach.com)

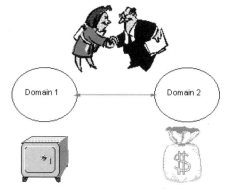

Figure 1-13
Trusts are not passed on to trusted domains. (Courtesy of www.ITcoach.com)

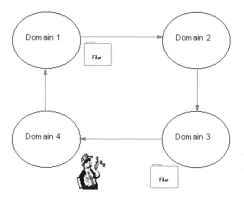

their own users access to the domain's file and print resources, but they can also grant permissions to users in any domains that are trusted.

When you're designing a Windows NT domain architecture for an organization, you must decide how many domains are required and how they will be managed. The simplest to manage is one large, single domain. Groups can be created to assign rights to many users, as is common with most network operating systems. Expanding the number of domains beyond the minimum required can add unnecessary complexity, thus making them very difficult to maintain.

For a company that is geographically dispersed, the entire company may be represented in one domain with backup controllers located at each geographically separate site. This arrangement would allow all users to be validated locally while administered centrally. Users from any one location can travel to another location and log on to the network using the single user names and passwords that they use at their home locations. Any domain members can be made members of the Administrator's group so that certain users can be permitted to add new users or manage server resources at each of the locations.

An alternative model would see each site become a domain on its own, with a trust relationship established between each domain. This arrangement would still allow visiting users to continue to access their files from a domain other than their own, or to log on to the network when they come to visit.

An organization may not be able to implement a single domain or a small number of trusted domains for political reasons, for example, or size. If this is the case, the domain model's weaknesses are exposed. The maximum number of users per domain according to Microsoft has increased form 10,000 to 40,000, but this number assumes that all accounts exist in one domain, whereas the remaining domains are resource domains.

To determine the number of trust relationships required between any number of domains, we must first determine how many domains there are in total. The number of trust relationships required for a company with n domains is

$$n * (n - 1)$$

If only a small number of domains exists, this number can be manageable, but as the number of domains increases, the number of trust relationships increases dramatically. This is illustrated in the following examples:

THE NUMBER OF TRUSTS IS 2 * (2 – 1) = 2 TRUSTS.

In the first example, as illustrated in Figure 1-14, domain 1 trusts 2 and domain 2 trusts 1 for a total of two trusts.

THE NUMBER OF TRUSTS IS 4 * (4 – 1) = 12 TRUSTS.

All domains trust each other, requiring 12 trust relationships to be set up among four domains, as shown in Figure 1-15.

HOW MANY TRUSTS ARE REQUIRED FOR 10 DOMAINS?

If something happens to one trust relationship, or if a server is renamed, all trusts may have to be reestablished.

By now, you should be getting the idea that the domain concept was a good one, but after we expand beyond a single domain, the level of management complexity increases considerably. Whereas NetWare 3.x servers were treated as peers of each other, NT has grouped them into a single logical server. When we expand beyond a single domain, because each domain is a peer of the other domains, we are back to some of the same issues we had with NetWare, but on a different scale. Microsoft has recognized this shortcoming and has stated that it will be coming out with

Figure 1-14
Trust relationships between two domains. (Courtesy of www.ITcoach.com)

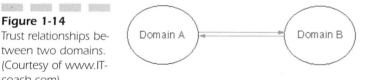

Figure 1-15
Trust relationship among four domains. (Courtesy of www.ITcoach.com)

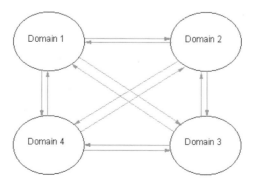

a new directory service to address this problem. In the meantime, we can use different domain models.

A single domain is easiest to manage; however, due to the size of an organization or political differences between groups within the organization, managing all servers centrally may not be feasible. Typically, we have found that corporate networks tend to evolve as islands of technology put in place as the result of an individual branch or department of an organization wanting control over its own data and resources. Each Windows NT LAN typically has been designed and administered independent of any central authority. If the organization was fortunate, it may have followed naming conventions that were in place. Eventually, as information was required by other groups, trust relationships were established on an as-needed basis. Eventually, they would grow to the point where no one was quite sure how certain people had or should be given access. This type of design, as illustrated in the previous example, is known as a *complete trust model* in which every domain trusts every other domain. The really bad news about a scenario like this is that domain servers must be reinstalled to join another domain, so consolidation is difficult.

If having a single domain is not practical for your organization, then the next best design is a *master domain model*. This model has all user accounts defined in one domain, and resources are managed in separate domains. (See Figure 1-16.) The domains containing the resources can then trust users from the master domain at the discretion of the administrator of the resource domain.

The advantage of a master domain model is that while dividing resources among many domains, it still allows users to be mobile. For example, resource domain 2 can be either be a domain owned by a separate branch or department within the organization, or it can be a separate location in the organization. To log on to a workstation in domain 2, users

Figure 1-16
Master domain
model. (Courtesy of
www.ITCoach.com)

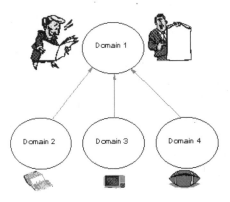

would log on as a user "FROM" the master domain. Because domain 2 trusts the master domain, any users who have been granted permissions can use the resources in domain 2. The same users could log on at any of the other resource domains, so using this model, users from anywhere can log on anywhere else, provided that they have been granted the appropriate rights.

Using the master domain model, each resource domain can have its own domain administrator who is responsible for managing the resources within the domain. So to review how a master domain works, the master domain contains user accounts. If two new users join the company, the administrator in the master domain is responsible for creating new accounts for those users. This domain typically is managed by the corporate MIS people. If the users will work in domain 2, then the users are given access to the local printers and necessary files in the domain in which they will be working. This job is the responsibility of the administrator in domain 2. If the users also need access to files in domain 3, then the administrator of domain 3 must grant them access. This scenario is all possible because accounts exist once for the entire organization and are located in the master domain. Because all other domains trust the master domain, all other domain administrators have access to master domain users and can manage their local access.

The most complicated model to manage is a multiple trust, or complete trust model, as discussed in the example. This model usually comes about as the result of islands of technology within an organization beginning to work together after working alone for some time. It is the least desirable model due to its complexity, and it is not usually the result of good planning.

If a complete trust relationship looks like the only alternative, then the best recommendation is to reduce the total number of domains, if possible. Also, you should implement a master domain model at the highest levels possible within the organization; for example, sales may have a master domain that includes the sales domains located at regional offices. A similar master domain model may exist for engineering. If a sales user needs access to a resource domain in engineering, a single trust would be required between the engineering resource domain and the sales master domain. The end result will be many master domains, but fewer trusts in all when compared to the complete trust model.

NETWARE 4.X NDS: NOVELL'S ANSWER TO MULTIPLE SERVERS As NetWare grew with LAN technology, it transformed from being a stand-alone LAN operating system used by small communities of users into a technology embraced by corporate IS managers. If LANs are to become corporate resources, then they must lend themselves to being centrally managed. Scaleability was an important issue that was not easily addressed using NetWare 3's management model. Novell answered the challenge by delivering NetWare 4, a product aimed directly at the corporate decision makers looking for an enterprise solution. (See Figure 1-17.)

NetWare 4 introduces the concept of NetWare Directory Services (NDS). The NDS allows access to information from a multitude of servers without having to go through the previously tedious task of attaching to multiple servers manually or the management task of automating this process. NDS provides a logical view of the network by depicting objects within the NetWare Directory Services tree. In a NetWare 4 environment, a company could create a services directory tree. (See Figure 1-18.) This tree structure would contain any number of file servers, printers, directories, and users. The top of the tree is called the *root*, and here the corporate LanManager would have control. From this point down, many branches of the tree could contain information for various departments within the organization. The tree structure could have branches based on the company's organizational structure or based on geographical locations. Network management therefore can be global or local depending on the requirements of the environment.

The advantages of the NetWare 4.x NDS are as follow:

- Users' login requests can be validated by any server in the organization.

- The NDS is a distributed database that can be replicated to all servers.

Figure 1-17
Network management models. (Courtesy of Learning Tree International)

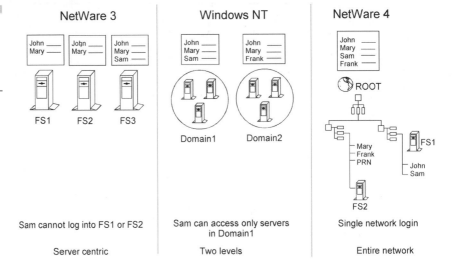

NetWare 3

Windows NT

NetWare 4

Figure 1-18
*User's view of direc-
tory tree. (Courtesy
of Learning Tree In-
ternational)*

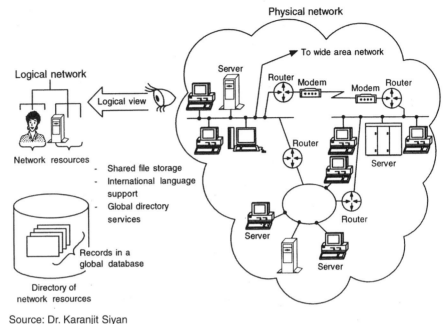

Source: Dr. Karanjit Siyan

- The NDS can be replicated in full or in part.
- Once logged in, users can access any resources in the network to which they have rights.
- Servers are transparent to the users. All they need to know is the name of the resource.
- Management is easier than managing individual servers.

An NDS tree contains three types of objects, and each contains properties unique to itself. Properties for users may include group membership, login names, and "nice to know" information such as addresses and telephone numbers and more. These three types of objects are

- Physical objects (such as users and printers)
- Logical objects (such as groups and print queues)
- Other objects (such as Organization Units) that can contain physical and logical objects

The directory tree itself is based on the international X.500 standard. Using it, you can organize information in a way that is logical and practical. It resembles an upside-down tree with a root at the top and branches below it.

NDS has container and leaf objects. Containers hold leaf objects, which automatically inherit all the characteristics of the container object. A printer or user is an example of a leaf object.

The container objects in NDS are called *organizational units* (OUs). Management of resources and assigning of rights can be performed at the OU level, much the same as managing based on groups. Any changes to an OU's rights are inherited by every user object in the OU automatically, including other OUs. Management is much simpler than managing individual objects; however, each object can be managed separately. Because container objects can be placed in other container objects, hierarchical object inheritance enables you to modify an entire organization by making simple changes at the top of the tree.

Every object on the tree can be uniquely identified by the combination of its name and location. For example, two users may have the same name. Both users can be uniquely identified in NDS by the OU they belong to; for example, Wayne in Accounting is different from Wayne in Engineering. See Figure 1-19 for another example, and note the following abbreviations:

C = Country

O = Organization

OU = Organizational Unit

CN = Common Name (given to leaf objects such as people and resources)

At the top of each branch, a LAN administrator can be defined. All resources for a particular branch could be under the control of the branch LAN administrator, or the LanManager could have complete control over the entire organization if required. An important note to make is that the branch LAN administrator could restrict the LAN Manager's access if the branch LAN contains sensitive information. The idea here is that the branch may be a highly independent group within the organization. Proper planning is critical in determining whether the LAN administrator should be able to prevent the LanManager from accessing or managing branch resources.

A good operational model would be based on a company's organizational chart, with the root of the chart being a controlling server managed by a central department responsible for maintaining the structure. This does not mean that the central department must have complete control over the other branch's configuration, but rather that a standard that must be adhered to be in place and some freedom given at the branch

Figure 1-19
NetWare Directory
Services Tree. (Cour-
tesy of Learning Tree
International)

The location of an object in the NDS tree is its context

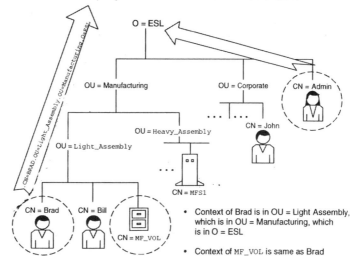

Source: Dr. Karanjit Siyan

level. This approach has been taken by the state of North Carolina. The NDS structure was developed at the top level, and information and specifications were then published for all other administrators to see. By taking this approach, all other government organizations in the state were encouraged to fit into the overall NDS tree while still being able to design and administer their own branches. You can find out more about how North Carolina accomplished this plan by visiting their Web site at `http://www.state.nc.us/SIPS/SIS/nw4x.htm`. (Note that this site URL is case sensitive.)

It is recommended that each company have only one root for which all organizations in the company are branches. Each autonomous group or branch can be installed as an organizational unit. Each unit can either be managed centrally or locally because security can be set to allow only a supervisor (Admin) to manage the level of the tree, preventing access to higher or lower levels. To ensure that branches and departments join at the correct level, the first NetWare 4.0 server installed should be configured by a central group that is in the position to set naming conventions, network addresses, directory structure, and so on. Each new 4.0 server will automatically search for an existing directory structure. If one does not exist, the server will be created with a default partition that includes a root. More than one root will be extremely difficult to manage, and merging of two roots, although possible, is highly inadvisable because limitations do exist:

- Organizations with the same name cannot be merged.

- Organizations with the same name cannot be merged"

- Organizations cannot be made organizational units; therefore, they must remain at the top of the tree.

Before servers are set up, the decision has to be made as to how all the servers will relate to each other. If users in one branch never expect to talk with or require information from another branch, then they can be set up independent of each other. Each branch or server can maintain its own directory partition; however, if they may join in the future, the time to include them in the overall plan is now. Starting the design properly is far cheaper and less time-consuming than trying to join and possibly rebuild in the future. Final product thereby reduces the development cost.

The NDS database can be replicated to enhance both performance and fault tolerance. The directory structure can be partitioned to allow each server to maintain the partition information for its own resources. Alternatively, one server can store the directory information for the entire tree. Depending on the organization's structure and how geographical dispersed, one or the other structure may be preferable. To increase performance in a wide area network environment, each regional server should maintain its own partition information and replicate this information to a central server. Replication means that more than one copy will be available in case of a server crash.

If an organization has branches that fall into a number of OUs, how do you determine which one fits where? One example is a branch within the head office that also has regional offices. Does the finance branch belong in OU Finance even if it's located in Vancouver and the head office is in Hull? Or does the branch belong in OU Vancouver? The NetWare 4 NDS design provides flexibility for either, although partitioning the database so that each partition is self-contained and does not span the WAN is advisable. Figures 1-20 and 1-21 show an NDS structure based on location and one based on the functional organization.

Based on the locational design, the local LAN administrator at each region may be responsible for administering every object at that site; however, it could be managed centrally, but more importantly, less WAN traffic would occur as a result of each partition being complete.

A functional design, as shown in Figure 1-21, would group users and other objects according to the organization's functional design. In the figure, an administrator could be designated for the marketing unit.

In summary, a NetWare directory tree is hierarchical and is very scaleable. It may not be as simple to understand during initial planning,

Figure 1-20
NDS partitions based on location. (Courtesy of Learning Tree International)

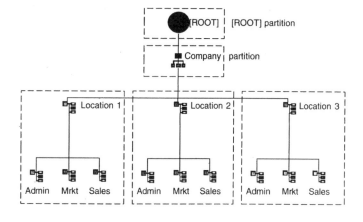

Figure 1-21
NDS partitions based on function. (Courtesy of Learning Tree International)

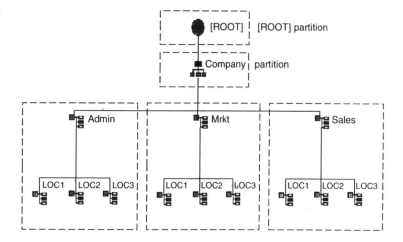

but once understood, it can be very powerful. From the end user's perspective, the complexity is transparent.

NOS Processing Methodologies

To complete the comparison of Windows NT and NetWare, we need to understand how the two operating systems make use of system resources because the two vendors themselves make a big deal of this capability. Specifically, we need to understand the differences in the way each NOS processes tasks.

NetWare has always had a speed advantage over its competitors by doing one thing well before moving on to the next. NetWare has taken advantage of available time and system resources by doing things such as caching disk information in memory, writing it to the hard disk when it has time to spare, and reusing cached information rather retrieving it a second time. Windows NT uses similar techniques. Performance differences between the two operating systems can be attributed to system overhead or how much of the server's resources are used up maintaining the operating system.

Whenever there are tasks to be performed, the desired results can be achieved in many ways. Efficient people tend to find the shortest steps to performing a task, whereas others may take a more roundabout path. Office efficiency experts tell us that when dealing with a task, the fewer times we have to touch that task, the more efficient the process. Network operating systems are no different.

When we are faced with an overloaded inbox, one school of thought suggests that we first sort and prioritize our mail, whereas others suggest that we make a decision and deal with each item as it comes to the top of the pile. Whichever method you prefer, the most efficient means of completing the task is to make sure that the task can be completed in the time allowed. Having mail strewn about while we move on to another task such as returning phone calls or preparing for a meeting is not efficient.

With operating systems, the best performance is usually gained by breaking down tasks into smaller bite- (not byte-) size tasks that can easily be completed in the time available. Both cruise missiles and video games take advantage of this principle. Rather than sampling a portion of each of the incoming pieces of information, sample one input and make a decision on it. The next time the operating system has the opportunity to take a sample, look at something else and make a decision. This process was explained to me by a programmer who has worked on both types of systems, which makes me wonder just how realistic video games are going to become.

Delegation is also a critical factor. If more help is available from an assistant such as a second processor, each processor has less work to do, therefore fewer tasks to juggle. Now if your assistant is not very capable, or you are not very organized, you may actually achieve less because you will spend more time managing your assistant than if you had completed the task yourself. As you can see, the more assistants you hire, the more time you will have to spend managing them. Eventually, you may need a full-time manager. Computers and operating systems are no different. The common view is that four processors give you the maximum efficiency. At this point, one processor is virtually spending all its time managing tasks for the other three.

Multitasking refers to the capability to do two or more things at once. A DOS user once commented to me after I explained the multitasking capabilities of Microsoft Windows, "Wouldn't it be great if we could multitask!" This person obviously couldn't walk and chew gum at the same time.

Two approaches to multitasking are *preemptive* and *nonpreemptive*. Preemptive multitasking means that the operating system can take control at any time just like your cable company preempting the regularly scheduled program that just happens to be the last Formula One race of the year just to bring you the National Bowling Championships. Nonpreemptive means that the operating system must wait until the task is completed before being interrupted to work on something else. (I am sure that most of you work in nonpreemptive mode, and all the users you support have agreed not to bother you when you are busy!)

Windows NT is a preemptive operating system. It can take control at any time if a problem or a more urgent task occurs. Managing tasks does take additional overhead and affects performance, but this compromise may be acceptable for the fault tolerance it provides.

NetWare is designed as a nonpreemptive operating system: an application can take control until it is ready to give back operation. This system takes less overhead to manage, which contributes to better performance. The risk is that an application such as a NetWare Loadable Module may misbehave if not designed correctly, thus causing all other tasks to wait and preventing the operating system from regaining control. Preemptive multitasking is available with NetWare SMP as discussed later in this section.

Multitasking is the ability of one processor to do many tasks, whereas *multiprocessing* is the ability to share the work with others. Multiprocessing is a processing strategy in which multiple processors are used in a single computer. Although NetWare has traditionally not supported multiprocessing, this capability has been available through selected system vendors such as Netframe when using their super server as the server platform. Windows NT has supported multiprocessing from the start.

Multiprocessing applications are written to allow tasks and subtasks, or threads, to be executed individually.

If you want to have a house built, you would probably hire a general contractor. The general contractor is responsible for getting the house built, the same way that your database application is responsible for storing information and responding to data queries. Several tasks are required for building a house. The foundation must be poured, the frame must be built, and the roof must go on. Inside, the heating and air conditioning systems, electrical wiring, plumbing, and wallboard must be installed before painting. If the wallboard is installed first, it would have to be torn down to install the electrical wiring behind it. Each of these jobs is a task, and tasks must be scheduled to provide results required by other tasks. Preparing a schedule and making sure that everyone sticks to it is the job of the general contractor. Each of these tasks has subtasks. In multitasking applications, they are known as *threads*.

The general contractor is not going to build the entire house; doing so would take too long. Instead, several subcontractors will be hired by the general contractor. The plumber and electrician can work on their tasks at the same time to get the job done quicker. Now we have multiple processors.

Multiprocessing strategies include *symmetrical* and *asymmetrical multiprocessing*. *Symmetrical multiprocessing* (SMP) occurs when any *central processing unit* (CPU) can perform any task; the work is shared evenly. Both applications and the operating system are spread evenly across all CPUs. *Asymmetrical multiprocessing* (ASMP) occurs when each CPU is dedicated to a specific task. In an asymmetrical multiprocessing system, a dedicated CPU may monitor disk I/O and another may monitor network I/O and yet another may monitor application processing and another may monitor the operating system itself. If the CPU supporting the operating system falls behind, all other processes could be left waiting for the operating system.

Adding additional processors does not always solve the performance problem; in fact, in many cases, the processor is not the cause of problem at all. The problem may be related to a number of other factors including disk throughput or the level of network traffic. Here are a few examples.

A few years ago when Windows 3.1 was just released, I was asked to participate in preparing a strategy for implementing Windows across a large government department. The goal was to automate the installation and minimize the support time. Options included installing Windows on each user's hard disk or keeping all the files on the server. At this time, a typical file server had a 1G hard disk and users had less than 100M. Along with determining the best Windows configuration and working through the various issues, we had to ensure that performance was acceptable. When we were ready to test the time it took to load Windows from the server, it was acceptable with one client connected over Ethernet, but the worst case would be when everyone arrived for work at 8:30 a.m. We set up a test with five simultaneous workstation connections, and the process slowed to a crawl. It looked like everyone would be taking long morning coffee breaks.

Our test configuration used a NetWare 3.1 server with a 386/33, 12M of memory, and an old 300M hard drive. A new 486 server had just been purchased for another project with the same amount of memory and a 1.2G hard disk. We performed the same tests on the new server and found no noticeable degradation in performance when one or five users were connected; in fact, we doubled the number of workstations, still with no noticeable differences. The immediate assumption was that the faster processor was the answer. However, we knew that the CPU was only one piece in the equation. We then repeated the test with the old server but this time with the new hard disk. Our results were the same as with the 486 server. The culprit was the slow hard disk in the old 386 server. Once again, we repeated the tests, but this time with the old hard disk in the 386 server and more memory. Again the results where the same.

- By replacing the hard disk, we removed the bottleneck.

- By keeping the slow hard disk and adding more memory, we provided the system with a larger disk cache, allowing the server to keep files required by the other workstations in memory longer instead of having to retrieve it from the disk a second and third time.

- By upgrading the CPU only, we kept the bottleneck; we just waited faster!

The conclusion is that any single component can have a negative effect on performance; using a faster CPU or more of them is not always the answer. In fact, the CPI is usually the last place we look for file server performance problems. The exception occurs when the file server doubles as a database engine or has some other application running on it, as is illustrated in this next example.

A few years ago, I was involved in the consolidation of a number of LAN segments supporting Windows NT servers. Before any changes were made, we measured the level of network traffic to determine whether moving all the servers to a central location would have any negative effects on that segment. At the same time, Windows NT Performance Monitor was used to look at each file server's performance statistics. Trends were recorded over a 24-hour period for each server to get a baseline measurement. Although all servers where relatively busy, of the five Windows NT file servers, only two showed any significant CPU utilization; as it turned out, they were the two servers supporting an SQL database. The other servers showed high numbers for disk access, and a few required more memory because the peak wait time for disk requests was high and could be solved by providing more memory for disk cache. In general, the bottlenecks were related to the network cards or the hard disk. The shortage of memory in some servers also had a negative effect due to the ability of Windows NT to use disk space as virtual memory. Items that we preferred would remain in memory were being swapped to the page file on the hard disk. Installing more memory solved this problem.

In general, to assess whether you will benefit from multiprocessing, you must determine whether your server applications are I/O intensive, as is the case with file services and includes a server supporting NFS, FTP, and can be the case with Internet Web servers (HTTP). You also must determine whether the applications running on the server processor are as intensive as client/server database engines tend to be. You should ask these questions:

- Do you need multiple processors?
- Are your server applications I/O intensive?
- Are your server applications processor intensive?

Windows NT Multiprocessing

Windows NT implements symmetrical multiprocessing. Windows NT controls multiprocessing at the operating system level and can take advantage of multiprocessor systems available from a variety of manufacturers including Compaq and DEC. With Windows NT, any task including operating system tasks can run on any CPU, and NT controls the show. The downside of how Microsoft has implemented multiprocessing is that managing all the processes does take some system overhead.

To determine which task is given CPU time, you can give each of the tasks threads a priority. (See Figure 1-22.) You can have 32 possible priorities (1–31). The range of priorities is divided in half with the upper 16 reserved for real-time threads and the lower 16 reserved for variable priority threads. A task with a priority level of 0 will only ever be able to execute if no other threads are ready.

As an example of high- and low-priority threads, consider first how a screen saver behaves. Earlier, we told the story of monitoring a number of Windows NT servers. After a 24-hour period, the data from all servers were analyzed. Even the busiest database servers had CPU utilization be-

Figure 1-22
*Windows NT priority
spectrum. (Source:
Microsoft Corpora-
tion)*

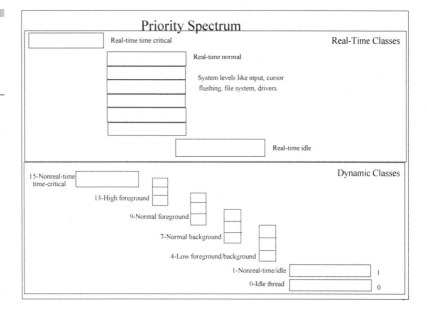

low 50 percent most of the time. We noticed an alarming trend when analyzing the data from one particular server. For 100 percent of the time, the server's CPU utilization was pegged at 100 percent! We found that a screen saver had been running on the server. We then stopped the screen saver, and utilization immediately dropped to only a few percent. This action caused a flurry of activity as users within earshot began disabling their screen savers. The good news is that although some screen savers can be very CPU intensive, they generally run at a low priority and easily give up the CPU when asked. Running more tasks on the server than necessary may not be the best idea, but no measurable degradation was found as a result of the screen saver. The downside was that we had to repeat the measurements.

At the other end of the spectrum is the cruise missile. Guidance systems rely on accurate data being available when it is required. Perhaps a shrewd programmer will build in some allowances for missing a few cycles; however, when the missile must turn, the system had better respond. Data acquisition is performed real time. If Windows NT is the operating system used, real-time threads run at the same priority for their entire lifetime. These threads run at higher priorities than all variable priority threads, which means that they must be used sparingly.

When a variable priority thread is created, it has its initial priority set based on the priority of the process that it belongs to. This priority can be dynamically adjusted up or down a maximum of two levels by the Windows NT kernel's dispatcher. The thread sits in the dispatcher's priority queue in standby state until it is ready to execute. (See Figure 1-23.) After the thread is ready to execute, it is switched to the ready state, at which time the dispatcher will bump or preempt any lower priority threads that are being serviced. To get an idea of how often this occurs, you can view the Context Switches Per Second counter from Windows NT Performance Monitor. A multithreaded application running on a single processor system will usually switch contexts quite frequently, which is not very efficient.

Figure 1-23
Thread states. (Courtesy of Learning Tree International)

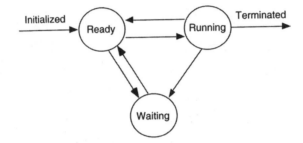

NetWare Multiprocessing

NetWare Symmetrical Multi-Processing is an add-on NLM for NetWare and is now bundled with NetWare 4.11. Previously, it was available through Novell system partners who manufacture multiprocessor servers. When NetWare SMP is installed, it provides a second operating system kernel that works preemptively to support SMP-aware NetWare Loadable Modules while providing backward compatibility for existing applications. Applications must be specifically written to take advantage of SMP.

In implementing SMP, Novell has removed the hardware-specific calls from the NetWare kernel and provided a *Platform Specific Module* (PSM), which acts as an interface between the hardware and the operating system. This PSM is provided to Novell by the hardware manufacturer and is included with NetWare 4.11. For SMP support in previous NetWare versions, this PSM must be obtained directly from the manufacturer. For each processor in the file server, a multiprocessor driver must be loaded. (See Figure 1-24.)

Non-SMP-aware applications will continue to make calls to processor 0 as usual. Calls to processor 0 are interpreted by the *Multi-Processor*

Figure 1-24
NetWare 4.1 SMP
architecture.
(Courtesy of www.
ITcoach.com)

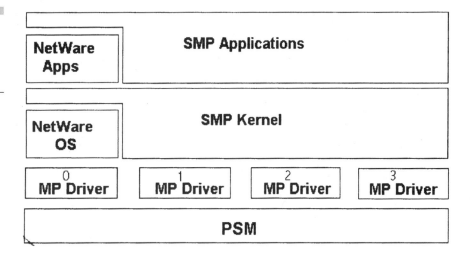

(MP) driver for that processor and passed on to the PSM that interfaces with the hardware. PSM modules written for UnixWare, of which there are many, can be recompiled to run with NetWare 4.1 SMP because the *Hardware Abstraction Layer* (HAL) specifications used are the same.

SMP-aware applications make calls to the SMP kernel, which takes care of scheduling tasks. Processes can be moved off processor 0 to another processor by the SMP kernel, allowing the non-SMP kernel to have the full processing power of processor 0. SMP applications can be written to take advantage of either Round Robin or *First In, First Out* (FIFO) processor scheduling. Round Robin is typically associated with preemptive multi-tasking. As discussed earlier, managing multiple tasks takes more system overhead if each one gets a piece of processor time as the Round Robin implementation allows; however, both methods are supported.

The following are three ways that processor 0 can be used with NetWare SMP:

■ Shared: The default setting is that the SMP kernel and the NetWare kernel share processor 0.

■ Dedicated: Processor 0 is used exclusively by NetWare and not shard with SMP.

■ Priority: The same as shared mode; however, NetWare is given a higher priority over SMP. Novell recommends this setting if you have seven or more processors.

To further optimize processor usage, you can move LAN traffic off processor 0. Doing so effectively eliminates the server's CPU from being the performance bottleneck when multiple high-speed LAN cards are installed in the server.

The following quotes have been taken from the June, 1996, Novell application notes that compare Web server performance on a single processor NetWare server to a quad CPU Windows NT server:

Unlike general-purpose operating systems such as UNIX and Windows NT, NetWare is a special-purpose operating system that is specifically designed to host network services. As such, it is a superior platform for special-purpose network applications such as database and Web servers.

As shown by the benchmark results presented in this appnote, NetWare is a superior platform for high performance network services and special-purpose applications such as database and Web servers. . . . NetWare provides significant strengths that general-purpose operating systems cannot match.

You can judge for yourself if this statement is true. File and print services have been Novell's strong points, and in general we would agree. But also consider this quote from Microsoft's Web Capacity Planning document:

Many IT administrators planning a Web site expect to find a simple formula that calculates the Web server's hardware based on a few simple assumptions about server usage. For example, the statement "The server's main task is to share static HTML documents" might determine the server's minimum processor speed, or "The average size of the shared HTML documents is 15K" might define the server's bandwidth requirements. If the process were this straightforward, there wouldn't be so many administrators wondering why they have never found that "simple formula."

The most important drain on a Web server's processor comes from additional applications that help the Web server produce dynamic pages. Applications written to the *Internet Server API* (ISAPI) specification often execute with one third to one fifth the CPU impact of *Common Gateway Interface* (CGI) applications. This is largely because ISAPI applications are loaded once, and run in the Web server service's process, whereas CGI applications run as separate processes and a new process starts every time the application is used.

FAULT TOLERANCE   One of the key concerns with any network operating system is how robust it is and what happens in the event of a systems failure. Any downtime in a corporate LAN can be very expensive in terms of lost productivity. Even worse is the loss of data that either cannot be re-created or will take a significant amount of time to do so. This situation becomes even more critical if the operating system is a source of revenue, as may be the case with an Internet server or database server.

Many backup solutions are available for both NetWare and Windows NT. Each manufacturer supplies a basic utility to perform backups, and several commercial backup products are also available for each operating system. Having a backup system in place is necessary; however, if the system does fail, some downtime will occur while any hardware repairs take place and the system is restored. In many cases, this downtime required to fix the problem is unacceptable. To address this concern, both Novell and Microsoft have developed "fault tolerant" features, which they have included in their products.

To show you how critical these issues are, consider the following scenarios:

One of my new clients had a financial system that was used to keep track of donations for this nonprofit organization. It stored not only financial data but also a database of names of people and organizations who had contributed in the past. To a large degree, the continued operation of this organization relied on the mailing list this system could generate.

I was initially contacted to review their requirements and recommend a shopping list of items for which they should budget over the next few years. When I first visited their site, I was concerned by the age of their equipment. The file server was over five years old, and this was at a time when hard drives were big, heavy, slow, and relatively unreliable by today's standards. I was pleased to see that the staff was religiously backing up the system each night and had a well-organized set of backups, which they were required to keep for a number of years for legal purposes. Their backup strategy involved taking full backups each Monday, with incremental backups the rest of the week. This process continued for a month at a time, and at the end of each month, the staff would keep the Monday tapes and recycle the others. After the next month passed, they would recycle all the previous months' tapes while keeping the last full backup of that month. Their tape collection included one full backup for each month over the last five years plus a full set of full and incremental backups for the current month.

The staff at this organization felt that maintaining this backup schedule was tedious and time-consuming. They also were concerned with the cost of tapes but realized that keeping them was necessary. I was impressed with how thorough they seemed to be in never missing a backup.

My first recommendation was to budget for a new server as soon as possible because I was concerned about the age of the equipment. They were also running out of disk space on their 100M hard disk (which was big in those days). They felt that the cost of a new hard drive was just too expensive at that time (almost $4000 for a 300M drive).

Within days of my initial visit, the server crashed. The organization was forced to bite the bullet, and we scrambled to get new hardware, a process that took over a week. A few late nights were spent configuring the server and getting things properly set up, but finally the worst was over, or so we thought. It was now time to restore the data from the last full backup . . . but the tape was empty! We went back to the previous month's tape, and it was empty as well. After going back through five years' worth of backups, we could not restore data from a single tape. Eventually, we sent out the hard drive to have the data recovered from it, and we were fortunate to get most of it back, although doing so was extremely expensive.

To review what happened here, the organization lost over a week of productivity due to a system crash. The staff were fortunate to recover most of their data at a considerable expense. They wasted considerable time performing backups that could not be used. In the end, they wondered what else they could have done to prevent what had just occurred. Do you test your restores regularly?

I know of a number of financial institutions that use local area network technology to run their equities trading systems. They could not tolerate the downtime I have just described and have gone to great expense setting up redundant systems with multiple backup strategies and hot swappable components that can be replaced on the fly. Although we all may not be able to justify this level of fault tolerance, it is an important consideration when selecting a network operating system.

DISK FAULT TOLERANCE Fault tolerance describes the server's ability to survive a component failure. Novell had a lead on the PC network operating system competition early on by providing disk fault tolerance. Initially, this capability simply involved providing a spare area on the hard drive known as a *hot fix* partition. Information was cached in memory before being committed to the disk. When the information was written to the disk, it was tested for accuracy. If a sector on the disk was found to be bad, the information was not removed from memory. Instead, the operating system would mark this sector bad so that it could never be used again, and a pointer to a new sector in the hot fix area identified where the data could now be stored. Only after it was successfully written to the disk would the information memory be discarded.

Windows NT supports two file systems: FAT and NTFS. If NTFS is used, the NT server will have the same level of fault tolerance as just described. Both Novell and Microsoft now support hot fixing. If a problem occurs with the disk, the end users likely will not experience any effects unless the failure is quite extreme. The danger with this strategy, of course, is that your hard disk could be slowly dying piece by piece, sector by sector, without your knowledge. Viewing the error logs to determine the number and frequency of disk errors is important. In addition, both NetWare and Windows NT configured with NTFS keep two records of the file directories on different locations of the hard disk in case one becomes corrupt.

With NetWare 2.15 came a product known as SFT II. This solution is now standard in all versions of NetWare and provides mirroring and duplexing capabilities. Windows NT was designed with this capability, so although Novell was first, both NetWare and Windows NT support disk mirroring and duplexing.

Disk mirroring refers to the configuration in which two identically sized disk drives are connected to the same disk controller. The operating system is responsible for managing the process of writing information to each drive consecutively to ensure that one is a mirror image of the other. This does create a slowdown compared to a nonmirrored drive configuration, because each time information is written, it is written twice. Also, if the disk controller were to fail, both drives would be lost.

Disk duplexing is similar to mirroring except it requires a separate controller for each drive; again information is written twice, but with two controllers, this process can occur simultaneously. With Novell's implementation of disk duplexing, there is an added advantage of being able to read data from either disk. Information is accepted from the disk that retrieves the information first.

Another solution that is available is *Redundant Array of Inexpensive Disks*, or RAID. In a RAID configuration, many disks are linked together to form the disk array. There are many levels of RAID protection. RAID can be implemented if you purchase from a hardware vendor a dedicated RAID system that plugs into the file server, or if you load software on the server that will manage the process. Both third-party hardware and software RAID solutions are available for NetWare and Windows NT; however, Microsoft has chosen to include this function in Windows NT from the factory.

According to Microsoft, RAID 0 includes a disk array that implements striping without any drive redundancy. This gives you a faster means of accessing your data; however, it offers no fault tolerance and is less reliable than a single-drive implementation. NT implements RAID 0 by linking all drives together to form one large volume. When a file is written, a portion of the file is stored on each disk. All of the disks read and write together, so just like when you have your friends over to help you with your electrical wiring in your new house we discussed earlier, many hands make light work! The problem with this configuration is that if one drive fails, you now have a big hole in your disk volume.

RAID 1 is disk mirroring, as we have already discussed. Two drives store identical information so that one is a mirror of the other. Windows NT also supports RAID 1. RAID 2, 3, and 4 are not available natively with either system.

RAID 5 dedicates the equivalent of one entire disk for storing check data but distributes the check data over all the drives in the group. The check data can be used to calculate the data on a missing drive. For example, sector 1 of disk 5 may be assigned to hold the check data for sector 1 of the remaining data drives and so on. Recovery of a single drive failure relies on the old data being available on an existing disk. As long as the old sector data and the old check data values are known, the new check data for a single sector write can be calculated. To implement RAID 5 to give you 2M of storage using 1M disks, you would require three disks. Although this solution works quite well and does speed up disk access, it places additional overhead on the server. A preferred solution is to use a hardware RAID disk array. Windows NT provides for RAID 5 natively.

SYSTEM FAULT TOLERANCE   Along with NetWare 3.11, in 1992 Novell offered a second version of this operating system to provide full SFT level III fault tolerance. NetWare SFT III 3.11 allows two servers to be configured as mirror images of each other. Data is written to both servers in the event that one server fails. If the primary server experiences a hardware failure, the second server automatically takes over servicing NetWare clients without missing a step because both disk and memory are mirrored. SFT III has been Novell's ace in the hole when dealing with competition from other network vendors in mission-critical installations.

Here's how SFT III works: One server acts as a primary while the other acts as a secondary or backup server. The primary server's main task is to respond to client requests, whereas the secondary server spends most of its cycles keeping up with changes on the primary. When the primary receives a request, it marks that request as a mirrored server event, which is then acted on by the primary server. At the same time, these events are sent to the secondary server, which also processes the event. If the primary were to fail, although the backup may not be at the same step as the primary, it does have all the requests queued and will soon get to the point where the primary was. Any additional requests will be received by the primary server directly.

Because the designation of primary server is dynamic and is determined by which server has been up the longest, the secondary becomes the new primary server. When the secondary server is placed back into service, the primary will synchronize both memory and hard disks.

Between the two servers is a high-speed link supported by placing a Mirrored Server Link card in each server. Each server can be of different hardware configurations as well because the NetWare SFT III I/O functions are handled separately. Only the server's Mirrored Server Engine (MSE) is common. This also means that existing NetWare NLM can run on SFT III without being modified unless they write to the hardware level.

Advantages of SFT III include the ability to service the hardware without bringing down the server. Each server can be serviced individually as long as one is always up, and the two servers are synchronized before one is brought down. If you are concerned about how your company will deal with a disaster such as an earthquake or fire, the two servers could reside at different locations. The maximum distance between servers is determined by the type of Mirrored Server Link selected.

Server performance is also enhanced using SFT III because data can be read from either server. Whichever server finds the information first can provide it to the client, so at any one time each server could be busy retrieving different information from the hard drive while other requests are in the queue. (See Figure 1-25.)

For a simpler solution for NetWare server fault tolerance, other third-party solutions are available. LANShadow is one solution that continuously mirrors individual files, directories, or entire server volumes to a designated backup server. LANShadow runs as an NLM and mirrors information over existing LAN and WAN connections, and backup can be continuous or scheduled. Individual files can be selected to include or exclude in the process based on their priority (which you set). LANShadow doesn't require dedicated hardware or that the destination server be physically connected to and configured exactly like a production server.

LANShadow's activity is transparent to the user. When first installed, LANShadow copies all designated files. After that, LANShadow copies only those files that have changed since the previous cycle and deletes from the destination server all files that have been deleted from the source server.

The LANShadow Bindery Phase mirrors bindery user information. In addition, trustee information is mirrored as files and directories are copied during the Copy Phase. Two NetWare file servers running NetWare

Figure 1-25
NetWare SFT III
architecture. (Source:
Novell, Inc.)

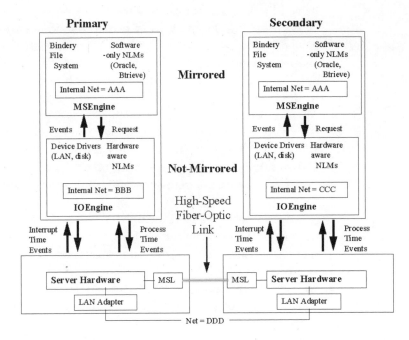

3.x or greater and enough available hard disk space on the destination file server are required. LANShadow requires a source and destination NetWare server. Typically, they are two separate file servers.

The servers used in a LANShadow configuration must be running NetWare, but it can be any version of NetWare. However, note that if a NetWare 3.x and 4.x server are paired, the bindery cannot be mirrored, as it can be when two 3.x servers are paired together.

If the primary server fails, users can continue to work by logging in to the backup server, or the backup server can be renamed and restarted so that users can continue to log in using the same server name. If users continue to work by logging into the backup server, LANShadow can convert user login script references from the source server to the destination server references using LANShadow's Convert login scripts option on the destination server.

NT System Fault Tolerance

Similar solutions exist for Windows NT Server to provide server fault tolerance. Although more will come in the near future, some good solutions exist today. With NetWare, SFT III provided a single "logical" server by mirroring two separate servers. The operating system was designed specifically for this job. LANShadow's product took existing servers that were treated separately and kept files synchronized between the two. In the NT world, Octopus Technologies provides similar functionality to LANShadow, and clustering provides similar functionality to SFT III.

Octopus Technologies provide what they describe as *automatic switch-over* technology for Windows NT. More information can be found on the Internet at **http://www.octopustech.com/product.html**.

The first feature of the Octopus product is that it can be used as an on-line backup of your NT server by automatically synchronizing files between the primary server and the backup server. This process can be scheduled to occur during off-hours or can be continuous.

The second feature is that in the event of a server failure the backup server can automatically switch over to become the primary server by renaming itself. The necessary Windows NT services are renamed and restarted. Effectively, Octopus provides server mirroring as well as automatic switch-over in the event of a server failure.

The following sequence of events was provided by Octopus Technologies:

1. The source system fails.

2. The target system does not receive an "I'm Alive" message from the source for 60 seconds.

3. The target system will try to access the registry of the source system.

4. The target system cannot access the source registry.

5. The target system will conclude the source system has failed and will begin the automatic switch-over process.

6. A "takeover" command will be executed if one was specified.

7. The target system will be renamed with the name of the failed source system.

8. All the services of the target system will be stopped and restarted.

9. A "post takeover" command will be executed if specified.

10. The new source system is now up and running.

11. All clients are automatically connected to the new source system.

Figure 1-26 illustrates this process.

Another solution that is beginning to get some media attention is NT Server Clustering. Clustered VAX computer systems from DEC have been around since the mid 1980s. Using VMS as the operating system, multiple CPUs could share resources such as hard disks. In the event of a failure, processing continued on the second processor. From the end user's perspective, the cluster was seen as one logical entity, and where the resources were physically situated was unimportant.

DEC has taken this technology and developed it for Windows NT Server; however, just recently Microsoft had a change of heart and chose to side with Stratus Computers, which is also developing a clustering product named RADIO. In conjunction with Microsoft, this product is code-named Wolfpack and will be released by Microsoft.

Today the solution is available from DEC if you purchase its Alpha servers; however, DEC has stated that it will provide an upgrade path to Wolfpack when it becomes available. More information is available from Digital at **http://www.windows.digital.com**, and RADIO server information can be found at **http://www.stratus.com/Stratus/ProdServ/ Hardware/Radio/radiobroch/**.

The Wolfpack project was first announced in October of 1995 with the product shipping date scheduled for early 1997. More information on the Wolfpack is available at **http://www.microsoft.com/ntserver/nts351/ cluster.htm**.

Initially, Microsoft's clustering will provide automatic "fail-over" to another server if the primary server fails. This will be transparent to the end user because the cluster is a group of servers that will appear as one log-

Figure 1-26
Octopus for Windows NT. (Courtesy of Octopus Technologies)

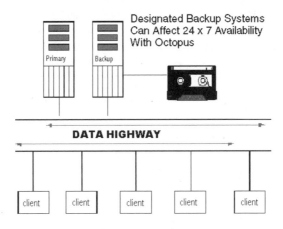

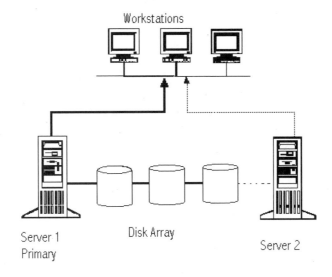

Figure 1-27
Windows NT cluster.
(Courtesy of www.IT-coach.com)

ical server. Eventually, Microsoft plans to provide scaleability by supporting multiple servers in the cluster. Both systems can share the same hard disks within a cluster. When a system in the cluster fails, the cluster software will recover by moving the work load to an available server within the cluster. (See Figure 1-27.)

Microsoft is hoping to standardize this solution by providing application developers with an Application Programming Interface (API) to access to allow them to build scaleable applications such as database engines.

Table 1-3 provides a comparison of NOS features.

Table 1-3

NOS Feature comparison. (Courtesy of Learning Tree

Feature	NetWare 3.12	NetWare 4.1	Windows NT Server
Architecture			
Preemptive multitasking	No	one additional CPU only	Yes
Multiprocessor support	No	Yes	Yes
Processors: Intel	Yes	Yes	Yes
Processors: RISC, MIPS, ALPHA, PPC	No	No	Yes
Virtual Memory	No	No	Yes

Continued

Table 1-3

Continued.

Feature	NetWare 3.12	NetWare 4.1	Windows NT Server
Microkernel architecture	No, boots from DOS	No, boots from DOS	Yes
Memory Protection for applications and subsystems	No	DOMAIN.NLM	Yes
TRANSPORT PROTOCOLS	IPX/SPX, TCP/IP	IPX/SPX, TCP/IP	NetBEUI, TCP/IP, NW Link IPX/SPX
File System			
Efficient Sub-block allocation	No	Yes, up to 64Kbytes	Static 512 bytes
File Compression	No	Yes	Yes , NT 3.51
Elevator Seeking	Yes	Yes	No
High-performance asynchronous I/O	No	No	Yes
Server Performance Optimization			
Cache	(Static cache)	(Dynamic Cache)	1 Gigabyte per process
Security			
C2 Security Level	No	Yes	Yes
Single Logon	No	Yes, NDS	Yes, Domain
Centralized security event auditing	No	Yes, client	Yes, client and server
Network Management			
GUI Utilities	No	Yes, but not at server	Yes
Remote administration, performance, and event monitoring	add-on	some and add-on	Yes
DHCP support	No	Yes	Yes
WINS support	No	No	Yes
BOOTP support	No	Yes	Yes
DNS	No	Yes	Yes

Table 1-3

Feature	NetWare 3.12	NetWare 4.1	Windows NT Server
Performance Monitoring			
Graphical remote performance monitoring or other servers	Yes, add-on	Yes, add-on	Yes
Fault Tolerance			
File system recovery log	No	No	Yes
Redundant server capacity	No	Yes - SFT III	No, but add-on provides mirrored shares and through clustering
Hot fix/bad block read after write verification	Yes	Yes	Yes
Disk mirroring/ duplexing	Yes	Yes	Yes
Disk striping	No	No	Yes
Raid Support	Yes, third party	Yes, third party	Yes, NT software or third party

SUMMARY

By now, you should have a good idea as to the strengths and weaknesses of NetWare and Windows NT Server. Entire books have been written on individual aspects of each operating system and how they work, because they are each very complex. To the noninitiated, NetWare's clunky interface conjures up the same emotions as UNIX does for Windows users; however, it is quite powerful. Windows NT has lulled many into a false sense of security by presenting them with a straightforward user interface when, in fact, it is equally as complicated under the hood.

We now end this brief history of PC networking and Windows NT Server-to-NetWare comparison. As both operating systems mature as products, we are beginning to see that the future of networking looks very different from the past. Gone are many of the proprietary standards as organizations buy into the global Internet technologies and begin to implement them internally as "intranets." The race is on between the two leaders to see who can successfully make the transition or at least overcome the onslaught of marketing hype surrounding the network arena. The role of a network file server is beginning to come into question as file and print services become a commodity item. For a network operating system to survive, it must not only provide superior file and print but also value-added services at a reduced maintenance cost. One issue that is easily overlooked but yet will have one of the biggest effects on your decision to integrate the two operating systems or fully migrate is application support. Many organizations have custom applications they have developed around their current technology. You may have commercial applications that do not function in one environment or the other. Be sure to give this issue due consideration and perform any application test necessary before making your decision.

Also, as technology advances, any shortcomings in one product or the other will be overcome. The latest trend for Directory Services is toward the *Lightweight Directory Access Protocol* (LDAP). LDAP is essentially a subset of the X.500 directory standard on which Novell based NDS and on which Microsoft based Exchange. Windows NT 5.0, scheduled for release in 1997, promises LDAP support, and Novell is making NDS LDAP compliant.

LDAP will also become the Directory Services for the Internet as other vendors embrace this standard. A company can maintain a single LDAP directory containing e-mail addresses and other network services. The battle Novell is hoping to win is for NDS to become the LDAP engine of choice. Novell has announced that it will license NDS to other vendors and will include NDS for Windows NT.

You may have already chosen your network operating system, which has no doubt brought you to this point. The issues we will address in the remaining chapters deal with how to make the two systems work together and how to eventually migrate from one to the other if that is what you want. We have included a number of references, including Internet Web sites, for you to find out more information as new products are released.

Integration and Migration Issues: Planning, Management, and Tools

This chapter covers the major areas of concern for integrating NetWare and Windows NT. It will set the stage for much of the rest of the book as it will provide an overview of all the different possible ways to integrate clients and servers in a multi NetWare and Windows NT network environment. Particular emphasis will be made on the project management and support issues involved. We will cover the migration processes and how to support a single network user login/logon in a multi NetWare and Windows NT network environment (although this issue is discussed more completely in Chapter 6). Finally, during any information systems integration and migration project, a number of basic steps or procedures should be followed. We will highlight these procedures and take you through actual case study examples.

Chapter Objectives

- Integrating NetWare and Windows NT
- Migrating user directory databases
- Integration and migration procedures
- Microsoft integration and migration software tools
- Novell integration and migration software tools
- Third-party tools

Why Support a Mixed-Platform Network?

There is not question that supporting a multiplatform network can generally involve a lot more work than supporting a single platform network. However, probably one of the most commonly accepted reasons for supporting different network platforms and workstation operating systems within an organization is the business requirements. Software applications and services that businesses require to remain competitive are not always available or supported on the same network hardware and software, or network architecture for that matter. Therefore, integration of disparate networking platforms will no doubt remain a key requirement for competitive businesses in the years to come.

Another main reason for supporting a heterogeneous network environment is that the cost of replacing legacy, or existing, infrastructures can be very expensive. Coming up with some level of integration that is acceptable and gets the job done is often easier (although this approach sometimes takes more work by the people supporting it, and subsequently the hidden costs are usually greater in the long run). Political issues may also have a very big impact on the technological direction of an organization. Let's face it, people have preferences and sometimes those preferences affect the strategic direction of an entire organization and its technology plan.

More specifically, an organization may decide to incorporate Windows NT within its information-providing structure because a particular application is available to meet its business requirements or because it gives the organization a platform on which to easily develop client/server applications. However, the same organization may equally decide that its existing investment in NetWare may be too significant to simply throw away. In our experience, the cost-versus-benefits analysis of a complete migration from one platform completely to another rarely demonstrates that migrating this way is economically feasible. Here again, personal preference or strategic direction is the often quoted reason for performing such a significant undertaking.

In any case, should an organization still choose to make such a migration, at some point in between it will have to deal with the integration of both platforms. Sometimes this integration phase will take place over the weekend only. In others, it will stretch out over several months or years. The scale of the network in question is usually the determining factor here.

Consider, for example, the network components in Figure 2-1.

In this figure, we have several network components that require some level of integration between them, both from a hardware and software perspective. Additionally, several network services that are available need to be shared, such as file and print, electronic mail, database access, and communication services.

Figure 2-1
NetWare and Windows NT integration. (Courtesy of Learning Tree International)

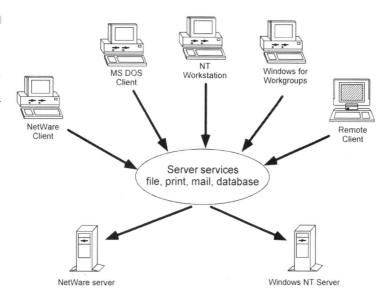

What do you foresee will be some of the potential integration challenges? Before you read on, take a moment to write down some problems on the following lines:

_____

_____

_____

_____

_____

On the surface, you can see some obvious issues. The ability to access resources from a single point using one single login/logon is probably the biggest issue. Anyone who has had to use different data terminals or manage multiple network user login/logon names and passwords will understand the importance of this issue. However, some other big concerns come to the forefront such as communication protocol selection, security, maintenance, training of support staff and users, terminology, network traffic, file system backups and post migration access to these backups, and finally the potential aspect of a complete migration to one platform or another.

Single Point of Access to Network Resources

Users on a network want to be able to access all network resources as easily and seamlessly as possible. Not long ago (less than 10 years now), I worked with clients who had to reboot their workstations every time they wanted to connect to a different network operating system server or host mini/mainframe computer. Throughout a network environment, printers and file systems may be connected to different lower-level physical hardware platforms as well as different server platforms (NetWare, NT, UNIX). However, end users don't care where the resources are located, nor should they. The network administrator's task is to provide access to these resources in a manner that is consistent across the network.

Even though the users may be attaching or connecting to several different server operating systems or platforms throughout a typical work day, they do not want to be encumbered with having to log out and log in or log on again to each server service they access. So a single point of access goes beyond just providing the users with one personal computer on their desktops. It involves providing them with access to all network resources through the single login/logon that they go through when they first begin their working day or each time they access the network.

Internetworking: Transport Protocols

If we start from the low end of the integration process, we will certainly need to ensure that users are on similar networks or have internetworking devices such as bridges or routers that allow them to interconnect. Above that, though, we will need some common transport protocol between the two platforms so that users can send and receive each other's packets of information and user requests generated from higher-level applications such as file and print services. An example of a protocol supported between both network operating systems is *Internetwork Packet eXchange/Sequence Packet eXchange* (IPX/SPX) from Novell, Inc. Although Novell created this protocol based on an earlier version of *Xerox Networking System* (XNS) protocol, both NetWare and Windows NT support this transport protocol. Given the recent success of the Internet (the real Internet with a capital "I"), both NetWare and NT support the use of the *Transport Control Protocol/Internet Protocol* (TCP/IP), which is also used exclusively in the UNIX and Internet environments. Here, however, NetWare and NT use TCP/IP to transport their own proprietary service level (that is, file and print) protocols.

Interoperability: Service Protocol

After we select a common transport protocol, we need to select a common service protocol so that clients from either platform can access network services like file and print. NetWare uses the *NetWare Core Protocol* (NCP) to provide access to these and other services by clients. Windows NT uses the Server Message Block protocol to provide access to similar services. The end result is that clients of their respective network operating systems get access to services the server provides. However, what if a client from one network operating platform (NetWare?) wants to access services provided on the other (NT?)

From a server perspective, this challenge can be solved in two main ways: one is through a gateway, and the other is by providing a service protocol that the client already supports. In the first instance, some device would intercept a file or print request and translate it to the service protocol the intended server supports. In this example, a NetWare client that uses the NetWare Core Protocol would submit a print job to an NT Server that supports *Server Message Block* (SMB). In the latter case, the server in question would support the service protocol that the client is currently configured to use. So, in the preceding example, the NetWare client supporting NetWare Core Protocol would submit a print job to an NT server that also supports the NetWare Core Protocol. In fact, the NT server would appear to the NetWare client as just another NetWare server.

However, we could also get the client to support multiple service protocol *stacks*, or *suites* as they are sometimes called. Although doing so has not been easy in the past, the new 32-bit, *Dynamic Link Library* (DLL) and Vxd-based systems are making this job much easier. In this case, the client would support both the NCP- and SMB-based service protocols.

Security

You may have some existing security configurations which ensure that your network and the services it provides are safe from both internal and external intrusion. A major question here is how the introduction of a new network platform and its clients will affect this existing security structure. Which operating system security will take priority, and which one will remain in effect? Will users accessing files on a NetWare server from a NetWare client have more access than when accessing the same files from a Windows NT client if they are using a different service protocol? Do NetWare rights translate equally to Windows NT permissions? Does Windows NT support some of the standard management capabilities that NetWare provides such as Workgroup Manager? Which NetWare Trustee Assignments does Windows NT not support if users migrate files to NT? Does the Windows NT Remote Access Server available on even the Windows NT Workstation version introduce a potential network dial-in access security threat?

As you can see, security issues pose many questions—questions that we did not have to consider when dealing with only one platform. Implementing strong security policies and procedures that do not cripple an organization's ability to use its technology is a difficult task as it is. We like to say, "We do not want to enable the organization's users by disabling technology," as was done at one company by disabling all the floppy drives to avoid virus infection. Further, new security loopholes are being discovered every day, and manufacturers such as Novell and Microsoft are continually racing to plug these holes. Security holes created by the integration of two platforms present an equally challenging problem in that you can rarely get a solution from one of the two NOS service support groups. This discussion usually becomes one of "Which way is the finger pointing?" Yet you still need to resolve the issue and close the security gap to protect your organization's information in a heterogeneous environment.

Maintenance

Hardware and software maintenance support issues are increased almost exponentially. In fact, the issue is not just a question of having twice as much network operating system software to install. You now have to perform ongoing software upgrades, patches, and fixes, and you have to implement new NOS versions as they become available (to fix problems the earlier ones created). As always, network services that worked before the upgrade may not work after an upgrade is performed. This simple situation is further compounded by the fact that upgrading software on one platform may, in fact, cause access by another network operating system server or client to stop working. These issues can be resolved with appropriate testing. However, you must realize that you will need to be testing access across multiple platforms, so even the task of testing the new configuration has become larger and more time-consuming.

Many companies have in the past standardized on one particular hardware platform to avoid the costs associated with a mixed personal computer environment (for example, PC and Mac). Given this one issue of maintenance in a mixed network environment, it is a wonder that anyone even suggests the idea in the first place. But we must remember that business-critical application requirements bring forward this challenge, not the desire to make different technologies work together!

Training

Remember that we're not just talking about another operating system. We're talking about the integration of the two. This, in turn, requires an understanding of how both of them work. More often than not, support staff will be coming from one camp or the other. They may have experience in NetWare but little in Windows NT (or vice versa). In fact, their experience may be limited to Windows for Workgroups, which is very different "under the hood" than Windows NT. Users, on the other hand, may not be particularly concerned about what server operating system you, as network administrator, are supporting. However, they may require training on the new client software if moving from DOS/Windows for Workgroups to Windows NT Workstation. They may also require training if the introduction of a new server presents a new method of access to the file or print services such as is introduced when using a gateway to access the NetWare server file system instead of accessing it directly as may have been done in the past. More likely, the network support staff will require more training on how to set up the new client environment properly than the end users will require to use it.

Of the two, network support staff will certainly require the most training. Additionally, you can expect that the type of training that they will require will be more expensive than end user training, given the level of technology that we are dealing with (network operating system software versus application software). After a new method of server service access has been established, network administrators can usually provide sufficient in-house training to provide end users with the information they require.

Terminology

When you get right down to crux of the matter, networks provide organizations with a similar set of services. Yes, different methods are sometimes used to provide these services, but under detailed inspection, the methods used are comparable (for example, Novell's Open Data Link Interface versus Microsoft's Network Device Interface Specification). All too often, the greater task is finding out how both NOS systems refer to the same service or function and what terminology they use to define it. This task is so great, in fact, that Microsoft even developed a Terminology Guide comparing Novell and Microsoft terms. After you know what something is called and what it compares to in the network environment you are used to working in, figuring out how it works is often much easier then.

Learning new terminology also goes hand in hand with training. A good course or reference material will help bridge the gap between the two NOS dictionaries by providing comparisons and links to facilitate comprehension of the new terms and what they mean. Unfortunately, not many exist, as you certainly can appreciate. Courses and books tend to focus on one or the other and leave you to create the link. Probably one of the better guides we have come across is the "Terminology Guide: The Novell to Microsoft Dictionary." We have included a copy in the appendix for your additional research.

Network Traffic

As an area of concern, network traffic has less to do with the introduction of some new network-connected devices than it does with the type of network traffic being introduced. In most integration or even migration scenarios, much of the existing network-connected devices will still be connected to the network. In other words, the number of devices connected to the network does not increase significantly. Moreover, it is usually the software running on these workstations that changes. The changes can include a new transport and/or service level protocol, and even a change in the workstation operating system.

However, the most significant impact usually comes from the addition of network traffic that is concerned with network configuration. For example, if a network is currently using Novell's *Internetwork Packet eXchange* (IPX) protocol for transporting user data and requests on the network and then introduces an additional protocol such as *Internet Protocol* (IP) to support the new Windows NT workstations and servers, the data portion of the network traffic is not increased significantly. However, the network traffic specifically concerned with tracking and updating network configuration is doubled. Both IPX and IP require a similar form of *Routing Information Protocol* (RIP) to announce changes to the network configuration. Not only must the routers now support both forms for RIP, which are not compatible with each other, but they must also do twice the amount of processing. Additionally, NetWare uses the *Service Advertising Protocol* (SAP) to advertise its services, and Windows NT uses browsers when configured with the Internet Protocol. Both provide the same service but for a different network operating system. The net result (pardon the pun) is more traffic on the network; this traffic is not user data, but traffic concerned with providing access to network services. Many organizations have experienced problems when introducing new protocols over slow wide area network links in particular. Essentially, the routers become flooded with the amount of traffic required just to keep themselves updated regarding network configuration, let alone to handle the actual forwarding of user data and request packets. As a result, network operating system and router vendors have developed "filter" applications that allow the network administrator to filter nonessential routing and service traffic to use the WAN and LAN links efficiently.

File System Backup

Networks grow and evolve over time. As they are used, information is stored and then periodically (we hope) backed up. One of the major considerations in any full-fledged migration from one platform to another is accessing information on the previous platform's backup system. For example, your company may perform backups of its data using one of the popular NetWare tape backup systems, and you have decided to migrate to NT. How will you retrieve information from the NetWare backup system if no NetWare servers are around after the migration period? Do you have a version of the existing backup software for Windows NT, and will it support the same tape format done on the NetWare servers? You need to address these and many other questions before migrating to the new platform.

Complete Migration

Although we said earlier that a full and complete migration from one network platform to another rarely makes economical sense, some companies are doing it for one of the reasons we stated: the task associated with managing two platforms is simply too expensive. The complete migration is usually justified more on the principles of strategic direction, application development, or ultimately personal preference (yes, it does happen).

In any event, any migration will involve some level of integration so that all the things we talked about will still be issues—some less so than others. The main issues in a migration will involve getting the information over to the other platform as completely as possible while creating a new network environment that requires minimal post migration reconfiguration. This information will include both user/group account and file data.

Finally, probably one of the more subtle areas that a network administrator will need to deal with in implementing the new technology is resistance to change. It's not a hardware or software issue; it's a people issue that you are probably all too familiar with. The level of resistance to change within an organization can be significantly reduced through proper testing of the integrated or migrated solution and by trying to reduce the level or magnitude of change that the end users actually experience in their day-to-day work routines. Ultimately, if significant change is required, then management should be prepared to train people properly to ensure that the organization receives the best return on investment.

Getting All the Systems to Work Together

In looking at the previous network diagram of integration components (shown in Figure 1-1), this question immediately comes to the foreground within any organization: What is it going to take to get all the systems to work together? A saying here is probably very appropriate: "Standardization is the key to simplicity." Try to select one common transport and service protocol if possible. Try to use one client workstation software package as opposed to supporting different client workstation software packages on different machines (for example, Novell NetWare Client for NT versus Microsoft NetWare Client for NT). Following these guidelines can simplify even a common network platform, but it can do wonders when you are working in a mixed environment where day-to-day fire fighting of network problems may lead you to often consider a different career path. You may be thinking, "Oh yeah, sure," and we agree that standardizing is not an easy task. However, generally you can set up categories of standardization to create pockets of conformity within your organization at least. This result is often the best you can hope for.

The OSI Reference Model

No book on network computing would be complete without its dissertation on the OSI Reference Model. (See Figure 2-2.) However, we will leave the details of the OSI Reference Model for Chapter 3. For now, we would like to highlight two main parts or aspects of the communication process that occur between communicating systems over a network: internetworking and interoperability.

Figure 2-2
The Open Systems
Interconnect (OSI)
Reference Model.
(Courtesy of Learning
Tree International)

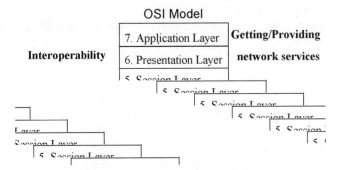

INTERNETWORKING AND INTEROPERABILITY *Internetworking* is the process of establishing and maintaining communications between entities or systems, and of transferring data among multiple networks. Ultimately, the major objective of internetworking is to get data from a source system to a destination system. However, internetworking alone does not provide access to resources or services on the destination host or system. It provides only a means to deliver the data requests, not a means of accessing the services that are located on the destination hosts.

Interoperability is the mechanism through which two systems can share their resources or provide access to services they offer. It also refers to the ability of two or more networks to work together even if they use different network architectures. Examples can include a DOS personal computer accessing a NetWare file server's file system or a Windows NT Workstation submitting print jobs to a Windows NT Server. Perhaps a more vivid example would be a Windows NT Workstation using the *Network File System* (NFS) to access files on a UNIX system, or a Windows NT Workstation that normally uses Server Message Blocks to access file system resources by using NetWare Core Protocol to access files on a NetWare server.

In summary, the main point to remember about these two concepts is that you cannot have interoperability without internetworking. You need to be able to transport data around the network to the destination host or system before you can have interoperability access to its resources. As we work through the book integrating and migrating between network operating system platforms, we will keep coming back to these two themes.

WHICH WAY ARE YOU GOING? This question is an appropriate lead-in to this section because the direction of your migration will have a significant impact on which integration and migration tools you use. Microsoft has taken a very early aggressive lead in this area by providing solid, working client workstation drivers and by supporting one of its main competitors own integration and interoperability protocols, mainly Novell's IPX/SPX and NCP. Although supporting IPX/SPX is, in hindsight, not such a big deal, Windows NT's ability to emulate a Novell NetWare 3.12 server for file and print services is a fantastic accomplishment. What is more is the fact that the product does what Microsoft marketing says it will do—and that is to provide existing Novell NetWare clients with direct access to a Windows NT Server using the Novell interoperability protocol (NCP). In other words, you do not have to change the NetWare client in any way, yet it can still access file and printer services on the Windows NT Server and the NetWare client thinks it is communicating with a NetWare server! We were indeed impressed with the Microsoft file and print services for NetWare the first time we used it. The degree of emulation of NetWare by NT is amazing. And if this one service or feature alone did not top it off, we will look at several others that are equally impressive as the first.

Not to be outdone, Novell, realizing the challenge, has stepped up to the plate recently and has provided similar tools to facilitate the integration or migration of NT into a Novell NetWare environment. In particular, these tools have facilitated the integration of NT into the NetWare 4.x *NetWare Directory Services* (NDS) environment as opposed to the NetWare 3.x bindery-based networks, and for good reason, because the Novell NetWare Directory Services is proving to be one of the best enterprisewide network directory services since Banyan Vines Street Talk Directory Service. Novell's integration and migration utilities include the tools required to make a NetWare server participate in a Microsoft network as a Server Message Block file and print server as well as tools to pull existing Windows NT Domain user and group information over to a NetWare Directory Service database. Tools that will be available by the time this book is available include the ability to run NetWare directory services on Windows NT directory, thus eliminating the requirement for Windows NT Domains all together. No, Novell has not laid down but rather has taken the bull by the horns and has been very aggressive in providing equally superior tools for NetWare users to integrate NT into their existing NetWare networks rather than migrating to Windows NT Domain networks that may not meet their enterprise network requirements.

As you can see, many options are now available to both Microsoft Windows NT and Novell NetWare network administrators. As is the purpose of this book, we are simply trying to point out all the options available to you and then let you make the decision as to which platform integration and migration strategy is best for you. We therefore present both sides.

What follows are examples of what options are available to you depending on whether you are migrating from Windows NT to NetWare or from NetWare to Windows NT, or just simply trying to get both of them to work cooperatively on the same network. We will start with bringing Windows NT into a NetWare network because this approach seems to be the major issue facing most corporations today. We will follow by introducing all the NetWare utilities available to integrate Windows NT into an existing NetWare network.

INTRODUCING WINDOWS NT INTO A NETWARE NETWORK ENVIRONMENT   NetWare users and resources can be integrated with or eventually migrated to Windows NT in many different ways:

1. A Windows NT Workstation can be placed into an existing NetWare network and access NetWare server services. To do so, you can use either the Microsoft or Novell client connectivity software drivers.

2. A Windows NT Server can be placed into an existing NetWare network and provide server services to existing NetWare clients by emulating a NetWare server. To do so, you can use the Microsoft *File and Print Services for NetWare* (FPNW).

3. A NetWare server can be placed into an existing Windows NT network and have Windows NT clients access it via a Windows NT Server gateway service; therefore, they do not have to support NetWare internetwork and interoperability protocols. The Windows NT *Gateway Services for NetWare* (GSNW) provide the Server Message Block to/from NetWare Core Protocol translator function.

4. A NetWare server's user and group information can be migrated to a Windows NT Server Domain. The Microsoft NT Migration Tool for NetWare will read a NetWare bindery and copy the user and group-related information into an NT Domain.

5. A NetWare server's user and group information can be updated from a Windows NT Server Domain primary server. To do so, you can use the *Directory Services for NetWare* (DSNW), which will update NetWare 3.x bindery databases or NetWare 4.1 Novell Directory Services databases that have bindery emulation support. This tool is also similar to the Novell NetSynch utility that is provided through Novell Directory Service to manage NetWare 3.x servers' bindery databases.

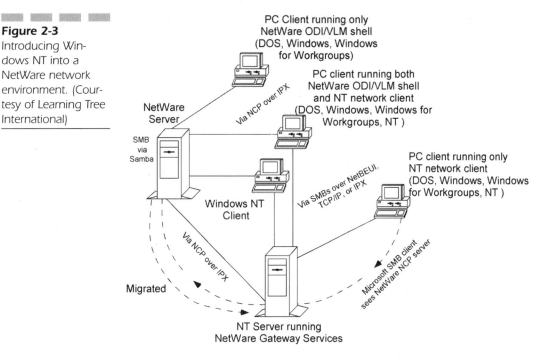

Figure 2-3
Introducing Windows NT into a NetWare network environment. (Courtesy of Learning Tree International)

Which one of these strategies you use depends on your particular integration and migration requirements. Figure 2-3 depicts several of these options in a mixed network environment.

INTRODUCING NETWARE INTO A WINDOWS NT NETWORK ENVIRONMENT   Equally powerful and viable alternatives are provided so that you can easily bring an existing Microsoft NT network into the world of Novell NetWare. Some of the services are provided by Novell directly, whereas others are provided by third-party groups.

1. You can configure your client workstation to support both Server Message Blocks and NetWare Core Protocol so that they can communicate directly with the new NetWare server. This is commonly done on Windows 3.11, Windows for Workgroups, and Windows 95. This solution is similar to the one presented in the preceding section (Item 1).

2. You can introduce a NetWare server into an existing NT network and run the SAMBA *Network Loadable Module* (NLM) on it. Doing so will provide Server Message Block access to the NetWare file and print services so that Microsoft clients do not have to be

reconfigured. This approach makes a NetWare server available in the Microsoft Network when looking in the File or Print Manager on a Microsoft client.

3. You can use Novell's Quiet Thunder Migration Utilities to support the migration of NT Domain objects, data files, and access control permissions from LAN Manager, LAN Server, and Windows NT Server. These utilities are similar in function to what Microsoft's Directory Services for NetWare provides as in the preceding section (Item 4).

4. You can manage NT Domain user/group databases from a Net-Ware 4.1 Novell Directory Services database. This amazing task can be accomplished through the use of an innovative third-party product called Synchronicity for NT by NetVision. Synchronicity for NT integrates Microsoft NT Servers with Novell Directory Services (NDS) by allowing administrators to seam-lessly manage users and groups across both networks. It is simi-lar in functionality to Microsoft's Directory Services Manager for NetWare described in the preceding section (Item 5). Addition-ally, Novell now has a similar product called NT Integration Utility, which is a "snap-in" to the Novell NetWare Administra-tor. It also allows you to manage your NT Domain user and group accounts from NDS.

5. You can support Novell Directory Services on Windows NT Do-main Servers. Banyan Vines has already converted its famous Street Talk Directory Service to Windows NT, and it has long been rumored that Novell Directory Services will also soon be available on Windows NT Servers. By running NDS on Windows NT Servers, you will no longer be required to maintain an NT Domain database.

Unfortunately, Novell does not provide any sort of a gateway function that will allow you translate between NetWare Core Protocol and Server Message Blocks. However, the almost universal file sharing services that are provided through Network File System are supported on both Net-Ware and NT and, as such, could be used to provide a common level of file access between these two, as well as other networking platforms sharing this requirement.

We will review these services in summary form only in this chapter. We will, however, describe each of them in detail in the following chapters of this book; we will include information on how to install and make use of the benefits they provide. Now that we have provided you with a glimpse of all the potential integration and migration options that are available to you, we would also like to provide you with a few points to consider.

If you add new servers to the network, you can migrate across the wire and keep some of your servers intact. This strategy is good as it provides you with a way to backtrack if you need to because something is not working. We don't see that there is any other way to perform a migration; however, some budgets seem to dictate that an organization should take unnecessary risks because the people involved don't understand the potential for downtime.

If you upgrade from NetWare 3.x to NetWare 4.x or Windows NT Server, you can maintain access controls. By this, we mean that through the use of an intelligent "upgrade or migration" tool you can maintain much, if not most, of the file system rights or permissions that you have set. Also, functions, rights, or abilities that the network administrator as delegated or assigned to other users such as Print Server Operator settings can be preserved during the upgrade or migration.

If you move management of NetWare 3.x servers' bindery databases to Novell Directory Service using the NetSynch or Microsoft Directory Services for NetWare, you get a mixed NetWare or mixed network operating system platform environment that lets you manage globally from one server and perform migration in phases. However, this is not a full and complete integration because DSNW does not yet provide full NDS support, although other third-party utilities do.

Many tools and utilities allow you to choose any one of several integration and/or migration strategies. The preceding few paragraphs begin to demonstrate this fact. However, they also begin to highlight the fact that with so many options come complexity and, as a result, the requirement for close definition of what sort of network your organization requires and how you are going to go about getting there and manage it after the fact.

MIGRATION   The decision has been made to migrate to Windows NT, so what now? Do you migrate NetWare accounts and continue to access both platforms of network operating system servers? And if so, for how long? Or do you migrate the NetWare file servers fully to Windows NT Domain Servers? But how will you access NetWare-based applications that are currently running on your NetWare servers? What about accessing NetWare-aware peripherals such as printers, fax servers, communication servers, and others? Are these peripherals supported in the Windows NT network operating system? Finally, what about backup tape systems?

How will we access files backed up using NetWare backup services after we have migrated to Windows NT?

PLAN YOUR WORK, WORK YOUR PLAN   Although introducing Windows NT into an existing NetWare environment is relatively easy, a lot of consideration should be given beforehand if integration and migration are to be successful.

The best approach for any successful integration or migration project is to simply sit down and plan out your organization's network requirements. After all the requirements have been defined, you will be in a better position to identify which network components (hardware/software) will need to be modified or changed altogether. This process of component identification will also start to build your implementation plan for you. Some of the component changes will need to be done before others, thus setting up, by default, a rough time line of events and project milestones.

The best place to start any project is by asking questions. Ask management personnel what they believe is required. Identify what end users will need as a result of any upgrades to their desktop platforms. Ask yourself what network infrastructure changes will be required to meet both management and end user requirements.

Here are some general questions:

1. What level of integration or migration do you want?

2. How will existing workstations access computers running Windows NT Servers?

3. How will users and groups be managed in a dual network operating system environment?

4. How will directories and files be accessed or migrated?

5. What will the new user menu and environment look like?

6. How will old files be restored onto the new server if required in the future?

Some large organizations have also found that after the migration was done, for whatever reason, they were not satisfied with the end result. In other words, Windows NT Domains did not provide the level of user and group information management they were looking for. How do you go back to your previous network configuration?

As the author pointed out in a July 15, 1996, *Information Week* article ("Reality Check, Early NT adopters are taking a second look at Novell's NetWare offerings."), several companies that made earlier decisions to migrate to Windows NT from NetWare have backed down. One organization highlighted in the article was going to migrate some 350 NetWare 3.x servers to Windows NT. Unfortunately, they found that the complexity of managing over 5000 users in a flat Windows NT Domain database was simply too difficult. The resulting network traffic caused during the migration also slowed the network to a crawl. Finally, management's expectations for the migration time frame were far too optimistic for a large organization. The main reason for the organization's backtracking to Novell's Directory Services solution instead of Windows NT Domains was what it estimated to be the cost of maintaining NT Domain Servers versus implementing Novell Directory Services.

Although it is not yet time to debate which is better at this point—NDS or Domains—we do want to bring to your attention, however, that it is equally important to have a backout strategy as it is to have an implementation strategy. Although some project managers may find this suggestion suspect, not all potential issues can be brought to the surface during testing and pilot projects. Some problems or challenges present themselves only as the network begins to scale and its full weight starts to show cracks in the underlying network operating system infrastructure that is trying to support its growth.

INTEGRATING AND MIGRATING NETWORK OPERATING SYSTEM PLATFORMS

Whether you are migrating from NetWare to Windows NT or the other way around (don't believe everything you read in the industry journals because it is happening!), some common points or steps in the process are highlighted in Figure 2-4. Essentially, you always start with your existing system. Some period during this process involves integrating the two platforms. During this stage, a common communication protocol will be

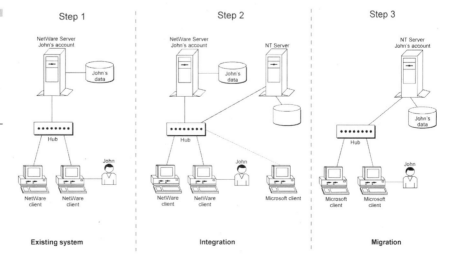

Figure 2-4
Integrating and migrating network operating system platforms. (Courtesy of Learning Tree International)

agreed upon, and some or all the user/group account or user file information will be migrated to the newly integrated system. For a brief period of time, users can access both systems using user accounts that are managed on two separate network operating system directory databases. Finally, the cost and requirements for supporting two systems or network platforms may no longer be justified, and you will migrate fully to one of them. Whichever platform it is, the process will be similar although the tools and utilities used may be different. In keeping with the objective of this book, we will present as many potential solutions as possible to assist you, depending on your integration and migration requirements.

MICROSOFT'S NT INTEGRATION AND MIGRATION TOOLS SPECIFICATION SHEETS Table 2-1 provides a list of all the tools and utilities that Microsoft provides to ease the integration of, and eventual migration from, NT to NetWare. The following pages will present summary reviews of each of these tools. The following chapters will provide in-depth coverage of the capabilities of each. You can find more information on the following tools at **http://www.microsoft.com**.

NWLINK INTERNETWORK PACKET EXCHANGE/SEQUENCE PACKET EXCHANGE (IPX/SPX) INTERNETWORKING (NWLINK) Of all the Microsoft utilities, NWLink Internetwork Packet eXchange/Sequence Packet eX-

Table 2-1.

Microsoft NT Integration and Migration Tools for NetWare. (Source: Microsoft Corporation)

Service	Description
NWLink IPX/SPX compatible transport protocol	Provides NetWare-compatible IPX/SPX transport layer protocol support for Windows NT.
Client Services for NetWare (CSNW)	Provides Windows NT workstation drivers for connecting to a NetWare server.
Gateway Services for NetWare (GSNW)	Allows a Windows NT Server to act as a gateway to NetWare servers for SMB-only clients. Also provides the client side access to NetWare servers for Windows NT Servers.
File and Print Services for NetWare (FPNW)	Allows a Windows NT Server to emulate a NetWare 3.12 server.
Migration Tool for NetWare	Migrates NetWare user and group accounts, login scripts, files, and directories, and security to a Windows NT Server.
Directory Services Manager for NetWare (DSNW)	Copies NetWare user and group accounts to a Windows NT Server for management and then incrementally propagates any changes in the accounts back to the NetWare server/bindery.

change Internetworking (NWLink) alone is required for all the others to function because it enables a Windows NT Server or workstation to support the NetWare network and transport layer protocols that Novell supports. (See Figure 2-5.) It provides the transport protocols that move and route upper-level file and print service requests over the network infrastructure. NWLink is a native 32-bit Windows NT implementation of IPX/SPX.

Probably the major benefit of implementing Novell's native networking protocols on Windows NT is that you can easily integrate Windows NT into an existing Novell NetWare network environment without having to change any of the network infrastructure. In other words, all the existing routers now can route Windows NT workstation and server service requests. In fact, as far as the routers are concerned, they won't even realize that anything is different except that a couple of new machines are on the network.

However, support of NWLink IPX/SPX alone will not enable you to share files and printer services between Novell and Microsoft clients. Additional upper-level protocols are required to facilitate this function. This process of internetworking and interoperability will be discussed in detail in Chapter 3, but for now we will look at the Microsoft tools that provide interoperability.

NWLINK FEATURES   The NWLink protocol includes many features that extend communication ability for Windows NT networks:

▪ SPX II NWLink supports Windows Sockets on the new Novell SPX II protocol. SPX II supports windowing and can set maximum frame sizes.

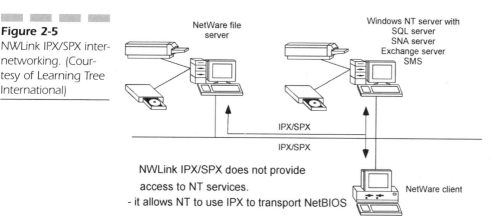

Figure 2-5
NWLink IPX/SPX internetworking. (Courtesy of Learning Tree International)

NetWare file server

Windows NT server with
SQL server
SNA server
Exchange server
SMS

IPX/SPX

IPX/SPX

NWLink IPX/SPX does not provide access to NT services.
- it allows NT to use IPX to transport NetBIOS

NetWare client

■ NWLink can be bound to support multiple network interface card adapters with multiple frame types.

■ NWLink automatically detects which frame type is being supported on the networking during initial start-up and uses that frame type. Although it will default to IEEE 802.2 frame type if multiple frame types are detected on the network, it can be manually configured to support all four Ethernet and two token ring frame formats.

■ The Windows NT Server service can support Direct Hosting over IPX, which allows Windows for Workgroup 3.11 clients to communicate up to 20 percent faster than they could using NetBIOS over IPX with Windows NT 3.5 computers.

CLIENT SERVICE FOR NETWARE (CSNW)   The *Client Service for NetWare* (CSNW) provides a fully native implementation of a NetWare redirector for Windows NT Workstations. (See Figure 2-6.) The Windows NT Server uses a different utility that will be described later in this chapter. On the surface, the tasks this service provides would appear to be difficult to accomplish given that Novell's redirector/server protocol NetWare Core Protocol is proprietary to Novell. (We are still wondering why Novell never took the issue of Microsoft implementing NCP on NT to the courts?) CSNW, which is implemented in Windows NT in native 32-bit code, includes a service and a device driver. Ultimately, it provides complete access to a NetWare server. Of course, the alternative would be to use Novell's NT client redirector software implementation.

Figure 2-6
Client Service for Net-
Ware. (Courtesy of
Learning Tree Inter-
national)

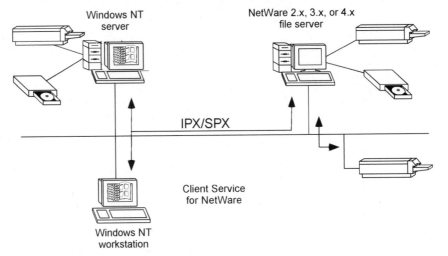

To access files or printers on a NetWare server, you need to use CSNW with NWLink. CSNW provides the following features:

- User access to NetWare file and print servers
- 16-bit NetWare application support for NetWare programs such as SYSCON, FCONSOLE, PCONSOLE, and RCONSOLE utilities
- Support for NetWare Core Protocol, which provides access to file and print services in a manner similar to Server Message Blocks
- Support for Burst Mode sliding windowing enhancements for large data transfers
- Support for *Large Internet Protocol* (LIP), which allows routed connections to negotiate the largest available packet size
- Support for *Long File Name* (LFN) when the NetWare server is running the OS/2 name space (OS2.NLM)

Client Service for NetWare supports access to NetWare 2.x and 3.x servers. CSNW for Windows NT 3.51 also supports access to NetWare 4.x servers using NDS where one of the containers is in Bindery Emulation Mode. Therefore, Windows NT 3.51 is not fully NetWare NDS compliant. However, Windows NT 4.0's CSNW does support full access to NetWare NDS server resources.

GATEWAY SERVICE FOR NETWARE (GSNW) Microsoft's *Gateway Service for NetWare* (GSNW) is truly an amazing utility as it allows non-NetWare clients to communicate with a NetWare server. (See Figure 2-7.) For

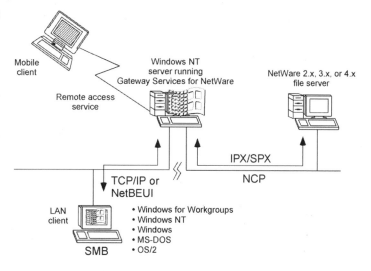

Figure 2-7
Gateway Service for NetWare (GSNW). (Courtesy of Learning Tree International)

example, Microsoft-only configured workstation clients (Windows NT, Windows 95, Windows for Workgroups, and even MS DOS) can access files and printers on a Novell server by accessing shares that are published on the Windows NT Server running GSNW.

As with the other utilities, it is a full 32-bit implementation configured to take advantage of NT's processing architecture. As stated earlier, it requires NWLink to function. GSNW can be used to access file and print services on NetWare 2.x and 3.x file servers, as well as on NetWare 4.x file servers running in Bindery Emulation Mode. It is anticipated that GSNW running on a Windows NT Version 4 Server will also allow the same Server Message Block based clients to access NetWare 4 Novell Directory Service based resources.

However, don't rush out and install GSNW on your NT Server as a way of moving your workstation clients to a single network protocol. GSNW is meant and designed to provide periodic access only. The Windows NT Server running GSNW takes a large performance hit when more than even three Server Message Block based clients try to access a NetWare server using its services. In fact, such a hit could easily increase server utilization to 100 percent.

FILE AND PRINT SERVICES FOR NETWARE (FPNW) Although Microsoft has long been known for its marketing and business prowess, one of the most amazing and aggressive marketing moves we have ever seen is its implementation of NetWare's NetWare Core Protocol file and print service on a Windows NT Server. File and Print Services for NetWare makes a Windows NT Server look like a NetWare 3.x file and print server to Net-

Figure 2-8
File and Print Services for NetWare. (FPNW) (Courtesy of Learning Tree International)

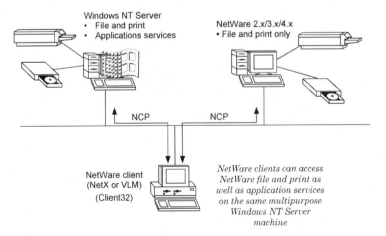

Ware-only-based clients. (See Figure 2-8.) We have used the product in many installations and training sessions, and it works every time.

The Gartner Group has created a Strategic Analysis Report regarding Novell NetWare and Windows NT. In it, the Gartner Group discusses how file and print services are becoming commodity items. (The Gartner Group study is serialized as R-NOS-103 by B. Gill, N. MacDonald, and A. Cushman; they can be reached at **http://www.gartner.com**). Indeed, there is a lot of truth to what these authors say and even predict. In fact, it has been happening for some time with the availability of Network File System as a means to provide a common file and print sharing protocol over multiple and disparate networking platforms. However, what is truly new is the concept of major competitors providing the file and print services facilities of competing network operating systems in an effort to facilitate integration and migration with their own products. Although slower out of the starting gate, Novell is also providing a Server Message Block service for Microsoft clients so that they can access NetWare server file and print services without supporting Microsoft's SMB protocols. Novell's solution will also be covered in this book.

Again, the File and Print Services for NetWare allows a Novell NetWare client running standard Novell client software to access file and print resources on a Microsoft Windows NT Server. No changes are required on the client side. Therefore, the server the client connects to can be a Windows NT Server; however, the server functions to the client like another NetWare 3.x server. FPNW is an optional add-on product (approximately $99 U.S.) that makes your Windows NT Server look like a NetWare 3.x server.

The following are some of the features of FPNW:

- Client workstations remain intact running existing client software.
- Simultaneous connections are made to Novell NetWare and Windows NT Server computers.
- Integration is made with the advanced computing platform of Windows NT Server for access to its applications.
- The migration from NetWare to Windows NT is facilitated.

MIGRATION TOOL FOR NETWARE (NWCONV)   The Migration Tool for NetWare allows you to migrate NetWare servers to computers running Windows NT Server with NT Domain database support. (See Figure 2-9.) The Migration Tool allows you to transfer user and group account information as well as directories and files from NetWare servers to Windows NT Server Domain controllers. Additionally, account information and file

Figure 2-9
Migration Tool for
NetWare (NWConv).
(Courtesy of Learning
Tree International)

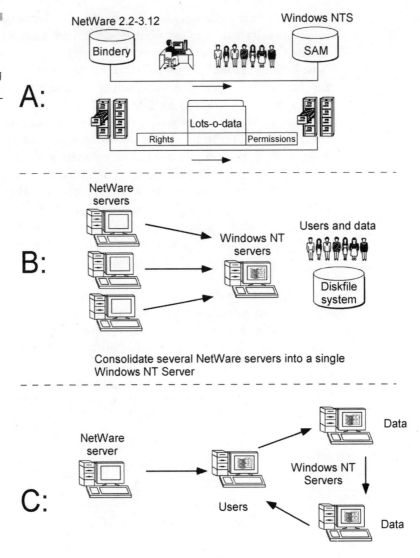

system information can be migrated to different NT servers. During the entire process, the NetWare server being migrated from is not affected or changed in any way.

The Migration Tool features

- Preserve appropriate user and group account information
- Configure how user and group names are migrated

- Set passwords for transferred accounts
- Control how system and user account restrictions as well as administrative rights are transferred
- Select the directories and files to be transferred
- Select the destination for transferred directories and files
- Maintain trustee assignments on transferred directories and files

The Migration Tool also allows the network administrator to run a trial migration that tests the migration settings that have been selected without actually implementing the migration or affecting the NT Server Domain controller. Extensive entries are made to the log file; these entries can then be reviewed and final changes made to the migration configuration before a live migration is run.

DIRECTORY SERVICES FOR NETWARE (DSNW)   Directory Service Manager for NetWare copies NetWare 3.x user and group account information to the Windows NT Server Domain database and then incrementally updates any changes made to these user accounts on the Windows NT Server Domain back to the NetWare server. (See Figure 2-10.) No software is required to be installed on the NetWare server. The network administrator can then centrally manage the NetWare 3.x servers' user and group account information from a single point. Only one user account and associated password for each user need be maintained.

Directory Service Manager for NetWare features include the following:

- A point-and-click *Graphical User Interface* (GUI) can be used for propagating user and group account information from NetWare

Figure 2-10
Directory Services for NetWare (DSNW). (Courtesy of Learning Tree International)

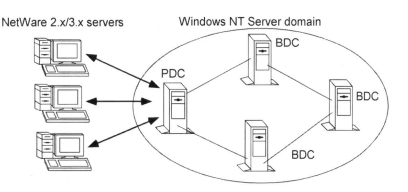

NetWare 2.x/3.x servers   Windows NT Server domain

Centrally manage NetWare 2.x/3.x users and group account information—maintain a single user account and password and enable a single logon access to file, print, and application resources

2.x/3.x and NetWare 4.x Bindery Emulation Mode servers to Windows NT Server Domain directory database.

■ Multiple options are available for setting up initial passwords, selecting user accounts to be propagated, performing account deletions, and running "trial propagation runs" for testing.

■ User accounts can be managed centrally from a Windows NT Server Domain directory database with changes automatically propagated back to the NetWare servers.

■ Propagated NetWare user account information is also copied to Windows NT Server Backup Domain Controllers for additional fault tolerance and fast disaster recovery.

■ User account information can be centrally managed from several different Windows NT client platforms including Windows NT Workstation, Windows 95, and Windows for Workgroups.

For end users, DSNW simplifies network access in the following ways:

■ They can use one common account and password for multiplatform access.

■ They can use the same common account and password for remote dial-in access through Windows NT *Remote Access Services* (RAS).

■ The same users can also access business applications running on the Windows NT Server even if they are logged on to a NetWare client.

■ They can use the Microsoft **CHGPASS** command to change their account passwords on both NetWare and Windows NT Domain server platforms.

INTRODUCING NETWARE INTO A WINDOWS NT NETWORK ENVIRONMENT
Table 2-2 highlights the tools and utilities that are available from Novell and several third-party groups to integrate or migrate Windows NT into a NetWare network environment. Not being the challenger for market share, Novell has unfortunately taken a less aggressive approach to providing tools for integrating Windows NT Workstation and Server into a NetWare environment. In fact, even Novell has admitted that early versions of its NetWare NT Client Driver were very unstable and simply did not work acceptably. However, it had several features that Microsoft's NT Client Services for NetWare did not have at the time of Windows NT 3.51. The main feature it had over Microsoft's client drivers was the ability to interface with NetWare 4.x Novell Directory Service, a feature that was available only with Windows NT version 4. However, despite its efforts,

Table 2-2.

Novell NetWare
and third-party
migration tools for
NetWare. (Courtesy
of WWW.NET-
WORKOLOGIST.
COM)

Utility	Description
LMIGRATE.EXE	This tool is used to migrate existing NT Server, LAN Manager, and LAN Server Primary Domain Controller objects to a NetWare 4.x server. It is also used to migrate the stated server's data files as well as user and group rights.
WINMIG.EXE and OS2MIG.EXE	These tools are used to migrate Windows and OS/2 clients to the Novell NetWare client driver software.
OS/2 Requester, NT Client Requester, and Client32 Requester	These tools are Novell NetWare client requesters for the individual client operating system platforms. Note that they can also coexist with existing LAN Manager, Windows NT, and LAN Server client drivers. However, they cannot exist with Microsoft's competing Client Service for NetWare or Gateway Service for NetWare on Windows NT; you must use one or the other.
NTAGENT.EXE	This Novell-developed tool is loaded at the NT Server to provide "Local" group information as well as permissions associated with files and directories during the migration process. Note that LMIGRATE.EXE will function without this utility; however, it will not process "Local" group and file system access permissions on the NT Server. Access permissions for the NT Server migration are supported only when migrating from Windows NT NTFS volumes, not HPFS or FAT file system volumes.
SAMBA.NLM	The SAMBA.NLM program is not required for the actual migration phase. However, it can be used to facilitate Microsoft client access to NetWare servers using NetBEUI, TCP/IP, and IPX protocols. It functions as a share emulator for NetWare 4.x servers to process file and print requests from LAN Manager, Windows NT Server, and LAN Server clients that are using SMB.

Novell has only just released a Beta copy of its Windows NT Client software, and it is still in testing as of the writing of this book. Novell currently seems to have failed to acknowledge that Windows on the end user desktop is here to stay and that it is responsible for developing fast and efficient NetWare clients in a timely manner (but I digress!).

For now, let's briefly review all the tools and utilities in Table 2-2. As always, you will find in-depth coverage of each tool in the following chapters.

NetWare Client 32 and IntranetWare Drivers for DOS/Windows/Win95/WinNT
Novell has provided client drivers for all the available or popular personal computer platforms including Macintosh. For the purposes of this book, we are most concerned with NetWare support for the Microsoft operating

systems. We will briefly review here the different client support that Novell provides with some focus on the Windows NT client software drivers. In Chapter 4, we will discuss all the client configurations required to support simultaneous access to both NetWare and Windows NT Servers by the various clients available.

NetWare NT Client Drivers Microsoft has already provided the ability for Windows NT workstations and servers to support Server Message Blocks. Novell provides its own proprietary NetWare Core Protocol for the Windows NT Workstation as well. Both SMB and NCP can be implemented at the same time, thus allowing a Windows NT workstation to communicate with a NetWare server and a Windows NT Server without having to reboot or otherwise disconnect from one or the other (or both and reboot like the old days). (See Figure 2-11.)

Novell NetWare's Client for NT provides the following features:

- It uses Novell standard *Open Data Link* (ODI) specification.

- It runs in requester mode.

- It supports file and print access through native NetWare Core Protocol.

- Versions of the software are available for RISC systems such as MIPS R4x00 and DEC Alpha AxP.

- It provides access to full Novell Directory Services.

Figure 2-11
Novell NetWare NT Client Drivers. (Courtesy of WWW.NET-WORKOLOGIST.COM)

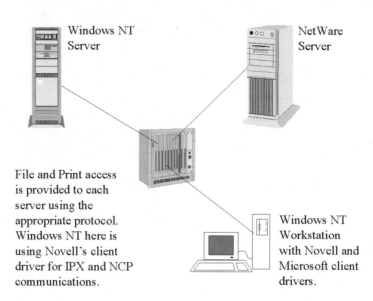

Windows NT Server

NetWare Server

File and Print access is provided to each server using the appropriate protocol. Windows NT here is using Novell's client driver for IPX and NCP communications.

Windows NT Workstation with Novell and Microsoft client drivers.

■ It supports NetWare login scripts.

■ It supports NWADMIN network management utility.

■ It supports dial-in, dial-out capabilities to NetWare and Windows NT through Remote Access Service.

A NetWare Server in an Existing Windows Network   Although not a Novell-developed utility, SAMBA allows a NetWare server supporting the Transmission Control Protocol/Internet Protocol to transport Server Message Block messages. (See Figure 2-12.) In effect, the NetWare server appears as another SMB server within a Microsoft network. Currently, SAMBA can only transport SMB within TCP/IP. However, Novell plans to release a redeveloped version of SAMBA for NetWare 4.1; it will support the transportation (or encapsulation) of SMB within Internet Packet eXchange/Sequence Packet eXchange or NetBEUI (NetBIOS Extended User Interface, or NBF). These protocol permutations and encapsulations are covered in detail in Chapter 3.

SAMBA has been available for some time for many UNIX systems and is freely available on the Internet. The main Internet warehouse for SAMBA-related source, binary, and documentation files is **http://lake.canbera.edu.au/pub/samba/**. Like the Network File System, SAMBA can be used to provide file and print sharing between or among different operating system platforms. A copy of the SAMBA.NLM files has also been included on the enclosed CD-ROM.

Figure 2-12
SAMBA. (Courtesy of WWW.NETWORKOL-OGIST.COM)

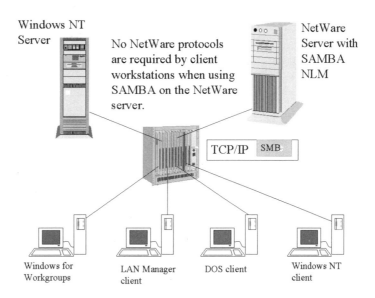

Migrating Windows NT Server Domain Directory Database to NetWare Novell Directory Services (NDS)   The Novell Consulting Services Group has developed the Quiet Thunder Migration Utilities, or simply Migration Utilities, set of utilities to facilitate the migration of Windows NT Server Domain Directory Database user and group accounts to a NetWare 4.1 Novell Directory Services database container. (See Figure 2-13.) The Migration Utilities also provide the capability to migrate domain databases from LAN Manager and LAN Server network operating systems as well. This is part of Novell's strategy to provide large organizations with the opportunity to migrate their existing domain-based directories to a unified Novell Directory Services database hierarchy.

The Migration Toolkit can be accessed on the Internet at `http://NetWare.Novell.com/corp/programs/NCS/toolkit/miggt.htm`   home page. The Migration Utilities are in a self-extracting compressed file. A copy of the utilities has also been provided on the enclosed CD-ROM. The main component and features of the Quiet Thunder Migration Utilities include the following:

- Migration utilities that support migration of domain-based objects, data files and access control information from LAN Server, LAN Manager, and Windows NT Server.

- DOS/Windows and OS/2 client workstation migration tools for migrating the networking software to the corresponding NetWare requester.

- A share emulation server for supporting LAN Server, LAN Manager, and Windows NT client workstations running their native client networking software drivers. (The share emulation is, in fact, the SAMBA application that has been ported to a NetWare Loadable Module.)

Figure 2-13
Quiet Thunder
Migration Utilities.
(Source: Novell Inc.)

A Vision for Network Integration of NetWare and Windows NT NetVision Inc., a company based in Lindon, Utah, has seen the future, and that future is the integration of probably the two most popular network operating systems platforms today. Unlike most of the media hype you probably read today, most organizations are not migrating one way or the other in a complete all-or-nothing approach. A more likely scenario is that the two NOSs will coexist for some time to come. The people at NetVision have seen this fact and have created a unique product that allows a NetWare network administrator to seamlessly manage users and groups across both networks. Impressive? You'd better believe it.

NetVision's product, called Synchronicity for NT, is just one of its new tools to ease the integration of NT into existing NetWare networks. (See Figure 2-14.) The company has a demonstration version that is available on the enclosed CD-ROM. However, you can also reach this company directly at **http://www.netvisn.com**.

The following are some of the many features this innovative product provides:

- It administers NT objects with NWAdmin (Novell's network management tool to administer user and group account information) for Windows 95 or Windows NT.

- It automates synchronization of relevant Novell Directory Services database changes to Windows NT objects.

Figure 2-14
Synchronicity for NT.
(Courtesy of NetVision Inc.)

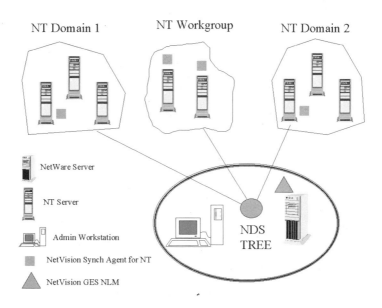

■ It reduces single sign-on difficulties.

■ It reduces Windows NT Domain management complexities.

In its most basic form, NetVision's Synchronicity for NT provides support for representing user and group accounts as NT-only or as NT-mapped Novell Directory Services (NDS) objects. This versatility allows administrators to identify which NT user and group objects can be managed with NDS and optionally which NT user and group objects will be synchronized with their NDS counterpart. It is truly an exciting product for NetWare network administrators, one that we will review in detail later in this book given its ability to create a seamless networking platform.

Novell's Administrator for Windows NT-NT Integration Utility   Although it is later out of the gate, Novell provides a similar product to NetVision's; it is called Novell Administrator for Windows NT-Integration Utility. The NT Integration Utility is an add-on component, sometimes called a "snap-in," that allows you to synchronize NDS and NT Domain user and group accounts. (See Figure 2-15.)

The following are some of the benefits that the NT Integration Utility can provide:

■ You can use one central user management utility, the NetWare Administrator, to manage users in your NT network and your Novell Directory Services tree.

Figure 2-15
The Novell Administrator for Windows NT - Integration Utility. (Source: Novell, Inc.)

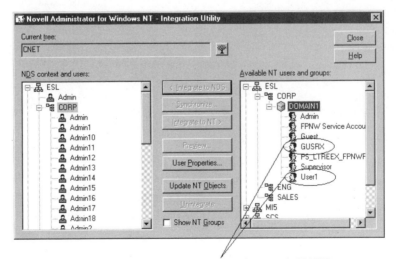

NT Domain users that have been integrated with NDS.

■ NetWare allows users to log in anywhere in the network and provide authentication to permitted servers.

■ Existing NetWare and Windows NT users can be migrated between platforms and synchronized at a later time.

Support Novell Directory Services (NDS) Directly on Windows NT Servers
Novell plans to provide support for its powerful Novell Directory Services on Windows NT Servers some time in the early part of 1998. It will, in fact, replace the need for a flat, two-dimensional domain directory database with the hierarchical Novell Directory Services directory database. (See Figure 2-16.) Since the inception of both NDS and Windows NT, many customers have wanted the reliability of Windows NT and the flexibility of NDS within their enterprise network. That day may soon come.

In the interim, Microsoft has started but then put on the back burner plans to support a hierarchical directory schema. Instead, Microsoft has chosen to allow others to export its directory schemes to Windows NT, preferring the *Open Directory Services Interface* (ODSI). ODSI is a set of *Windows Open Services Architecture* (WOSA) *Application Programming Interfaces* (API) that will make it easier for customers and developers to build applications that access, manage, and register across multiple directory database services. Users identified within NDS could then be

Figure 2-16
Novell Directory Services (NDS) on Windows NT Server.
(Courtesy of WWW.NETWORKOLOGIST.COM)

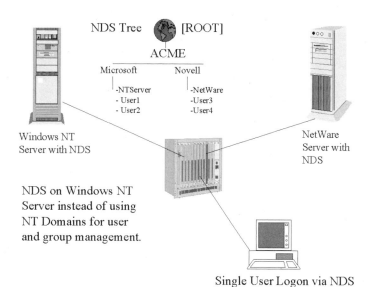

NDS Tree   [ROOT]

ACME

Microsoft   Novell

-NTServer   -NetWare
- User1   -User3
- User2   -User4

Windows NT
Server with NDS

NetWare
Server with
NDS

NDS on Windows NT
Server instead of using
NT Domains for user
and group management.

Single User Logon via NDS

Figure 2-17
Microsoft's Open
Directory Service
Interface. (Source:
Microsoft Corpora-
tion)

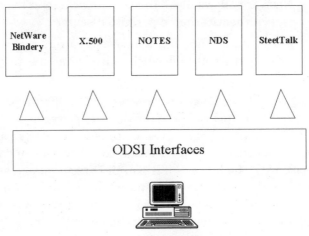

given access to services running on a Windows NT Server via ODSI. (See Figure 2-17.)

The problem with ODSI is that it is not a directory database service. It is, in fact, a tie-in to Microsoft's proprietary WOSA standard, which requires buy in and acceptance from marketplace developers so that end users can make use of it—something we suspect will not have a major impact in the market. However, through the use of ODSI and other special Windows NT APIs, companies such as Banyan and Novell have been able to port their directory services to Windows NT.

At the heart of the matter, however, is the fact that some organizations and many who watch the industry feel strongly that Microsoft's NT Domain strategy is weak when used in large organizations and that its flat or two-dimensional structure is limiting. However, until Microsoft develops a more flexible approach to directory services that appeals to large enterprise customers, the thought of running Novell Directory Services on Windows NT instead of the domain directory service is very appealing. Although little information is available to date, we will present as much as we can on this very interesting issue.

Are There Any Other Options?   Yes, in fact, several other options have been in use for some time now. The most popular one is Network File System.

Figure 2-18 demonstrates a Network File System configuration using several products specific to Novell NetWare and Microsoft Windows NT. In common with these products is the fact that they provide support for an industry standard file and print sharing protocol that was first devel-

Figure 2-18
Network File System.
(Courtesy of
WWW.NETWORKOL-
OGIST.COM)

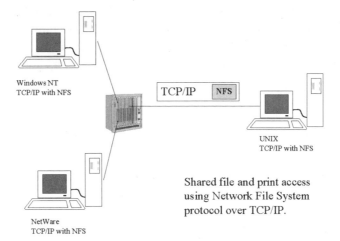

Windows NT
TCP/IP with NFS

TCP/IP NFS

UNIX
TCP/IP with NFS

Shared file and print access
using Network File System
protocol over TCP/IP.

NetWare
TCP/IP with NFS

oped in the UNIX network environment. It was later ported, or moved, to several other network operating system platforms including the two we concentrate on in this book.

On a NetWare server, you could use Novell's NetWare NFS to export (make available over the network) NetWare File System volumes. However, one of the limitations with the NetWare NFS is that it can export only NetWare File System volumes. It cannot, for example, import other file server file systems and then make them available to its own NetWare-connected clients. The NetWare NFS service, however, can be used to make NetWare File System volumes available to Microsoft Windows NT clients that are using client NFS-based products such as Hummingbirds NFS Maestro, Intergraph and SunSoft's codeveloped PC-NFS, or Distinct NFS. These NFS client products will allow end users to access NetWare file systems within their own Windows NT File Manager as if they were local.

Inversely, you can run a freely available *Son of Stan's Own Server for Windows NT* (SOSS-NT), which will allow you to turn your Windows NT Workstation or Server into a Network File System server. A copy of SOSS-NT is provided on the enclosed CD-ROM, or you can retrieve the file named SOSSNTR4.ZIP from **http://ftp/winsite.com/pub/pc/winnt/ netutil**. A commercial version of an NFS server for Windows NT by Intergraph Software Solutions is also available; a demo evaluation copy is provided on the enclosed CD-ROM, but you can always find an update at **http://www.intergraph.com/nfs**. It allows NetWare clients that also support some version of client NFS to access Microsoft Windows NT Workstations and Servers that provide NFS server services—although, realistically, simply supporting Server Message Blocks on the client is probably easier than supporting NFS. There may be a larger network access requirement and different platforms other than the two main ones addressed in this book; however, that's a story for another McGraw-Hill book.

SUMMARY

The purpose of this chapter was to highlight the many integration and migration issues you will face when planning and managing your network with NetWare and Windows NT. Although we cannot do project management justice in one chapter—or even this entire book—we have highlighted many of the issues and areas of concern that you will be required to deal with. In doing so, you are now aware that you can take many potential integration and migration roads depending on which direction you are headed or on which existing networking platform you are now supporting.

Finally, this chapter provided you with a brief overview of all the different utilities, tools, and products that you can use to facilitate your integration and migration project. In the chapters ahead, you will be provided with detailed information on how to evaluate and implement them depending on your requirements. As you can now appreciate, many options are awaiting you.

3

Protocol Integration

In this chapter, we identify all the network communication protocols used in NetWare and Windows NT network environments. Considering that organizations will potentially need to support multiple network communication protocols, we will discuss the challenges associated with multiprotocol network environments and provide heterogeneous solutions that will create efficient use of the underlying network infrastructure. Given that we can communicate from several directions over the network, we will review procedures to configure multiprotocol support on NetWare and Windows NT client workstations and servers. You will see that both systems support a range of networking transport and service protocols. We will focus particular attention on what each protocol can do because, although both *network operating systems* (NOS) will support the same lower-level Transport protocol for internetworking, such support does not imply the ability to access services (file and print) running on both of the same systems. Although this chapter covers the details about network protocols, Chapter 4 will go into the details of implementing the many protocol variations. We cannot stress enough that a good understanding of the *Open System Interconnection* (OSI) Reference Model and the functions it describes is critical to later understanding the protocol solutions that vendors such as Novell and Microsoft provide.

Chapter Objectives

■ Review the Open Systems Interconnection Reference Model

■ Differentiate between internetworking and interoperability

■ Identify protocols used in NetWare network environments

■ Identify protocols used in Windows NT network environments

■ Evaluate various network transport and service protocols with the goal of identifying the one most applicable to your network requirements

■ Identify implementation and management issues for multiprotocol networks

An Overview of the Communication Process

Before we jump right into how computers communicate, let's review the communication process and try to divide the task into three manageable areas. Communication between two computing systems and the devices in between that interconnect them can be put into three categories. Because the lower-level network components that a computer connects to (such as Ethernet or Token Ring on 10BaseT) are standard and common to most popular network and client operating systems (in other words, you can run NetWare and Windows NT on the same network infrastucture), we will concentrate on the areas of NOS implementation.

The three categories that facilitate the communication between computing systems on a network include the following:

■ Operating system support for peripheral devices that attach them to the network. This component instructs the operating system to support a particular *Network Interface Card* (NIC) and the methods used to interpret the digital information that the NIC receives. NetWare and Microsoft use different methods to instruct an operating system about a NIC and how to transmit bits through it.

- Transport services. This category is made up of the various protocols that allow the operating system to transport requests for services (that is, file and print access) over an internetwork. Many different protocols are associated with the function of transporting datagrams or packets of information over the network, although you will probably find in the end that you want to use only one.

- Server services. This category is made up of the various protocols that allow operating systems to request services (clients) or provide services (servers). Both NetWare and Windows NT use different protocols to provide or access services available on a computer system (that is, file and print). These protocols make operating systems interoperable so that they can share access to server resources.

An Analogy

The process of two computers communicating is similar to two people having a telephone conversation, as illustrated in Figure 3-1. If we look at the first category, we see a telephone system (network infrastructure) and a person who knows how to use it (operating system peripheral access). One phone is a rotary phone, and the other is a touch tone phone. One person telephones another person, and an initial connection is established, but still no communication is taking place.

To facilitate communication, the people need to have a language to convey ideas. The language used can be called the *transport service*. It will be used to transport the requests to the other person. Many different languages are available for use, just as many Transport protocols are available in the computer industry. Given the fact that two people are trying to communicate successfully with each other, using the same language is probably a good idea. Now that they both have a connection and a common language with which to relay a request, they need to ask for or provide a certain service. At this point in the call, one person has picked up the phone, a telephone directory assistance operator has answered, and the two have agreed on the same language to transport service requests.

Figure 3-1
Internetworking and
interoperability.
(Courtesy of Stu Ack-
erman at Learning
Tree International)

- **Interoperability**
    - Getting / providing network services

- **Internetworking**
    - Transporting / moving service requests or replies around on the
      network

Figure 3-1
Internetworking and interoperability. (Courtesy of Stu Ackerman at Learning Tree International)

However, something interesting happens now. The two people need to be using or supporting the same server services request options. If not, they can hear each other but cannot effectively communicate service requests to each other. So now that the operator has answered, if the other person asks for information about the weather instead of directory assistance, the operator will not be able to provide that service as it is one the operator does not support nor will the operator even understand the request.

In summary, although the we may have different telephones and different ways of using them (NICs with Open Datalink Interface or Network Device Interface Specification), we need to use the same language (transport services such as Internetwork Packet eXchange/Sequence Packet eXchange or Transmission Control Protocol/Internet Protocol) to convey requests and the support, or to understand the same service protocols (Server Message Blocks or NetWare Core Protocol) if we are to communicate successfully.

Addressing

In the same way we dial a telephone number to call a company, ask for a company department, and then ask to speak to a specific person about a specific topic (customer complaints), *addressing*, or component identification, is an important aspect of network communication. Addressing occurs at every level of communication from the Network Interface Card all the way up to the applications themselves. Each component has a form of addressing that identifies it to other processes running at the same level or to processes running at lower or higher levels of the communication process. (See Figure 3-2.)

At the lowest layers or levels is an Ethernet address that resides in the Network Interface Card. The received transmission comes in the form of an Ethernet frame. The Ethernet frame carries in the control field a number corresponding to the EtherType, which identifies the type of upper-level network protocol data unit (datagram or packet). So the EtherType is the address of the multiple network protocols that might be waiting for a packet. The network protocol that will receive the packet in Figure 3-2 will be *Internet Protocol* (IP). Within the network packet is an identifier that allows the IP program to deliver the contents of the packet to the appropriate protocol even further up the communication process. That identifier is call the Protocol ID. In the figure, IP will either deliver it to *Transmission Control Protocol* (TCP) or to *User Datagram Protocol* (UDP).

In the current case, let's say that TCP is the receiver of the content of the packet. TCP itself will be able to identify which service protocol—*File*

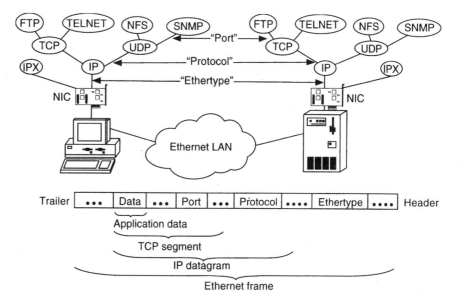

Figure 3-2
The use of multiplexing addresses. (Courtesy of Learning Tree International)

Transfer Protocol (FTP) or Telnet—is meant to receive the message contents of the segment. The type of address used to identify the waiting service protocol in the case of a TCP/IP network is the identifier *port*. In other protocols, address names such as *port* are called another name such as *socket*. However, they still perform similar functions.

In summary, the main issues facing network administrators as they begin to integrate and migrate network operating systems lies specifically with internetworking and interoperability. In a nutshell, you can have two computer systems supporting the same transport service protocols and be able to see each other on the network yet still not be able to access each other's file and print services because they do not support the same server service protocols. This issue will become apparent as we review transport and server service protocols supported by both NetWare and Windows NT. Definitions of these two main areas were provided in Chapter 2, so let's move on to how the Open Systems Interconnection Reference Model breaks down these two tasks into more detail.

The Open Systems Interconnection (OSI) Reference Model

No discourse on networking would be complete without some level of review of the Open Systems Interconnection Reference Model. (See Figure 3-3.) It is a sometimes painful yet necessary process. Fortunately, we are going to make it fun. Our view is that a well-grounded understanding of the OSI Reference Model can assist you greatly as you go about integrating and migrating networks because all networking protocols in use today have some relationship to it.

In this section, we will cover in detail the function the OSI Reference Model plays in modern network data communication. We will then extend the concepts presented in the model and relate them to the specific protocol solutions that Novell and Microsoft as well as the industry in general have implemented to facilitate the process of communicating between two network-attached computers.

Many network communication models existed before OSI; however, they were all proprietary. IBM's SNA and *Digital Equipment Corporation's* (DEC) DNA were represented by similar models. The TCP/IP protocol was represented by the *Department of Defense* (DOD) model but was public domain. All these models facilitated one goal: end-to-end communication of computer-based network applications. Although each model

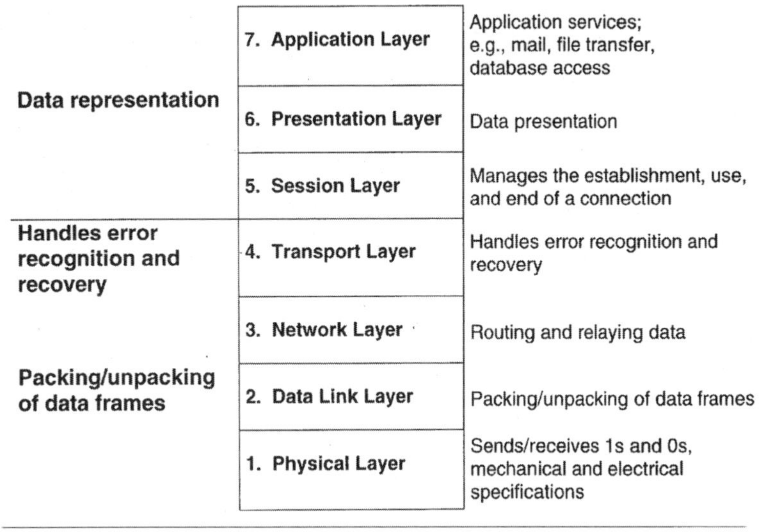

■■ ■■ ■■ ■■

Figure 3-3
The OSI Reference
Model. (Courtesy of
Learning Tree International)

	7. **Application Layer**	Application services; e.g., mail, file transfer, database access
Data representation	6. **Presentation Layer**	Data presentation
	5. **Session Layer**	Manages the establishment, use, and end of a connection
Handles error recognition and recovery	4. **Transport Layer**	Handles error recognition and recovery
	3. **Network Layer**	Routing and relaying data
Packing/unpacking of data frames	2. **Data Link Layer**	Packing/unpacking of data frames
	1. **Physical Layer**	Sends/receives 1s and 0s, mechanical and electrical specifications

was represented logically on paper somewhat differently, they all strived to achieve this same objective.

In 1977, the International Organization for Standards created a subcommittee of members of other standards organizations, vendors, and end users to develop standards for more open systems that would facilitate multiplatform interconnectivity and interoperability. Since then, most, if not all, network-related manufacturers have built products whose functionality fits within the OSI Reference Model.

The OSI Reference Model has been divided into seven layers, or categories, of functions. The seven layers divide the enormous task of protocol development into easier, more manageable subtasks. These subtasks can be optimized individually and tailored to specific functions. The layers are not protocols, but rather they state guideline tasks of the protocol components to be implemented.

Many people wonder why the model has seven layers and not more. Why not fewer? The answer becomes apparent as we look at the functions that each layer is responsible for during the complete communication process, as you will see in the following summary. (However, we have also read that this number was chosen because seven numbers are easier to remember; for example, consider telephone numbers.) The OSI Reference Model is also defined by the *International Telecommunications Union*

(ITU) X.200 Standard. The X.200 Standard document is provided in detail on the enclosed CD-ROM.

Before we move on to a summary review of the seven functional categories of the OSI Reference Model, we have found some of the following key phrases to be helpful in remembering their order.

Model Layers	Phrase Top to Bottom	Phrase Bottom to Top*
Application	All	Arnold
Presentation	People	Presented (by)
Session	Seem	Session
Transport	To	Training
Network	Need	Network
Data Link	Data	Dynamic
Physical	Processing	Pretty

*Note: Thanks to Mr. Chris Cauthier for this phrase.

The Physical Layer

The Physical Layer is the lowest common denominator of all network communication. (See Figure 3-4.) Eventually, all messages transmitted from one host to another will appear in the form of electromagnetic signals over a cable (or through the air with wireless forms of network communication, as related in Chapter 2). The electromagnetic signals are transmitted (or interpreted) as bits of information. Bits are the main element addressed at the Physical Layer.

Both this layer and the Data Link Layer are predominantly hardware-based standards. The main responsibility of the Physical Layer is the management of the signal bits through the mechanical and electrical specifications of the transmission medium (cable) and the network interface. Signal patterns for 0s and 1s including voltage levels of the signals, clocking, cable and adapter pin assignments, and types of cables are all included at this layer.

Signal patterns and voltage levels detail how bits of 0s and 1s should be interpreted by the network interface. Different transmission media support different voltage levels, and as such, the Network Interface Card must be compatible with the medium in use. The timing we use while we mon-

Figure 3-4

The Physical Layer.
(Courtesy of Learning
Tree International)

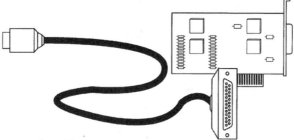

- **Manages data bits**
    - Mechanical and electrical specifications of medium and interface
    - Signal patterns for 0s and 1s, voltage levels, clocking, pin assignments, and types of cables
    - Example: RS-232-C, RS-449, CCITT/ITU X- and V-series recommendations

CCITT/ITU = International Consultative Committee for Telegraphy and Telephony/International Telephone Union

itor electromagnetic signals on the cable is called *clocking*. Faster clocking techniques allow for an increase in a transmission medium's potential bandwidth. Coax uses different wire pin assignments than UPT does, and we need to establish, given a specific medium, which wire pin will be responsible for receiving or transmitting information. Finally, the physical characteristics of the network interface connector are handled at this layer. This aspect entails the shape of the connector and location of pin outs.

A sample protocol associated with this layer would be an RS-232-C serial cable often used to connect a modem to your computer. With an RS-232-C cable, Pin 2 handles bit transfers, and Pin 3 handles bit receives. RS-232-C type connectors, DB-25, or DB-9 are pin type interface connectors. Another example is a UTP cable with an RJ-45 type connector. RS-449, CCITT/ITU X-, and V- series recommendations are still more sample protocols in use at the Physical Layer.

The ITU X.200 document defines the services of the OSI Physical Layer as follows:

The physical layer provides mechanical, electrical, functional, and procedural means to activate, maintain, and deactivate physical connections for bit transmissions between data link entities. A physical connection might involve intermediate open systems, each relaying bit transmissions within the physical layer. Physical layer entities are interconnected by means of a physical medium. The mechanical, electromagnetic, and other media-dependent characteristics of physical media connections are defined at the boundary between the physical layer and the physical media.

From a NetWare and Windows NT perspective, this statement simply means that either they both need to be supporting the same physical layer characteristics or that some upper layer protocol is acting as an intermediary between them. In other words, if the two systems are not on the same coax, 10BaseT, or fiber optic network cable, then an internetwork connection device such as a bridge or router or gateway (all of which work at higher OSI model layers) is facilitating communication between the two. These devices are moving the electromagnetic signal required at this level onto the end system's network cable medium.

This layer also deals with the *physical topology* of the network cable medium. The physical topology of the network is what the cabling segments actually look like: ring, bus, star. It, however, does not deal with how information or bits are actually transmitted around on the network, which is the responsibility of the Data Link Layer.

The network interconnection device that works at the Physical Layer is the *repeater*. One of the problems associated with network cable media is that of distance limitations. Electromagnetic signals start to deteriorate (or attenuate) as the signal travels ever further down the cable. The repeater takes in a weak signal and repeats it on an attached network cable segment as a newly regenerated signal. One of the terms often used to describe this process is *digital regenerative repeater*. Finally, one important point to remember about a repeater is that it does not look at the bit stream. It deals or works with one bit at a time and is not aware of any structure in the bit sequence. The first bit in is the first bit out. Starting to put a structure on the bit stream is the responsibility of the Data Link Layer.

The Data Link Layer

The Data Link Layer is responsible for managing frames (groups) of bits. (See Figure 3-5.) This layer frames bits of data together into coherent groupings. In computer communication, this means framing a series of 0s and 1s together and then interpreting them. As this grouping is derived from original electromagnetic signals, and because these signals are susceptible to outside interference, the Data Link Layer must also detect errors in transmitted frames. The Data Link Layer is also mainly hardware-related, although it also deals with the way or sequence in

Figure 3-5
The Data Link Layer.
(Courtesy of Learning
Tree International)

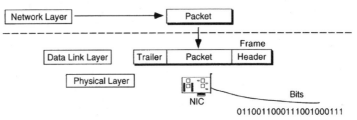

- **Manages frames**
  - Frames data, detects errors, flow control, adds physical addresses
  - Organizes 0s and 1s into frames, encapsulates packets (datagrams)
  - Example: Ethernet, 802.5, Attached Resource Computer NETwork (ARCNET), Fiber-Distributed Data Interface (FDDI)
  - Implementation of a channel access scheme

which electromagnetic bits are converted to binary information and then framed for interpretation.

Depending on the type of network in use, workstations will be vying for turns to transmit a frame worth of bits or will be waiting in line for their turn. The manner in which the workstation accesses (gets its turn) the network transmission medium through the Network Interface Card is called the *channel access scheme*.

After a workstation begins sending frames of bits, the receiving workstation may not be able to process the frames as quickly as sent. The sending station needs to be able to determine when this is the case and then change its transmission speed. This process is called *flow control*.

With multiple workstations or hosts directly connected to the same transmission medium, we require a method to identify each one individually. Unique physical addresses are added to each Network Interface Card. The address information of the sender and receiver is included in the frame of bits that are transmitted.

Finally, the Data Link Layer encapsulates information packets or datagrams from the Network Layer located directly above it. The packets become the payload or cargo of the frame.

Examples of protocols providing Data Link Layer functionality are Ethernet or 802.3, Token Ring or 802.5, *Attached Resource Computer NETwork* (Arcnet), and *Fiber Distributed Data Interface* (FDDI). Channel access schemes used by these protocols are token passing or collision detection based.

The ITU X.200 document defines the services of the OSI Data Link Layer as follows:

The data link layer provides functional and procedural means to establish, maintain, and release data-link connections among network entities and transfer data-link-service data units. A data link connection is built upon one or several physical connections.

The data link layer detects and possibly corrects errors that might occur in the physical layer.

In addition, the data link layer enables the network layer to control the interconnection of data circuits within the physical layer.

Both NetWare and Windows NT uses different methods for framing bits within their operating systems. Although Ethernet and Token Ring produce the same results on both systems, the technology used to implement them is different, as you will see in this chapter. Specifically, NetWare uses the *Open Data Link* (ODI) interface to implement data link frame format support, whereas Windows NT (and Microsoft operating systems in general) uses *Network Device Interface Specification* (NDIS). Both provide the capability for the network operating systems in question to support all the standard Ethernet, Token Ring, Fiber Distributed Data Interface, and other frame formats. This issue is particularly important when you are configuring your Windows NT *File and Print Service for NetWare* (FPNW) to support an existing NetWare client workstation that already supports a particular frame format.

Besides frame formats, the Data Link Layer is the place where we will also start to deal with *logical topology* (as opposed to physical topology). Logical topology is the way the network actually works, not how it looks. For example, a Token Ring network today is usually run on a star configured physical topology. However, a logical ring is working through the physical star configured wiring.

MEDIA ACCESS CONTROL   The *Media Access Control* (MAC) component of the Data Link Layer is responsible for how the computer systems on the same network cable share access to the cable medium itself. Ethernet uses a "contention-based" nondeterministic approach to accessing the cable medium. In other words, the workstations fight it out to see which one will get to transmit first. The problem with this method, and one of the reasons that it is called nondeterministic, is that the contention between systems for transmit on to the cable medium produces a nonorderly scheme of access. As a result, with Ethernet we cannot determine how long it will take for a workstation computer system to transmit its frame successfully. Token Ring or Fiber Distributed Data Interface, on the other hand, use a form, or "token passing," to determine which workstation computer system will be next to transmit. The token is passed in an orderly fashion around the ring so that each system has an opportunity to transmit. As such, it is called deterministic because we can calculate how long before a given system on the ring has an opportunity to transmit its information.

Additionally, individual computer system addressing is done at this layer as well as determining the framing technique used. Each Network Interface Card within a network connection computer system or device will have a unique network address. The address scheme used in most *local area networks* (LAN) is administered by the *Institute of Electrical and Electronics Engineers* (IEEE), and a formula is given to each NIC manufacturer to ensure that every NIC card produced is unique.

The *frame* is the basic unit of information created and transmitted by the data link protocol. A frame indicates how the bits that arrive from the physical layer are ordered and interpreted. When the bits are put together, a frame structure is created. A basic frame is composed of four components: an address field, a control field, a data field, and an error-check field. Figure 3-6 shows a generic frame format.

The important aspect of the frame (although there are many) is the NIC address. As two systems work together to communicate at the Data Link Layer, key elements in the process are the Source and Destination MAC addresses. Essentially, when a source system builds a frame to be transmitted to the intended recipient system, the destination MAC address placed in the frame *must* be reachable on the physically attached network cable medium; otherwise, the frame will not be received.

LOGICAL LINK CONTROL   The *Logical Link Control* (LLC) component, or sublayer, of the Data Link Layer is responsible for identifying the class of service (connection or connectionless) and for transport layer protocol multiplexing. This sublayer determines which network layer Transport protocol is supposed to receive and process the payload of the frame.

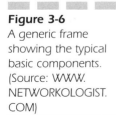

Figure 3-6
A generic frame showing the typical basic components. (Source: WWW. NETWORKOLOGIST. COM)

Finally, and perhaps most importantly from an integration perspective, a common network interconnection device called a *bridge* works at the Data Link Layer. Bridges are used to link LANs. They do so by transferring frames from one LAN to another based on the MAC addresses in the frame. In general, the two types of bridges are *transparent bridges* that are used to link Ethernet LANs and *source routing bridges* that are used to link Token Ring LANs. Extending the physical cable medium segment is the main function or purpose for employing a bridge within a network. It does so by providing the same function that a repeater does at the Physical Layer, except that it also builds frames to make its filter or forwarding decision. You will see later in this chapter that certain Transport protocols are dependent on the services that a bridge provides and will not work over a router or gateway.

The Network Layer

The Network Layer manages the flow of packets that have been delivered within the frames from the lower layer. (See Figure 3-7.) As we move to the Network Layer, software begins to play a dominant role in the communication process. One of the main functions of the Network Layer is to route packets throughout multiple network segments. This type of service is required because the physical workstation we want to communicate

Figure 3-7
The Network and
Transport Layers.
(Courtesy of Learning
Tree International)

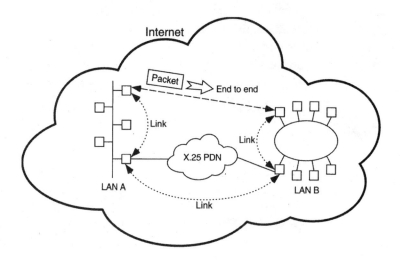

PDN = public data network

with may not be on the same physical transmission medium we are connected to. To facilitate the routing process, a logical networkwide address scheme is implemented. Several different routing methods and protocols will be highlighted in Chapter 4.

Packets are created at this layer to carry Transport Layer segments of information. The Network Layer protocols are usually unreliable, connectionless-oriented in LAN environments (IPX and IP) and connection-oriented in the WAN environments (X.25). By connectionless-oriented, we mean that we do not check at this layer to ensure that the packet arrived successfully at its destination. We rely on other, higher layers to perform this function.

Sample protocols in use at the Network Layer are *Internetwork Packet eXchange* (IPX), *Internetwork Protocol* (IP), and *ConnectionLess Network Protocol* (CLNP for OSI protocol suite).

The ITU X.200 document defines the services of the OSI Network Layer as follows:

> The basic service of the network layer is to provide the transparent transfer of data between transport entities. This service allows the structure and detailed content of submitted data to be determined exclusively by layers above the network layer.
>
> The network layer contains functions necessary to provide the transport layer with a firm network/transport layer boundary which is independent of the underlying communication media in all things other than quality of service. Thus the network layer contains functions necessary to mask the differences in the characteristics of different transmissions and subnetwork technologies into a consistent service.

The Network Layer is of particular concern to network administrators when integrating NetWare and Windows NT because it is critical to providing access to interoperable services in an enterprise network environment. Both network operating systems can use different Network Layer Transport protocols to deliver upper-level service requests.

As described previously, some of the main areas of responsibility for the Network Layer include logical network addressing and routing of datagrams or packets. Addressing is a feature used at all layers of the OSI Reference Model to uniquely identify entities, devices, and processes. At the Network Layer, addressing uniquely identifies logical networks throughout an internetwork of LANs. As will be demonstrated later in this chapter, different network protocols implement network addressing differently; however, they still provide the same basic functionality as defined by this layer. The complete network address is composed of the logical network address given to the network segment of computer systems as well as an address associated with the individual computer system on that network. The individual computer system address can be manually configured as is the logical network address or, depending on the protocol, can use the NIC address instead to uniquely identify each network computer system within a logical network. The approach all depends on the network protocol you select.

After a logical network addressing scheme has been selected, routing of datagrams or packets will need to be done to ensure that the right packet gets to the appropriate logical network and subsequently to the appropriate computer system on that logical network. This function is facilitated through routing protocols. *Routers* are network interconnection devices that perform this function. Routers are also commonly called *gateways* in many UNIX books and journals; however, for the purpose of this book, we will refer to the Network Layer interconnection device as a *router*. These devices are dependent on the Network Layer address to perform the functions of moving datagrams or packets among different logical networks. Routers use route discovery and route selection techniques to facilitate the packet forwarding process. Network routers can be updated statically by making manual entries into a routing table or dynamically through the use of special routing protocols. However, in the case of dynamic routing, the system in question needs to support this kind of service (which both NetWare and more recently Windows NT do).

Sequencing and flow control are two additional functions that occur at the Network Layer. A large file that is being transferred over the internetwork can be segmented into many smaller size datagrams or packets. These packets can take several different paths enroute to the destination system (some faster than others) and as such can arrive at different times. Therefore, sequencing of packets is very important. Flow control, on the other hand, ensures that the sender does not flood the receiver with packets that it is not able to process. The receiver controls or sets the pace of the communication flow (number of packets transmitted) and tells the sender to slow down.

Finally, network administrators should be aware that three Transport protocols are available to both NetWare and Windows NT. However, only two of them are supported on both platforms (IPX/SPX and TCP/IP) at the time of this writing, although Novell has stated it will support the third in the near future (NetBios Extended User Interface, or NetBEUI). These protocols will be reviewed in detail later in this chapter.

Figure 3-8
Transport Layer.
(Source: WWW.
NETWORKOLOGIST.
COM)

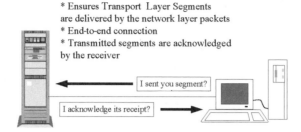

* Ensures Transport Layer Segments
  are delivered by the network layer packets
* End-to-end connection
* Transmitted segments are acknowledged
  by the receiver

The Transport Layer

The Transport Layer ensures the reliable end-to-end delivery of message segments across an internetwork. (See Figure 3-8.) Segments are the main element used here. This layer compensates for the unreliability of lower layer functionality. To accomplish reliable delivery of segments of information between hosts, acknowledgments are used.

An interesting aspect of Network Layer packet delivery is that packets can take different routes to get to the same destination. As such, Transport Layer segments can arrive at the receiving workstation in a different order than they were sent. Sequencing of segments assures that the eventual message is reassembled in the proper, intended order. Flow control is also used at this layer, like the Data Link Layer, to ensure that information travels on the network at an optimal speed at which the sending and receiving hosts can process it without flooding the underlying network segments.

The ITU X.200 document defines the services at the OSI Reference Model Transport Layer as follows:

> The transport service provides transparent transfer of data between session entities and relieves them from any concern with the detailed way in which reliable and cost-effective transfer of data is achieved.
>
> The transport layer optimizes the use of the available network service to provide the performance required by each session entity at minimum cost. This optimization is achieved within the constraints imposed by the overall demands of all concurrent session entities and the overall quality and capacity of the network service available to the transport layer.

The transport layer is relieved of any concern with routing and relaying because the network service provides network connections from any transport entity to any other.

The transport layer uniquely identifies each session entity by its transport address. The transport service provides the means to establish, maintain, and release transport connections.

The following services are provided by the transport layer:

a. transport-connection establishment

b. data transfer; and

c. transport-connection release.

What the preceding statement really says is that the Transport Layer's responsibility is to hide the details of the networking performed by the lowest three layers from the rest of the upper layers. Transport programs add functionality to the lower layers by providing these important and needed services. The Transport Layer protocols also make the underlying networking protocols more reliable.

A common way of differentiating the Transport Layer from the Network Layer services is by comparing the telephone system (transport) to the postal system (network). With the postal system, you need to know only what the address is of the destination you are trying to forward your package to, and you don't need to find out whether anyone is home to receive it before you send it. With the telephone system, however, a connection has to be established before communication can proceed. Transport Layer protocols are commonly referred to, therefore, as being connection-oriented (although some operate in a connectionless manner), whereas Network Layer protocols are commonly referred to as connectionless-oriented.

Network administrators don't really have much to worry about at this layer because, unlike the Network Layer where you need to possibly select one specific protocol over another, the Transport Layer protocol is chosen for you by virtue of your Network Layer protocol selection. For example, if you decide to use Novell's Network Layer *Internetwork Packet eXchange* (IPX) protocol, you will, in turn, be forced to use its *Sequence Packet eXchange* (SPX) protocol for Transport Layer functionality.

The Session Layer

The Session Layer manages a dialogue between computers, or actually, between applications running on two computers. (See Figure 3-9.) It sets

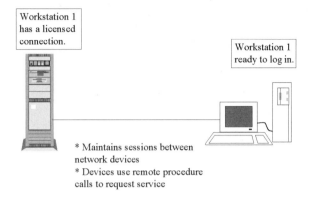

Figure 3-9
Session Layer.
(Source: WWW.
NETWORKOLOGIST.
COM)

Workstation 1
has a licensed
connection.

Workstation 1
ready to log in.

* Maintains sessions between
network devices
* Devices use remote procedure
calls to request service

the rules for the beginning and end of segment transmissions. The Network and Transport Layers provided interconnectivity between the two computers. The Session Layers begin to provide interoperability services where we can begin to access applications residing on other hosts. Not all protocol families support a component at this layer but rather support its functionality at high layers. For example, this layer is generally not referred to by the NetWare series of protocols where higher layers provide similar functionality.

Session Layer functionality provides services through *Remote Procedure Calls* (RPC) in which one computer system sends an RPC to the other requesting some form of service such as a file transfer. Sample protocols implemented at the Session Layer include Remote Procedure Calls such as NetBIOS, *International Standards Organization* (ISO) 8237, and Novell's *NetWare Core Protocol* (NCP). However, some of these protocols also perform functions at other higher layers.

The ITU X.200 document defines the services of the OSI Reference Model Session Layer as follows:

> The purpose of the session layer is to provide the means necessary for cooperating presentation entities to organize and synchronize their dialogue and to manage their data exchange. To do this, the session layer provides services to establish a session connection between two presentation entities, and to support orderly data exchange interactions.
>
> The following services are provided by the session layer:
>
> **a.** session-connection establishment;
>
> **b.** session-connection release;

c. normal data exchange;

d. quarantine service;

e. expedited data exchange;

f. interaction management;

g. session-connection synchronization; and

h. exception reporting.

Dialog types and dialog administration are two main areas of concern for Session Layer protocols. Dialog types deal with the flow of the conversation including simplex, half-duplex, and duplex forms of communication. Dialog administration deals with the establishment of a connection, data-transfer, and connection release. Following the telephone analogy earlier in this section, establishing a connection would be like telephoning someone and having that person answer the phone. Data transfer would be the process of talking to each other. Dialog type would then come into the process as we either talk one at a time, each taking a turn on the line (half-duplex) or if we are able to both talk at the same time and still understand each other (duplex). Finally, when the call is done, the connection would be released by hanging up the phone.

A final way of looking at the functions of the Session Layer that network administrators can relate to is in a situation in which a workstation boots up and establishes a connection with the server. No users have yet logged on to the server in question. However, the server and workstation know that each of them are visible on the network, and the server has already granted the workstation access by giving it a connection upon which users can send their login/logon information.

The Presentation Layer

The Presentation Layer is responsible for syntax and grammar rules. (See Figure 3-10.) Up until this layer, we have been dealing with bits or groupings of bits of information. This layer converts a group of 0 and 1 bits into alphanumeric formats that are more easily understood by humans. Character code tables are used to determine what alphanumeric characters are represented by a group of bits.

Data compression and expansion are performed Presentation Layer protocols. Long patterns of 0s and 1s are compressed into shorter representative patterns, which are then expanded at the receiving application. Finally, data encryption facilities are provided at this layer. Data encryp-

Figure 3-10
Presentation Layer.
(Source: WWW.
NETWORKOLOGIST.
COM)

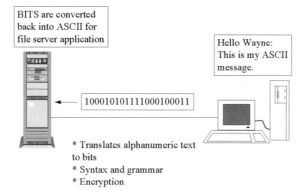

BITS are converted back into ASCII for file server application

Hello Wayne: This is my ASCII message.

100010101111000100011

* Translates alphanumeric text to bits
* Syntax and grammar
* Encryption

tion scrambles data into incoherent streams of data bits that require special keys to unencrypt by a receiving station or application.

Note that many gateway services function at this layer to act as translators between computers that are using dissimilar protocol suites or stacks. Sample protocols in use at the Presentation Layer are the conversion of ASCII to EBCDIC (or vice versa), *Data Encryption Standard* (DES), and *eXternal Data Representation* (XDR).

The ITU X.200 document defines the services of the OSI Reference Model Presentation Layer as follows:

> The presentation layer provides for the representation of information that application entities either communicate or refer to in their communication.
>
> The presentation layer covers two complementary aspects of this representation of information:
>
> **a.** the representation of data to be transferred between application entities; and
>
> **b.** the representation of the data structure which application entities refer to in their communication, along with the representations of the set of actions which might be performed on this data structure.

Network administrators don't have much to worry about at this layer unless they are starting to employ data encryption services running on one network operating system platform and they want to share the data with users on another. In this case, they will need to ensure that the encryption software runs on both NOSs before they can share data. Data compression is taken care of by each NOS respectively in that the file will be decompressed before being transmitted. If communicating between a personal computer and a mainframe, gateway software will facilitate ASCII to EBCDIC translation. Remember simply that the translation occurs at the Presentation Layer.

Finally, why perform these functions at the Presentation Layer and not some other lower or higher layer? At the Presentation Layer, higher Application Layer alphanumeric information is translated into binary 1s and 0s. The 1s and 0s are easier and more flexible to manipulate and work with.

The Application Layer

The Application Layer manages users and application access or interfaces to the network services. (See Figure 3-11.) This layer is often confused with applications that users run at their client workstations, but it is not the same. The applications users run use the services provided by this layer to copy files to the network file server hard disk drive system, for example.

Functions provided by the Application Layer include file access and transfer, virtual terminal emulation to host computers, directory services, network management, and mail transfer. The main element of this layer is messages in the form of requests and replies for services.

Sample protocols providing this functionality include File Transfer Protocol file transfer; *File Transfer, Access, and Management* (FTAM); NetWare Core Protocol; X.400 Mail protocol; *NetWare Directory Services* (NDS); and Telnet for terminal emulation in Terminal/Host-based computer environments.

The ITU X.200 document defines the services of the OSI Reference Model Application Layer as follows:

The application layer contains all functions which imply communication between open systems and are not already performed by lower layers. These include functions performed by programs and human beings.

As the highest layer of the reference model of Open Systems Interconnection, the application layer provides a means for the application-processes to access the OSI environment. Hence the application layer does not interface with a higher layer. The application layer is the sole means for the application processes to access the OSI environment.

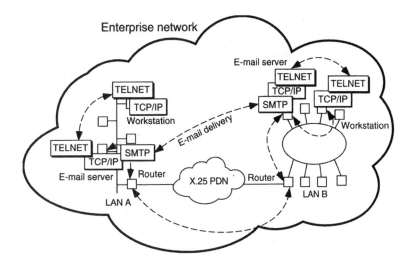

Figure 3-11
The Session, Presentation, and Application Layers in action. (Courtesy of Learning Tree International)

SMTP = Simple Mail Transfer Protocol

The purpose of the application layer is to serve as the window between correspondent application processes which are using the OSI to exchange meaningful information. The application services differ from services provided by other layers in neither being provided to an upper layer nor being associated with a service access point.

In addition to information transfer, such services might include, but are not limited to the following:

a. identification of intended communication partners (that is, by name, by address, by definite description, by generic description);
b. determination of the current availability of the intended communication partners;
c. establishment of the authority to communicate;
d. agreement on privacy mechanisms;
e. authentication of intended communication partners;
f. determination of cost allocation methodology;
g. determination of adequacy of resources;
h. determination of the acceptable quality of service;
i. synchronization of cooperating applications;
j. selection of the dialogue discipline including the initiation and release procedures;
k. agreement on the responsibility for error recovery;

l. agreement on procedures for control of data integrity; and

m. identification of constraints on data syntax (character sets and structure).

Although the Network Layer protocol selection is probably the first and most important area for enabling internetworking, the Application Layer protocol selection is the component that enables interoperability. For network administrators, this often means configuring clients and servers to support the same Application Layer service protocol, or alternatively, as Microsoft has taken initiative with, getting the server to support multiple Application Layer protocols so that it can provide server service access by different client configurations.

We have stated that server services are provided by the Application Layer. To access services on the network by a *local operating system* (LOS) or *disk operating system* (DOS), we need to inform them of the various services that are available. This is accomplished through the advertising of the services by the server. The two methods used to advertise these services are *active* and *passive*. An active advertisement of services is done by the server periodically broadcasting to notify all possible clients of the services it can provide. The passive approach has servers register their services with a *directory server*. When clients require a service, they first check with the *directory server*, or *browser* as it is commonly called in Windows NT, to see whether the required service is available and learn where they should go to get it. Finally, the software components that implement Application Layer services on a client need to provide the client with the ability to access the services from a server. Most client components do so by implementing a form or redirector or requester component that intercepts the request for nonlocal or rather remote services and forwards it in the appropriate manner.

The Complete OSI Model

The Complete OSI Model introduces two main components in addition to the seven layer model: End Systems and Intermediate Systems. (See Figure 3-12.) End Systems are the actual clients and hosts or servers. Intermediate Systems are the devices in between the clients and hosts or servers that facilitate the relaying of packets of information between separate, logical networks.

As systems process information created by protocols, information flows from a sender's application to the receiver's application in the following manner:

Figure 3-12
The Complete OSI
Model. (Courtesy of
Learning Tree Inter-
national)

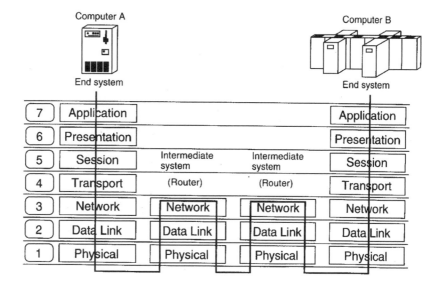

1. Information is processed by the upper layers of the sender.
2. It is passed to the lower layers of the sender (down the stack).
3. It eventually becomes an external signal on the cable.
4. The upper layer information is assisted toward its destination by router.
5. It is processed by the receiver's lower layers.
6. The information is handed up through the upper layers to the receiver's application.

Senders and receivers are considered *End Systems* (ES), and routers (or gateways) are considered *Intermediate Systems* (IS). The process of passing information from one layer to another is called *protocol layering and encapsulation*. For example, as we saw in Figure 3-2 earlier (protocol multiplexing), the source or sending End System sends a Telnet message that gets passed from the upper three layers to the Transport Layer and encapsulated inside the *Transmission Control Protocol* (TCP) segment. The TCP segment is then passed from the Transport Layer to the Network Layer and encapsulated inside an *Internet Protocol* (IP) packet. The IP packet is then passed down to the Data Link Layer and encapsulated inside an Ethernet frame. The whole package or series of *Protocol Data Units* (PDU) is then passed down to the Physical Layer and sent out on the network cable segment as one long stream of 1s and 0s depending on

Figure 3-13
Protocol encapsulation and layering. (Courtesy of Learning Tree International)

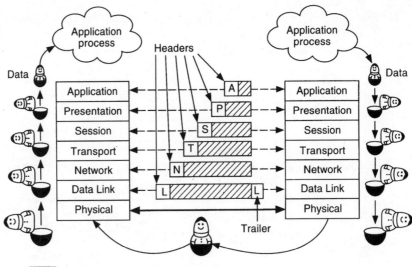

Payload or "data" field at each layer

Encapsulation is similar to using "Russian dolls" to transport data

the contents. If necessary, as the message travels down the network segment, Intermediate Systems will pick up and relay it until it reaches the destination End System where the process will then reverse itself. (See Figure 3-13.)

A Trekky Analogy

Here is yet another analogy. For the many *Star Trek* fans out there, Mr. Neil Hollingum (a famous Learning Tree International instructor) developed an analogy comparing the Star Trek Transporter process to the OSI Reference Model; we wanted to share this analogy with you to shed some light on the whole process.

> Captain Kirk jumps on to the transporter pad at the Application Layer and shouts "Beam me up, Scotty!" At this point, Scotty pushes a lever, and Captain Kirk goes down through the Presentation Layer that converts objects into bits (anti-matter). The Session Layer sets checkpoints for the transmission. The Transport Layer prepares to handle error recognition and recovery. The Network Layer routes him to the correct planet and remote transporter pad. The Data Link Layer verifies the *Cyclical Redundancy Checks* (CRC) and recovers any potential errors as a result of an asteroid passing through the transporter beam transmission. (Remember the *Next*

Generation episode in which the people get stuck in the transporter beam buffer?) The Network Layer then checks to see whether he has arrived at the correct planet and transporter pad. The Transport Layer puts things that are out of sequence back in the right order, as it could be painful if a person's bits are reassembled out of sequence. The Session Layer checks its checkpoints. The Presentation Layer converts the bits (anti-matter) back into objects (matter). And Captain Kirk reappears on the planet's transporter pad.

We've now concluded the review of the OSI Reference Model. By now, you should have a really good feel or understanding of what is taking place when two computer systems try to talk to each other over a network. As well, you now can appreciate the functions specified by the seven OSI Reference Model layers and subsequently what is expected of any protocol solutions implemented by vendors such as Novell or Microsoft. In the following sections, we will review in detail the protocol solutions that are available to facilitate the integration of these two NOSs.

Comparing Novell and Microsoft Networking Protocols

Figure 3-14 demonstrates the most important and popular potential solution protocols that each network operating system can support. For the following sections of this chapter, we will proceed through the protocol stacks starting with the lower layers and then proceed to the upper layers of each protocol family (also called *stacks* or *suites*). We will start with the NetWare-supported protocols and then proceed through the Windows NT protocols. Although it is supported equally by both network operating systems, we will close the protocol comparison section with a look at how *Transmission Control Protocol / Internet Protocol* (TCP/IP) is supported in both environments and investigate how it can be used to support the transport of NetWare and Windows NT service protocols NCP and *Server Message Blocks* (SMB), respectively, while also enabling internetworking and interoperability capabilities between the two NOSs.

A brief glance at Figure 3-14 will begin to reveal some similarities both in format and in actual protocols supported on both NOSs. For example, you can see that both NetWare and Windows NT support the Transmission Control Protocol/Internet Protocol. You can see three sections of functionality: Adapter Card Drivers/Network Interface Cards, Transport Protocols, and Network Services. We have already discussed briefly in this

Figure 3-14
Windows NT and
NetWare protocol
stacks compared.
(Courtesy of Learning
Tree International)

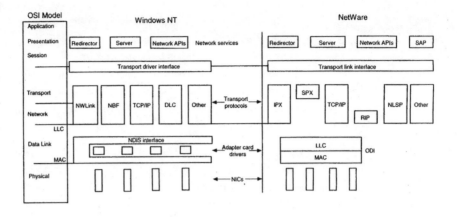

API = application program interface
DLC = data-link control
LLC = logical link control
MAC = media access control
NBF = NETBEUI frame

NLSP = Network Link Services Protocol
ODI = open data-link interface
OSI = open systems interconnection

chapter how these three categories relate to internetworking and interoperability. The adapter driver instructs the operating system about the
existence of the Network Interface Card. The Transport protocols provide
the ability to relay upper-level messages for service requests around on
the internetwork. The network services provide server and client services
like remote access to a server's file system or printer resources. Note that
both network operating systems, in fact, provide the same services.
The differences are the methods and mechanisms they use to accomplish
this task.

Novell NetWare Protocols

The NetWare protocol suite of protocols is based on the *Xerox Network
System* (XNS) protocols that were developed in the 1960s at the *Palo Alto
Research Center* (PARC). (See Figure 3-15.) As you will see with the
Transmission Control Protocol/Internet Protocol protocol stack, Net-
Ware's protocols do not match up exactly beside the seven-layer OSI Ref-
erence Model as was shown in Figure 3-14.

The Open Data Link Interface specification is Novell's proprietary
means of instructing the operating system about the existence and support for Network Interface Cards and their frame formats. The main pro-

Figure 3-15
NetWare protocol stack. (Courtesy of Learning Tree International)

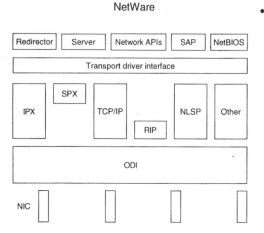

NetWare

XNS = Xerox Network Systems

- **Internetwork Packet Exchange (IPX) Protocol**
  - Is a connectionless protocol concerned with routing and network addressing
  - Evolved from XNS's Internetwork Datagram Protocol (IDP)

tocols NetWare implements are Internet Packet eXchange, *Sequenced Packet eXchange* (SPX), and NetWare Core Protocol. IPX and SPX provide the internetworking capabilities for NetWare network devices and function at the Network and Transport Layers, respectively. The Session, Presentation, and Application Layer functionality is provided by the NCP protocol. Through NCP, client network devices access NetWare NOS file and print services. *Network Basic Input Output* (NetBIOS) is an IBM client/server protocol, which is also supported by encapsulating it inside IPX. It provides functionality similar to NCP but is not required for NetWare-only access. However, as we begin to discuss the Windows NT integration side, NetBIOS will become an important protocol. Other support protocols such as *Routing Information Protocol* (RIP) and *NetWare Link Services Protocol* (NSLP) provide network routing and route status information to clients and servers on the network. The *Service Advertising Protocol* (SAP) advertises the availability of network services. (See Table 3-1.)

The Open Data Link Interface was codeveloped in 1989 by Novell and Apple Computer. ODI provides a similar function to the Network Device Interface Specification. The ODI specification resolved a major problem facing customers and end users of network operating systems—namely that they could support only one protocol stack at a time. When a Network Interface Card is directly linked to one communication protocol stack, other protocol stacks cannot be supported. This, in turn, meant communication over the network was limited to one (usually proprietary) group of network services. Some patchwork solutions did evolve, but they

Table 3-1

NetWare Protocol topics and methods. (Courtesy of Learning Tree International)

Protocol	OSI Layer	Topics	Methods
MLID (Multiple Link Interface Driver)	Data Link MAC	Media Access	Contention, Token Passing, Polling
LSL (Link Support Layer)	Data Link LLC Specification	Protocol	Interface between MLID and upper layer protocols
IPX (Internetwork Packet Exchange Protocol)	Network	1. Addressing	1. Logical Network Service
		2. Route Selection	2. Dynamic
		3. Connection Service	3. Connectionless
RIP (Routing Information Protocol)	Network	Route Discovery	Distance Vector
NLSP (NetWare Link Services Protocol)	Network	Route Discovery	Link State
SPX (Sequence Packet Exchange Protocol)	Transport	1. Addressing	1. Connection Identifier
		2. Segment Development	2. Division and Combination
		3. Connection Services	3. Segment Sequencing Error Control End-to-End Flow Control
NCP (NetWare Core Protocol)	1. Transport	1. Connection Services	1. Segment Sequencing Error Control End-to-End Flow Control
	2. Session	2. Session Administration	2. Data Transfer
	3. Presentation	3. Translation	3. Character Code File Syntax
	4. Application	4. Service Used	4. OS Redirector Collaborative (depends on client redirector or requestor)
SAP (Service Advertising Protocol)	1. Session	1. Session Administration	File Transfer
	2. Application	2. Service Advertisement	2. Active

were often cumbersome and always required lots of memory on the client workstation. To overcome this problem, the ODI specification was developed. With ODI, one NIC on a single workstation can transparently support several different protocol stacks, using just the one NIC driver. This solution, in turn, required less memory and processing resources at the client workstation. An example of ODI implemented on a client workstation would be the ability for its user to access TCP/IP services such as Telnet while accessing a NetWare file server over IPX.

However, the problem is not resolved by simply supporting the Network Layer and upper parts of the protocol stack because TCP/IP and IPX support different lower-level Data Link Layer frame formats. Therefore, the ODI specification also provides the workstation with the capability of transmitting upper-level protocol stack components using various low-level frame formats. For example, TCP/IP's default and de facto standard frame format is Ethernet_II, whereas NetWare's is currently IEEE802.2 (Institute of Electrical and Electronics Engineers). The issue of supporting various frame formats is important to integrating network administrators because when two NOSs are on the same Data Link Layer network segment (joined by a bridge or switch), the same frame format must be supported on both NOSs and clients to ensure that they can communicate with each other at this level. The ODI specification allows a NetWare client or server to support the following frame formats:

Ethernet:	Ethernet II, 802.3 RAW, IEEE 802.2, Ethernet SNAP
Token Ring:	IEEE 802.5, Token Ring SNAP
FDDI:	FDDI, FDDI SNAP
Apple:	Local Talk

An additional function is that one Network Layer protocol can be supported or transported in different frame types. For example, the Internetwork Packet eXchange protocol can be transported or encapsulated inside IEEE 802.2 and 802.3 RAW. Frame format selection will depend on which server the client is trying to communicate with and the frame format that server supports. This capability will become important as network administrators integrate older NetWare clients and servers that may be using 802.3 RAM Ethernet frame formats to access a Windows NT Server on the same network segment that is also running the File and Print Service for NetWare. NetWare 2.x and 3.11 support 802.3 RAW frame formats by default, whereas NetWare 4.x defaults to the IEEE 802.2 frame format.

The ODI architecture, as illustrated in Figure 3-16, consists of the following components:

- Multiple Link Interface Driver (MLID)
- Link Support Layer (LSL)
- Communication protocol stacks

The ODI specification not only allows the support for multiple frame formats to be processed by the same NIC, but also provides the capability of supporting multiple upper layer protocols within the same frame format. In other words, the Ethernet II frame format can be used to support both Internetwork Packet eXchange and Internet Protocol. Essentially, these transport layer protocols are selectively bound to the frame formats that are supported through the ODI configuration. However, one really interesting limitation is that a Transport Layer protocol can be bound to only one frame format on NetWare client workstations. For example, after IPX is bound to the Ethernet II frame format, it cannot be rebound to also simultaneously support IEEE 802.2. Now, in all honesty, trying to support multiple frame formats on your network infrastructure is probably not a wise idea anyway. However, the situation to do just that does arise in many instances within organizations, and sometimes we wish we could have done so. To get around this limitation, multiple frame formats must be supported at the server instead of at the client workstation. Doing so has unfortunate implications and effects on network traffic in that all the network routing and server service information is now broadcast twice. What is important for network administrators to remember is that when integrating NetWare with Windows NT, a common frame format will sometimes be required—in particular when the computers in question are not the same physical network segment.

Figure 3-16
ODI architecture.
(Source: Novell, Inc.)

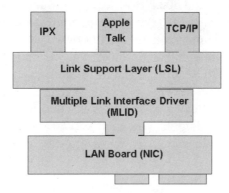

Internetwork Packet eXchange (IPX)

Functioning at the network layer of the OSI Reference Model, Internetwork Packet eXchange is a connectionless network protocol. It is proprietary to Novell and is a subset of the Xerox XNS specification. IPX performs routing of packets based on routing table information maintained via the Router Information Protocol. IPX also provides a networkwide addressing scheme. The IPX packet is the protocol data unit of the Data Link Layer frame.

IPX provides a common format for network addressing of NetWare networks. The IPX network address is used to identify all the computer systems and devices that are on the same logical network operating at the Network Layer. The addressing is also used by the IPX enabled routers to identify and route IPX packets. The full IPX address is composed of the following three components:

1. IPX Logical Network Number
2. NIC Media Access Control (MAC) Address
3. Application Socket Number

A complete IPX network address would have the format

`FFFFFFFF:FFFFFFFFFFFF:FFFF`

or more practically

`F0000001:0000C0123456:0451`

The Application Layer socket number is used to relay the IPX protocol data unit payload up to the appropriate higher layer.

Sequenced Packet eXchange (SPX)

Sequenced Packet eXchange is Novell's proprietary Transport protocol. It is a connection-oriented packet delivery service that functions similar to Transmission Control Protocol. SPX was derived from the *Xerox Sequenced Packet* (XSP) protocol. The protocol performs flow control, sequencing, and acknowledgment of packets. Not all client/server services provided by a NetWare server require SPX, and for this reason, it does not cross the entire protocol stack. In other words, an Application Layer service can deposit its message directly in IPX and bypass the SPX protocol component altogether.

Three main applications make use of the reliability of the SPX protocol in a NetWare environment: RCONSOLE (Remote Console), RPRINTER (Remote Printer), and *System Network Architecture* (SNA) Gateways for mainframe access from the local area network.

NetWare Core Protocol (NCP)

NetWare Core Protocol is the protocol that provides the interoperability within a NetWare network. The main function of NCP is to provide file and print service access by client workstations. In addition, it also manages file and record locking, security, and network file server access. Workstation or network devices use redirector or requester (shell) software that makes the file server services appear as a transparent extension of the local operating system. NCP calls are made by the NetWare (shell). NCP calls are proprietary to Novell. This issue is important when you consider that Microsoft has implemented support for these calls on an NT Server. (See Figure 3-17.)

Unlike in Microsoft network environments, in NetWare only servers are assigned unique logical name identifiers. NetWare clients are not assigned unique logical names and are instead referred to or communicated with via their IPX network/NIC numbers. NetWare server names can be

Figure 3-17
NetWare IPX, SPX, and NCP protocols. (Courtesy of Learning Tree International)

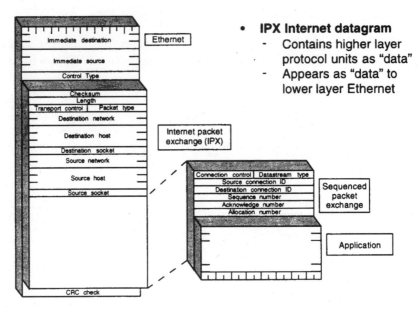

- **IPX Internet datagram**
  - Contains higher layer protocol units as "data"
  - Appears as "data" to lower layer Ethernet

up to 32 alphanumeric characters long. The server's logical name is then used with NetWare end user commands that allow or facilitate access to NetWare server resources over the network. An example would be when you use the NetWare **MAP** command to redirect a local workstation drive letter to a NetWare server file system volume (**MAP G:=SERVER_NAME\ VOLUME:DIR\SUBDIR**).

NetWare IP

NetWare IP is Novell's response to the user community's demand for support of the industry standard TCP/IP Transport protocol as a method for accessing NetWare servers. NetWare IP uses encapsulation of IPX/NCP within standard IP packets as well as standard IP packets. The design approach allows NetWare users to continue working with the same server technology while using the IP Transport protocol to communicate with the NetWare servers. NetWare's IP is composed of the following components:

- NetWare IP client
- NetWare 3.1x or 4.x servers
- Domain Name System (DNS) servers
- Domain SAP Servers (DSS)

The NetWare IP Client Architecture

NetWare IP uses the same standard NetWare client architecture at the hardware, ODI, and applications layers. Only the Transport Layer is different. Rather than using IPX to transmit information, NetWare IP clients use the User Datagram Protocol in the Novell implementation of the TCP/IP protocol stack. (See Figure 3-18.) Unfortunately, given the original design of the IPX/NCP combination, it was not simply an issue

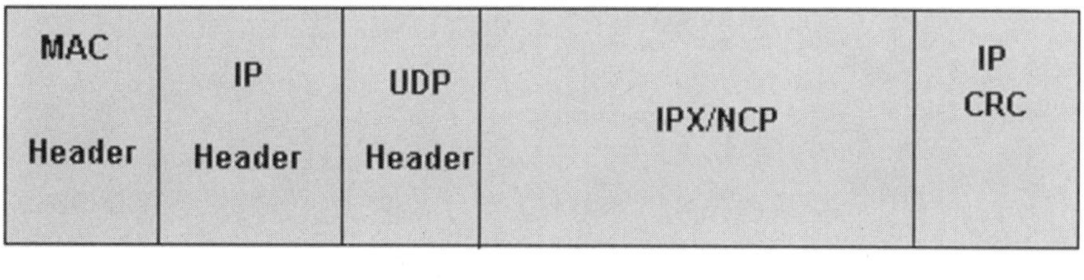

Figure 3-18
NetWare IP with IPX/NCP encapsulation. (Source: Novell, Inc.)

MAC Header	IP Header	UDP Header	IPX/NCP	IP CRC

of replacing IPX with IP, so modifications had to be made to allow Net-Ware's IP client implementation to work over TCP/IP. Applications, in turn, talk to NCP, which makes calls to an NWIP software driver. NWIP then makes its calls to TCP/IP.

Network administrators must understand that, although both Net-Ware and Windows NT support TCP/IP, they do so for different reasons. Also, although TCP/IP will provide access by its respective clients to the server services they offer, it will not facilitate integration directly. Here, NetWare supports its own NetWare Core Protocol encapsulated inside TCP/IP. You will see that Microsoft's TCP/IP implementation is to support Server Message Blocks encapsulated inside TCP/IP. Therefore, the two are not fully compatible and do not provide integration. Interoperability would require a solution such as SAMBA running on a NetWare server to support SMB encapsulated in TCP/IP to facilitate access to NetWare services.

Routing Information Protocol (RIP)

Similar to TCP/IP's RIP, NetWare *Routing Information Protocol* (RIP) was derived from XNS's *Internetwork Datagram Protocol* (IDP). RIP is a distance vector-based routing protocol that uses hop counts to assign a cost to network routes. The protocol functions at the Network Layer and is assigned its own unique socket number.

NetWare Link State Protocol (NLSP)

NetWare Link State Protocol (NLSP) is a link-state route discovery protocol that is based on the ISO's *Intermediate System to Intermediate System* (IS-IS) protocol standard. NLSP provides better router information update processes and supports the more reliable mesh and hybrid mesh network topologies. NSLP will no doubt replace NetWare's RIP as the router information protocol of choice.

Service Advertising Protocol (SAP)

Service Advertising Protocols (SAPs) are the advertisements to client workstations about the services that network servers provide. Although the main servers are file and print, many other server services are available, such as database, communication, and mail delivery. Service information is maintained in SAP tables on each server. SAPs are broadcast every 60 seconds and can, in large networks with many services, cause a lot of traffic on the network infrastructure (including LANs and WAN links). NLSP also incorporates SAP information and reduces the frequency of SAP broadcasts.

Network Basic Input Output System (NetBIOS)

Network Basic Input Output System is a protocol that emulates the standard IBM NetBIOS and provides some, but not all, of the specification's services. The main benefit of using Novell's implementation of NetBIOS in a NetWare environment is that NetBIOS messages are encapsulated in IPX packets. NetBIOS command messages are submitted using *Network Control Blocks* (NCB). Because IPX is a Network layer protocol, NetBIOS can then be routed throughout an organization's internetwork. IBM's *NetBIOS Frames Protocol* (NBFP) is not a routable protocol and as such does not work in a routed network environment. The disadvantage is that NetWare does not support all the NetBIOS Network Control Blocks and therefore is not compatible with IBM's NBFP. We will describe NetBIOS in more detail in the Windows NT protocols section.

NetWare Remote Procedure Call (RPC)

Novell's implementation of Remote Procedure Call is used predominantly by the NetWare *Network File System* (NFS) product. NetWare NFS provides a standard way of sharing files with other network operating systems and operates over Novell's NetWare implementation of Transmission Control Protocol/Internet Protocol.

Apple Talk

Novell also supports the full range of Apple Talk protocols starting with Local Talk Frames at the Data Link and Physical Layers, moving up through the Network Layer with Apple Datagram support, and finally by supporting Apple File Talk and Printer Access Protocol server services protocols. In fact, if you are curious, you could actually use Apple Talk protocols on both NetWare and Windows NT as a way of providing inter-operability and internetworking between the two. However, doing so would not be pretty and would certainly not be the most efficient approach, nor would it address issues concerning migration.

The NetWare Communication Process in Action

Figure 3-19 depicts the steps that a computer workstation sending information over the network will take to encapsulate its message request and forward it to the receiving server.

In addition to IPX, NCP protocols can also be transmitted or encapsulated in the Transmission Control Protocol/Internet Protocol for relaying over an internetwork. Therefore, network administrators can provide access to NetWare servers without using the IPX protocol. We will investigate the capability in the TCP/IP section later in this chapter.

Windows NT Networking Protocols

Starting with *Microsoft Network* (MS-NET), Microsoft has provided a means of being able to communicate between computer systems on a network cable segment. Early versions supported only one protocol stack and were limited in the number of computers that could be located within one network segment (as with Novell's NetWare). Novell and Microsoft in conjunction with IBM were pioneers in the area of network development. Although Novell had a definitive market lead and advantage during the late 1980s and early 1990s, that lead is now being challenged by Microsoft's newer network implementations. We will cover Microsoft's client and server operating systems in future chapters. For now, let's look at the protocols that Microsoft has started with to enable network communication and then turn our attention to the ones they now support and recommend that you use.

Figure 3-20 highlights some of the protocols that Microsoft's Windows NT uses for network communication. However, they are also supported on Microsoft's client operating systems such as Windows for Workgroups and Windows 95. Although working initially with a very limiting networking protocol stack, Microsoft has taken a strong initiative in providing excel-

Figure 3-19
NetWare computer
system sending and
receiving network
communication.
(Source: Novell, Inc.)

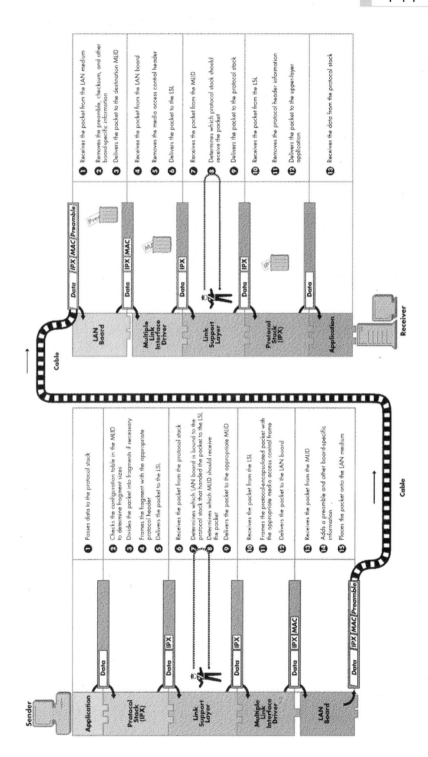

Figure 3-20
Microsoft networking
protocol stacks.
(Courtesy of Learning
Tree International)

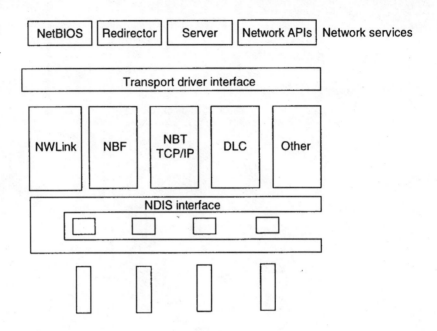

Windows NT

NBF = NetBIOS frames
NBT = NetBIOS in TCP/IP

lent support for other proprietary and industry standard networking
Transport protocols. We believe this initiative is probably due to a reluc-
tant acknowledgment of the market share reality as well as pressure from
the customer community at large for better Internet integration (much
the same way Novell has had to make changes). In the former instance,
Microsoft now supports Novell's internetworking protocol as a transport
vehicle for its own server service protocols (and you will see that Microsoft
takes NetWare integration even further). In the latter instance, Novell
supports the Internet's standard TCP/IP Transport protocol to carry both
its own service protocols and to also facilitate access to and integration

with the Internet. Along the way, it has also maintained the capability of supporting access by the large Macintosh community.

In a broad sense, Microsoft's network architecture includes the following components:

- Transport protocols that define the rules for network communication

- *InterProcess Communication* (IPC) that allows applications to communicate with each other over a network

- File and print sharing services that allow resources to be made available over the network

- The *Multi-Provider Router* (MPR) and *Multiple Uniform Naming Convention* (UNC, also called Universal Naming Convention by the rest of the networking world), which facilitate network communication by applications using a single *Application Programming Interface* (API) over any network vendor's redirector or Transport protocol

Starting from the lower-levels of Figure 3-18, the Network Device Interface Specification implements support for multiple protocol stacks and frame types on the same Network Interface Card. It, in effect, provides for Windows NT (and other Microsoft clients) what ODI does for NetWare. NDIS is the link between the NIC and the various potential Transport protocols that are supported on NT link IPX/SPX, TCP/IP, NetBEUI, and others. The *Transport Device Interface* (TDI) provides a similar function to NDIS, but instead of providing a multiplexing interface to the NICs, it provides an access point for the numerous server services to select and transmit over one or more of the transport protocols. This mechanism allows an application to transmit over TCP/IP to one client while possibly transmitting the same information to another client over IPX/SPX or NetBEUI. NDIS and TDI are generally referred to by Microsoft as a *boundary layer*, which is a unified interface between the layers in the Windows network architecture that facilitates third-party application development. Unlike NDIS, TDI does not have a specific software driver that is a standard for passing messages between layers in a network architecture.

Unlike NetWare, Windows operating systems, since Windows for Workgroups, can act as both server and client. This duality of functions allows them to create a Peer-to-Peer network in which one computer can provide a server service by sharing its printer yet also be a client by running an executable application that resides on another computer's file system. The

Windows Workstation Redirector and Server service provide these capabilities. And although Windows for Workgroups does not allow you to tune
or optimize a computer for one of the two rolls, Windows 95 and Windows
NT do. Finally, you can use methods and protocols to access higher-level
interoperability services on Windows NT systems; they will be reviewed
in the following section.

It is important to understand that Microsoft's network communication
is based on the NetBIOS Application Programming Interface specification. One of the peculiar aspects about NetBIOS is that it requires all
clients and servers to have a unique identifying name, unlike NetWare,
which requires only the servers to have names. The main reason for this
requirement is that Microsoft's network operating system functions predominantly in a Peer-to-Peer mode in which every machine can provide
workstation (client) or server services.

Network Device Interface Specification (NDIS)

The Network Device Interface Specification was codeveloped by Microsoft and 3Com in 1989. Like ODI in the NetWare environment, NDIS
is a standard for defining an interface for communication between the
Media Access Control layer and the Transport protocols. The NDIS specification defines the software interface used by the Transport protocols
to communicate with the Network Interface Cards in a computer system.
(See Figure 3-21.) Windows for Workgroups uses NDIS 2.0, and Windows
95 supports both NDIS 2.0 and 3.0 specifications. Windows NT uses
NDIS 3.0. The NDIS 3.0 specification allows an unlimited number of

Figure 3-21
NDIS Wrapper. (Cour-
tesy of Learning Tree
International)

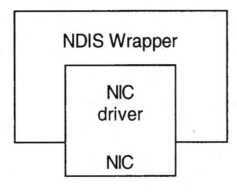

NICs in a computer system. Additionally, an unlimited number of Transport protocols can be attached or bound to a single adapter card. Probably one of the main differences between NDIS 2.0 and NDIS 3.0 is that the latter implementation uses an NDIS Wrapper. The NDIS Wrapper is composed of a piece of software code that surrounds all NIC device drivers. The main purpose of the NDIS Wrapper is to provide a common interface between protocols and the NDIS device drivers.

NDIS also facilitates the support of various frame formats for Microsoft clients and servers and in turn supports their binding to upper-level Transport protocols. Over time, Microsoft operating systems have supported different frame formats as their default installation modes. We will investigate frame format support provided by NDIS for Microsoft operating systems in Chapter 4. You should note that NDIS provides support for Ethernet, Token Ring, FDDI, ARCnet, and WAN links (switched virtual circuits, ISDN, X.25, and dial-up or dedicated asynchronous links).

Transport Level Protocols

Following is information about the various Transport Level protocols.

NetBIOS Extended User Interface (NetBEUI)

The NetBIOS Extended User Interface was first introduced by IBM in 1985. The goal of the NetBEUI implementation was to provide an efficient network protocol stack that did not require a lot of computer resources and was well suited for a small network environment. Some of the original assumptions that went into the design of NetBEUI eventually led to its unpopularity. However, used in the correct network setting, it provides more network performance than other, bulkier Transport protocols. Some of the original design specifications assumed that it would only ever be used in a local workgroup setting in which under 200 workstations would be connected to the same network segment. If access to mainframes or mini computers was required, then some form of a gateway service would be provided by a network-connected device. Microsoft's Windows NT *NetBEUI Frame* (NBF) transport driver implements the IBM NetBEUI 3.0 specification.

NetBEUI's development was also based partially on the original Network Basic Input Output System protocol, which was developed for IBM by Sytek. The development of NetBIOS and subsequent development of NetBEUI are very important when reviewing Microsoft network solutions because the network components of the operating systems are all based around it. Microsoft has supported the NetBEUI protocol in all the networking products it has produced since MS-NET was first available in the 1980s. At a basic level, NetBIOS support allows applications to be developed to a common interface for access to network resources. NetBIOS has two main components:

■ A Session layer interface implements a standard Application Programming Interface set for applications to use to submit network resource access requests and pass them down to the underlying networking protocol. (NetBIOS commands are issued as Network Control Blocks.)

■ A session management and Transport protocol commonly called NetBIOS Frames Protocol is responsible for transporting the NetBIOS NCB over the network infrastructure.

In the first component, NetBIOS provides interoperability access by applications to network resources through the use of a common set of APIs. In the second component, NetBIOS Frames Protocol transports these requests over the network. Today, NBFP is no longer required because it has been replaced by NetBEUI Frames. However, NBF implemented in Windows NT is based on the original NetBEUI specification. There is often a lot of confusion about NetBIOS and NetBEUI. The thing to remember really is that the interoperability capability of NetBIOS is supportive of NetBEUI frames, so the NetBIOS Frames Protocol is no longer used. NetBIOS remains in NetBEUI. However, NetBEUI can support a number of other upper-level interoperability access mechanisms such as the X-Open Server Message Blocks, Windows Sockets, or UNIX-like Remote Procedure Calls.

As stated previously, NetBEUI makes use of IBM's NetBIOS 3.0 specification as the upper-level interface to the network by applications and the NDIS boundary at the bottom level for access to the network infrastructure. Through NDIS, NetBEUI supports the 802.2 Logical Link Control protocol frame format. (See Figure 3-22.)

NBF provides for both connectionless and connection-oriented forms of network communication. Although connectionless network communication can be further made to be reliable or unreliable, NBF and NetBEUI support only the unreliable connectionless form, which is similar to the postal system of communication in that the recipient need not be home

Figure 3-22
NetBEUI frame
format with
encapsulated Net-
BIOS request.
(Source: WWW.
NETWORKOLOGIST.
COM)

Destination Address	Source Address	Lenght	DS/LP	SS/LP	Control	NetBIOS
00 00 C0 65 43 21	00 00 AA 12 34 56	00 2F	F0	F0	03(00)	Code - 0h, ADD_NAME_QUERY

for you to send a package. Connection-oriented communication is like making a telephone call in which no session is established unless someone answers at the other end.

NBF Limitation

As you look at Figure 3-22, you will notice that there is no Network Layer information. This is probably NetBEUI's biggest downfall as a Transport protocol because it means that the protocol is not routable over internetwork links. Therefore, the network-connected computers you may want to communicate with need to be on either the same physical segment, or access is facilitated through a bridge internetworking device that functions at the Data Link Layer. However, this same limitation makes NBF such a fast network transport mechanism because there is no overhead in the protocol associated with maintaining logical network addressing information, nor does the system need to perform additional levels of address resolution because there is only the NetBIOS name of the computer system and its associated NIC address.

We stated that NBF was the original transport and service level protocol that Microsoft supported in its oriented operating systems and that it is capable of transporting NetBIOS and other upper-level interoperability protocols. However, given its limitations in large enterprise network systems, Microsoft has engineered the ability for its operating system to use other popular Transport protocols such as Novell's IPX/SPX and the industry standard TCP/IP. We will now look at those two protocols from a Microsoft perspective.

NWLink Internetwork Packet eXchange (NWLink IPX or NetWare Link Protocol)

Developing a truly ingenious idea given the popularity of Novell's NetWare NOS and its undeniable market share, Microsoft has taken the bold initiative of supporting the NetBIOS compatibility layer over Novell's IPX Transport protocol. Microsoft includes support for IPX, SPX, RIPX, and NBIPX. NBIPX is NetBIOS over IPX and is also called NWLinkNB in Windows NT 3.5 and NWNBLink in Windows NT 3.1. NWLink IPX supports both IPX/SPX Sockets, NetBIOS APIs, Remote Procedure Calls, and SPX-based client/server applications. NWLink also supports the latest version of Novell's SPX II, which supports a large packet size sliding window version of the SPX protocol. A computer system running NWLink can support MS-DOS-, OS/2-, and Win32-based applications that use IPX/SPX Application Programming Interfaces such as Sockets, NetBIOS, or even Novell's proprietary communication APIs that use Even Control Blocks. (See Figure 3-23.)

Because Microsoft is supporting Novell's IPX, which we reviewed earlier in the chapter, we do not need to go into detail on IPX here. However, you can really look upon NetBIOS encapsulated inside IPX (NBIPX) as being similar in functionality to NetWare Core Protocol in IPX. The end result is that they both provide access to server resources on a network. However, the NWLink/NBIPX combination simply allows Microsoft clients using this service and Transport protocol combination to talk with other like-configured Microsoft computer systems on an IPX network. It does not provide for interoperability with NetWare servers. However, because it does support IPX/SPX Sockets, it also can support the NCP protocol, which would provide for that level of integration. The NCP protocol support is provided through the Microsoft's *Client Service for NetWare* (CSNW) and *Gateway Services for NetWare* (GSNW) software and will be discussed in the Chapters 4 and 5, respectively.

Figure 3-23
NWLink IPX/SPX support. (Source: WWW. NETWORKOLOGIST. COM)

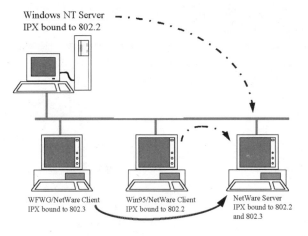

Windows NT Server
IPX bound to 802.2

WFWG/NetWare Client
IPX bound to 802.3

Win95/NetWare Client
IPX bound to 802.2

NetWare Server
IPX bound to 802.2
and 802.3

As we highlighted in the NetWare protocols section of this chapter, Net-Ware's Open Data Link Interface can support many frame formats. Although frame formats are not an issue with NetBEUI Frames (because it uses only 802.2), frame formats are an issue when internetworking with NetWare. Furthermore, because NDIS supports several frame formats and Transport protocols simultaneously, the concept of *binding* becomes important. As with ODI, upper-level Transport protocols are bound to a lower-level frame format. However, NDIS allows a Windows NT system to support IPX bound to several different frame formats. Binding of protocols in Windows NT allows you to determine not only which frame format will support a particular Transport Level protocol, but also which server service protocols can use which Transport Level protocols. Binding can have some effect on performance, so we will investigate this issue further in Chapter 4.

Through NDIS, NWLink can interface with several frame types including Ethernet II, 802.3 RAW, 802.2, and Ethernet SNAP. (See Figure 3-24.) Token Ring and FDDI support 802.2 and SNAP formats. ARCnet supports ARCnet frame format. We stress this fact of multiple and variable frame support because it is often a source of frustration when trying to integrate NetWare and Windows NT. In the following chapter, we will walk through the process of configuring NWLink to support multiple frame formats and highlight which ones are appropriate for a given network configuration.

NWLink uses broadcasts to resolve NetBIOS names to IPX addresses. Using caching of the NetBIOS name to IPX address mappings, NWLink does manage to reduce the number of broadcasts. Currently, NWLink does

Figure 3-24
NWLink IPX/SPX
Properties.
(Source: Microsoft
Corporation)

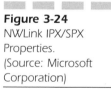

NWLink IPX/SPX Properties   [?][X]

General

In most cases, you should choose Auto Detect. You should manually configure the Frame Type/Network Number only if Auto Detect does not work in your environment. If you experience problems, contact your network administrator.

Adapter: [1] SMC (WD) ISA Adapter

Frame Type: Auto Detect

Network Number:

              OK   Cancel   Apply

not support static files (such as HOSTS or LMHOSTS) or name services such as Windows Internet Name Service for name resolution. Such a feature is unlikely to be implemented in the future because Microsoft appears to be moving more toward Internet Protocol support, as is Novell.

NetBIOS in TCP/IP (NBT)

Windows NT supports an implementation of Transmission Control Protocol/Internet Protocol to act as a Transport Level protocol over internetworks in the same fashion that NWLink IPX does. However, TCP/IP usually refers to a number of additional protocols, and Microsoft's implementation supports many of them as well, such as User Datagram Protocol, *Internet Control Message Protocol* (ICMP), and *Address Resolution Protocol* (ARP). Although we will cover the TCP/IP suite of protocols later in this chapter, you should understand that to link NWLink IPX, the main purpose of NBT is to provide internetworking interoperability between Microsoft clients and servers, and not between UNIX and Microsoft operating systems residing on an internetwork.

NetBIOS support over TCP/IP was first introduced in the Internet's Request for Comments (RFC) documents 1001 and 1002 titled RFC NetBIOS or NBT (included on the CD-ROM). It provides for a means of implementing the NetBIOS 1.0 API set over the TCP/IP Transport protocols. (The original intent was to provide an interface to LAN Manager resources over an IP internetwork.) In Figure 3-25, you see that NetBIOS can be encapsulated in TCP and UDP. However, for a majority of the functions that NetBIOS supports, UDP is used. TCP is used for special Net-

Figure 3-25
NetBIOS in TCP/IP
(NBT). (Source: Microsoft Corporation)

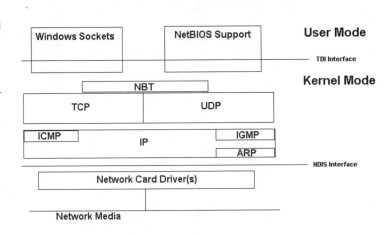

BIOS-based applications that require reliable network connection services such as communication servers but not for simple file and print transfers.

Because we are using TCP/IP, the Windows computer system will need to be configured with at least the IP Address, IP Subnet Mask, and Default IP Gateway information, as would any other computer using the TCP/IP protocol stack. However, many other issues are involved in supporting NetBIOS over TCP/IP, and they can have an effect on your Windows NT network as well as any network it is integrated with, including NetWare. Let's look at some of these issues now. We will concentrate on TCP/IP configuration for Windows NT in the next chapter.

One of the key functions stated in RFC 1001 and 1002 for NetBIOS in (or over) TCP/IP is name resolution. NBT is responsible for resolving NetBIOS names used by Microsoft clients and servers to reference network resources. The RFCs define these methods for implementing NBT:

- Broadcast Node (B-Node)
- Point-to-point Node (P-Node)
- Mixed Node (M-Node)
- H-Node

In a B-Node system, NetBIOS names are resolved to an IP address using a local broadcast. In a P-Node system, broadcasts for name resolution are not used. Rather, the *NetBIOS Naming Service* (NBNS) and *NetBIOS Datagram Delivery Service* (NBDD) are used. Together, both protocols provide name lookup and datagram delivery.

Microsoft's implementation is based on a hybrid to the B-Node implementation as outlined in the previously noted RFCs. Although Windows NT fully supports the B-Node implementation, it also supports added functionality for communication with TCP/IP hosts on the network. NBT requires that Windows NT computes supporting TCP/IP implement name discovery, name registration, and name release.

Name discovery is the process used to determine whether a particular TCP/IP host is on the network. A broadcast NetBIOS "name request frame" is broadcast on the network. Name registration is used by computer hosts as they initialize their TCP/IP stack. The computer host broadcasts a preconfigured NetBIOS name on the network. If another computer host is already using this name, it will reply to the broadcast. The result at the originating host is that it cannot start its workstation or server services. Effectively, it cannot participate in the network. One of the major disadvantages, in our opinion, is that the NetBIOS name space used by Microsoft is flat, so all the workstations and servers in an enterprise must have a unique NetBIOS name. Having a unique name can become a significant challenge in large network environments. When a workstation service is stopped, the computer host will stop replying to NetBIOS Name Registration requests for that unique NetBIOS name, and therefore the NetBIOS name is "released" from use on the network until it is registered again.

Because NetBIOS name registration and resolution broadcasts can have a serious effect on network traffic, they are restricted to their local subnetwork. This restriction presents a problem when trying to use the broadcast method. At this point, the additional nodes of operation come into play.

Although the normal method used for B-Node NetBIOS name resolution is to broadcast onto the local subnet, one of the enhancements Microsoft has made to its implementation of NBT includes support for name resolution from an ASCII text file. LMHOSTS is a text file that contains the NetBIOS names and their corresponding IP addresses. It is similar in format to the UNIX HOSTS file.

Additionally, Windows NT can support *Windows Internet Name Service* (WINS, which is a NetBIOS Name Server, or NBNS) and *Domain Name Service* (DNS) as alternative methods for name resolution. WINS servers contain dynamic databases mapping computer NetBIOS names to IP addresses. The Domain Name Service also provides a method for looking up name mappings to IP addresses; however, it is used predominantly in the UNIX "hostname" to IP address resolution area. It can, however support NetBIOS name resolution over TCP/IP in a manner similar to WINS, with the exception that DNS uses static database files.

M-Node and H-Node implementations for NBT are hybrids that facilitate name resolution when B-Node and P-Node cannot do so. They also dictate the method selection for name resolution. For example, in an M-Node network environment, a computer will first try name registration and resolution using the B-Node method. If not successful, it will then switch to P-Node operation and attempt to register with a NetBIOS Name Server. H-Node, which is still under development, improves on M-Node by using P-Node first for name registration and resolution with a NetBIOS Name Server, thus creating less traffic on the network. However, if the NBNS is down, the computer will switch to B-Node operation to register and resolve names on its local network segment. Finally, an H-Node system can use LMHOSTS files as a last resort, should broadcasting for name registration and resolution fail.

Although the issue of NetBIOS name resolution is not significant to NetWare unless you are running a NetBIOS server service like SAMBA on it, name resolution can have an impact on network administrators' ability to provide an integrated network environment. This issue must be carefully planned out during implementation. Perhaps the best method for name resolution is WINS; we recommend strongly that you consider configuring the service on one of your Windows NT servers that is not as busy as the rest because the service itself will consume some CPU processing time.

Table 3-2 provides a summary of Windows NT Transport protocols.

Transport Driver Interface (TDI)

The Transport Driver Interface is the second and upper-level boundary of the Microsoft networking architecture model. (See Figure 3-26.) You will remember that NDIS was the lower boundary interface between the NIC and the Transport protocols. TDI, on the other hand, is the interface between the Transport protocols and the upper-level applications interfaces. The TDI thus provides a common access point and interface for all the networking components that communicate with applications at the Session Layer of the OSI Reference Model. The main objective of providing a common interface was to facilitate development of distributed applications without having to worry about the myriad of lower-level network communication facilities. As a result of this common interface between the Transport protocols and the upper levels of the communication model, software components running above and below the TDI boundary layer can be intertwined without additional programming for each possible implementation.

Figure 3-26
Transport Driver
Interface (TDI).
(Source: Microsoft
Corporation)

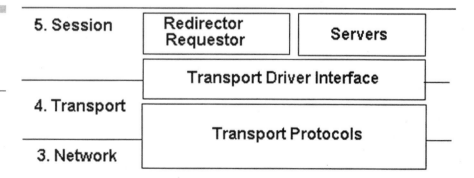

Table 3-2

Windows NT
Transport protocols
summary. (Source:
Microsoft
Corporation)

Transport Protocol Comparison Summary	NBF	NWLink	TCP/IP
Industry acceptance	Limited to IBM and Microsoft networks	Primary protocol in PC networks	Most popular in UNIX-based and now with the Internet (Fast becoming the standard)
Open versus Proprietary	Proprietary, but published	Proprietary	Open
Interoperability	Limited to IBM and Microsoft PC networks	Available on many platforms	Available on nearly every platform
Simplicity of client configuration	Simple	Simple	Can be difficult
Simplicity of administration	Simple	Simple	Can be difficult
Network Segmentation			
Differentiates between networks	No	No	Yes
Hierarchy of subnets within networks	No	Yes	Yes
Routing capabilities	No	Yes	Yes
Name Resolution requirements			
Application Layer to Network Layer	Uses NetBIOS names natively	Resolves NetBIOS names to IPX addresses	Resolves NetBIOS names to IP addresses
Network Layer to Data Link	Resolves NetBIOS names to MAC addresses	IPX address contains MAC address	Resolves IP addresses to MAC address
Network Traffic			
NetBIOS Name Registration	Broadcast	Broadcast	WINS, Broadcast
NetBIOS Name Resolution	Multicast	Cache, Broadcast	Cache, WINS, WINS Proxy, LMHOSTS, Broadcasts, HOSTS, DNS
Router Broadcast	N/A	Dynamic routers and NetWare file servers issue RIP broadcasts every 60 seconds	Dynamic routers issue RIP broadcasts every 30 seconds
SAP Broadcasts	N/A	IPX servers issue SAP broadcasts every 60 seconds	N/A
DHCP Broadcasts	N/A	N/A (but is available on NetWare servers supporting DHCP)	Client IP configuration negotiated via broadcast
WINS Replication	N/A	N/A	Replication traffic when using multiple WINS servers
Network Status Reporting	No	No	Yes
Performance			
Small LANs	Fastest	Fast	Fast
File and Print Operations	Fast	Fastest	Fast
Application Services	Fast	Fast	Fastest

No software program executables are associated with the implementation of the TDI interface. Rather, TDI is a protocol specification to which device driver developers adhere when writing their applications. It is through TDI that upper-level protocols such as Server Message Blocks, NetWare Core Protocol, and Windows sockets, and so on can use multiple lower-level Transport protocols such as IPX and IP. The Windows NT implementation of the NetBIOS interface is probably the best example because Network Control Blocks can be encapsulated inside any of the lower-level transports that Windows NT supports including IPX (NWLink) and IP (NBT). If TDI were not available, multiple device drivers and application interfaces would have to be created for each lower-level transport that the system provides. TDI is the single interface, then, that allows redirector and server services to communicate with supported Transport protocols.

ACCESSING CLIENT AND SERVER SERVICES So far in our journey through the Windows NT networking model, we have passed through the network cable, formatted a Data Link Layer frame, and had the frame's protocol data unit (packet, datagram, or message) removed by the NDIS driver interface, passed to the Transport protocol level, and retrieved the upper-level service request message for the TDI interface to process. At this point, we still don't have a protocol that will allow us to access the various services provided by the server, nor a means of redirecting a client's request for remote server services.

The computer uses the Windows NT Redirector to access remote network resources located on another computer. The redirector concept is also supported on other versions of Microsoft's operating systems. The redirector maintains network connections for the computer and reestablishes them when they are lost. The Windows NT Server service provides connections or allows clients to connect to it using their "redirectors" and subsequently allows them access to the resources available to them. Figure 3-27 represents the redirector and server processes that occur when a client uses its redirector to access a server service. Server services include file, print, browsers (to locate server services), message services, dynamic data exchange (as is used by the network-enabled Clipboard application), and Remote Procedure Calls.

When the Windows NT Workstation tries to open a file that resides on a remote computer, the following steps occur:

1. The process calls the I/O Manager to request that the file be opened.

Figure 3-27
Redirector and server
processes. (Courtesy
of Learning Tree In-
ternational)

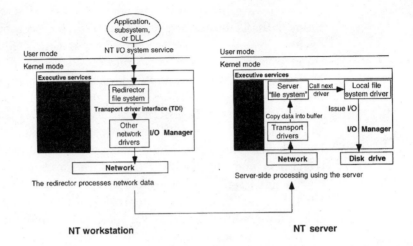

NT workstation　　　　　　　**NT server**

2. The I/O Manager recognizes that the request is for a file on a remote computer, so it passes it to the redirector file system driver.

3. The redirector passes the request to lower-level network drivers,
which in turn transmit the request to the remote computer's
server service for processing.

When the Windows NT Server services receive a request from the remote workstation asking them to read a file that resides on the local hard
drive, the following steps occur:

1. The low-level network drivers receive the request and pass it to
the server driver.

2. The server passes a file read request to the appropriate local file
system driver.

3. The local file system driver calls lower-level disk device drivers to
access the file.

4. The data is passed back to the local file system driver.

5. The local file system driver passes the data back to the server.

6. The server passes the data to the lower-level network drivers for
transmission to the client computer requesting the file.

Because we have already gone through all the possible lower-level network drivers and Transport protocols, you should be able to identify which
protocols are used at which stage of the communication process. Now that
we have seen the process used by clients to access server services, let's
look at how they locate services in the first place.

LOCATING RESOURCES ON THE NETWORK We saw earlier how Windows workstations and servers announce themselves on the network by using a unique NetBIOS name. The name they choose is broadcast on the network, or a file is looked up, or a NetBIOS name server is queried. But what protocols or standards do they use to locate, identify, and access network resources in the first place?

The server service on Microsoft network-enabled operating systems will listen for broadcasts or requests from clients. The clients will issue the broadcast as a result of end users typing in a NetBIOS name into some command line prompt or by clicking on a graphical list of computer-running server services on the network. The former is the broadcast method of access, and the latter is provided through a browser function that is itself a service running on some computer on the network.

As stated earlier, the broadcast method of resource access is limited to the specific IP subnetwork on which the computer is located, and therefore it does not see the resources outside its own subnet. We saw earlier how the type of node implemented to support NetBIOS over TCP/IP determined the method used for name resolution and eventually resource access. However, certain nodes can be configured to use a static file (LMHOSTS) to facilitate access to resources on the network, both on the local and remote subnetworks.

Browsing introduces a concept of dynamic resource location identification and access. Viewing all the computer resources on the network is called *browsing* the network. Windows systems, even Windows for Workgroups, will act as browsers and maintain a list (browse list) of all computer-running server services. Then, when users try to access a particular server on the network using the File Manager, Print Manager, Windows Explorer for the 95 interface (not Internet Explorer), the users will be presented with a *browse list*. The WNet component of the Windows NT WIN32 subsystem is responsible for providing computers with the ability to connect to multiple networks, browse the resources of computers on the networks, and transfer data between computers on those networks. The "browse list" has been forwarded to it from the server currently running as the browser. Depending on the size and configuration of the network in question, several and many types of browsers can be running at the same time. One such example is a Domain Master Browser, which facilitates the updating of Master Browsers located in each IP subnetwork. Without the Domain Master Browser, computers would not see servers in other subnets as part of the "browse list."

Not all systems support integration or access to the Windows browser service to facilitate access to network server services. Additionally, browse lists take some time to be updated. When the browse service is not available, computers can refer to servers by using a Uniform Naming Convention, which is also sometimes called a Universal Naming Convention. The UNC naming convention is a method for specifying a location of a resource on the network. The UNC format is as shown in Figure 3-28.

Now that we now how Windows computers use protocols to provide access to resources on a server or to redirect requests from a client to those remote computers, let's look at the protocols that actually supply the services we access.

APPLICATION SUPPORT PROTOCOLS In addition to redirectors, Windows also provides a few other methods to facilitate links to remote network computers. Redirector and server services mainly provide access to file and print resources. (See Figure 3-29.) Network Basic Input Output Systems and Windows Sockets are also provided to assist developers in building distributed applications and to provide access to server resources from clients. A distributed application consists of two parts: one on the client (front end) and one on the server (back end). NetBIOS and Windows Sockets are commonly called *InterProcess Communication* (IPC) facilities. We will also look at several other IPCs later in this chapter.

NETWORK BASIC INPUT OUTPUT SYSTEM (NETBIOS) Network Basic Input Output System is a session layer service used to communicate with NetBIOS-supported Transport protocols such as NetBEUI Frame, NBT (NetBIOS in TCP/IP), and NWLink IPX (NetBIOS in IPX). (See Figure 3-30.) (At this point in the chapter, you should have a better understanding as to the difference between NetBIOS and NetBEUI.) Since Sytek's original development of NetBIOS, many other vendors

Figure 3-28
Uniform naming convention. (Courtesy of Learning Tree International)

A UNC name format:
\\server name\share\subdir\file

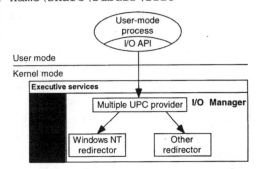

Figure 3-29
Application process
access to network
services. (Courtesy of
Learning Tree Inter-
national)

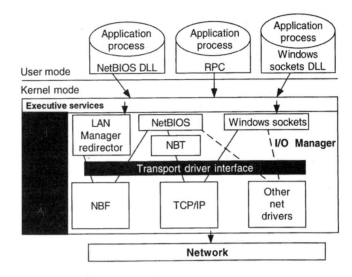

RPC = Remote procedure call
NBT = NetBEUI in TCP/IP
NBF = NetBIOS frames

Figure 3-30
NetBIOS Interface to
NBF, NBT, and
NWLink (not shown).
(Courtesy of Learning
Tree International)

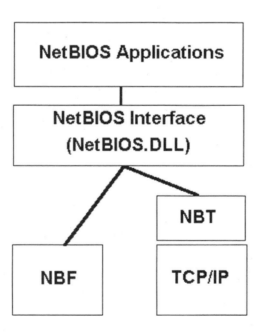

including Novell have produced derivatives of the protocol. Microsoft originally developed a NetBIOS interface for its early MS-NET and LAN Manager and Windows for Workgroup products.

NetBIOS provides both connection-oriented (virtual circuit) and a connectionless (datagram) service. It supports broadcast and multicast methods of communication. NetBIOS provides three basic types of services:

- Name Service
- Session Service
- Datagram Service

However, from a Microsoft perspective, NetBIOS is really used only for Session and Name Service services because, in their implementation, Net-BEUI provides the Datagram service (Transport protocol).

The Windows NT Redirector is a NetBIOS application. As stated earlier, NetBIOS is also the protocol responsible for establishing unique logical computer names when systems communicate on a network. It also creates session links between communicating computers on the network. Finally, and this is a most important aspect, it makes up for the unreliability of the underlying Transport protocols that deliver its messages.

Creating unique NetBIOS names for a large number of computers on a network can be a real challenge. Unlike UNIX computer naming conventions, NetBIOS uses a "flat" name space. This means that there is no way of categorizing or grouping computers with the same name in different areas because they are all on the same directory level (kind of like using DOS version 1.0 when you could not have directories or subdirectories for your files). NetBIOS names are limited to 15 alphanumeric characters. A 16th character is actually available, but it is reserved for identifying the type of NetBIOS service being offered. Each NetBIOS node maintains a table of all names currently owned on the network. To facilitate communication, NetBIOS creates a logical link or session between two computers. The two computers can then transfer data between each other using NetBIOS Network Control Blocks or using Server Message Blocks.

Many sites on the Internet can provide significantly more information than we can go into in this book. However, on the CD-ROM, we have included Request For Comments #1001, "Protocol Standard for a NetBIOS Service on TCP/UDP Transport - Concepts and Methods," which has a detailed explanation of the NetBIOS protocol. RCF 1002, which is available on the enclosed CD-ROM provides an even more-detailed description of NetBIOS in a TCP/IP environment. Although these documents may be specific to NetBIOS in TCP/IP, they do provide you with a good overview of the NetBIOS protocol functionality itself. Another good source is IBM's own Web site at **http://www.software.ibm.com/openblue**; here you can find a lot of information on networking protocols and NetBIOS.

SERVER MESSAGE BLOCKS (SMB) Jointly developed by IBM, Microsoft, and Intel, the Server Message Block is a specification providing several commands that allow information to be exchanged between network computers. (See Figure 3-31.) It is a protocol for sharing files, printers, serial ports, and communication abstractions such as named pipes and mail slots. SMB is a client/server request and response protocol. Servers make their resources available to clients on the network. Clients connect to servers using NetBEUI, TCP/IP, or IPX/SPX Transport Level protocols. After a session is established with the server, clients can send requests (SMB commands) to the server to access its resources.

In Figure 3-31, notice that when NetBIOS uses either TCP/IP or NetBEUI to communicate, it needs to pass through the NetBIOS API. Also, notice that IPX/SPX supports NetBIOS API calls directly.

Several SMB protocol variations are available. The number and implementation of these variations can be particularly frustrating when you're trying to integrate NetWare and Microsoft networking products because different variations use different variants. Unfortunately, as you might expect, they are not all fully compatible. For example, when you're integrating NetWare and Windows NT using SAMBA on a NetWare server, you must ensure that they are using the correct SMB protocol variant (although the default usually works). But there is good justification for the different versions because they were developed to handle new challenges that arose with ever-expanding network complexity.

Figure 3-31
Server Message Blocks (SMB) interface to NetBIOS, TCP/IP, NetBEUI, and IPX/SPX. (Courtesy of Learning Tree International)

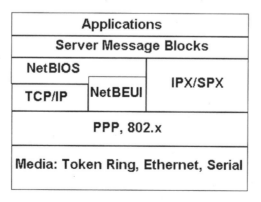

The original version of SMB was Core Protocol or PC Network Program 1.0. It could provide very basic network operations including the following:

- Connecting to and disconnecting from file and print service shares
- Opening and closing files
- Opening and closing print files
- Reading and writing files
- Creating and deleting files and directories
- Searching directories
- Getting and setting file attributes
- Locking and unlocking byte ranges in files

Several variations have been made available since then. Table 3-3 provides a fairly complete list.

SMB implements both Share Level and User Level security access. Share Level access is essentially open to anyone in the workgroup and requires only a password. User Level access implements security at the user level. In other words, a user is required to be on the access list before the

Table 3-3

SMB protocol variants.

SMB Protocol Variant	Protocol Name
PC Network Program 1.0	Core Protocol
Microsoft Networks 1.03	Core Plus Protocol
Microsoft Networks 3.0	DOS LAN Manager 1.0
LANMAN 1.0	LAN Manager 1.0
DOS LM1.2X002	LAN Manager 2.0
LM1.2X002	LAN Manager 2.0
DOS LANMAN2.1	LAN Manager 2.1
LANMAN 2.1	LAN Manager 2.1
Windows for Workgroups 3.1	LAN Manager 2.1
NT LM 0.12	NT LAN Manager 1.0
SAMBA	NT LAN Manager 1.0
CIFS 1.0	NT LAN Manager 1.0

network resource can even be seen. Only valid users can access the resources, and an appropriate user level password is required to be logged on to the network in the first place.

The main SMB client and server protocol implementations are from Microsoft products including MS-DOS, Windows for Workgroups, Windows 95, and Windows NT. Other SMB clients and servers are also provided through products like "smbclient" from SAMBA, "smbfs" from LINUX, SCO Windows File and Printer Service (VisonFS), DEC Pathworks, LAN Server from IBM, and TotalNET Advanced Server from Syntax.

You also should note that SMB will be one of the main protocols used to provide interoperability between NetWare and Windows NT.

WINDOWS SOCKETS Windows Sockets is an implementation of the University of California Berkeley Sockets for the Windows operating systems. Berkeley Sockets are widely used through the network community and are supported by Microsoft's TCP/IP, NWLink, and AppleTalk Transport protocols. Windows Sockets enable Microsoft Windows users to use network resources such as e-mail, Usenet news, talk or relay chat, FTP, and other Internet services within their own Windows environment. Windows Socket utilities integrate the Windows environment to make interacting with the network the same as using any other Windows application. The Windows Socket API is tailored for use by programmers developing applications in the Windows environment. A public specification, its goal is several-fold:

- To facilitate network application development by providing a familiar API set for Windows and UNIX programmers alike
- To provide application binary compatibility
- To support connection-oriented and connectionless protocols

Windows Sockets are a great, open concept for application development. Unfortunately, and no doubt as you may have encountered, many versions of the Windows Socket implementation are available. Vendors, using the latest Windows Socket software interface, have added their own features and distributed their implementations with their software. Multiple applications running on the same computer did not always like or work with different versions. However, one vendor's version would simply be overwritten by another during installation of the latter. As the problem evolved and new applications were released, you then had the option of configuring each application to use a particular version of Windows Sockets (or WinSock, as it is commonly called).

NAMED PIPES AND MAIL SLOTS   Named Pipes are based on OS/2 API calls but with some additional features under Windows NT, and the Mail Slots API set is based on those available in Microsoft OS/2 LAN Manager. An interesting aspect of Named Pipes and Mail Slots is that they are treated as file systems and not as device drivers, which is the norm for other Application Level service protocols. Look in the Windows NT Registry (configuration database), and note that the entry for Named Pipes is actually Named Pipes File System and the entry for Mail Slots is Mail Slots File System. (This information is trivial, but it may be helpful to remember when you are searching through the massive Windows NT Registry looking for information on either.) Perhaps one of the greater advantages of the file system approach to Application Level service provision is that this approach does not use networking components directly but rather goes through the redirector. Once again, this approach assists developers in writing applications because they do not need to be troubled with the lower-level networking issues. They write their applications to work with the Named Pipes or Mail Slots facilities, which, in turn, deliver the request to the redirectory. An additional benefit of using a file system approach is that similar functions are available to both including the ability to cache requests as they arrive at the destination computer system, for example.

Windows NT's implementation of Named Pipes has the added functionality of providing *impersonation*. This function allows a server to change its security identifier to match that of the client's. This feature is used predominantly with back-end database servers in which the server process itself has significant access to the database files, but it impersonates the client trying to access the database to establish a level of security that is appropriate for the client.

Windows NT's implementation of Mail Slots is limited to "second-class" mailslots. Second-class mailslots provide only for connectionless, broadcast-oriented messaging. In a connectionless-based network, delivery of a message is not guaranteed. This mechanism is used predominantly for the identification and advertising of computers or services on those computers on a network.

REMOTE PROCEDURE CALL (RPC)   Although they were originally created by Sun Microsystems, current development and support of Remote Procedure Calls are now carried out by the *Open Software Foundation* (OSF) in conjunction with its *Data Communications Exchange* (DCE) standard. Microsoft RPC is compatible but not compliant with OSF/DCE standard implementation of RPC. In other words, it supports all the OSF/DCE RPC standards; therefore, it is fully interoperable with other OSF/DCE RPC systems. However, it is noncompliant because Microsoft has also added to it some specific features for its own group of operating systems. (See Figure 3-32.)

RPCs use other InterProcess Communication methods to create a communication link between the client and the server. In fact, RPC can use the Named Pipes, Windows Sockets, or even NetBIOS IPC mechanisms mentioned previously to support communication with remote computer systems. The Windows NT Local Procedure Facility is used when client and server processes on the same computer need to transfer information between them.

You have now reviewed both the Transport and Application Level of protocols that Windows NT and Microsoft operating systems in general support. Table 3-4 provides a summary of which Application Level protocols are supported by which Transport Level protocols.

Figure 3-32
Client/server RPC
interaction. (Source:
Microsoft
Corporation)

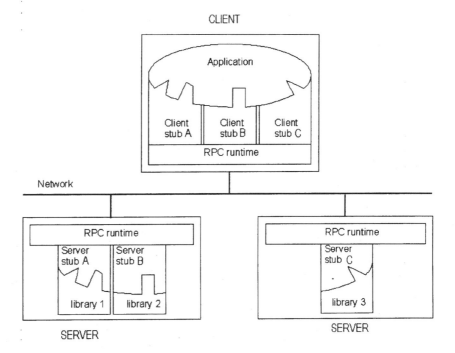

Table 3-4

Application Level
protocol support
by Transport Level
protocols. (Source:
WWW.
NETWORKOLOGIST.
COM)

Application Programming Support	NBF	NWLink	TCP/IP
NetBIOS	Yes	Yes (NBIPX)	Yes (NBT)
Named Pipes	Yes	Yes (NBIPX)	Yes (NBT)
Mail Slots	Yes	Yes (NBIPX)	Yes (NBT)
NetDDE	Yes	Yes (NBIPX)	Yes (NBT)
Sockets	No	Yes (NBIPX)	Yes (TCP/UDP)
RPC over NetBIOS	Yes	Yes (NBIPX)	Yes (NBT)
RPC over Named Pipes	Yes	Yes (NBIPX)	Yes (NBT)
RPC over Sockets	No	Yes (IPX/SPX)	Yes (TCP/UDP)

REMOTE ACCESS SERVICE (RAS) AND WINDOWS PROTOCOL SUPPORT AND POINT TO POINT PROTOCOL (PPP) AND SERIAL LINE IP (SLIP)   PPP and SLIP are two important industry standard protocols that are used to provide remote access to Windows NT and their interconnected networks. Although they are not Microsoft protocols, highlighting them here is important because of their positive implications on NetWare and Windows NT integration.

Remote Access Service provides remote computers to dial into and establish a link with Windows NT Servers and Workstations providing the RAS service. RAS is not a remote control program that sends screen and keyboard information to the remote computer such as Symantec's PC Anywhere or Cubix. Instead, RAS gives the client a redirected link between the workstation and the remote server much in the same way the Workstation or Redirector service does in a local area network through the NIC. However, in a RAS connection, the local drive letter pointing to the remote service uses the slower asynchronous dial-up telephone lines to provide its underlying network infrastructure. As such, it is a much slower means of transferring files than when you are working on a network.

PPP and SLIP are two protocols that can be used by RAS. However, only PPP is used by the RAS server to provide remote access to RAS clients because of the enhanced network configuration and encryption features that PPP offers over SLIP. (See Figure 3-33.)

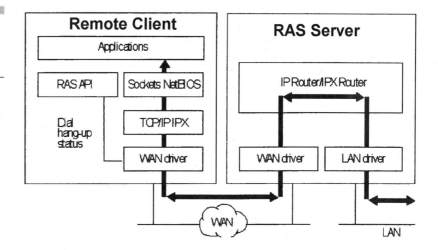

Figure 3-33
PPP architecture of
RAS. (Source: Mi-
crosoft Corporation)

As you can see in Figure 3-33, RAS allows the remote client to support any of the standard Windows Support Transport and Application Level protocols such as NetBEUI, TCP/IP, IPX, NetBIOS, or Windows Sockets. One of the real benefits that the RAS service provides is the NetBIOS Gateway. This feature allows clients dialed in using one protocol to access services provided by another protocol on the other side of the NetBIOS Gateway. The RAS service is similar in functionality to the Gateway Services for NetWare, which will be discussed in Chapter 5.

Serial Line IP (SLIP) was really the precursor protocol upon which PPP was based. It is supported extensively through the UNIX networks in which the UNIX servers provide dial-in capability to support sessions like Telnet. It is used only by Windows NT RAS clients as a means of accessing the UNIX-oriented SLIP servers.

THE TCP/IP PROTOCOLS   The Transmission Control Protocol and Internet Protocol are arguably the most widely used protocols throughout the world. together as a public domain protocol suite, it continues to surpass proprietary vendor protocols and ISO-defined OSI protocols. TCP/IP offers true internetworking and interoperability between disparate network operating systems and host platforms. In one way or another, every major operating system supports an implementation of TCP/IP.

The TCP/IP suite of protocols is also very tightly integrated with the UNIX operating system. (See Figure 3-34.) TCP/IP packet driver software

Figure 3-34
TCP/IP protocol suite.
(Courtesy of Learning
Tree International)

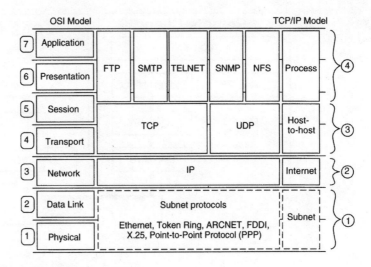

TELNET = Terminal Network Protocol
UDP = User Datagram Protocol

has been written for almost all Network Interface Cards (if not all of them). Also, TCP/IP supports all major lower layer wide area network protocols and services (for example, X.25).

One of right side of Figure 3-34, notice the TCP/IP Model (sometimes called the Department Of Defense, or DOD, Model). The TCP/IP Model, when lined up with the OSI Reference Model, does not match the seven layers. However, the protocols that fit within each of the four TPC/IP Model layers perform the functions described in each layer of the OSI Reference Model.

TCP/IP MODEL   Layer 1: Subnet: The Subnet Layer protocols provide the same functionality as the OSI Physical and Data Link Layers. Protocols in use at this layer include Ethernet, X.25, and Token Ring. The Subnet protocols were covered in the IEEE Project 802 section earlier in this chapter, and additional protocols like X.25 that TCP/IP supports will be covered at the end of this chapter.

Layer 2: Internet: The Internet Layer protocols provide the same functionality as the OSI Network Layer. Implementation of IP, ICMP, RIP, OSPF, and ARP occur at this layer.

Layer 3: Host-to-Host: The Host-to-Host Layer protocols provide the same functions as the OSI Transport Layer and some functions of the Session Layer. TCP, UDP, and DNS are the main protocols implemented at this layer.

Layer 4: Process/Application: The Process/Application Layer provides the same functions as some of the Session Layer and predominantly those functions at the Presentation and Application Layers. Protocols implemented at this layer include FTP, NFS, SMTP, TELNET, SNMP, and NFS.

TCP and IP are regarded as protocols that provide internetwork functionality. IP has become the de facto standard for routing of packets in network environments both large and small, but it excels in large networks. IP defines the composition of the Network Layer packet, services. and networkwide addressing. The IP packet's protocol data unit is TCP or UDP.

TCP provides for reliable connection-oriented communication between networking devices. IP packets, once sent, do not check to verify that the packet reached its intended destination. The TCP protocol must provide for more reliable transmission over IP networks. Some communication services, however, do not require reliable end-to-end transmissions because the higher-level information is not critical in nature, or can always be retransmitted at a later time. User Datagram Protocol provides connectionless transmission of data. Domain Name Service is a distributed database service that provides IP addresses to host name resolution for client applications.

Additional higher-level protocols provide application-based services. The application-based services allow for interoperability between network devices. Briefly, the upper layer protocols providing interoperability between network devices include File Transfer Protocol, Simple Mail Transfer Protocol, Telnet, Simple Network Management Protocol, Network File System, External Data Representation, and Remote Procedure Call. These protocols will be individually reviewed later in this chapter.

TCP/IP PROTOCOL SUITE DEFINITIONS, INTERNETWORKING, NETWORK LAYER PROTOCOLS, AND INTERNET PROTOCOL (IP) The IP protocol works at the Network Layer and therefore defines the composition or structure of the packet (or commonly called the *datagram* in the UNIX environment). The Internet Protocol provides connectionless delivery of packets in that the protocol does not establish a connection with the destination network device before transmitting packets to it. The connectionless delivery of packets or datagrams is sometimes called a "best efforts" service, or it is compared to the postal system for delivering the mail. The routing function uses packet switching to route packets throughout the internetwork. IP packets can also be fragmented into smaller portions and reassembled at the remote destination host. Every IP packet has a header and is the protocol data unit of the Data Link Layer frame.

As highlighted in Figure 3-35, the IP packet is composed of a number of fields. The Version identifies the revision of IP protocol being used. The Type of Service designates how a datagram is to be handled (slow, fast, high reliability). The Length field value is the entire length of the packet including IP header information. Flags are used to indicate whether the packet can be fragmented. The Time To Live counter ensures that packets do not travel endlessly around the internetwork. The Protocol indicates what Transport Layer protocol process (port or socket) is to receive the protocol data unit (TCP or UDP). The Header Checksum is an error check for the IP header only and is recomputed after each hop because it may change. Source and Destination Addresses are the 32-bit IP network address fields. Options is a variable-sized field to support additional capabilities such as source routing.

Several routes through which the packet can be routed or switched are available. IP will always try to choose the best route or available path. To facilitate this process, IP routers make independent routing decisions. Using additional Network Layer protocols, the routers keep each other informed of the status of each connected logical network and the number of hops required to reach them. Routing tables are continually updated to ensure that available paths are kept current.

Figure 3-35
IP packet structure.
(Courtesy of Learning Tree International)

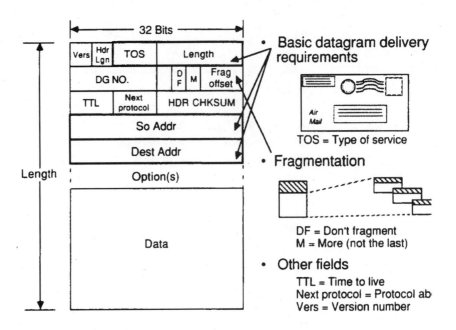

Finally, IP defines a networkwide logical addressing scheme. The network address numbers are maintained by the network administrator. This logical address uniquely identifies the host network device and network the device resides on. An isolated network may use any range of network and host device addresses the network administrator chooses. However, when a network or host is connected to the worldwide Internet, specifically assigned network addresses must be used. Internet addresses are assigned by the Internet Activities Board. (See Figure 3-36.)

IP uses three main classes of addressing: Class A, Class B, and Class C. (See Figure 3-37.) Class D and Class E are also available but reserved by IAB for future use. IP addresses can also be subnetted for even further network addressing flexibility.

Additional Internet Protocols implemented at the Network Layer are *Routing Information Protocol* (RIP) or *Open Shortest Path First* (OSPF), *Internet Control Message Protocol* (ICMP), and *Address Resolution Protocol* (ARP).

ROUTING INFORMATION PROTOCOL (RIP) The Routing Information Protocol is a distance vector route discovery protocol used to advertise which

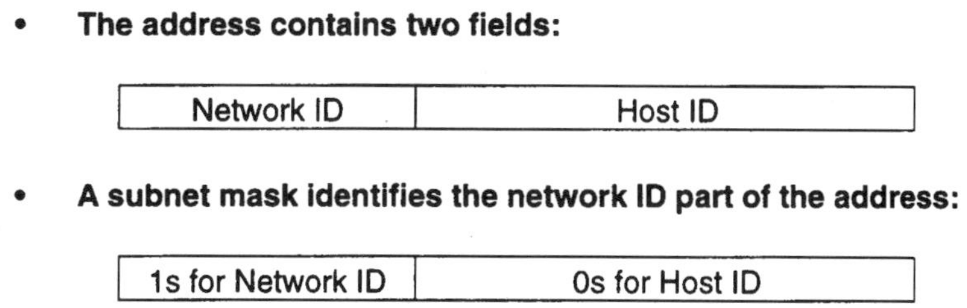

Figure 3-36
IP addressing assignment example.
(Courtesy of Learning Tree International)

• **The address contains two fields:**

Network ID	Host ID

• **A subnet mask identifies the network ID part of the address:**

1s for Network ID	0s for Host ID

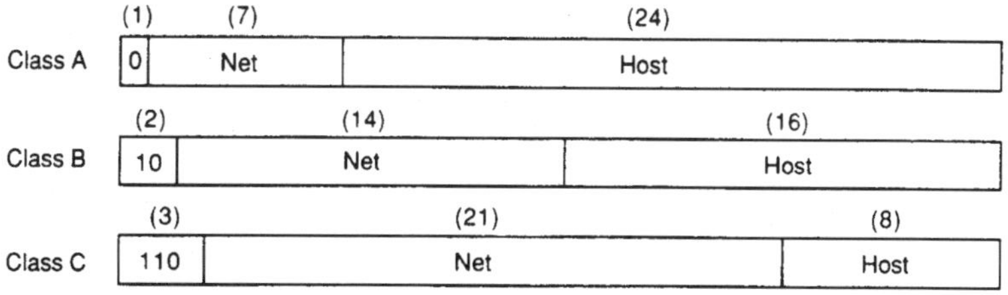

Figure 3-37
IP addressing classes.
(Courtesy of Learning Tree International)

networks can be reached by a router and at what cost. RIP broadcasts are periodically sent out to advertise their routing tables throughout the network. The broadcasted routing tables include information on the destination networks and their distances from the transmitting router in terms of the number of routers (hops) that must be crossed. Although it performs its job sufficiently, RIP has a number of setbacks—in particular, in large, complex internetworks.

OPEN SHORTEST PATH FIRST (OSPF)   Open Shortest Path First is a link state route discovery protocol that was designed to address some of the weakness or limitations of RIP. One of the major benefits of OSPF over RIP is that routing table updates do not need to occur as frequently, reducing the overhead traffic created to maintain network routing information. With a link state discovery protocol, routing information is transmitted only on an as-needed basis or at a preconfigured interval of time, usually every two hours. Additional OSPF features include load balancing and class-of-service-based routing. Load balancing allows multiple Network Interface Cards to be directly connected to the same hub service devices on the same logical network. Class-of-service-based routing allows routing decisions to be made depending on the type of network service required. There is no doubt that OSPF will eventually replace RIP as the routing protocol of choice.

INTERNET CONTROL MESSAGE PROTOCOL (ICMP)   The Internet Control Message Protocol is used by routers to provide error and flow control information. One common use of ICMP is the "ping" protocol, which employs an "echo request" ICMP message. Although ICMP is not more reliable than IP as a protocol, it does facilitate in making it more efficient by making better paths available for routing of packets.

HOST-TO-HOST LAYER PROTOCOLS   Transmission Control Protocol is a connection-oriented protocol. Unlike IP, for TCP protocol data units to be delivered to a remote network device, a connection must first be established between it and the transmitting device. As such, TCP compensates for the connectionless, unreliability of the lower layer IP protocol. It uses full-duplex communication, acknowledgments, and flow control to do so. TCP also is responsible for accepting messages for the upper Process/Application layer protocols (Telnet, SMTP, FTP) and can support numerous simultaneous conversations between these processes. TCP protocol data units are sent as a continuous, unstructured byte stream.

The TCP protocol data unit also has many fields like IP. (See Figure 3-38.) The Source Port is a 16-bit field designating which process (FTP, TELNET, and so on) in the host device initiated the message. Each of these processes has well-known port numbers. If you have access to a UNIX host, these numbers are displayed in the SERVICES file located in the ETC directory. The Destination Port is the port number of the communicating process on the receiving device. The Sequence Number is used by TCP for fragmentation and reassembly of the byte stream. The Acknowledgment Number is the sequence number of the next TCP message the sender expects to receive, and the Data Offset is the length of the TCP header in 32-bit words. Flags are used by TCP for control messages and indicate, like IP's Type of Service, the type of processing the TCP protocol data unit requires. The Windows field is used for TCP's sliding flow control protocol data unit transmission service. Options provide for the capability to support special functions such as the maximum TCP segment size. The Data field contains the upper layer protocol data unit.

Figure 3-38
TCP Protocol Data
Unit Structure.
(Source: Learning
Tree International,
Inc.)

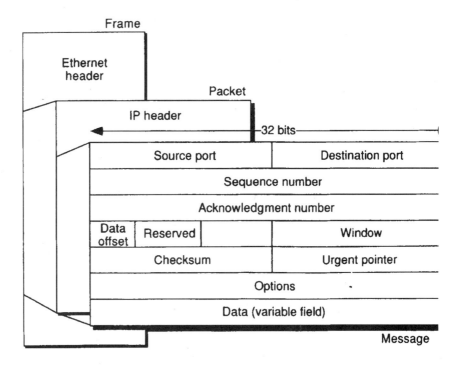

User Datagram Protocol (UDP)   Some Process/Application Layer protocols do not require the reliability that TCP provides and can be handled by a Host-to-Host protocol that has less connectivity overhead associated with it. The User Datagram Protocol provides this service. This connectionless-oriented protocol (which does not require a connection to the remote host before transmitting) does not acknowledge receipt of protocol data units sent. The protocol, while functioning on a network device, simply sends and receives packets as required. Rather than establish a virtual circuit connection between two network devices, a port is set up as a pointer to a local running process. Because UDP does not require the overhead associated with establishing remote connections before transmission and ensuring reliable delivery, it is usually faster than TCP.

Domain Name Service (DNS)   The last Host-to-Host Layer protocol is Domain Name Service. DNS servers on the network maintain a hierarchical naming convention and structure through a distributed database system. DNS allows IP network addresses that the computers understand to be mapped to host names that humans understand.

INTEROPERABILITY: PROCESS/APPLICATION LAYER PROTOCOLS AND FILE TRANSFER PROTOCOL (FTP)   File Transfer Protocol is a process protocol that enables users on one host to copy (move) a file or files to another host. The neat aspect of FTP is that it provides for transparent interoperability between different host operating environments. FTP, when implemented, looks the same to all users, regardless of the workstation operating system they are using. The same FTP command set is available to each user.

To access the remote file system, users must have established user login accounts on the remote system and be provided with the account passwords. This account determines which areas of the file system users can see, and whether the users can upload files to the remote system. A low level of remote system access is also provided through the *Trivial File Transfer Protocol* (TFTP). TFTP is like a read-only access level to the remote file system so that users can copy files to their own local file systems.

Simple Mail Transfer Protocol (SMTP)   Simple Mail Transfer Protocol is probably the most widely used protocol in the world given the daily electronic mail traffic that takes places each day on the Internet. SMTP is the electronic mail workhorse used between network hosts. Although users access an electronic mail front end application, it is SMTP that shuttles (routes) the mail around the Internet from host to host until it reaches its final destination. Despite what most people think, SMTP requires the reliability and connection-oriented TCP protocol to deliver the mail. A review of message switching in Chapter 2 will highlight the reason that this is the case. Essentially, a connection is established between intermediate hosts as mail is routed to its final destination, which could be several hosts away. However, for the period of time that mail is transferred from one host to another during its journey, a reliable connection is established to ensure that the mail message is delivered successfully, in its entirety, to that host. This host, in turn, establishes a reliable end-to-end connection to the next host mail must be routed to.

Remote Terminal Emulation (Telnet) Remote Terminal Emulation allows users to access terminal/host-centralized computing system applications on the network. The original terminals were "dumb" in that they did not have any local centralized processing unit (CPU) and relied on the host to provide all application computer processing. Today, personal computers emulate terminals to connect to centralized host computers. Telnet provides connectivity to host systems by allowing users to log in to and run applications. In this sense, Telnet provides some degree of interoperability. However, the personal computer must emulate the terminal type that the host supports, and the session does not appear simply as an extension of the native operating system. As such, a Telnet session to a DEC VAX system is not the same as a Telnet session to an IBM Mainframe system.

Simple Network Management Protocol (SNMP) Simple Network Management Protocol specifies the communication between network listening agents and network management systems. Agents are devices that sit out on a network and collect information on the health of the network. Network management stations collect information from agents and allow network management staff to better maintain network operations and availability. While SNMP is the protocol used to communicate between agents and network management stations, information statistics are collected in a Management Information Base (MIB) on the agent for forwarding to the network station.

Network File System (NSF) The Network File System was developed by Sun Microsystems. NFS is most often associated with Sun's suite of protocols that make up *Open Network Computing* (ONC). Although the protocol was originally developed by Sun, it was released into the public domain, an event that helped promote and solidify its position in the computing industry. The three ONC protocols used most often are NFS, XDR, and RPC. All three protocols work together to provide true interoperability between dissimilar host operating and file systems. After the system is set up, the local user sees the remote file system as an extension of itself. For example, a DOS-based personal computer with NFS would see a UNIX host file system as just another DOS drive letter to be accessed.

Although NFS provides great interoperability features, you must be aware that it does not automatically convert the underlying file formats to that of the local operating system. If DOS users copy text files created by UNIX users to their local file systems, the DOS users will still need to run conversion utilities to put the files into formats that they can work with locally.

External Data Representation (XDR)   External Data Representation is a group of C programming language routines that allow for machine-independent description and encoding (formatting) of data. The C programming routines allow programmers to describe various data structures.

Remote Procedure Call (RPC)   A Remote Procedure Call allows programmers to request services, regardless of the type of underlying operating and file system. This capability simplifies the process of sending and receiving files from dissimilar host machines. A redirector or shell filters calls made by a host process. Local calls are passed on to the local operating system for execution. Remote calls are forwarded via TCP/IP for remote execution.

Note that many network operating systems use RCPs. Novell NetWare, Banyan Vines, Microsoft's LAN Manager, and Windows NT Server all use a form of RPC. However, not all RPCs are fully compliant with the OSF/DCE standard.

We've now concluded our review of all the standard protocols supported by Microsoft and NetWare. In the following section, we will present some of the concerns and issues that will need to be addressed when implementing a multiprotocol network environment.

NETWARE AND WINDOWS NT PROTOCOL COMPARISON: ODI VERSUS NDIS
Novell's ODI specification has always tended to be a bit faster than Microsoft's NDIS specification. The main reason for this speed difference is that the ODI specification has been written to interface directly with the hardware NIC, whereas NDIS must go through an NDIS Wrapper or additional software driver first. However, NDIS drivers in the past tended to be more flexible, although this advantage is quickly disappearing with the new Novell 32-bit client drivers. Although direct access to the hard-

ware by Novell's client drivers is a fast and efficient feature within regular DOS/Windows 3.11 and Windows for Workgroup clients because of the use of ODI, it was not so with the original client drivers for Windows NT.

As was demonstrated in Chapter 1, Windows NT does not allow software outside the Kernel Mode to access the hardware directly. Instead, client redirectors must pass through the NDIS Wrapper first, which tends to slow down the process a little yet increases operating system reliability. Novell's original Windows NT client drivers tried to implement their standard ODI architecture through a little-known feature whereby Microsoft allowed developers to make calls directly to hardware interrupts. This implementation proved to be very unstable and caused Windows NT to crash frequently when using Novell's client drivers. As a result, many users implemented Microsoft's Client Services for NetWare client drivers and stuck with them. However, this is no longer true because Novell has implemented 32-bit client drivers for Windows NT, and as we will see, you might want to seriously consider using Novell's client drivers today if you are installing NT in a predominantly NetWare or NetWare NDS network environment.

Certainly, newer 32-bit protocol implementations have elevated the competition between the two vendors because both provide ease of installation, increased flexibility in application layer services support, and increased performance to the desktop for network I/O. Novell's Network Input/Output System (NIOS) standard is based on the ODI concepts and fundamental building blocks, whereas Microsoft continues its implementation of NDIS, only now with full 32-bit support.

Finally, although both vendors claim their client implementations are easy, when you're trying to implement multiple protocol stacks, the ease of integration quickly disappears. It is even more difficult to acquire support from one vendor to support the other vendor's services despite numerous efforts to create joint and reciprocal end user (network administrator) support services by both vendors. So if you find something that works in your network, chances are that you should stick with it! However, as we stated earlier, the implementation issue is starting to become easier.

Transport Protocols Selection Many performance and benchmark studies have been done in the past with regards to the three main protocols at play when integrating NetWare and Windows NT. However, we will not go into the numbers and statistics here because they are not as important. Although NetBEUI may indeed be a faster protocol for small networks, not too many small networks are left out there. What about the small 20-user network companies, you say? Well, many of them are connecting to the Internet, which requires a TCP/IP internetwork configuration. The next question is why Microsoft supports NWLink IPX at all when even many of the companies that have NetWare networks will need to support an interface to TCP/IP. The answer to that question is one of marketing.

What is important to remember is that interoperability requires support from internetworking protocols. Therefore, supporting just IPX/SPX or TCP/IP is not sufficient to create a fully heterogeneous network. However, choosing a common internetworking protocol remains a critical factor in how your network infrastructure performs.

Both NetWare and Windows NT support TCP/IP, so why not just standardize on this industry standard protocol? Well, although they both support the TCP/IP Transport Level protocol, what they do not generally support is a common Application Level protocol that uses TCP/IP. For example, Windows NT will support the Application Level NetWare Core Protocol encapsulated (or bound) to the NWLink IPX protocol, but it will not support it encapsulated inside TCP/IP, as does Novell's NetWare IP protocol. Therefore, NetWare and Windows NT cannot use NCP encapsulated in TCP/IP to accomplish both internetworking and interoperability. However, we must not lose hope yet because the SAMBA product has been implemented on NetWare, and both Windows NT and NetWare can internetwork over TCP/IP and interoperate using Server Message Blocks encapsulated inside TCP/IP. In fact, if you are planning on migrating your Windows NT Domains to NetWare Directory Services, you will need to do so.

The two main issues you will most likely face as you try to provide internetworking and interoperability services between NetWare and Windows NT will be with respect to the Transport and Application Level protocols you choose. Microsoft has made it incredibly easy for you to provide NetWare Core Protocol services over IPX/SPX to service your existing NetWare clients. It has even gone a step further and provided existing Microsoft computer systems using NetBEUI with access to NetWare servers through the Gateway Services for NetWare service. Unfortunately, Novell has not yet made the integration as easy. Although it does support the IPX/NCP combination on Windows NT Workstations and Servers, it does not support Microsoft's standard networking protocol NetBEUI. The rumor is it that Novell will be supporting it with the next implementation of SAMBA, when they will support TCP/IP/NetBIOS, IPX/NetBIOS, and NBF/NetBIOS. The latter supports ease of integration of existing Windows for Workgroups clients whose default networking protocol is NetBEUI.

Simplicity of Implementation   NBF requires very little configuration or network administration to implement. IPX also requires very little configuration on the client because it uses the client's Network Interface Card as the NODE part of the IPX network address. The Network part of the network address is configured only at the server. This, in turn, eliminates the requirement to configure addressing at each node. TCP/IP is the most cumbersome to configure and subsequently administer. However, paradoxically enough, it is also the most popular given its widespread use. IP addresses require configuration of each host to support unique host NODE addressing. Further, the node address is generally configured by a human, which leads to the potential for duplication—a common problem in IP networks. A further agreement must be made on the common network address that all nodes on a network or subnet will use. If, in fact, subnetting is used, then a subnet address must be configured. Although you probably see the additional complexity of managing an IP network, we believe strongly that the benefits far outweigh the configuration and maintenance issues.

Segmenting the Network   NBF, which is not a routable protocol, uses a flat host name space. Therefore, network segmentation is only possible at the Data Link layer of the OSI Reference Model, which requires bridging. This is not efficient for large networks.

IPX is routable but uses only one part of its address to identify the network component. Although this means that IPX networks can be segmented into multiple subnets, it does not provide for hierarchical subnets as is true with TCP/IP when subnet masking is used. IPX works at the Network layer of the OSI Reference Model, which requires the use of routers. Routers provide the best enterprise network support.

IP is routable and also uses only one part of its address to identify the network component. Like IPX, it can be segmented into multiple subnets. However, IP can further divide the host NODE component of the IP address into a subnetwork identifier, which allows it to logically segment large networks into individual, smaller interconnected subnetworks.

Memory Requirements   Depending on its implementation, NBF generally can be configured to use a very small amount of system memory. TCP/IP and IPX, on the other hand, have usually required more system memory than NBF. Today, both TCP/IP and IPX protocol stacks are implemented, thus making better use of system resources. As a result, both can be installed with less than 5Kbytes of system memory required at the desktop. However, some protocol vendors have chosen to make use of extended system RAM—and use it they do. One protocol vendor's implementation requires 2M of Extended RAM to be run on a DOS/Windows 3.11 system and the same amount when run on Windows NT. Newer versions are VxD (Virtual Driver) and DLL (Data Link Library) based and require little, if any, memory at all.

Which One Is Faster?   As was stated earlier, NBF is definitely faster when implemented on a small local area network. It is not designed to use in a wide area network environment. IPX and IP tend to perform relatively the same, with probably the most distinguishing difference being that IPX tends to be faster for file and print services, whereas IP tends to be faster for application service access.

Which One Should We Choose?   So which protocol combination is best? Well, we would like to give you the straight answer, the silver transport bullet as it were, but the answer really depends on your requirements. Overall, we recommend that you try to use TCP/IP as much as possible, not necessarily because it is a better protocol than IPX/SPX (because that could seriously be debated) but because it is more of an industry standard and because it facilitates integration with the Internet. Novell has gone to great lengths, as has Microsoft, in providing gateways to the Internet with IPX to IP gateways, but gateways only slow down processes because a translation of protocols is involved. Therefore, choosing one main protocol is always better, if at all possible.

Multiprotocol Network Issues   From a network administrator's perspective, the network world would probably be great if we were limited to supporting just one protocol stack within our network environment. Alas, this just does not seem to be reality because in many corporations we are required to support several protocols at the same time. Although some network administrators have made a good case for limiting multiprotocol proliferation, we are generally simply given the challenge of making the new "business-critical application" that uses the protocol we have never heard of work on the organization's existing network infrastructure. You then might wonder what are the main issues of supporting multiple protocols on the network.

Let's use a case model network example in which we have one server and 100 clients on the network. No routers or bridges are involved in the network because it is an isolated physical network segment. In this example, we will demonstrate the impact of supporting multiple protocols over the physically isolated network. During the case study implementation, we will not add or subtract from the number of network workstations. We will, however, change the network protocols that they use and add only two more servers

In the example shown in Figure 3-39, the network is supporting IPX packets over Ethernet 802.3 frames. In this example, network traffic is composed mainly of the following:

- IPX routing information sent over the Ethernet 802.3 frame format
- User data transmitted in IPX packets over Ethernet 802.3 frame format

You now know, having read through this chapter, that IPX uses Routing Information Protocol and Service Advertising Protocol to disseminate information about the network configuration and the services offered on it. These RIP and SAP broadcasts occur on a somewhat repetitive basis every 30 and 60 seconds (using the older NetWare standards). For this example, suppose that in the network, we are currently experiencing a split of network traffic in which 10 percent of all traffic is for RIP and SAP broadcasting and 90 percent is for actual user data.

The organization is starting to integrate new NetWare and Windows NT server systems that will require support for additional Network and Data Link layer protocol capability over the same physical network segment. Currently, based on the preceding network configuration, the first phase of integration will require the installation of a new NetWare 4.x server and that 30 percent of the clients migrate to a new protocol stack consisting of IPX and Ethernet 802.2. What impact will this have on the network?

Figure 3-39
Multiprotocol sample
network one.
(Source: WWW.
NETWORKOLOGIST.
COM)

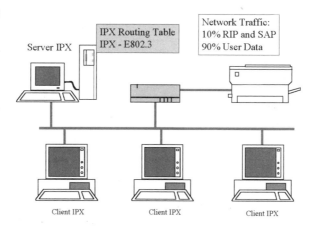

Well, that is a good question. Essentially, all the RIP and SAP broadcasts that were previously made with IPX in Ethernet 802.3 will now have to also be made with Ethernet 802.2. This will have the effect of doubling the RIP and SAP traffic loads on the network and therefore reducing the amount of usable network bandwidth for User Data traffic. Configuring both servers to support IPX over both Ethernet 802.3 and Ethernet 802.2 means that they are each also broadcasting double the RIP and SAP traffic. We will say for conservative measures that this addition only increases overall network traffic to 25 percent RIP and SAP broadcasts and reduces user data traffic to 75 percent. (See Figure 3-40.) As you can see, starting to support even the same Network Layer protocol over two different Data Link Layer protocols has an impact on network traffic and, as a result, the amount of available network segment bandwidth for user data.

Let's now take the example to a final stage in which we will add a Windows NT Server that supports TCP/IP with encapsulated NetBIOS and migrate another 30 percent of the clients to this protocol stack. Because these migrated clients will also need to continue to communicate with the NetWare servers, we will also configure the NetWare servers to support TCP/IP encapsulated in Ethernet_II. In doing so, the NetWare servers will now be broadcasting RIP and SAP in IPX over Ethernet 802.2, RIP and SAP in IPX over Ethernet 802.3, as well as RIP in IP over Ethernet_II. Additionally, the Windows NT server will also be configured to actively participate in the IP RIP network routing broadcasts, and subsequently it will broadcast IP RIP over Ethernet_II as well.

What is the final estimated impact on the network? Well, a lot more of the network traffic will now be simply to keep everyone informed as to

Figure 3-40
Multiprotocol sample
network two.
(Source: WWW.
NETWORKOLOGIST.
COM)

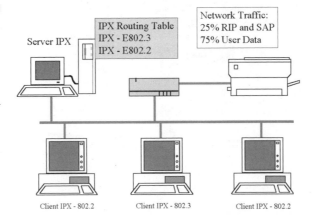

the state of the network's routing configuration and the services available on it as opposed to actual user data. In fact, the current configuration may even increase IPX RIP and SAP traffic as well as IP RIP traffic to a total of 30 to 35 percent of the total network bandwidth utilization. Although this number may not have a significant impact initially on the users within this small network segment, you can see the decrease in usable network bandwidth for user data even though we have added only two servers and have not changed the number of workstations. (See Figure 3-41.)

Additionally, routers on the network, of which the NetWare and Windows NT servers are performing this duty in our example, will be required to support multiple routing tables. The processing of these routing tables will require more CPU resources and, as a result, will slow down processing.

In summary, the effect of supporting multiple protocols over an existing network is quite obvious. It has the impact of adding additional network support protocols while reducing the available network bandwidth for actual user data traffic. This problem is even further compounded by virtue of the fact that even the network infrastructure has its own line overhead associated with just maintaining an Ethernet network, for example. Figure 3-42 further demonstrates how the actual throughput for a network segment, which is called Payload Capacity, is affected by the LAN/WAN Circuit requirements and Line Overhead.

Figure 3-41
Multiprotocol sample network two. (Source: WWW. NETWORKOLOGIST. COM)

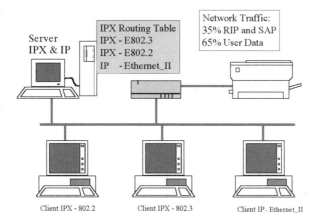

Figure 3-42
Network communications overhead versus data throughput.
(Courtesy of Learning Tree International)

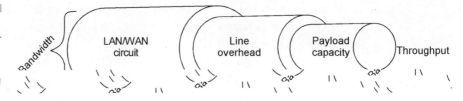

The moral of the story is that you should support as few protocols as necessary on your network. Given that you have now seen, in theory, that Novell NetWare and Microsoft Windows NT both support TCP/IP, it is a pretty good assumption that this would be the preferred network Transport protocol to use. This finding is further justified by the fact that TCP/IP can be used to transport such diverse Application Level protocols for file, print, communication, database, and application access as NetBIOS, NCP, Windows Sockets, and RPC.

SUMMARY

We've now concluded the chapter on the OSI Reference Model, Networking Protocols, and Multiprotocol Network Issues. In this chapter, we identified all the network communication protocols used in NetWare and Windows NT network environments. We discussed the challenges associated with multiprotocol network environments and provided heterogeneous solutions that will create efficient use of the underlying network infrastructure. We also reviewed procedures to configure multiprotocol support on NetWare and Windows NT client workstations and servers, and how to configure both systems to support a range of networking transport and service protocols. In the following chapter, we will show you how to implement these protocols on NetWare and Windows NT server clients.

CHAPTER **4**

Client Connectivity

This chapter covers NetWare and Windows NT client workstation connectivity options. Particular emphasis will be placed on highlighting connectivity from any side of the network: NetWare clients to Windows NT server, and Windows clients to NetWare server. Access to the NetWare server will be reviewed through two possible methods: directly through NetWare client software or indirectly through the Windows NT Server Gateway. After the services are connected, we will demonstrate how NetWare command utilities function differently depending on which of the two connection methods are used and why the differences exist. From the Windows NT perspective, we will cover how the Performance Monitor can be used to monitor the client driver throughput to assist us in determining which client connection method best addresses our requirements. Finally, we will look at some of the alternative methods NT such as *Network File System* (NFS), Macintosh Appellate, and File Transfer Protocol that can be used to connect network clients to either NetWare or Windows.

Chapter Objectives

■ Overview of multiplatform connectivity from a client perspective

■ Client connectivity in a heterogeneous network environment

■ DOS/Windows connectivity options

■ Connecting the DOS/Windows client to NetWare and Windows NT

■ Another alternative: change the Windows NT Server instead!

■ Integrating Windows for Workgroups with NetWare and Windows NT

■ The Windows NT network connection from WFWG

■ Making the Novell NetWare connection from WFWG

■ The latest thing for Windows for Workgroups

■ Coordinating user names and passwords

■ Integrating Windows 95 with NetWare and Windows NT Servers

■ Windows 95 client networking support for NetWare and Windows NT networks

■ A quick overview of the Windows 95 logon process

■ Communicating with Windows NT is easy

■ Profiles and policies

■ Communicating with NetWare: two options

■ NetWare communications the Microsoft way

■ Integrating NetWare login and Windows NT logon scripts

■ Common problems with Microsoft's client for NetWare networks

■ NetWare Communications the Novell way

■ Common problems with Novell NetWare Workstation Shells 3.x and 4.x

■ Novell's new client network solution: Client 32 for Windows 95

■ Windows 95 profiles and policies in a mixed server network

■ Some final thoughts on the Windows Client/NetWare Client question

■ Things are not what they appear to be: Windows 95 acting like a NetWare server

■ Integrating Windows NT Workstation with NetWare and Windows NT Servers

- Overview of the Windows NT Logon Process
- Windows NT Workstation is tightly integrated with NT Domains
- Microsoft's Client Services for NetWare (CSNW)
- Accessing NetWare Server volumes and directories
- Accessing NetWare print queues
- Support for NetWare-aware applications and utilities
- Running NetWare-aware applications
- Monitoring CSNW performance
- General CSNW troubleshooting tips
- Windows NT Workstation 4.0 and Client Services for NetWare
- Are profiles and policies still supported?
- Novell NetWare Client Software for Windows NT Workstation
- Novell's NetWare Client 32 for Windows NT
- Novell's IntranetWare Client for Windows NT
- Windows NT Server as a Client
- Additional connectivity options
- Apple Talk, File Transfer Protocol, and Network File System
- If we can't change the client, change the server!

Overview of Multiplatform Connectivity from a Client Perspective

Two main options are available when we reach the stage in which we need a single workstation, regardless of the operating system it is running, to communicate with multiple servers (that is, NT and NetWare). The first option is to simply load the client software required by that particular server platform to all direct connectivity. The second option is to use some form of translating gateway to allow the existing client software to communicate with the alternate server operating system indirectly. Both options have advantages and disadvantages that we will explore in this chapter. Alternatively, we could change the server to support the networking language the client currently supports, but that approach will be the topic of the next chapter.

In the first option, the disadvantage is that we are required to configure and load two networking protocols on the client workstation. Configuration was the first big challenge, and although it was a real problem in the early days of the DOS/Windows 3.1 operating system combination, the issue is less daunting with Windows 95 or Windows NT. However, even though configuration is much simpler, the issues of supporting multiple protocol stacks are still present. We discussed this issue in some detail in the preceding chapter, so we will not repeat ourselves here. The advantages seem to outweigh the disadvantages, however, in that by supporting the client software the remote server platform is expecting us to use, we are, in turn, treated as real clients with full access to all the file and system management utilities (given the appropriate logon/login, of course) that are available.

Back to the configuration issue, how would you like to have to maintain multiple protocol stacks on over 1000 or even 10,000 workstations? As the scope and scale of the network increases in size, so too does the complexity of managing more protocols on the desktop. Simplicity is really the key to maintaining large network environments whenever possible. At this point, option number two becomes very appealing. Instead of changing literally thousands of client workstation configurations, we simply add some form of a translating gateway that allows a server to act as a go-between for the client and remote server, which are supporting different networking protocols. Implementing such a gateway is also the focus of the next chapter. For now, we will look at both options from the client workstation's perspective.

Which client software is installed, if any, will depend mainly on the current network configuration. If we have a predominantly Novell NetWare client and server network, and are in the process of installing a Windows NT server that we want the existing NetWare clients to communicate with, then we are going to have to configure the clients to support the Windows NT client protocols. This new configuration will quite possibly require software at both the internetworking and interoperability layers (for example, NetBEUI and NetBIOS, or IPX and NetBIOS). Similarly, if we have a predominantly Windows network environment (DOS/Windows 3.x, Windows 95, Windows NT), and we are about to introduce NetWare server into this network, then we will need to change the existing Windows systems (clients and servers) to support the NetWare protocols (for example, IPX and NCP). Alternatively, with the latter scenario, we can also configure Windows NT server to act as a gateway to the NetWare server. Ultimately, our choice will probably be based on our requirement for ease of implementation and maintenance, as well as a long-term strategic plan.

Client Connectivity in a Heterogeneous Network Environment

DOS/Windows Connectivity Options

As described earlier, the most straightforward approach is to configure the client workstation to support the required protocol for each server platform it needs to communicate with. In Figure 4-1, the DOS/Windows client connectivity to a NetWare server is fairly easy because Novell provides the required installation disks, files, and setup procedures. Under this scenario, it is assumed that the DOS/Windows client already has the Microsoft network drivers (NDIS) installed. The basic DOS/Windows NDIS client software provides for NetBEUI as the transport protocol with NetBIOS/Server Message Blocks encapsulated inside it and acting as the service request protocol. Unfortunately, we have only one choice when

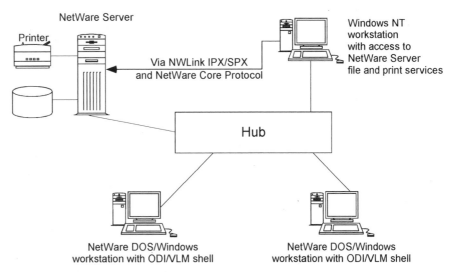

Figure 4-1
Connecting to a NetWare server. (Courtesy of Learning Tree International)

configuring the DOS/Windows 3.x client workstation to access NetWare server file and print resources directly, and that's Novell's client software.

Installing the DOS/Windows 3.x NetWare Client Drivers

Figure 4-2 displays the NetWare client installation screen for client driver software. Earlier versions of the NetWare client driver used a program called NETBX.EXE as the main client redirector component. Newer versions provide a much more flexible alternative client architecture for the DOS/Windows combination called Virtual Loadable Modules. This version is based on a similar concept to the NetWare Loadable Modules that are used on the NetWare server.

The NetWare client installation software will add all the necessary client software to the DOS/Windows 3.x workstation. It will also modify the required AUTOEXEC.BAT and CONFIG.SYS files on the client workstation. One of the major problems with the older NETBX.EXE configuration was the requirement it placed on the workstation's conventional memory. After it was loaded, NETBX.EXE took over 70 K of conventional memory and could not successfully be loaded into upper memory. The subsequent VLM.EXE and its related modules could be loaded into upper memory, thus freeing up significant areas of conventional random access memory for other client applications.

Supporting Multiple Protocol Stacks

How do we support both protocol stacks to allow us to communicate with either the NetWare or Windows NT servers? Well, with DOS/Windows 3.1, the answer is not so simple and requires some heavy editing of the

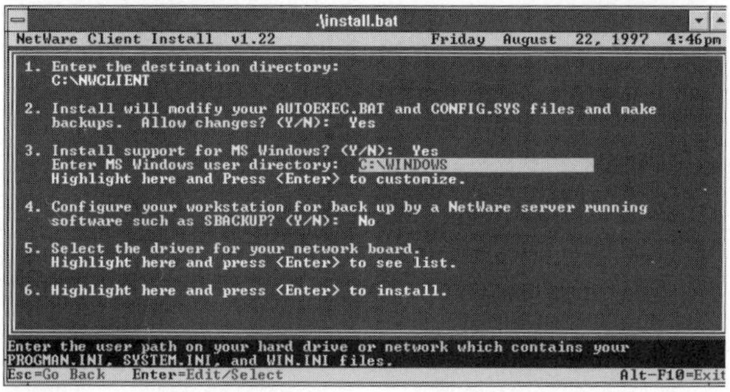

Figure 4-2
NetWare Client install utility. (Source Novell, Inc.)

NetWare *Open Data Link* (ODI) configuration files (NET.CFG). We would load the standard NetWare ODI client software and then proceed to implement drivers that allowed the ODI stack to support *Network Driver Interface Specification* (NDIS) networking components. Frequently, however, we would run out of workstation random access memory required to run any decent-sized application—that is, if we got past the configuration file editing stages successfully. For anyone truly interested in getting a DOS/Windows 3.1 computer to support both NetWare and Microsoft networking protocols, we highly recommend that you research some of the earlier NetWare Application Notes available on the *NetWare Support Encyclopedia* (now called *NetWare Connection*). Novell offers some well-documented steps to create this setup. Given that the DOS/Windows 3.1 combination is really starting to become outdated, we will not concentrate on this issue here. However, after we complete this setup (and doing so is indeed possible), we can access both platforms fairly seamlessly. Because Windows 3.x is based on DOS, it does require that we log on to both the NetWare and Windows server services in advance of starting Windows 3.x.

In applying this configuration, however, we remove the Microsoft NDIS client configuration software because both cannot coexist easily. After the DOS/Windows client workstation has been configured to support Novell's ODI drivers, we can use a technique that is often called a *shim or program code* to support both the ODI and NDIS protocol stacks on the same Network Interface Card. The combination is called DOINSUP by Novell for NDIS support within the ODI stack. This feat will allow our existing DOS/Windows client to communicate with both the NetWare and Windows NT servers. Figure 4-3 demonstrates the ODI network drivers supporting the NDIS stack.

The following information from Novell, Inc., describes how to set up ODINSUP support at a DOS/Windows 3.x client:

1. If the ODI network is not installed, do so to provide the ODI drivers. If you are installing a NetWare client, a STARTNET.BAT file is created during product installation. This file will load your ODI drivers, the SERVER.EXE file (if you selected to make this machine a server or to share its resources), and the client software (CLIENT.EXE or VLM.EXE files). The following is an example of part of a STARTNET.BAT file:

```
    LSL   <-Link Support Layer driver -+
    NE2000 <-MLID (Hardware) driver    +- ODI drivers
    IPXODI <-IPX protocol driver      -+
    SERVER <-driver for sharing resources (used only
with NetWare Lite/Personal versions)
    VLM   <-driver for using shared resources
```

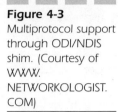

Figure 4-3
Multiprotocol support
through ODI/NDIS
shim. (Courtesy of
WWW.
NETWORKOLOGIST.
COM)

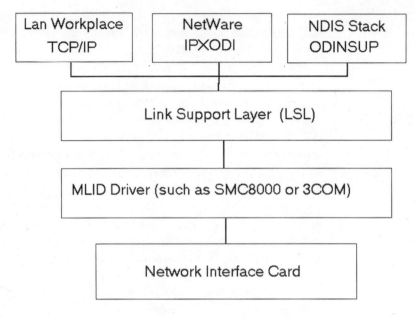

Test and verify that the NetWare Lite or PERSONAL NetWare
network is functioning correctly. If it is not functioning, contact
your normal lines of technical support for this NetWare product to
receive assistance.

2. Reboot without loading the NetWare network drivers. When the
NetWare client was installed, a line was added to the AU-
TOEXEC.BAT file to run the STARTNET.BAT file. You should insert a remark at the beginning of this line before you reboot. The
following is an example of the AUTOEXEC.BAT file:

```
PATH=C:\WINDOWS
C:\WINDOWS\SMARTDRV.EXE
CALL C:\NWCLIENT\STARTNET.BAT
C:\WINDOWS\NET START
SET TEMP=C:\TEMP
N:
```

3. Install the NDIS network. If the NDIS network was already installed, verify that all the drivers are set up to load properly;
then load them. Run the NDIS network and verify that it is functioning correctly. If it is not functioning correctly, contact your
normal lines of technical support for this NDIS product to receive
assistance.

4. The ODI and NDIS hardware drivers cannot share the Network Interface Card. ODI will take control of the hardware and pass the NDIS packets up to the NDIS stack. Insert a remark on the NDIS MAC driver line. This line is probably in your CONFIG.SYS file. For details on what this driver is called, consult the documentation supplied with the NDIS network.

5. Verify that the PROTMAN driver is loading in the CONFIG.SYS file. Also verify that the PROTOCOL.INI file is in the path specified on the PROTMAN load line. (For example, if the load line reads DEVICE=PROTMAN.DOS /I:C:\NET, then the PROTOCOL.INI file should be in the C:\NET directory.) The PROTMAN.DOS file is loaded from within the CONFIG.SYS file. The following is an example of the CONFIG.SYS file:

```
FILES=30
BUFFERS=30
DEVICE=C:\WINDOWS\PROTMAN.DOS /I:C:\WINDOWS
DEVICE=C:\WINDOWS\WORKGRP.SYS
LASTDRIVE=P
DEVICE=C:\WINDOWS\HIMEM.SYS
STACKS=9,256
```

6. Modify the PROTOCOL.INI file. Disable the Bindings statements for the NDIS MAC driver line by putting a semicolon at the beginning of the line, and add a Bindings statement for the ODI MLID driver. The following is an example of part of a PROTOCOL.INI file:

```
[PROTOCOL_MANAGER]
  DriverName = PROTMAN$
[ETHERAND]
DriverName = DXME0$
Bindings = NE2000
; Bindings = x3C523
; Bindings = ne22
```

7. Edit the STARTNET.BAT file, and add a line to load ODINSUP. The ODINSUP driver should be loaded after the MLID driver and before the IPX protocol driver. The following is an example of part of a STARTNET.BAT file:

```
LSL
NE2000
ODINSUP      (to support the NDIS stack)
IPXODI
SERVER       (only used with NetWare Lite/Personal
              NetWare Peer to Peer Network)
VLM
```

8. ODINSUP requires that all possible FRAME types be installed with the driver. To do so, edit the NET.CFG file located in your NWLITE or NWCLIENT directory. If you are using a Token Ring driver, you need to load both of the following frame types:

```
TOKEN-RING
TOKEN-RING_SNAP
```

If you are using Ethernet, you need to load the following frame types:

```
Ethernet_802.2
Ethernet_802.3 (not needed, but recommended for
               compatibility)
Ethernet_snap
Ethernet_ii
```

You add these frame types by adding **FRAME** lines under the **LINK DRIVER (MLID)** section. Unless you have a bind statement in the **LINK DRIVER** section, make sure that the frame type being used by your ODI-based network is the first frame type listed.

To tell ODINSUP what driver it is going to bind to, you must also add a protocol section. The following is an example of part of a NET.CFG file:

```
PROTOCOL ODINSUP
     BIND NE2000
     LINK DRIVER NE2000
     INT 5
     PORT 340
     FRAME Ethernet_802.2
     FRAME Ethernet_802.3
     FRAME Ethernet_snap
     FRAME Ethernet_ii
```

9. To allow STARTNET to run again when the computer is rebooted, edit the AUTOEXEC.BAT file to remove the remark in front of the **STARTNET** line. Also, make sure that the **NETBIND** and other NDIS network commands are executed after STARTNET has loaded.

10. Double-check the setups specified in the preceding steps to verify that everything is set up properly; then reboot the machine. When your machine comes up, you should be able to connect and use both the ODI-based and NDIS-based network.

Here are some common troubleshooting tips:

- If the ODINSUP driver doesn't load, check the NET.CFG file for syntax errors or missing information.
- If the **NET BIND** fails, check the PROTOCOL.INI file for syntax errors or incorrect **Bindings=** lines.

Connecting the DOS/Windows Client to NetWare and Windows NT

After the ODINSUP combination of ODI and NDIS client software has been installed, we will then need to connect to the two (or more) network servers before we start the Windows 3.x application. In addition to the ODINSUP entries in the NET.CFG file, several other entries will be specific to the NetWare redirector software (NETBX.EXE or VLM.EXE). These entries will instruct the NetWare client software to leave a number of drive letters at the top of the alphabet for the Windows network software to use. After the client workstation has been booted up, and both the ODI and NDIS client software drivers have been loaded successfully, we can then proceed to log on to both the NetWare and Windows NT servers using the appropriate login/logon commands. For NetWare, this action would involve running the LOGIN.EXE command, which is usually located on Drive F:. Drive F: was assigned to the client workstation when the NETBX.EXE or VLM.EXE (and modules) was loaded. After we are logged in, we can proceed to use the MAP.EXE command to redirect additional drive letters to the NetWare server. Additionally, the NetWare CAPTURE command could be used to redirect printer output, as is usually done. A typical MAP and CAPTURE command would be as follows:

Syntax: **MAP drive:=SERVER\VOLUME:directory**

Actual: **MAP G:=NWSERVER\SYS:PUBLIC**

Syntax: **CAPTURE print_port:=SERVER\PRINT_QUEUE**

Actual: **CAPTURE LPT2:=NWSERVER\HPLASERQ**

Our DOS/Windows 3.1 client workstation is now connected to a NetWare server. Of course, all this activity has been done at the DOS prompt before we start Windows 3.1. The next phase of this process would be to start the Microsoft networking client redirector software (NetBIOS and SMB). We do so by using the **NET START** command at the client; invoking this command connects us to a server specified in our Microsoft networking client configuration files. The NET.EXE command is used for a variety of network services in the Microsoft network environment. These services include mapping or redirecting local workstation drive letters and printer ports to remote server file system and printer services.

NET Command Syntax

The following is a list of the options that the NET.EXE command supports:
Command: `NET.EXE /?`

`NET CONFIG`	Displays information about our workgroup settings.
`NET DIAG`	Runs the Microsoft Network Diagnostics program to display diagnostic information about our network.
`NET HELP`	Provides information about commands and error messages.
`NET INIT`	Loads protocol and network-adapter drivers without binding them to Protocol Manager.
`NET LOGOFF`	Breaks the connection between our computer and the shared resources to which it is connected.
`NET LOGON`	Identifies us as members of a workgroup.
`NET PASSWORD`	Changes our logon passwords.
`NET PRINT`	Displays information about print queues and controls print jobs.
`NET START`	Starts services.
`NET STOP`	Stops services.
`NET TIME`	Displays the time on or synchronizes our computer's clock with the clock on a Microsoft Windows for Workgroups, Windows NT, Windows 95, or NetWare time server.
`NET USE`	Connects to or disconnects from a shared resource or displays information about connections.
`NET VER`	Displays the type and version number of the workgroup redirector we are using.
`NET VIEW`	Displays a list of computers that share resources or a list of shared resources on a specific computer.

For more information about a specific NET command, type the command name followed by /? (for example, **NET USE** /?).

The configuration file related to our Microsoft networking redirector configuration is called SYSTEM.INI. The following is an example of the SYSTEM.INI file:

```
[network]
filesharing=no
printsharing=no
autologon=yes
computername=LTREE1
lanroot=C:\NET
username=Administrator
workgroup=
reconnect=no
directhost=no
dospophotkey=N
lmlogon=0
logondomain=NTPARIS    #Windows NT Domain Name
preferredredir=full
autostart=full
maxconnections=8
[network drivers]
netcard=smcmac.dos
transport=ndishlp.sys,*netbeui
devdir=A:\NET
LoadRMDrivers=yes
[Password Lists]
*Shares=a:\net\Share000.PWL
```

Accessing NT Server Drives

After we have initiated the NET START client software and logged on to the Windows NT Domain, we can then continue to map drive letters to the Windows NT server by using the **NET USE** command. The following command would perform this function:

Syntax: **NET USE drive: \\SERVER_NAME\SHARE_NAME**

Actual: **NET USE X: \\NTPARIS\USERS\Wayne**

The preceding command would map the current client workstation's drive X: to the Windows NT server called NTPARIS, to the USERS share on that server, and subsequently to the directory called Wayne on the USERS share.

Accessing Windows NT Printers

Similarly to the NetWare **CAPTURE** command, the Microsoft **NET** command can also be used to redirect printer output from the client to the Windows NT server. The following is an example of this command use:

Syntax: **NET USE LPT2: \\SERVER_NAME\PRINT_SHARE_NAME**

Actual: **NET USE LPT2: \\NTPARIS\HPLASER**

Finally, after all the NetWare and Windows NT remote drive and print connections have been established, we can then start Windows itself. Because all the drive and print connections have already been set up at the DOS level, the Windows utilities such as File Manager and Print Manager will automatically see the underlying network resources that DOS sees. Within Windows itself, many additional items that can be configured will affect the applications interface with the network resources.

Another Alternative: Changing the Windows NT Server

Loading all this additional software takes memory, which on a DOS/Windows 3.x client is a scarce resource. So what if we required the NetWare client workstation to access files on a Windows NT server, but we did not want to change the client configuration to support the "ODINSUP shim"? We would then have to configure the Windows NT server to receive network resource requests from the client in the client's networking language. (See "File and Print Services for NetWare" in the next chapter.) This approach was the latter option we presented in the introduction. Figure 4-4 demonstrates how to connect to a Windows NT File and Print Services for NetWare service from a NetWare-only client.

Using the NetWare MAP Command to Access a Windows NT Server Running File and Print Service for NetWare

Connecting the existing DOS/Windows 3.1 workstation to the Windows NT server that is running Microsoft's *File and Print Server for NetWare* (FPNW) on a Windows NT server would be no different than connecting to any other NetWare server. The same NetWare **MAP** command would be used in both cases. The following **MAP** command would connect our Net-Ware-only client in Figure 4-4 to the Windows NT server:

Syntax: **MAP drive:=COMPATIBLE_NWSERVER\VOLUME:directory**

Actual: **MAP G:=NTPARIS_FPNW\SYS:users\userXa**

Figure 4-5 demonstrates the results of this command.

As you can see, we now have the DOS/Windows 3.1 client workstation with a drive mapping to both the NetWare server and Windows NT server displayed in Figure 4-5. The FPNW service running on a Windows NT server supports most of the client commands available on a NetWare server. In fact, after we are logged on to the FPNW service, we can even use the standard NetWare SYSCON.EXE or NETADMIN.EXE utilities to add users to the NT server. However, we will encounter some functions that we are used to performing on a NetWare server from a client work-station that are not supported by the FPNW service, so be forewarned. But the main reason for using FPNW is not to allow us to administer the Windows NT server, but rather to provide seamless access to multiplat-form network servers without having to change the client networking con-figuration. In this case, when we introduce a Windows NT server into a mainly NetWare environment, FPNW does the trick.

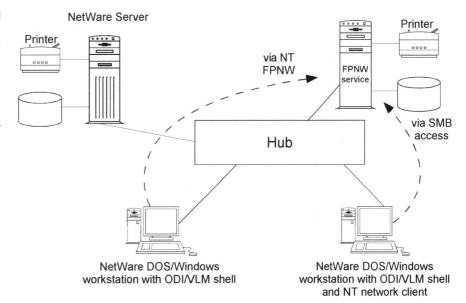

Figure 4-4
Connecting to a Win-dows NT server from a NetWare-only client. (Courtesy of Learning Tree Inter-national)

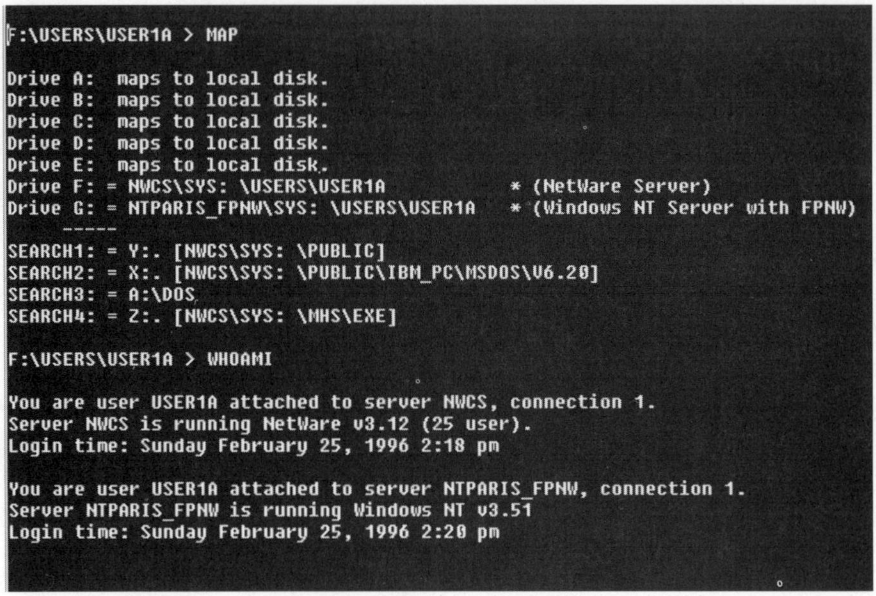

Figure 4-5
Connecting to a Net-
Ware-compatible
Windows NT server
using the **MAP** com-
mand. (Courtesy of
Learning Tree Inter-
national)

```
F:\USERS\USER1A > MAP

Drive A:  maps to local disk.
Drive B:  maps to local disk.
Drive C:  maps to local disk.
Drive D:  maps to local disk.
Drive E:  maps to local disk.
Drive F: = NWCS\SYS: \USERS\USER1A          * (NetWare Server)
Drive G: = NTPARIS_FPNW\SYS: \USERS\USER1A  * (Windows NT Server with FPNW)

SEARCH1: = Y:. [NWCS\SYS: \PUBLIC]
SEARCH2: = X:. [NWCS\SYS: \PUBLIC\IBM_PC\MSDOS\V6.20]
SEARCH3: = A:\DOS
SEARCH4: = Z:. [NWCS\SYS: \MHS\EXE]

F:\USERS\USER1A > WHOAMI

You are user USER1A attached to server NWCS, connection 1.
Server NWCS is running NetWare v3.12 (25 user).
Login time: Sunday February 25, 1996 2:18 pm

You are user USER1A attached to server NTPARIS_FPNW, connection 1.
Server NTPARIS_FPNW is running Windows NT v3.51
Login time: Sunday February 25, 1996 2:20 pm
```

Integrating Windows for Workgroups with NetWare and Windows NT

Fortunately, when Microsoft came along with *Windows for Workgroups 3.11* (WFWG), it improved the whole networking side of the application significantly. (Remember, WFWG is only an application relying on the DOS operating system underneath.) Configuring WFWG to support multiple networking protocols is much easier than configuring Windows 3.1 was. With the exception of preinstalling the NetWare client drivers, much of the configuration for multiplatform support (NetWare and Windows NT) can now be done from within Windows for Workgroups itself. However, this job is still no walk in the park.

After the NetWare client drivers are installed, the remaining part of the network configuration is done through the Windows Setup program located in the Main Program group. After we launch the Windows Setup program, or applet, we can select to Change Network Settings from the Options menu item. The screen in Figure 4-6 is then displayed.

From the Network Setup screen, we can finish configuring both the Microsoft and NetWare client configuration. Doing so will, in turn, allow us to connect over the network to either network operating system platform. The first thing we will need to do is select the Networks button to choose which networks we will support access to from this client. In this screen, we are, in fact, configuring WFWG to support both the NetWare Core Pro-

Figure 4-6
The WFWG Network
Setup screen.
(Source: Microsoft
Corporation)

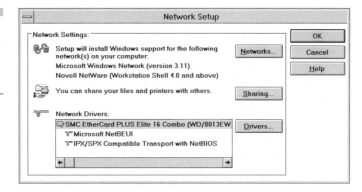

tocol and NetBIOS/SMB protocols for file and print server access on Net-Ware and Windows NT or compatible servers.

Selecting the Microsoft network support is fairly straightforward as we simply select the Install Microsoft Windows Network radio button. After the configuration process, Windows will install all the required files down to the client hard drive and will also change the required INI configuration files such as PROTOCOL.INI, AUTOEXEC.BAT, and CONFIG.SYS. The PROTOCOL.INI file replaces the SYSTEM.INI file that was used with the earlier client support software for DOS/Windows 3.1, but it looks similar. The following is an example of the PROTOCOL.INI file:

```
[network.setup]
version=0x3110
netcard=ms$w13ew,1,MS$W13EW,4
transport=ms$nwlinknb,NWLINK
transport=ms$netbeui,NETBEUI
lana0=ms$w13ew,1,ms$netbeui
lana1=ms$w13ew,1,ms$nwlinknb
[net.cfg]
PATH=C:\nwclient\net.cfg
[NWLINK]
BINDINGS=SMC8000
MAX_SOCKETS=50
MAX_CONNECTIONS=100
SOURCE_ROUTING=60
FRAME=ETHERNET_802.2
[NETBEUI]
BINDINGS=SMC8000
LANABASE=0
[MS$W13EW]
[Link Driver SMC8000]
data=   Frame Ethernet_SNAP
data=   Frame Ethernet_802.2
data=   Frame Ethernet_II
data=   Frame Ethernet_802.3
```

As you can see, the PROTOCOL.INI file uses the same standard nomenclature that all the INI files seem to use and therefore is not something we want to have to edit manually.

Supporting Non-Microsoft Windows Networks

To use a network other than the Microsoft Windows Network, we need to install the device drivers for the network before we start. Here's how:

1. From the Main group, select the Windows Setup icon.

2. From the Options menu, select Change Network Settings.

3. Choose the Networks button from the Change Network Settings dialog box. The Change Networks dialog box appears. The screen should look similar to the one in Figure 4-7.

4. Ensure that the Install Microsoft Windows Network is selected. Then select Other, open the list, and select the network you want to use. Select the Novell NetWare Workstation Shell. If you are using Virtual Loadable Modules, select Shell 4.0 and above. Note that if you want to use this network only, rather than the Microsoft Windows Network, select Install Windows Support For The Following Network Only. Then open the list and select the network.

5. Select the OK button.

6. In the Network Setup dialog box, select the OK button. A dialog box may appear, requesting that you insert a disk.

Figure 4-7
Configuring Microsoft and Novell NetWare client support. (Source: Microsoft Corporation)

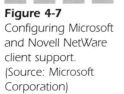

Networks

○ No Windows support for networks.

● Install Microsoft Windows Network:

    You have the options of sharing your files and printers with others.

    You can use files and printers on Microsoft Windows NT, Microsoft LAN Manager and other Microsoft-compatible servers.

    You can also install Windows support for an additional network:

        ○ No additional network

        ● Other: [Novell NetWare (Workstation Shell 4.0 and above) ↓]

○ Install Windows support for the following network only:

[↓]

[OK] [Cancel] [Help]

7. Insert the disk in drive A, and then select the OK button. Alternatively, you can type the drive letter and directory where the network driver is located, and then select the OK button. If you selected Unlisted or Updated Network, a dialog box appears, listing the network drivers on the disk. Select the driver you want to use, and then select the OK button.

8. You will need to restart the computer eventually to have the changes take effect. You can do so by selecting the Restart Computer button when prompted for the changes to take effect. However, before we do this, we will need to configure the network adapter.

The Network configuration takes care of the protocols responsible for the upper layers of the OSI Model communications. In other words, it installs the client redirector software. Before we continue, however, we also need to install a Network Interface Card or adapter card. At this stage, we should be looking at the Network Setup dialog box once again. Select the Drivers button to install a network interface or adapter card driver. When we do so, we should see a screen similar to the one in Figure 4-8.

To add a network adapter driver, we will need to perform the following steps:

1. Select the Windows Setup icon from the Main group.

2. From the Options menu, select Change Network Settings.

3. In the Network Setup dialog box, select the Drivers button.

Figure 4-8
Configuring the WFWG network adapter. (Source: Microsoft Corporation)

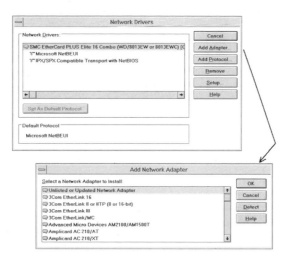

4. In the Network Drivers dialog box, select the Add Adapter button.

5. In the list of network adapters, select the one you want to add, and then select the OK button. If your network adapter is not listed, select Unlisted or Updated Network Adapter.

6. Insert the requested disk in drive A, and then select the OK button. Alternatively, you can type the drive letter and directory where the driver is located, and then select the OK button. If you selected Unlisted or Updated Network Adapter, a dialog box appears, listing the supported network adapters on the disk. Select the network adapter you are using, and then select the OK button.

7. If the network adapter driver requires additional settings, a dialog box appears, displaying the default (preset) settings for your network adapter. In most cases, the default settings should work. However, sometimes they may conflict with other devices, such as a mouse, sound card, or memory managers installed on your system. For information about settings, see the documentation for your devices and for your network adapter.

8. If you need to change advanced settings, select the Advanced button, and then complete the dialog box. After you are finished, select the OK button.

9. In the network adapters settings dialog box, select the OK button.

10. In the Network Drivers dialog box, select the Close button.

11. In the Network Setup dialog box, select the OK button.

12. For your changes to take effect, select the Restart Computer button.

Within the Network Drivers dialog box, we can also configure both the NetBEUI and IPX/SPX Compatible Transport protocols. These protocols, however, support only Windows-to-Windows communications through NetBIOS encapsulation. Remember that to support Novell NetWare Core Protocol, we still require the NetWare client redirector software. We set and tune the NetWare client software through the NET.CFG file. (See Figure 4-8 for small sample of this file.) The screens in Figure 4-9 show the items that can be configured for the two Microsoft Networking protocols.

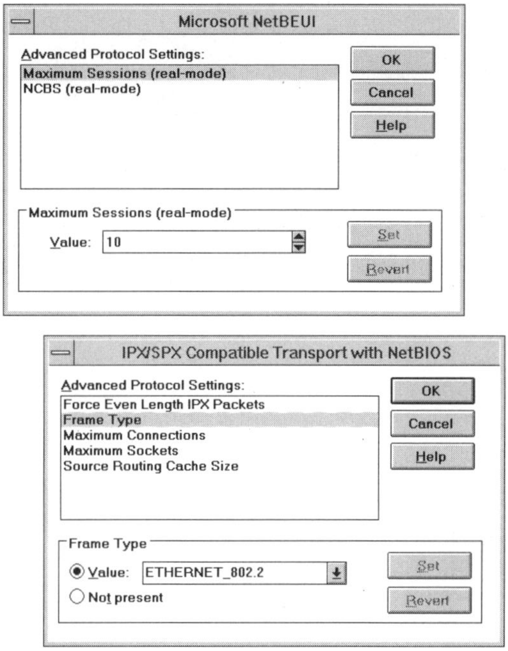

Figure 4-9
Configuring the
WFWG networking
protocols. (Source:
Microsoft
Corporation)

Figure 4-9
Configuring the WFWG networking protocols. (Source: Microsoft Corporation)

Making the Windows NT Network Connection from WFWG

Configuring the Logon

After the client workstation restarts, we should then be able to use the network server utilities within WFWG to connect to the NetWare and Windows NT (or compatible) servers on our network. We can configure our WFWG computer to automatically connect and log on to our Windows NT servers through the Network icon of the Control Panel. This application allows us to specify the NetBIOS name of the computer, the workgroup our computer initially belongs to, and the comments the other network users will see when they list our computer in their browse lists within File Manager. It also tells us our current logon status, as well as allows us to configure the Microsoft logon or start-up options. We will also the Net-Ware configuration button. Figure 4-10 shows the Control Panel's Network icon configuration screen.

Figure 4-10
Configuring WFWG
Network logon
options. (Source:
Microsoft
Corporation)

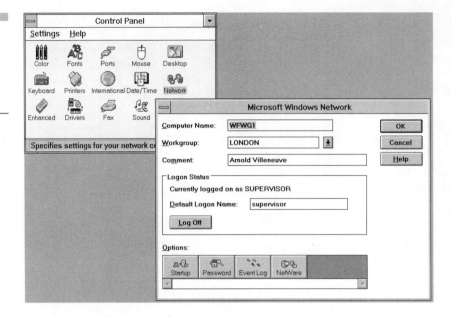

One of the options we want is to be able to specify which Windows NT domain we would like to authenticate our logon to, as opposed to simply being part of a workgroup. Using the Startup options button, we configure this item as well as the automatic logon at start-up of the WFWG workstation. In Figure 4-11, we have clicked on the Startup options button displayed in Figure 4-10 of the Microsoft Windows Network dialog box. Under the Options for Enterprise Networking, we can enable our WFWG computer to search the network for the Windows NT Domain Controllers. In our example configuration, we have specified that this workstation should establish authentication connections with one of the OTTAWA Domain Controllers.

Logon Startup Settings

During a logon process, the logon application knows which Domain Controllers to search for by looking at the Startup Settings configuration information. (See Figure 4-11.)

Also in the Startup Settings screen is the Set Password button option, which allows us to change our Windows NT Domain user account password. However, we must be successfully logged on already before we can change our passwords.

Figure 4-11
Configuring the
WFWG Microsoft
Network startup
settings. (Source:
Microsoft
Corporation)

The Logon to Windows NT

Now that we have configured WFWG to support network connections to the Windows NT server (as well as other LAN Manager and LAN Server network operating systems), we can initiate a logon. After we are logged on, we can access other resources such file and print shares. If we have configured Log On at Startup in the Startup Settings box, then the logon will occur at the time of bootup for our workstation. However, if we want to initiate a logon at a separate time after the workstation has started up, we can do so by using the Network program group. The Log On/Off icon is located within the Network program group that is installed when we configure the Network Settings to support Microsoft networks. The Log On/Off icon will present us with a Welcome to Windows for Workgroups dialog box in which we will be prompted for our user names and passwords. Provided we have typed everything correctly, we will then be told of our successful logon to the Windows NT server. Figure 4-12 details this process.

Accessing File and Print Services

Upon a successful logon to the Windows NT server, we can now proceed to connect to a shared network resource located on the Windows NT server. Accessing network resources from WFWG can be initiated within

Figure 4-12
Logging on to
Windows NT from
WFWG. (Source:
Microsoft
Corporation)

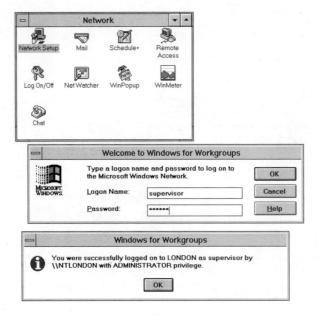

the File Manager or Print Manager. Selecting the File Manager for our example, we can connect to a remote network file system in two ways: select the Connect Network Drive item from the Disk menu or select the Connect Network Drive button. Either method to start the Connect Network Drive feature will allow us to redirect a local drive letter to the remote Windows NT file system share. Because we are already logged on to the Windows NT server, it will use our Domain user account to validate our access. If we are not already logged on, we will be prompted to log on during our attempt to connect to the network shared resource.

Figure 4-13 highlights access to the Windows NT server from WFWG File Manager. Here, we are about to connect the local workstation's drive D: to the Windows NT file server \\NTLONDON and the file system share called Users. In the Connect Network Drive dialog box, we have the option of specifying whether we want to have the local drive letter automatically connect to the remote server at start-up. The Show Shared Directories on: window displays all the computers with server services running on them (both workstations and servers can be running server services). The Shared Directories on \\NTLONDON displays which remote file system shares are available for us to connect to.

After we are connected, the drive letter we selected—in this case, D:—will appear in our File Manager program. It is important to point

Figure 4-13

Connecting to Windows NT file system share from WFWG. (Source: Microsoft Corporation)

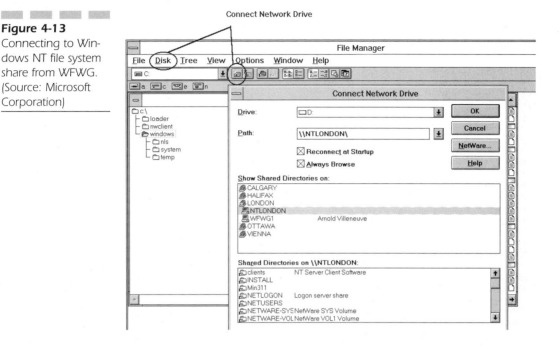

out at this point that even if we were not logged on to the Windows NT server at the time of connection, we would be prompted to do so at that time. The logon screen would be the same as was highlighted in Figure 4-12. We can then easily move files between our WFWG workstation and the Windows NT file server. Accessing shared printer resources from the Windows NT server would be done in a similar manner. And now that we have successfully logged on to the Windows NT server and accessed the file system, configuring the printer side would be relatively simple. Using the Printer Manager, we would select the Connect Network Printer option and the same screen would be presented as was done with the remote file access. Figure 4-14 demonstrates the WFWG client connecting to the Windows NT remote shared printer.

One part of the networking integration puzzle is solved. Now we need to move onto connecting our WFWG workstation to a NetWare file server. Unlike Windows 95 and Windows NT, the NetWare networks are not displayed in the browse list, only the Microsoft network servers are displayed in the Show Shared Directories on: window. To access NetWare servers, we need to select the NetWare button. We will investigate this feature next in this chapter.

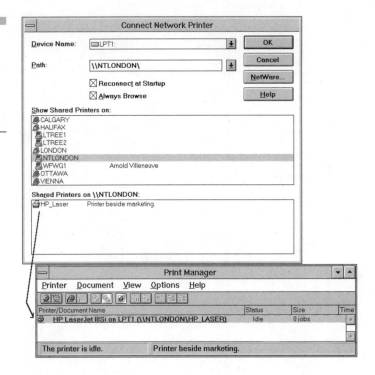

Figure 4-14
Connecting to Windows NT remote shared printer from WFWG. (Source: Microsoft Corporation)

Making the Novell NetWare Connection from WFWG

The NetWare Login

Everything has been configured for Microsoft network access. The WFWG client workstation is now in a position to access shared file system and printer resources on remote Microsoft Windows NT, LAN Manager, and IBM Lan Server network operating system servers. The client workstation can even access other Windows for Workgroups and Windows 95 workstations. And if we really wanted to push the envelope, we could configure a UNIX host to support the NetBIOS/SMB protocol (such as LinULX running SAMBA or SCO with SCO Vision), and our WFWG client workstation would be able to access it as well. However, now we need to finish the WFWG workstation so that it can access the Novell side of the network. The NetWare client software was installed initially from DOS and then completed within the WFWG Windows Setup program. The NetWare client software is in place before WFWG starts up. During the start-up process, the configuration changes we made earlier in the Windows Setup program instruct WFWG about the fact that it is now "NetWare aware." We can check the current NetWare settings by selecting the Network program from the Control Panel. Figure 4-15 details the NetWare settings.

NetWare Client Redirector Options

Like the Microsoft Startup options button, several sections within the NetWare option dialog screen can affect the capabilities of the NetWare client redirector software. In particular, the Resource Display Options dialog box allows us to configure WFWG to access NetWare Personal/Lite workstations, NetWare 3.x Bindery-based servers, as well as NetWare 4.x and IntranetWare Directory Services servers. Also similar to the Microsoft start-up, the NetWare client software can be configured to restore previous NetWare server connections.

Figure 4-15
Configuring NetWare settings for WFWG. (Source: Microsoft Corporation)

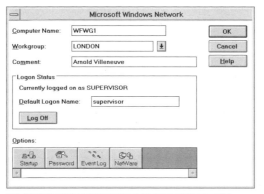

The initial login to the NetWare server can be done before WFWG is loaded on the workstation. The benefit here is that the user's logon script can execute before WFWG is started. Thus, all the NetWare resources will be available within WFWG. However, this capability would only be useful if we were running complicated login scripts that performed special loops depending on our user group's membership. Newer versions of the NetWare client software for Windows supports full login within Windows itself (more on this subject later). Alternatively, we can attach to the NetWare server after WFWG is started. This is similar to a login; however, no login script is actually run. After it is attached, the WFWG client can restore its previously connected drive letters.

The main control or configuration program is NetWare Connections. Through this utility, we can configure which NetWare servers we want to log in to, which remote file system volumes and directories we want to connect to, as well as which remote print queues we want to connect to. You may have noticed a NetWare Hotkey dialog box in the previous NetWare Settings figure. This Hotkey can be used to invoke the NetWare Connections software with one keystoke. The NetWare Connections screen can also be invoked from the Connect Network Drive or Connect Network Printer dialog boxes. Figure 4-16 shows the NetWare Connections configuration application program called NetWare User Tools.

Figure 4-16
Log on to a NetWare server from WFWG. (Source: Novell, Inc.)

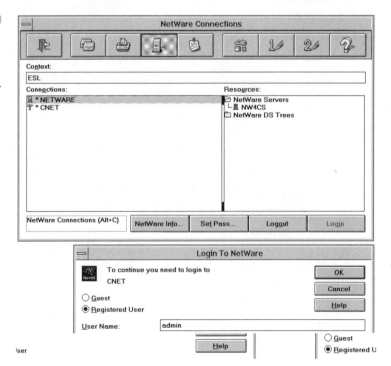

In Figure 4-16, we can see that the WFWG client workstation can see the NetWare 4.x server on the network. The server is called NWSERVER, and it is part of the ACME *NetWare Directory Services* (NDS) tree. We can initiate an attach login to the server by clicking on the Login button. After we are logged in, we can select the NetWare Info button at the bottom of the screen to get information about the server that we are currently connected to. In the following example, you can see that we are connected to the NWSERVER as the ADMIN user. We have also been authenticated by Directory Services.

The NetWare User Tools

Figure 4-17 highlights all the features of the NWUser Tool options by each individual button.

The NetWare User Tools can allow us to perform all sorts of NetWare client workstation functions from one source. We can map local drive letters or redirect printer output to currently connected servers. We can attach or log in to NetWare servers we are not already connected to. We can send messages to other NetWare users on the network. The "key" button is used to change the client's NetWare server connection configurations. This is the same screen that we called from the Microsoft Windows Network | NetWare Settings button earlier in Figure 4-14. Finally, we have user-definable buttons in which we can place pointers to our favorite programs (like shortcuts) that we can access directly while within the NetWare User Tools menu. The last button is for help (which is appropriate because it is usually the last place we look when we are having problems!). (See Figure 4-18.)

Figure 4-17
Using the NetWare
User Tools. (Source:
Novell, Inc.)

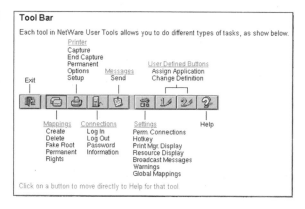

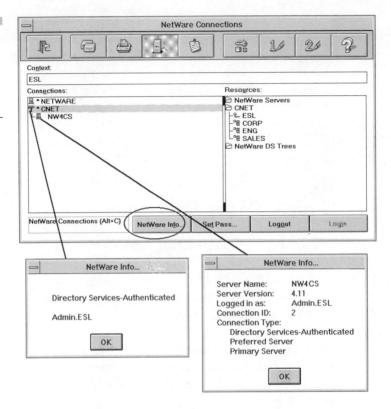

Figure 4-18
Displaying the
NetWare server con-
nection information.
(Source: Microsoft
Corporation)

Accessing NetWare File and Print Services

Now that we have successfully logged in to our NetWare 4.x server, we can begin to attach to remote NetWare file and print services. We do so by selecting the Disk Drives button (to the right of the open doorway). This option will display all the current local drives and drive mappings on the left of the screen while providing us with the available NetWare resources on the right. In our example, we already have drive N: mapped to NWSERVER SYS volumes LOGIN directory. This connection was created at start-up of the WFWG workstation before WFWG was loaded. When the VLM's drivers load through STARTNET.BAT file, one drive letter (specified in the NET.CFG file) is used to create an initial connection to the LOGIN directory. From here, the LOGIN.EXE command can be run. Alternatively, the ATTACH/LOGIN can be performed from within the NetWare Connections application, as was demonstrated earlier. Figure 4-19 displays how we can map a new drive letter to a NetWare volume\directory.

The result of mapping a drive letter to the NetWare server from WFWG is that our computer now has a connection to both a NetWare and Win-

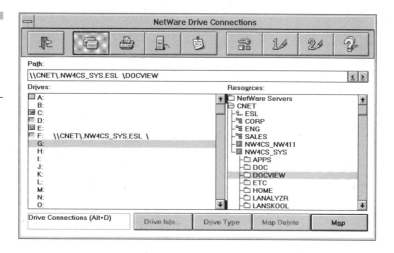

Figure 4-19
Displaying the
NetWare Drive Con-
nection information.
(Source: Novell, Inc.)

dows NT server. This can be aptly demonstrated in the File Manager program. In Figure 4-20, we can see that the File Manager highlights the two
server connections that we have made so far in this chapter. The first one
was to a Windows NT Domain server using the Microsoft client software.
As you may remember, the Microsoft client software uses NetBIOS/Server
Message Blocks for file and print service access over the network. The second connection was to a NetWare 4.x server using the NetWare client software. The NetWare client software uses the NetWare Core Protocol for file
and print service access over the network.

At this stage, we could easily copy files back and forth between two
servers in question. If we were copying a file from the NetWare server to
the Windows NT server, it would first be copied to our own workstation's
random access memory using the NCP protocol. After it is delivered, the
file data would be taken out of the NCP protocol message at the top of the
OSI Model (Application Layer). It would then be placed inside a Net-
BIOS/SMB message and sent down the protocol stack out to the Windows
NT server. We would be limited only by our access privileges, Windows NT
permissions, or NetWare rights on either server.

The Latest Thing for Windows
for Workgroups: 32-Bit Network Drivers

Both Microsoft and Novell have moved to provide newer client connectivity software for Windows for Workgroups. Microsoft has created a
Win32S TCP/IP client for WFWG. This client software allows WFWG to

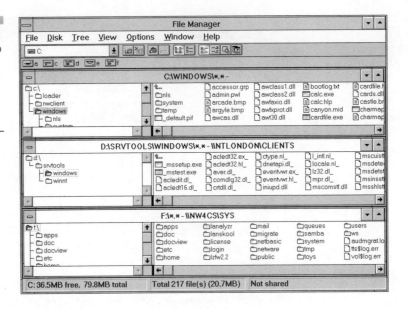

Figure 4-20
WFWG connected to
both a Windows NT
and NetWare server
simultaneously.
(Source: Microsoft
Corporation)

internetwork using TCP/IP as the transport driver instead of NetBEUI. After it is installed, however, the software provides similar access to that displayed previously in this chapter. Only the installation is a little different. Microsoft usually refers to the process of encapsulating Net-BIOS/SMB inside TCP/IP as NBT. As was detailed in Chapter 3, TCP/IP is a much better transport protocol that NetBEUI.

Novell, meanwhile, has developed the Client 32 for DOS/Windows 3.x. Like Microsoft's product, this is a 32-bit implementation of the client software. Both client software packages allow support for a new generation of Network Interface Cards, PC motherboards, and BIOS versions, and better dynamic loading and reconfiguration of protocol stacks. Although Microsoft continues to provide GUI network client configuration, Novell's Client 32 for DOS/Windows 3.x uses a new GUI installation interface over the older character-based installation screens. As a result, the entire installation can now be done within Windows itself for both protocol stacks. Novell's Client 32 is based on the *Network Input/Output System* (NIOS) client architecture. NIOS performs better memory management of network redirector utilization, services for NLMs, and reads the NET.CFG. Finally, the Client 32 provides a new GUI login facility that allows you to execute login scripts from within Windows 3.x itself.

However, the 32-bit client driver software developed by both vendors was a little late of the mark given that Windows 95 had been released by this time and provided significantly better multiprotocol support. For the sake of reference, we include Table 4-1, which lists the differences between the Novell NetWare Virtual Loadable Modules and the new NetWare Client 32. Remember that Microsoft does not provide a complete NetWare client for WFWG (NWLink IPX/SPX is used for transporting the Server Message Blocks between Microsoft clients, so their 32-bit client software does not assist us here), and as such you must use Novell's client software. Therefore, if you are still using WFWG, Table 4-1 may help convince you of the benefits of upgrading to the Client 32 client drivers. Although the early versions of the software were not very stable (as is true with any new software release), the current versions of Client 32 are very stable and work extremely well. Additionally, many new client applications facilitate using WFWG in a NetWare network environment. All the Microsoft network tools are already there, so we don't need to make a further comparison between Microsoft's 16-bit and 32-bit client software.

For more detailed information, refer to Novell's Web site at **http:// netwire.novell.com/home/client474-000113-001**. (Note: This URL may have changed since this book was printed.)

Table 4-1

NetWare Client 32 and Virtual Loadable Modules comparison. (Source: Novell, Inc.)

Item	Client 32	VLM
General		
Conventional memory required	4K	100K (estimated)
Point of logon	DOS/Windows	DOS
Provides automatic client update from the server	Yes	Yes
Client-side caching	Yes	35 Max
Advanced NCP support	Yes	No
ODI Driver	32-bit and 16-bit	16-bit
32-bit NetWare Client API libraries	Yes	No
16-bit NetWare Client API libraries	Yes	Yes
NetWare Windows diagnostic tool (NWD2.EXE)	Yes	No
Install		
Unattended install, Automatic Client Update (ACU)	Yes	Yes
Windows install program (setup.exe)	Yes	No

Continues

Table 4-1

Continued.

Item	Client 32	VLM
DOS Install program (install.exe)	Yes	Yes
Install advanced client features Login	Yes	No
Graphical user interface		
Log in to multiple trees	Yes	No
Search and specify a NetWare server	Yes	No
Search and specify a NetWare NDS tree	Yes	No
Specify Context	Yes	No
Specify Login script at Login	Yes	Yes
Drop-down list of the last servers, trees, and contexts	Yes	No
Specify login script variables at login	Yes	Yes
Clears other connections at login option	Yes	Yes
Login via NDS or Bindery	Yes	Yes
Save settings on exit	Yes	No
GUI for mapping of search drives	Yes	No
GUI for updating environment variables	Yes	No
Provider		
NetWare User Tools	Yes	Yes
Map search drives via NWUser	Yes	No
Position search drive in path	Yes	No
Limit options available to users in NWUser	Yes	No
Leverages NLM technology at the client	Yes	No
Supports NAL application management	Yes	Yes
Select default capture parameters	Yes	No
Multitree support	Yes	No
Auto Reconnect	Yes	Yes
Restore Capture Status	Yes	Yes
Reconnect to servers	Yes	Yes
Reconnect to NDS tree	Yes	Yes
Reconnect drive mappings	Yes	Yes

Table 4-1

Item	Client 32	VLM
Restore open files	Yes	No
Restore file locks	Yes	No
Configuration		
Customizable configuration	Yes	Yes
On-line documentation/Configuration Help	Yes	No
Dynamic Updates	Yes	No
NDS Support		
Login to multiple trees	Yes	No
Supports extended NDS schema: view additional objects	Yes	Yes
Supports application object extensions via NAL	Yes	Yes
Protocols		
Named Pipes	Yes	Yes
NetBIOS	Yes	Yes
SMB	Yes	Limited
NetWare / IP	Yes (32-bit mode)	Yes
NetBEUI	Yes	Yes
IPX/SPX	Yes (32-bit mode)	Yes
TCP/IP	Yes (32-bit mode)	Yes
Packet Burst	Yes	Yes
Large Internet Packets	Yes	Yes

As you can see by the comparison, the NetWare Client 32 drivers for Windows 3.x provide some really nice features over the older client software. Granted, the 32 drivers do nothing for connecting to the Windows NT servers; however, Microsoft already does a good job of that on its own, so we don't need to expand on it here. Windows for Workgroups version 3.11 also provides for Microsoft's 32-bit client drivers, which greatly improve WFWG connectivity to Windows NT and other versions of Windows over the network.

NetWare Client 32 drivers also provide better support for interfacing with NetWare 4.x NetWare Directory Services and provides better Windows utilities. For example, using the NetWare Client 32 drivers will allow us to log in to a NetWare server from within Windows and support the processing of login scripts. We can have the GUI login automatically appear on the WFWG desktop at the time of login by placing the LOGINW31.EXE icon in the WFWG Startup program group. It will also allow us to connect to services available inside different NDS trees. And, most important of all, the NetWare Client 32 drivers ship with an installation help file to help us troubleshoot any installation and configuration problems.

Coordinating User Names and Passwords

Now, in all this multiplatform connecting, one thing we have not made obvious is the fact that user names and passwords must be coordinated throughout the entire system. On all servers, users must ideally have the same user names and passwords. Unlike the standard DOS/Windows 3.1 combination, because WFWG is based on its ability to perform Peer-to-Peer networking with some ease, it stores the user name and password in a *.PWL file. The cached user name and password is then used each time users try to connect to another User Level Access resource so that they do not have to keep typing in user names and passwords. Figure 4-21 demonstrates a first-time user logging on to a WFWG workstation. Although the WFWG workstation will take any user name and password that is typed, it will not, however, do this user much good when trying to connect to a NetWare or Windows NT server Domain if the user's name and password have not been set up on that system. In this example, we have tried to connect to a Windows NT server network resource through the File Manager's Network Connection option.

The Hidden User Name and Password File

As we eluded to earlier in this chapter, WFWG saves or caches the user name and password in a USER_NAME.PWL file in the Windows directory on the local hard drive. An individual file is saved for each user. The cached password file is saved in encrypted format. You can search for these files on your hard drive by searching for *.PWL. Deleting old password files when they are no longer required is a good idea because they

Figure 4-21
A first-time logon to
WFWG and Win-
dows NT Domain.
(Courtesy of WWW.
NETWORKOLOGIST.
COM)

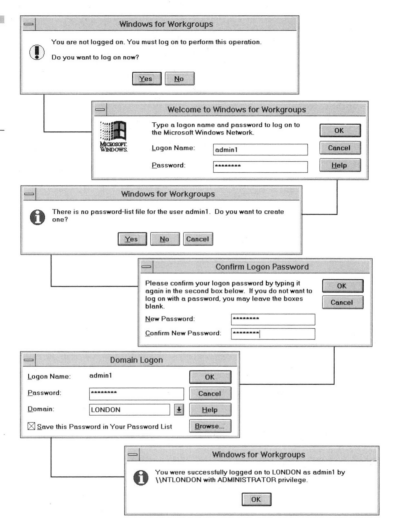

present a security hazard. If users are able to access the file and unencrypt it, they can then use the information to access resources on other
parts of the network and on other servers. Several programs have been
made freely available on the Internet to crack these files. Figure 4-22
shows a list of all the cached password files on our WFWG computer.

Now that you know how WFWG stores client passwords on the local
system, as well as how it uses them to initially connect to network servers,
the question you are probably asking is "How do we maintain coordinated
user names and passwords on both NetWare and Windows NT servers simultaneously?" Another obvious question when integrating these two

Figure 4-22
List of locally cached
password list files.
(Courtesy of WWW.
NETWORKOLOGIST.
COM)

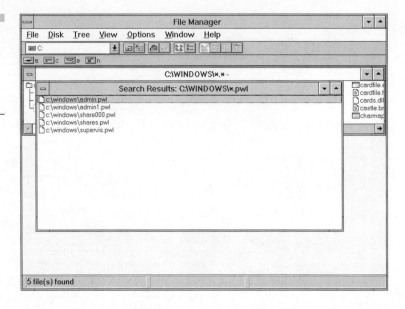

server platforms is "Is there any way to get my current server user list (be it NetWare or Windows NT) over to the other server?" Or "What happens if users change their passwords on one server but not the other?" These are very important questions for network administrators faced with multiplatform integration to be asking. We will answer these questions and more in Chapter 7 when we address the issue of migration. For now, however, you should be aware that to provide the end users with as seamless as possible integration between the two network server platforms, you need to maintain identical user names and passwords on all servers (Bindery, NDS, or Domain) that the users will connect to.

Much of this information is equally true of Windows 95 with respect to accessing Share Level and User Level network resources. Perhaps one of the major differences is the ease with which we can now configure Windows 95 to access multiplatform network resources. Let's investigate how we can integrate Windows 95 into a heterogeneous NetWare and Windows NT network environment.

Integrating Windows 95 with NetWare and Windows NT

Resistance to change seems to be a standard human characteristic (but don't tell the Borg ;-) . And so it is with adapting to Windows 95. Despite its many shortcomings in the early releases, it truly is a much improved version of Windows when compared to Windows 3.1 and Windows for Workgroups 3.11. Although the new graphical user interface was a great leap for many people, the internals of Windows 95 are truly the place where the operating system provides many benefits to both network administrators and end user alike. Before we begin a detailed look at how we can best integrate Windows 95 into NetWare and Windows NT networks, let's do a quick comparison of Windows 3.x and Windows 95, covering some of the areas that will be important from our integration perspective. Table 4-2 provides a summary of the differences.

Table 4-2

Comparison of Windows 3.x and Windows 95. (Source: Microsoft Corporation)

Windows 3.x	Windows 95
Multiprotocol network support is difficult to implement.	Multiprotocol network support is native.
No built-in network management support.	Built-in network management support for HP OpenView, Novell NetWare Management Service, Microsoft Systems Management Service; Simple Network Management Protocol support, Desktop Management Interface (DMI) support.
Workstation configuration management is done separately at each workstation through many individual .INI files.	Workstation configuration management is done through a central Registry database.
Securing desktop security through Program Manager requires technically advanced editing of the .INI files	System Policy Editor is a Graphical User Interface program to facilitate the security configurations of the workstation desktop.
No logon authentication security to the workstation desktop; anyone at the keyboard can access the hard drive.	Can be configured to require NetWare or Windows NT server authentication for workstation desktop logon access.
Hardware setup requires some level of personal computer knowledge.	Supports Plug-and-Play hardware that is easily recognizable and configurable by Windows 95.
Support for 16-bit Network Interface Card drivers (with only very recent support for 32-bit versions).	Support for 16- and 32-bit network drivers with considerable performance improvements from the 32-bit drivers.
Network Data Link layer frame type must be specified on each workstation's configuration to maintain consistent network communications.	Automatic detection of frame type supported by network during installation

Continues

Table 4-2

Continued.

Windows 3.x	Windows 95
NetWare and Windows NT login/logon scripts must be executed prior to starting Windows. Non-native support for NetWare connectivity within Windows is provided by NWUSER.EXE from Novell. Allows server ATTACH function with drive mapping and printer redirection.	Native support for NetWare and Windows NT login/logon scripts within Windows 95.
Must redirect local printer port output and local drive letters to NetWare and Windows NT printers and remote file system prior to starting Windows.	Local drive and printer redirection support within Windows 95 through the Desktop Explorer and browse capability. Native support for Click, Drag-and-Drop printing.
Peer-to-Peer networking support for Microsoft network clients only. NetWare clients cannot access the Microsoft client server service shares.	NWServer support within Windows 95 allows it to emulate a NetWare 3.x-compatible server. NetWare configured clients can access the Windows 95 NWServer service by mapping drives, capturing printer ports, and sharing files as though Windows 95 were a NetWare server.
Workstation network connections must be reestablished outside Windows. Disconnection produces an error that usually halts Windows processing.	Automatic network drive disconnect and reconnect allows workstation to continue functioning despite loss of a noncritical server connection.
Network drivers require conventional and upper memory that can be used up quickly.	32-bit virtual device drivers (VxD) architecture provides network drivers with access to memory above 1 megabyte.
Support 16-bit applications.	Supports 32-bit and 16-bit applications for Windows and NetWare.
16-bit nonpreemptive environment because it is based entirely on DOS.	Supports 32-bit preemptive environment for performance enhancements.

SUPPORTED PLATFORMS FOR WINDOWS 95 INTEGRATION

Although our main concern in this book is with supporting the Windows 95 connections to NetWare and Windows NT network servers, the operating system also supports seamless integration with many other network operating systems including the following:

IBM PC LAN Program: part of Microsoft networking

IBM LAN Server: part of Microsoft networking

Microsoft LAN Manager: part of Microsoft networking

3COM 3+OPEN and 3+SHARE: part of Microsoft networking

Figure 4-23
Windows 95 integrates well into a multiserver, multiplatform network operating system environment. (Courtesy of WWW. NETWORKOLOGIST. COM)

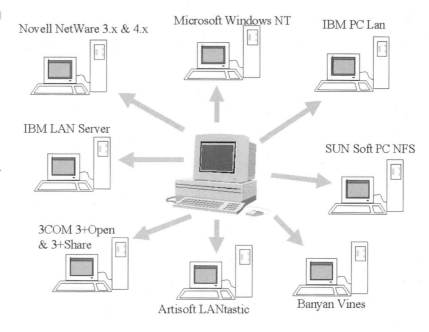

Novell NetWare 3.x & 4.x

Microsoft Windows NT

IBM PC Lan

IBM LAN Server

SUN Soft PC NFS

3COM 3+Open & 3+Share

Artisoft LANtastic

Banyan Vines

Digital Equipment Pathworks: installed as a protocol

Banyan VINES: Version 5.52 and greater

Artisoft LANtastic: Version 5.0 and greater

SunSoft PC-NFS: Version 5.0 and greater

Novell NetWare: Version 3.11 and greater

Figure 4-23 shows how this integration works.

WINDOWS 95 NETWORK REGISTRY ENTRIES Support for these different network operating system environments is built in and is relatively easy to set up. All the setup is done through the typical wizard or point-and-click interfaces. Fortunately, there is much more to it than that. Whereas in the DOS/Windows combination, everything had to be configured from within several *.INI files, Windows 95 places all the configuration information in the Registry. (See Figure 4-24.) However, this fact alone is not what makes configuring networking support for Windows 95 easier. In fact, if we had to begin editing the Registry by hand through the Registry Editor, the task would be a lot harder than editing INI files (or maybe we just got used to editing INI files). The difference is really that Microsoft, as well as the other vendors, now does a much better job

Figure 4-24
The Client for
Microsoft Networks
Registry keys and
values for Windows
95. (Source:
Microsoft
Corporation)

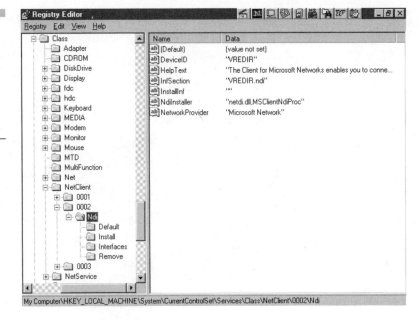

of installing the software components so that we don't have to hack configuration files to bits and piece to get the stuff working after it is installed. Installing these components is easier certainly because of the more flexible networking architectures the operating system now provides to support multiple network platforms.

From the user perspective, access to the various underlying networks could not be easier. From the network administrator's viewpoint, installation and support of the various networks is infinitely easier than the old DOS/Windows combination. After it is installed by the network administrator, the Windows 95 Windows Explorer interface to the various underlying networks hides the complexity and differences. (See Figure 4-25.) As you will see, access to NetWare and Windows NT servers is easy to configure. As with the Windows for Workgroups File Manager, the Windows Explorer provides a common look and feel to remote file system access, regardless of the destination network operating system or the differences in protocols used to get there.

WINDOWS 95 CLIENT NETWORKING SUPPORT FOR NETWARE AND WINDOWS NT NETWORKS NetWare and Windows client networking support is provided natively within Windows 95 by Microsoft. Microsoft has actually developed a compatible IPX/SPX transport protocol

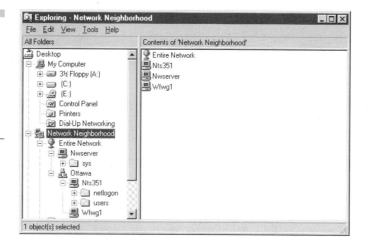

Figure 4-25
Windows 95 Windows Explorer with connections to the entire network. (Courtesy of WWW. NETWORKOLOGIST. COM)

to carry its network communications around on the network. The NWLinkNB enables Windows 95 to transport NetBIOS/SMB messages around on the network using the IPX/SPX transport protocol. However, it takes more than using the right Network Layer packets to interoperate with a NetWare server. To this end, Microsoft has also designed a compatible NetWare Core Protocol to provide its client operating systems with NetWare server access natively. In other words, we do not need any software from Novell to talk to a NetWare server. It's one-stop shopping for all NetWare connectivity needs, and the solution works very well.

Figure 4-26 highlights the network architecture that is used by Windows 95 to support heterogeneous network operating system access. You may be familiar with a similar network architecture demonstrated in Chapter 3— that of Windows NT. The main areas of the figure to focus on are the Transport and Redirector sections. In the Transport section, you can observe that Windows 95 supports IPX/SPX natively. In addition to IPX/SPX, it can also support both NetBEUI and TCP/IP for transporting Server Message Blocks. IPX/SPX can be used for transporting both Server Message Blocks to enable Microsoft-to-Microsoft network communications as well as NetWare Core Protocol for Microsoft to NetWare communications.

WINDOWS OPEN SERVICES ARCHITECTURE (WOSA) The Windows 95 network architecture is based on Microsoft's *Windows Open Services Architecture* (WOSA) model. The WOSA model is made up of a service provider, a routine module, and an Application Programming Layer. When combined with network drivers and transport protocols, the WOSA model allows multiple software components to coexist on the same system.

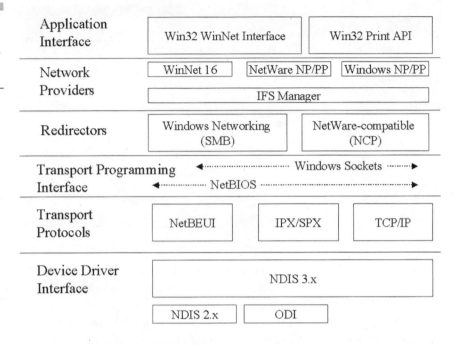

In the grand scheme of this model, the API layer is independent from its underlying services or hardware. The routing module services the API and directs the API calls to the appropriate service provider interface. The service provider interface, in turn, works with the operating system to perform the required service functions.

The WOSA model is composed of the following components:

- Application Programming Interface (API)
- Multiple Provider Router (MPR)
- Service Provider Interface (SPI)
- IFS Manager
- Network Transport
- Network Driver Interface Specification

APPLICATION PROGRAMMING INTERFACE The Windows 95 API consists of a 32-bit WinNet interface that is called the WinNet APIs. The API layer functions with a range of supported networks, thus allowing us to log in to any Windows 95-based peer server. This includes, for example, Windows NT, NetWare, and Banyan Vines servers with the same API function calls. Windows 95 supports two main APIs, which we are particularly concerned about when integrating Windows 95 with Windows NT and NetWare servers: WinNet APIs and NetWare APIs. We will look at both of these APIs now in more detail and then move on to describing the rest of the WOSA components.

The WinNet API set as been around since Windows 3.0 and has been continually enhanced since its introduction. The WinNet interface provides for network platform-independent APIs. The LAN Manager version of the API introduced a multinetwork DLL that provided the capability to route requests from the interface to both LAN Manager and NetWare networks. Windows for Workgroups expanded on the API set and added common network dialogs that used the WinNet interface. When Windows NT was introduced (before Windows 95), the API was further extended to incorporate Windows browsing and different network naming conventions.

Windows 95 incorporated all the previous WinNet API features and added a few more. First, the goal was to support Win32 WinNet, which was in use already by Windows NT. Like Windows NT, the interface provides seamless browsing of network resources (file systems, printers, and resource directories). To support access to these resources that may be located on different network platforms, Windows 95 provides a consistent authentication methodology for multiple networks. It also provides backward compatibility with Windows for Workgroups.

WINDOWS WINNET COMPONENT APIS   The following is a list and brief description of the various WinNet component APIs:

Authentication Dialog API: The network provider uses the Authentication Dialog API to make a consistent login/authentication interface available.

Password Cache API: This API allows the various network providers to access and use the Windows 95 password cache file information. Note that the system can also be configured to prevent them from using the password cache as well.

Uniform Naming Convention API: This network provider interface allows UNC paths to be treated in a consistent fashion. Note that UNC is also referred to in the industry as *Universal Naming Convention,* which means roughly the same thing.

Local Device Name API: This additional network provider interface helps standardize device naming through API calls.

Error Reporting API: This API is used for transmitting and receiving error codes and used only by the network providers.

Enumeration API: This API provides the client with the ability to browse the network for resources. Is used by programs such as File

Manager or Windows Explorer to display a list of network resources and details about these resources.

Connection API: This API provides applications with the ability to create, manage, and remove connections to network resources.

NETWARE API SUPPORT IN WINDOWS 95   NetWare APIs provide support for client operating systems to access and manage Novell Net-Ware file servers and their resources. The two main types of NetWare APIs are MS-DOS-based and Windows-based NetWare APIs. Microsoft's NetWare client software supports all MS-DOS-based NetWare API calls and functions. As Windows became the predominant desktop operating system, Novell created better Windows-to-NetWare server client/server interfaces through a series of Windows-based APIs. The Windows-based NetWare APIs are provided through programming interfaces included in Novell's DLL files for Windows, as well as through the NETWARE.DRV driver. Novell provides the DLL files on its NetWare Client installation kit. A special version of NETWARE.DRV is provided with Windows 95 to provide better client integration with NetWare servers. Although many of the Windows-based API calls go through the same interrupts as the MS-DOS API calls. However, the Windows-based APIs are passed to the NET-WARE.DRV supported by Windows instead of directly to the NetWare NETBX or VLM client software. These calls are, in turn, passed to a NWREDIR.VXD driver, which is the Windows 95 handler for the NetWare Core Protocol calls.

The end result is that Windows 95 does a really good job of supporting applications that were designed to run on Windows 95 yet talk to Novell NetWare servers. The one exception to that run is server management utilities designed to manage and configure the NetWare servers themselves. Although Microsoft Client for NetWare supports really good interfaces to the older NetWare Bindery-based servers, when the Novell Windows-based utilities used for managing NDS are run onto the Microsoft Client for Net-Ware drivers, real problems being to arise (in our experience).

MULTIPLE PROVIDER ROUTER (MPR)   The Multiple Provider Router supports all the Windows 95 network operations. The MPR handles all the 32-bit WinNet API calls and routes the requests to the right service provider depending on the function requested. The files that provide MPR capabilities are 32-bit DLLs.

SERVICE PROVIDER INTERFACE (SPI)   Network platform functionality is provided by each network provider. Each of them uses the service provider interface. Login/Logout, driver mapping, and printer redirection operations are provided by the *Service Provider Interface* (SPI). The only WOSA component to call on the SPI network provider is the MRP.

IFS MANAGER   Windows 95 supports what is called an *Installable File System* (IFS). The IFS Manager is responsible for routing requests to the specific network file system driver. Therefore, each network platform must have its own unique network provider and file system driver. The benefit here is that it allows Windows 95 to talk to different network server platforms by supporting multiple redirectors. While accessing the remote servers file system, you can expect better access reliability and improved file system performance due to the fact that IFS caches incoming requests. It does so by caching the client side of the network redirector requests. The files that provide IFS Manager capabilities are 32-bit VxDs.

NETWORK TRANSPORT   As is highlighted in Figure 4-26, which shows Windows 95 network architecture, Windows 95 supports several transport protocols to carry the upper layer service requests around on the network. (For a detailed comparison of the pros and cons of the various transport protocols, refer to Chapter 3.) The main three transport protocols are NetBEUI, IPX/SPX, and TCP/IP. The Network file system drivers use the network transports to send and receive data from the network. The transport protocols can also be used by applications that are programmed to use transport-independent programming interfaces like NetBIOS and Windows Sockets. The files associated with network transport are 32-bit VxDs.

NETWORK DRIVER INTERFACE SPECIFICATION (NDIS 3) Originally designed by 3COM and Microsoft, the Windows 95 version of NDIS is a 32-bit, vendor-independent specification for interfacing between a network device driver and a network transport protocol. This version of NDIS, which is supported by several Network Interface Card vendors, also includes support for Plug and Play. Plug-and-Play capability is an important feature because it allows you to dynamically load and unload the drivers themselves. As was the case with the DOS/Windows 3.x combination, 16-bit ODI drivers are also supported by interfacing them with the NDIS drivers. The ODI driver interfaces with NDIS through a "shim" called ODIHLP.EXE, which is loaded before the IPXODI.EXE driver is. Older NDIS 2 drivers are also supported; however, they interface directly with NDIS without the requirement of a "shim."

A GOOD FIT?   The reason it works well is because Microsoft designed the operating system and, thus, can probably design a better networking transport to run on it. And although it runs very smoothly on the client, the story changes when the client starts talking to the server. The problems particularly start to arise when communicating with Novell's newer network operating system versions like NetWare 4.11 and IntranetWare.

But as you may appreciate, the people who designed the Novell NetWare operating system also know a thing or two about how a client can best communicate with its server to get the most out of it. So, although Microsoft has some level of advantage when designing the client drivers for the Windows 95 operating system, certainly Novell has an equally great advantage when designing how the client communicates with the server and the utilities it uses to do so. You wouldn't use a Novell client driver to talk to a Microsoft Windows NT server unless it did a better job, would you?

In the following sections of this chapter, we will investigate how to configure Windows 95 to support integration with both NetWare and Windows NT server operating systems. Initially, we will configure Windows 95 to use its native Windows NT and NetWare client connection software. Then we will keep the Windows NT client connection software but replace the Microsoft version of the NetWare client drivers with Novell's Client 32 for Windows 95. Along the way, we will explore the advantages and disadvantages of each method—information that will hopefully allow you to draw your own conclusions.

AN OVERVIEW OF THE WINDOWS 95 LOGON PROCESS   Windows 95 does not have a local user database. Therefore, you might ask why it prompts you for a user name and password when it starts up. (See Figure 4-27.) From the outset, it was envisioned that Windows 95 should function as an integrated networking client. During network access in a basic workgroup configuration of WFWG or Windows 95, user names are not really required because the form of network resource access they use is based on Share Level Access. In Share Level Access, only a password is required to access a network resource. Two levels of access are Read Only and Full. Each level can have a separate password associated with it. Figure 4-28 shows how to set up Share Level Access on a folder in Windows 95 from the Windows Explorer.

So if Windows 95 supports Share Level Access, why the need to log on first? Well, we don't need to! We could simply bypass the logon altogether. Then when we go out over the network to access resources on other share level servers (that is, other Windows 95 or WFWG computers in your

Figure 4-27
Logging on to
Windows 95.
(Source: Microsoft
Corporation)

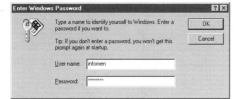

Figure 4-28
Configuring Win-
dows 95 Share Level
Access on a folder.
(Source: Microsoft
Corporation)

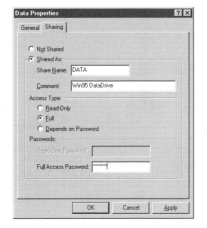

workgroup), we can simply type the password at the time of access. Now notice we said "other share level servers."

Alternatively, we can also configure Windows 95 at least to provide some level of centralized user level access to its shared resources by specifying that users and groups who have access to each shared resource be authenticated against a central server database. This central server database can be either a NetWare or Windows NT server. Although the default level of access for Windows 95 is Share Level Access, this feature can be configured in the Access Control tab of the Control Panel's Network program icon. Figure 4-29 highlights where this is done.

LOGON AUTHENTICATION Both Windows NT and NetWare server have user databases. Both Windows NT and NetWare server access is based on User Level Access security. With WFWG, you usually log on to the two server platforms from DOS before we start the WFWG program. However, with Windows 95, you do not go into DOS first and therefore must provide the servers with a user identifier at the time of access. The two forms of logon are logging on at the local workstation and then attaching to the server by presenting a local user name and password, or

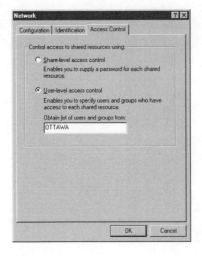

Figure 4-29
Configuring Access
Control in the Con-
trol Panel's Network
program icon.
(Source: Microsoft
Corporation)

logging on to the server itself using a centrally stored user name and password at the server. In either instance, the server from which you are
requesting services can identify you. Windows 95 supports both of the
preceding methods using the first one by default until you configure it to
use server-based user names to authenticate initial local access to the
workstation.

Whether you are using a central server to authenticate your logon,
Windows 95 will take the user name and password you specify and cache
(save) it on the local hard drive in a hidden file. (Yes, some people have
even developed a program that will allow you to crack the hidden file and
see the user names and passwords!) The user name and password are
then used for a "network logon" whenever you try to access a User Level
Access network resource. So rather than having to retype a user name
and password every time you try to access a User Level Access network
resource located on a Windows NT or NetWare server, Windows 95 caches
the one you type and then uses it by default for your network resource
access.

We will look at configuring Windows 95 to use either a Windows NT
or NetWare server for logon authentication in the following sections.
However, one of the main themes that arises here is that to provide a
user sitting at a Windows 95 workstation with ease of access to both network operating system platforms, then we are going to have to ensure
that the user's account and password are duplicated on all the User Level
Access servers that this user will attempt to access. If not done, the user
will continually be prompted for a user name and password at each access attempt.

COMMUNICATING WITH WINDOWS NT IS EASY For the most part, configuring Windows 95 to communicate with Windows NT Server is fairly straightforward. In fact, the services themselves are installed during the initial installation process of Windows 95. Windows 95 is Microsoft network-ready you might say. Windows 95 can autodetect your Network Interface Card and subsequently install the Client for Microsoft Networks. This client software allows you to basically support any number of Microsoft network connections to computers that are supporting NetBIOS/SMB-compatible services (that is, WFWG, Windows 95, Windows NT). However, our particular concern is with Windows NT client connectivity, so we will concentrate on this area.

In the Windows 95 Control Panel, you can configure the Client for Microsoft Networks through the Network icon program. In fact, that is the place where we will be doing pretty much all our network configuration work over the next few pages as we configure both Microsoft and NetWare protocols and services. Figure 4-30 represents the default configuration for our Windows 95 Workstation after installation. By selecting the Client for Microsoft Networks and then the Properties button, we can configure Windows 95 to look to the Windows NT Domain Controller for initial logon authentication or validation. We could also choose to have Windows 95 validate the user name and password at a NetWare server.

After this is done, the user will need to provide a valid Windows NT Domain user name and password to log on to the Windows 95 computer. Now, in reality, the default Windows 95 configuration would simply allow the user to bypass the logon screen altogether by simply pressing the Escape key or by clicking on the Logon screen cancel button. However, this minor security hole can be plugged by implementing a policy that will

Figure 4-30
Windows 95 Control Panel and Network applet. (Source: Microsoft Corporation)

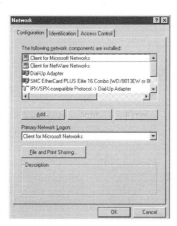

force the user to provide a valid user name and password; otherwise, the system will not allow the user to proceed beyond the logon screen. (For more information on implementing policies on Windows 95, see the documentation as it is actually quite good on this subject.) Additionally, you can configure Windows 95 to perform a fast logon by not reestablishing any of the previously used network connections from the last logon session. However, if you don't want to run a login script (simple batch file), you can have Windows 95 remember all your previous network connections in your User Profile and reestablish them at the time of logon. Figure 4-31 highlights how this can be done.

More often than not, when you save your configuration in the Control Panel's Network program, you will be asked to restart your system. You should always do so to ensure that the recent changes take effect. When you reboot, Windows 95 will provide you with a Logon dialog box similar to the standard one, but now it has an additional entry for the Domain Name information. This domain is the one you entered in the Client for Microsoft Network's Properties form. When you type your user name and password, Windows 95 will attempt to establish a connection to one of the Windows NT Domain Controller servers for the OTTAWA domain. It will do so instead of looking at the locally cached user name and password file. If successful, Windows 95 will log you on to the domain and allow you to continue to access the Windows 95 workstation. If not, you will be given another opportunity to reenter your user name and password. (See Figure 4-32.) If the system has not been configured with a policy to force server validation of user accounts, then you could simply cancel the logon request and continue to access the workstation. However, you will not be able to access any Windows NT server resources.

Figure 4-31
Changing the Client for Microsoft Network's properties. (Source: Microsoft Corporation)

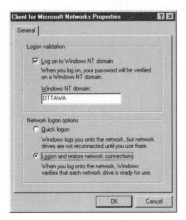

Figure 4-32
Logging onto the
Windows NT Domain
from Windows 95.
(Source: Microsoft
Corporation)

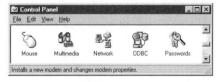

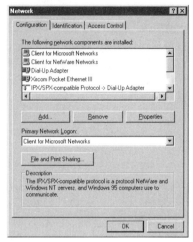

Figure 4-33
Accessing the Win-
dows NT NETLO-
GON share during
logon. (Source:
Microsoft
Corporation)

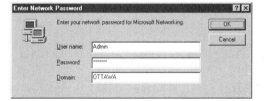

Now that we have configured Windows 95 to perform logon validation
from the Windows NT Domain (OTTAWA), we are attaching to one of the
OTTAWA Windows NT Domain Controllers. The Windows NT Domain
Controllers provide a special share called NETLOGON, which is the file
system share to which all clients initially connect. The NETLOGON share
is actually the \%SYSTEMROOT%\SYSTEM32\REPL\IMPORT\
SCRIPTS directory on the NT server in question. (Note: %SYSTEM-
ROOT% is a variable that tells the system the directory from which Windows NT is running; to find out which directory this is, start an MS-DOS
Command Prompt window and run the **SET** command.) Figure 4-33 shows
that we have connected to this share.

PROCESSING THE WINDOWS NT LOGON SCRIPT The NETLO-GON share has several special purposes. The main purpose is to provide a directory into which we can place logon scripts for users. A logon script is simply a batch file (for DOS/Windows clients) or a command file (for OS/2 clients). In a Microsoft Windows NT Domain network, one central Primary Domain Controller is responsible for maintaining the original copy of the user database. This database is then copied to other Windows NT servers that act as Backup Domain Controllers. The Backup Domain Controllers provide a way for offloading logon authentication from the Primary Domain Controller, especially over wide area network links. Although the original user database is replicated or synchronized from the Primary Domain Controller out to the Backup Domain Controllers, the user logon scripts are not. So the second important role the NETLOGON share plays is to act as a receiver for the Backup Domain Controllers. The %SYSTEMROOT%\SYSTEM32\REPL\EXPORT\SCRIPTS directory on the Primary Domain Controller is used by the network administrator to place original copies of the users' logon scripts. The scripts are then copied to the Backup Domain Controllers where they are made available to Windows NT Domain clients. Figure 4-34 highlights this process.

You can tell the user is connected to the Windows NT server's NETL-OGON share by looking at the Control Panel's Server Manager program

Figure 4-34
Windows 95 Client connecting to the Windows NT Server's NETLOGON Share for logon script processing. (Courtesy of WWW. NETWORKOLOGIST. COM)

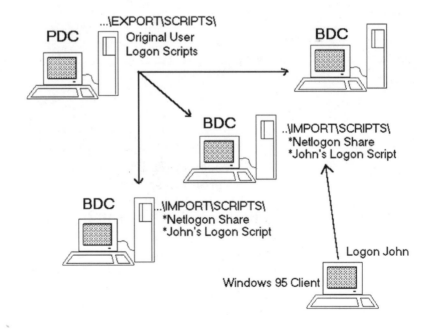

icon on the Windows NT server. This program will highlight which users are currently connected to the server. The connection to the NETLOGON share does not require a local drive letter at the client workstation because it is done through a network API built into the logon/connection process.

Although the process of getting the logon script is a bit different from that of the DOS/Windows client as it is done from within Windows, the end result is still the same. The logon script can be used to connect to additional network server-based resources. Additionally, logon scripts can be used to run a virus scanner, send the Message of the Day, or even distribute software down to the client for remote updating.

The user's Windows NT Domain account is configured with the User Manager for Domains. Here you can configure the user to have a logon script processed at the time of logon. The User Manager for Domains can be run from the Windows NT server itself, or a Windows 95 version of the User Manager for Domains can be loaded down at the client. After you are in User Manager for Domains, click on the Profile button. Type the name of the login script file in the Login Script Name dialog box. (See Figure 4-35.)

Note that you need to type only the name of the logon file, not the path to the file itself. You do so because, by default, Windows NT will be looking into the \%SYSTEMROOT%\SYSTEM32\REPL\IMPORT\ SCRIPTS\ directory of the Domain Controller server that authenticates the user's logon. However, be forewarned that after typing the name of the user's logon script, you still need to create the script itself. To do so, use the Notepad program and create your logon script. Then save it in the \%SYSTEMROOT%\SYSTEM32\REPL\IMPORT\SCRIPTS\ directory.

Figure 4-35

Configuring the Windows 95 user's logon script on the Windows NT Domain server and saving it in the \%SYSTEMROOT%\ SYSTEM32\REPL\I MPORT\SCRIPTS directory. (Source: Microsoft Corporation)

Now, the next time you log on to the Windows NT Domain server, your logon script will be processed. But remember, if you have a large network with many Backup Domain Controllers, you will need to ensure that the Primary Domain Controller is replicating the logon scripts to the Backup Domain Controllers. For the sake of accuracy, you should know that the original logon scripts could be placed on any Windows NT server and then replicated to the appropriate Domain Controllers. However, most people place them on the Primary Domain Controller and then replicate them from there. Although the entire process is beyond the scope of this book, a brief overview of configuring the replication between Domain Controllers is as follows:

1. Create a Windows NT Domain account, and give it the Right to Log On As A Service (in the User Manager for Domains Policy - User Rights area).

2. Place all of your Domain users' logon scripts in the \%SYSTEM-ROOT%\SYSTEM32\REPL\EXPORT\SCRIPTS directory.

3. Configure the Primary Domain Controller Directory Replication service to export files from the \%SYSTEMROOT%\SYS-TEM32\EXPORT\SCRIPTS directory (which is the default). Configure the Directory Replication service through the Control Panel's Server Manager program icon to start up automatically. Additionally, configure the Directory Replication service on the Primary Domain Controller to import files and use the default of \%SYSTEMROOT%\SYSTEM32\REPL\IMPORT\SCRIPTS. This way, you have to place only the original logon script files in the ...\EXPORT\SCRIPTS directory, and they will automatically be placed by the Directory Replication service into the ...\IMPORT\ SCRIPTS directory for your users to access through the NETLOGON share.

4. Configure the Backup Domain Controllers to import files only. Use the same procedure as described for the Primary Domain Controllers in step 3.

5. Configure the Backup Domain Controllers Directory Replication service to start up automatically as well.

Although the preceding instruction summary should work fine, refer to your Windows NT Server documentation for a more detailed explanation of the process. Figure 4-36 shows a Windows 95 user logged on to the Windows NT Domain server. The LOGON.BAT logon script is processed, and an important message is displayed.

Figure 4-36
Processing the Windows NT Domain logon script on the Windows 95 client. (Source: Microsoft Corporation)

Profiles and Policies

KEEPING A LOW PROFILE   In addition to the logon script, the next most important item the users may want is to have *profiles*. A User Profile is used to save a user's preferred desktop settings. Desktop settings include the screen colors, desktop appearance (Rainy Day, Pumpkin, and so on), screen saver mode, wallpaper, and background settings. Alternatively, network administrators may decide to enforce a mandatory profile that everyone is forced to use to maintain some level of a corporate standard. If profile settings are not made in the users' Windows NT Domain User Account Profile Settings dialog box, then the users will use the default settings of the local Windows 95 workstations at which they are logged on. From the default, personal profiles will be made for those users. However, the profiles will be available only if the users are logged on locally at that machine.

To provide the users with *roaming profiles*, the network administrator can configure the Windows NT Domain user account profile settings to save the users' profiles on a network server somewhere on the network. First, though, you will need to configure Windows 95 to allow the users to customize their preferences and desktop settings. This is done through the Passwords program icon in the Windows 95 Control Panel. This process is called *enabling User Profiles* in the Microsoft Windows 95 Resource Kit. Once profiles are enabled, you can also set Profile User Settings. These options allow you to control what should be included as part of users' profiles. After these settings have been configured, you will be required to restart the Windows 95 computer. In addition to enabling User Profiles on Windows 95, you will also need to ensure that the Client for

Microsoft Networks is selected as the Primary Network Logon Client. This is done through the Control Panel's Network program icon on the Windows 95 client. Figure 4-37 highlights how the User Profiles can be enabled in the Passwords Properties dialog box.

Now we're ready for the Windows NT side of the equation. On the Windows NT Server, you will need to create a USERS directory, which is, in turn, shared as a network resource. Each user will have a personal sub-directory under the USERS directory. You can create the USERS directory (or folder in Windows NT 4.0) in the File Manager (or Windows Explorer) and share it from there.

Then, in the User Manager for Domains, pick the user account that will be used on the Windows 95 workstation, and change the Profile information. In the User Environment Profile, you can configure the user's Home Directory to point to the Windows NT Server USERS shared directory. In the Home Directory dialog box, configure the settings to connect to a drive letter (the default is Z:). The drive letter should point to the Windows NT Server USERS share using the UNC name. For example, in Figure 4-38, the UNC name is \\NTS351\USERS\ARNOLD.

Then, when users log on to the Windows 95 workstation using the Windows NT Domain user account, they will begin to save their settings to the Windows NT server specified in their user account profile information. A series of subdirectories will then be created under the users' home directories on the Windows NT server. The main profile file is called USER.DAT. Now, the users can log on at other Profile Enabled workstations through the network and still receive their own desktop settings.

Figure 4-37
Configuring Windows 95 to provide users with profile customization. (Source: Microsoft Corporation)

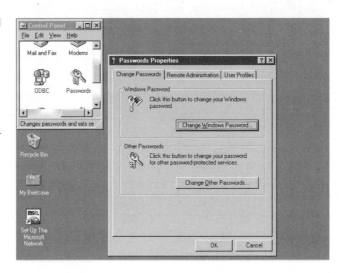

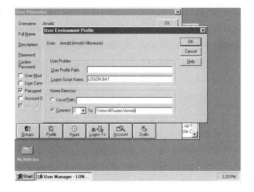

Figure 4-38

Configuring the User Environment Profile to save the Windows 95 User Profile on the Windows NT server. (Source: Microsoft Corporation)

Figure 4-39

Windows 95 User Profile saved on the Windows NT server. (Source: Microsoft Corporation)

They are usually called *roaming profiles*. Figure 4-39 displays the subdirectories and USER.DAT file that is saved on the Windows NT server. These subdirectories and the USER.DAT file contain a user's personal Windows 95 desktop settings.

MANDATORY PROFILES The process of providing mandatory profiles on your network is very simple. Log on as a user, and create the desktop look and feel that is required for your company. Set the desktop appearance and colors. Place the corporate logo in the background. Make all the changes that are required to the desktop. Then log off as that user. Go to the Windows NT server where the profile was saved, and rename the USER.DAT file to USER.MAN. Then distribute the USER.MAN file to all users' personal directories that are required to have mandatory profiles.

A MATTER OF POLICY: SYSTEM POLICIES Policies could be considered a step up from profiles in that they enable you to set more restrictions than you can with a User Profile. For example, you can restrict access to the Control Panel options, restrict what users can do from the desktop, hide the Network Neighborhood, customize parts of the desktop, and even configure network settings. Policies are quite a bit more challenging to configure and implement, and they are certainly beyond the scope of this book. However, suffice it to say that they can be configured and centrally stored on the Windows NT server. Then they can be applied uniquely and individually to users when they log on at Windows 95 workstations.

After a policy has been created, the Windows 95 workstation can be configured for automatic downloading of the system policies. The local Windows 95 workstation Registry is edited through the Policy Editor to download a policy file from the network. The policy file is created and saved on the Windows NT Domain Controller into the directory that is shared out as NETLOGON (\%SYSTEMROOT%\SYSTEM32\REPL\IMPORT\SCRIPTS) as CONFIG.POL. When the users log on to the Windows 95 workstation, the local Registry entry kicks in and downloads the policy file from the network. The policy file is dynamically applied to the local Registry, and changes are enforced before the user logon process continues. For more detailed information on policies, refer to the Windows 95 Resource Kit. However, let us add a word of caution. After you start to use policy files, you should always use policy files to make subsequent changes or to reverse local Registry settings previously made through the Registry itself. Performing this process any other way tends to be difficult to reverse.

COMMUNICATING WITH NETWARE: TWO OPTIONS FOR WINDOWS 95 After all these pages on Windows 95 and Windows NT, you were probably wondering when Novell NetWare came into the picture. Well, that time is now. Windows 95 can be configured to communicate with NetWare 3.x and 4.x servers. Both Microsoft and Novell provide client software for Windows 95. Windows 95 comes with Microsoft provided native NetWare client support using 32-bit drivers. It is fast, efficient, easy to install, and works well. For normal access to a NetWare 3.x server, the Microsoft NetWare client drivers will probably do everything you need and more. However, NetWare 4.x integration by Windows 95 using Microsoft's client drivers has not been as good. The main reason is NDS support. Novell's NDS is a much more complicated directory service than the old NetWare 3.x Bindery, which has been around for almost a decade now. In the following section of this chapter, we will look first at the Microsoft client and then at the Novell client driver software. In the end, we hope to provide you with enough information so that you can make your own decision based on your particular circumstances.

If there are two potential clients, which one do you choose? As we explained previously, the answer really depends on how you are planning to access the NetWare servers from the Windows 95 clients. If you plan only for straightforward file and printer access, then we suggest that the Microsoft client is more than adequate, easy to install, and provides seamless access. If, however, you are planning to manage your NetWare server from a Windows 95 client, then further consideration needs to be given. The Microsoft client works well with NetWare 3.x Bindery-based servers. However, this is not the case when working with Novell Directory Services.

The main reason is that to develop a client redirector for NetWare, Microsoft had to emulate everything that the NetWare client redirector does. Given that at the time of the initial development of Windows 95, NetWare 3.x was still the most popular network operating system platform, the choice to provide tight integration with NetWare 3.x servers was obvious. So, Microsoft developed its client redirector (service provider) software on the NETBX and VLM network communication solutions with Bindery-based access as the focus. So if you are managing NetWare 3.x servers from Windows 95, then the Microsoft Client for NetWare Networks will work reasonably well. All the commands such as SYSCON.EXE for user management and PCONSOLE.EXE for print server, printer, and print queue management work well because they are based on the MS-DOS NetWare API call sets.

But, as you can appreciate, things get more complicated when you try to get Windows 95 to talk to a NetWare 4.x server. Here Novell has a definite advantage over Microsoft because Novell developed NDS and knows best how to get a client to talk to it. Novell has developed the tools and administrative utilities to manage NetWare 4.x network server from Windows 95. Not surprisingly, the NetWare 4.x utilities work only on top of its own client redirector software. And although there are certainly many technical reasons for this result, it is nonetheless a fact, and you will need to install Novell's Client 32 drivers if you want to manage NetWare 4.x network servers from Windows 95. Additionally, as we will review, many nice features of Novell's Client 32 for Windows 95 may lead you to implement it as your preferred NetWare server client software.

From a practical standpoint, the ultimate objective of every network administrator is to keep network, workstation, and server management as simple as possible. Running software drivers from two different vendors on the same client workstation is wrought with the potential for problems. Therefore, many of our clients weigh the pros and cons within their own network environment before making any hasty moves.

However, a fair characterization of many of the installations we have worked on is that the Microsoft Client for NetWare works fine in a NetWare 3.x server environment, and therefore, moving to a Novell version of the client driver is not necessary. However, for migrating to or already supporting a NetWare 4.x server environment, most people have chosen to implement Novell's Client 32 for Windows 95 as the NetWare client redirector software.

PICKING THE RIGHT CLIENT REDIRECTOR TO MEET YOUR NEEDS   To assist you in making the best choice in client redirector software combination for your network environment, you should perform a certain number of tests. You can take several approaches:

- Pick a suite of applications and services that are accessed over the network and use them for your benchmark.
- Create a standard set of exercises or tests to be performed on the various client configurations you are about to install including the following:

  Mapping local drive letters

  Capturing local printer ports

  Accessing files from the NetWare server

  Submitting print jobs

  Using applications that are NetWare-aware so that you can test support for the MS-DOS and NetWare API calls

  Using network performance utilities for benchmarking pure file transfers over the network

  Running login scripts

- Install each one of the potential Windows 95 NetWare clients and test access to your suite of applications.
- Perform NetWare server administration from the Windows 95 client and test that you can do the following:

  Create and manage new user and group accounts (Bindery and NDS-based)

  Create and manage printer services

  Run NetWare command-line utilities such as BINDFIX and BINDREST

- Create default User Profiles and/or system policies if you plan to use them.

■ After you select your client configuration, roll out the implementation of the redirector in question with any special settings you have configured to do the following:

Decide on local manual installation or automatic installation from the network

Test any subsequent network installation of the client redirector software before final roll out

■ Begin the roll out to the client workstations.

While you're performing the testing, be on the lookout for any Terminate and Stay Resident programs that may be required for application access over the network. You may need to ensure that they are installed in the workstation's AUTOEXEC.BAT, CONFIG.SYS, or Windows 95's WINSTART.BAT before starting Windows 95. Finally, be on the lookout for certain existing workstation NetWare-originated TSRs that are not compatible with Microsoft's Client for NetWare.

NETWARE COMMUNICATIONS THE MICROSOFT WAY When initially installed, Windows 95 will try to detect the underlying physical network connections (Ethernet, Token Ring, FDDI, and so on) and install the appropriate network adapter driver. It will also listen to the traffic on the network and then automatically install the appropriate network client. The Client for Microsoft Networks will be installed by default. However, if a Novell NetWare server is detected on the network, then the Microsoft Client for NetWare Networks will also automatically be installed. The Microsoft Client for NetWare provides many benefits for Windows 95 workstations integrated with NetWare networks. First and foremost, it is installed without much of a fuss. Configuring it takes more time, however, if you are to set it up to connect to your favorite server and run your NetWare user login scripts. (See Figure 4-40.)

THE MICROSOFT CLIENT FOR NETWARE Of course, if you are installing Windows 95 on a NetWare network, Microsoft recommends that you use its NetWare client software—and with good reason. Microsoft wrote the operating system. Therefore, the client software it designed uses all the best features of the Windows 95 internal operating system architecture. Microsoft's client, therefore, delivers fast, 32-bit high-performance

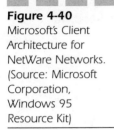

Figure 4-40
Microsoft's Client
Architecture for
NetWare Networks.
(Source: Microsoft
Corporation,
Windows 95
Resource Kit)

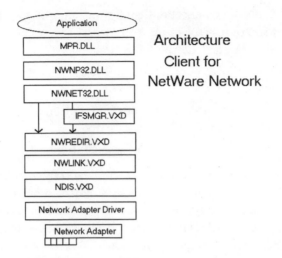

Architecture
Client for
NetWare Network

networking protocol implementations. It takes advantage of Windows 95's multitasking capabilities and ensures better reliability by running the client driver software in protected mode.

Microsoft's client also takes advantage of the operating system's memory architecture and uses no conventional memory. The end result is that the Microsoft Client for NetWare Networks is very stable and delivers between 50 to 200 percent faster network file transfers (according to Microsoft) than the standard DOS/Windows 3.x and NetWare VLM client combination.

The Microsoft Client for NetWare Networks also supports full NetWare login script capability with NetWare 2.15, 3.x, and 4.x servers. The NetWare 2.15 and 3.x servers are accessed via their Bindery, whereas the NetWare 4.x servers are accessed via Bindery emulation in NDS. A login script processor is supplied with Windows 95 to accomplish this function.

On the protocol level, Microsoft's client supports Packet Burst Protocol and Large Internet Packet. Packet Burst Protocol, which is a feature supported by the NetWare Core Protocol, makes network communications more efficient by resending only the packages of information that require it and not everything after that point. This feature is called a *sliding window* implementation of protocol communications. Large Internet Packet (LIP) support ensures that packets do not get broken up into smaller components when they go through an IPX router. IPX routers used to break down a large packet carried inside an Ethernet frame into smaller ones in case any Arcnet-supported Network Interface Cards were on the network. Additionally, LIP is used by the client and server to negotiate the largest potential packet than can be transferred over the network. This allows for the greatest, most efficient use of the network.

The Microsoft Client for NetWare Networks also supports all "documented" MS-DOS and NetWare API calls. This capability allows you to run NetWare-aware applications on the Windows 95 client without purchasing new versions of the application in question.

In general, the Microsoft Client for NetWare also supports all the many networking enhancements that the Microsoft Client for Networks supports, including enhanced client-side caching of network communications, remote access to NetWare networks, roaming User Profiles, and long file name support on the local workstation, Windows NT servers running File and Print Services for NetWare, and NetWare 3.x and 4.x volumes configured to support the OS/2 name space.

Finally, if not most amazingly, Windows 95 can be configured to emulate a NetWare 3.x server! And it really works. However, it can also create a lot of havoc in an existing network if configured haphazardly without regard for current NetWare clients (more details on this issue later). Windows 95 can thus be configured to provide File and Print Sharing for NetWare network clients. After it is configured, it can share its local file system, including CD-ROM drives, to NetWare-only clients (client workstations that are running only the NetWare client driver software—Microsoft's or Novell's).

IMPLEMENTING THE MICROSOFT CLIENT FOR NETWARE NETWORKS ON WINDOWS 95 So you have made the decision to use Microsoft's Client for NetWare Networks on your Windows 95 workstations to provide NetWare server access to your users. You have already configured Windows 95 to access Windows NT Domain servers, so that part is taken care of. What now? Well, if the NetWare servers were on the network at the time of installation, then Windows 95 will most likely have detected them and performed an installation for you. If you need to install the Microsoft Client for NetWare Networks, the process is fairly straightforward. Let's look at that now. The following steps provide a summary overview of the process for adding the Microsoft Client for NetWare Networks after Windows 95 has already been installed:

1. Select the Network program icon for the Control Panel, and verify which networking components are installed already.

2. If the NetWare NETBX or VLM drivers are already installed, they can be removed by selecting the NetWare Workstation Shell client from the list of installed components and clicking on the Remove button.

3. Click on the Add button to install in the Select Network Components dialog box. (See Figure 4-41.)

4. Select Microsoft from the Manufacturers list, and then click on the Client for NetWare Networks. (See Figure 4-42.)

5. Select the OK button.

When you are prompted, restart your computer workstation. You must restart the system for the new configuration to take effect. The internal configuration of the Microsoft Client for NetWare is fairly transparent in that it makes the appropriate Registry entries. In particular, Windows 95 will make a `lastdrive=32` entry in the Registry to allow for additional drive entries in the drive table. Although both Microsoft and Novell clients use Z as the last drive letter, NetWare uses six additional drive settings that are used by NetWare-aware applications only. (See Figure 4-43.)

Figure 4-41

Installing the Microsoft Client for NetWare Networks. (Source: Microsoft Corporation)

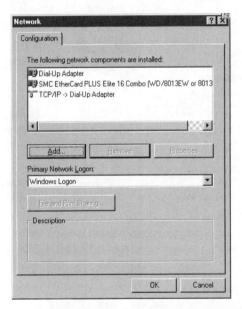

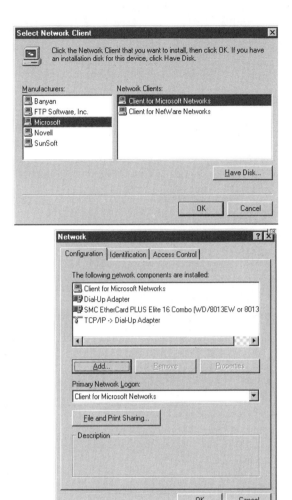

Figure 4-42
Selecting the
Microsoft Client for
NetWare Networks.
(Source: Microsoft
Corporation)

**MICROSOFT CLIENT FOR NETWARE NETWORKS CONFIGU-
RATION** Configuring the Microsoft Client for NetWare Networks is the
point at which the work comes in. Microsoft's Client for NetWare Networks redirector can work with Microsoft's 32-bit protected mode network
adapter driver or with Novell's ODI network adapter drivers. We would
suggest that if you are using Microsoft's client redirector, then you should
also use its 32-bit protected mode network adapter driver because you will
receive many performance benefits. Using this adapter makes sense given
the tighter integration between the two, seeing that they are both made
by Microsoft.

You can change which network adapter drivers the Microsoft Client for
NetWare Networks will use by opening the Properties of the Network

Figure 4-43
Registry entries made for the Microsoft Client for NetWare Networks. (Source: Microsoft Corporation)

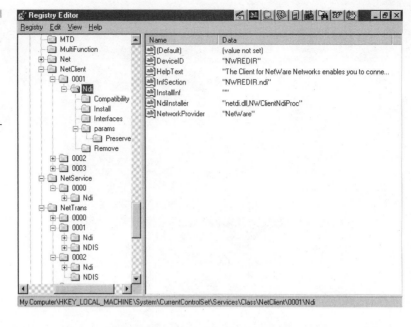

Figure 4-44
Configuring which network adapter driver type the Microsoft Client for NetWare Networks will use. (Source: Microsoft Corporation)

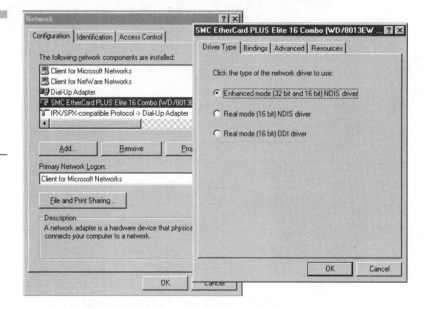

Adapter using the Network program icon. The Network program icon is within the Control Panel options. Select the Driver Type tab and then change to the Enhanced Mode for the 32-bit and 16-bit NDIS Driver selection. Figure 4-44 shows how you can perform this process.

You will notice that this is also the place where you can configure the Microsoft Client for NetWare Networks to use the Real Mode 16-bit NDIS driver or the Real Mode 16-bit ODI driver. You might use the 16-bit NDIS or ODI drivers because you have an old Network Interface Card that does not have newer 32-bit versions of the drivers for it; in fact, that might be the only reason. If you are doing some serious networking in your office, you will certainly want to replace these Network Interface Cards with newer, more supported models. Furthermore, the 16-bit ODI drivers have some limitations in that you are required to use conventional memory on the workstation, workstation performance will not be as good, the Plug-and-Play capability is not supported, and you cannot support a shared network installation of Windows 95 (many clients running the same Windows 95 operating software from the network server as is done with diskless workstations). After you finish selecting the Enhanced Mode NDIS adapter drivers, you will need to restart your Windows 95 workstation for the changes to take effect.

CONFIGURING MICROSOFT'S CLIENT FOR NETWARE AS THE PRIMARY NETWORK LOGON   Finally, you need to ensure that by using the Networks program icon of the Control Panel, you select Client for NetWare servers as the Primary Network Logon server. If you do not, then Windows 95 will try to log you on to a Windows NT Domain server, and not a NetWare server. People often forget to configure this feature and wonder why they are able to connect to the NetWare server but their NetWare login scripts are not running.

To configure this feature, simply go to the Control Panel's Network program icon, and then click on the Primary Network Logon dialog box. From there, you can select the Client for NetWare Networks. The Primary Network Logon is used to validate your user name and password, process login scripts from the selected client server, and perform additional start-up tasks as may be configured by the network administrator. Additionally, you will need to configure the Client for NetWare Networks Properties to point to the user's preferred NetWare server and enable the processing of the NetWare login scripts. Figure 4-45 details where this change can be made.

WE'RE CONNECTED! NOW WHAT?   After the preceding process has been completed, you can now log in to your NetWare Bindery-based server (NetWare 3.x Bindery or NetWare 4.x with Bindery Emulation). All the normal network functions can then be performed. However, as was done earlier with Windows 95 on a Windows NT Domain, you may want to have your Windows 95 Profiles stored centrally on the NetWare server so that

Figure 4-45
Configuring the
Microsoft Client for
NetWare Networks
as the Primary Net-
work Logon Server.
(Source: Microsoft
Corporation)

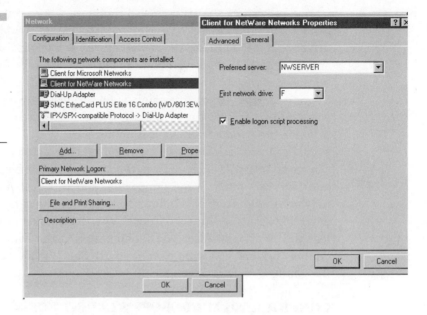

you can have your desktop follow you as you move to other Windows 95
workstations on the network.

**MAINTAINING WINDOWS 95 PROFILES ON THE NETWARE
SERVER** The process of maintaining Windows 95 profiles on the Net-
Ware Server is much the same as was described earlier in the Windows 95
section. However, instead of using the Windows NT Domain user's Home
Directory as defined in the User's Profile configuration screen to store the
Windows 95 desktop profile information, NetWare uses the MAIL subdirectory that is created for each NetWare user. When the user account is
created, each user is given a unique User ID (for example, 10002). A subdirectory is created in the NWSERVER\VOLUME:MAIL directory with
the user's unique ID as the subdirectory name. It is also in this directory
that the user's NetWare login script is placed. (See Figure 4-46.)

First, you will need to enable the Enable User Profiles option in the
User Profiles tab of the Passwords program icon in the Control Panel (use
the same process described for Windows NT). You should have already selected the Client for NetWare Networks as the Primary Network Logon
server for this workstation. Although you should not have to, you may
want to make sure that the NetWare user account has a valid MAIL directory. You can verify this by locating the user's unique User ID in the
NetWare SYSCON program under User Information and then verify that
the directory exists. Alternatively, you can look at the users' Trustee As-

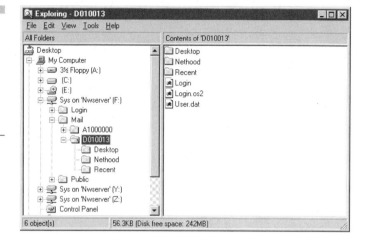

Figure 4-46
The Windows 95
User's Profile stored
on the NetWare
server in the user's
MAIL directory.
(Source: Microsoft
Corporation)

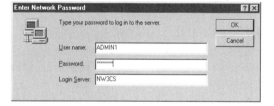

Figure 4-47
Logging on to the
NetWare server
NWSERVER. (Source:
Microsoft
Corporation)

signments in the NetWare SYSCON program wherein they should have a rights assignment to their own mail directory. Note that you do not need to specify where the User Profile file will be saved as you do with Windows NT Domains. The Client for NetWare Networks is automatically preconfigured to figure out the NetWare user's User ID and place it in the appropriate directory.

Upon rebooting, the user will be presented with a familiar logon screen. However, instead of Domain for logon, the user will be directed to the Net-Ware server that was specified as the Preferred Server earlier in the configuration of the Client for NetWare Networks. Note that the user could enter in a different default logon server at this point. This capability is helpful if you are the network administrator and you are moving around to different Windows 95 workstations all the time. Remember, the Client for NetWare Networks from Microsoft supports only Bindery-based Net-Ware servers, so your users need to be pointed to the NetWare server that has their login names and passwords. Figure 4-47 highlights login into a NetWare server from the Windows 95 Network logon screen.

Now the first time users log in to the NetWare server, they will receive a message explaining that the system is processing the NetWare Login Scripts. All the standard NetWare login script commands are supported.

COMMON NETWARE LOGIN SCRIPT COMMANDS   Common NetWare login script commands are as follows:

ATTACH: Connects to a Bindery-based NetWare server

#: Indicates an external program that will execute and return control to the login script

COMSPEC: COMmand SPECifier setting specifies the directory where the DOS command processor should look for the COMMAND.COM file

EXIT: stops the login script execution of the LOGIN utility

FIRE PHASERS: Sounds an electronic space gun (most favorite)

IF...THEN: A conditional statement used to perform actions based on certain conditions

MAP: Maps drives and search drives to network directories (folders) and NDS directory objects

PAUSE: stops the execution of the login script and waits for the user to press any key

SET: Sets DOS and OS/2 environment variables

WRITE: Displays messages on the screen

For more information regarding NetWare login script commands and internal variables that can be used within the login script process, consult the NetWare documentation. Figure 4-48 highlights what Windows 95 users will see when they log in to the NetWare server.

SUPPORTING LONG FILE NAMES ON THE NETWARE SERVER VOLUMES   One major item you need to make sure you configure on the NetWare server side when you are saving User Profiles on the NetWare server is support for the Long Name Space on the SYS: volume where the

Figure 4-48
The NetWare login script is processed. (Source: Microsoft Corporation)

```
■ Login Script Processor for NetWare          _ □ ✕

HELLO WINDOWS 95 USER
THIS IS A NETWARE LOGIN SCRIPT


IMPORTANT MESSAGE FROM THE INTERNET

TRY  WWW.NETWORKOLOGIST.COM   TODAY!

TRY  WWW.ITCOACH.COM   TODAY!

Press any key to continue . . .
```

MAIL directory resides. Windows 95 uses long file names for certain desktop folder files. Depending on the server you have, the following commands will do the trick:

Syntax: `server_prompt: load name_space_name`

Syntax: `server_prompt: add name space NAME_SPACE_NAME to`
           `           volume_name`

For NetWare 3.x, type the following at the server console:

```
NWSERVER: LOAD OS2.NAM
NWSERVER: ADD NAME SPACE OS2 TO SYS:
```

For NetWare 4.x, type the following at the server console:

```
NWSERVER: LOAD LONG.NAM
NWSERVER: ADD NAME SPACE LONG TO SYS:
```

You should verify that your server supports the Long Name Space before you try to log in to the NetWare server from a Windows 95 client; otherwise, you will run into a few problems—namely that the Windows 95 Logon process tries to create LFN files within the desktop folder/directory of the user's unique MAIL subdirectory and can't if the NetWare Volume does not support the Long Name Space. The user will then get an error message. If the Long Name Space is not supported on the NetWare server, the Windows 95 logon process will still create the User Profile folders on the NetWare server, and it will even save the USER.DAT profile file. However, several critical files will be missing from the desktop folder.

Now when the user logs on for the first time, Windows 95 will look at the NetWare server and discover that no Windows 95 User Profile or supporting subdirectories exists. It will create the supporting directories at that time. Then, when the user logs off, the Windows 95 USER.DAT profile file for that user will be saved to the NetWare server.

INTEGRATING NETWARE LOGIN AND WINDOWS NT LOGON SCRIPTS Now the fun starts. You have managed so far to configure your Windows 95 workstation to connect to a Windows NT Domain using the Client for Microsoft Networks. Then you configured the Windows NT Domain account to have both a Logon script and store a User Profile on the Windows NT server. Then you configured the same Windows 95 workstation to support NetWare connectivity through the Client for NetWare Networks. You changed the User Profile configuration information for Windows 95 and told it that you wanted to store your roaming User Profile on the NetWare server. You also configured your NetWare user account to have a login script. The Windows NT and NetWare user name and password are the same on both servers. What happens when you login/logon now?

Well, a very interesting thing happens. Here is the current configuration based on our work so far:

Windows NT Domain Server:

■ A user account exists in the Windows NT Domain.

■ The user account profile information has a logon script specified.

■ The user account profile information has a Home Directory specified and the Home Directory points to the Windows NT Server.

NetWare Server:

■ A duplicate account exists on the NetWare server (in this case, a NetWare 4.11 server with Bindery emulation) with the same user name and password as the one on the Windows NT Domain.

■ The NetWare server SYS volume supports Long Name Space file names.

Windows 95 Client Workstation:

■ This workstation is configured to support Client for Microsoft Networks with a selected NT Domain.

■ This workstation is configured to support Client for NetWare Networks with a preferred server.

■ This workstation is configured to support individual User Profiles.

■ This workstation is configured to use Client for NetWare Networks as the Primary Logon Server for user validation and authentication.

■ This workstation is configured to store the user's User Profile on the NetWare server by virtue of the fact that both "individual User Profiles" and "Primary Logon Server" have been configured.

THE FLOW OF LOGON/LOGIN TO BOTH NOS PLATFORMS The flowchart in Figure 4-49 details the logon process when NetWare validation is used as the Primary Logon Server. Notice that even though the Windows 95 client is configured to go to the NetWare server for User Account validation, it will go to the Windows NT Domain server because the Client for Microsoft is configured. Subsequently, it will log the user onto

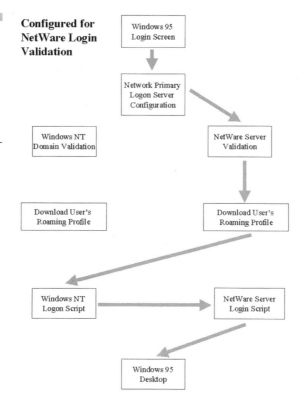

Figure 4-49
Login process when configured for Net-Ware Login Valida-tion. (Courtesy of WWW. NETWORKOLOGIST. COM)

the Domain server and process the user's logon script if it has been configured within the User's Profile information screen.

The reverse is also true in that if we had configured Windows 95 to use the Client for Microsoft Networks as the Primary Logon Server, then it would have gone to the Windows NT Domain Controller for user account validation and authentication first. Second, it would have downloaded the client's User Profile from the Windows NT server and then processed the NT logon script. Finally, before bringing up the user's desktop, it would have attached the user to the NetWare server and processed the user's NetWare login script. The following flowchart details the logon process when Windows NT validation is used as the Primary Logon Server.

Which server platform you use for Windows 95 validation will really depend on your existing network infrastructure. If you have a predominantly NetWare server network operating environment, then you will most likely configure the Client for NetWare as the Primary Logon Server. If you have a predominantly Windows NT Domain server network operating environment and are trying to integrate NetWare servers with your

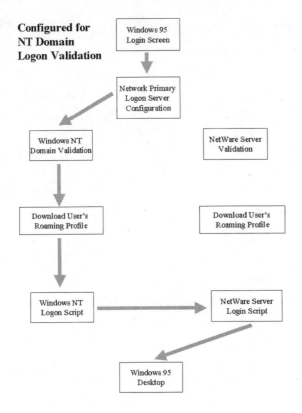

Figure 4-50
Login process when
configured for Win-
dows NT Domain Lo-
gon Validation.
(Courtesy
of WWW.
NETWORKOLOGIST.
COM)

existing Windows 95 client workstations, then you will most likely choose the Client for Microsoft Networks as your Primary Logon Server.

However, in either situation, you now realize (we hope) that you can also have the best of both worlds. In other words, you can have logon/login scripts execute from both server platforms from the one Windows 95 client. This feature is extremely powerful in that it allows you to attach to two initial servers, one from each platform, and then from there branch out to other network resources through the processing of these joint logon/login scripts. After you are connected to each server platform, the logon/login scripts can subsequently attach you to a host of other resources on the network through the various **NET USE** (Microsoft) and **MAP/CAPTURE** (Novell) commands that can be run from within the scripts. And, of course, you can get pretty fancy within the logon/login scripts and have the scripts perform network resource attachments based on group memberships, day of the week, time of the day, and so on. Many network administrators also try to do a lot of the server or network resource attachments from within the Windows 95 User Profiles. Although this approach works reasonably well, we still find that some tasks cannot be done this way, so we must resort to logon/login scripts. (See Figure 4-51.)

Figure 4-51
Multiserver platform access from Windows 95. (Courtesy of WWW. NETWORKOLOGIST. COM)

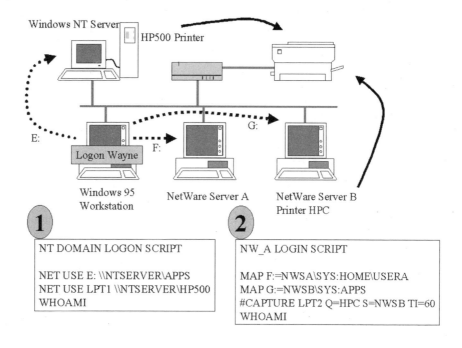

```
NT DOMAIN LOGON SCRIPT

NET USE E: \\NTSERVER\APPS
NET USE LPT1 \\NTSERVER\HP500
WHOAMI
```

```
NW_A LOGIN SCRIPT

MAP F:=NWSA\SYS:HOME\USERA
MAP G:=NWSB\SYS:APPS
#CAPTURE LPT2 Q=HPC S=NWSB TI=60
WHOAMI
```

COMMON PROBLEMS WITH MICROSOFT'S CLIENT FOR NET-WARE NETWORKS Always finding the latest and greatest versions of whatever drivers you are currently using is advisable. In particular, Microsoft recommends that you have the most recent NETWARE.DRV, which should be about 2K in size and no larger.

If no network is available after Windows 95 starts up, you should obviously verify that the Windows 95 Client for NetWare Networks did, in fact, install after you configured it; then you should restart the system because sometimes the configuration change will not take effect. This problem is usually an operator error; after operators finish configuring the Client for NetWare networks, they often click on the X button in the top-right corner of the screen or on the Cancel button—both events result in a cancellation of the configuration changes requested.

If the login scripts don't process, verify that the Enable Login Script check box is checked in the Client for NetWare Networks Properties screen.

If NetWare servers cannot be located on the network, you may have any one of several problems. Before you continue, however, make sure you can access the server over the network from another workstation just to make sure it is indeed up and accessible; this trick isolates the problems to the workstation. These problems can include the incorrect Ethernet or Token Ring Frame type, the fact that you are trying to connect to a NetWare 4.x server that does not have Bindery Emulation turned on and set correctly, or that maybe you have a Network Interface Card conflict with another workstation adapter. To verify the frame format that you are using, look in the IPX Compatible Protocol properties and ensure that the Frame Type is set for Auto (detection).

RESYNCHRONIZING YOUR PASSWORDS If you are continually prompted for passwords, the problem is most likely the result of the fact that your user passwords that are stored individually on separate server platforms have gotten out of sync. It could also be that your Windows 95 workstation is not connecting to the right NetWare server. Ensure that the passwords are synchronized for Windows 95, the NetWare server, and the Windows NT Domain Server. You can do so by using the Control Panel's Passwords program icon. (See Figure 4-52.)

Figure 4-52
Resynchronizing your multiserver passwords. (Source: Microsoft Corporation)

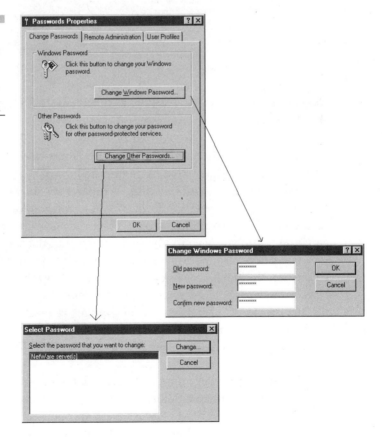

Note that passwords will only be synchronized on the NetWare servers that you are currently attached to, *not* all NetWare servers on which you actually have an account. If access to NetWare servers is denied, then you have a validation and authentication problem. When you select a server to act as the Primary Logon Server for initial Windows 95 logon, the user name and password that you use from that server to initially log on is then used as your validation user name and password for access to other network resources. If it is not in synch with your user identification on the other servers (that is, you have a different user name and password on the other servers), then you will have problems connecting to them.

All is well and good. The preceding scenario is typical for many organizations. It works well and provides the end users with seamless access to both networking platforms. However, what if your network is made up of predominantly NetWare 4.x servers and Windows 95 is simply a client workstation platform within your organization? What if you have a lot of very tightly integrated NetWare applications? What if you would just rather use the NetWare client software instead? Well, let's have a look at that now.

NETWARE COMMUNICATIONS THE NOVELL WAY Windows 95 can be configured to support NetWare client redirector software in essentially three ways, or rather, three NetWare client redirectors can be used to support Windows 95 communications to NetWare servers. No matter how you look at this situation, the first two solutions are the same client redirector software drivers that you would use if you were working with DOS/Windows 3.1 or Windows for Workgroups. In fact, you will require all the Novell-supplied Windows 3.x drivers for the Windows 95 installation. And as was the case with the DOS/Windows and WFWG, you should log in to your NetWare server before starting Windows 95. Therefore, if you are upgrading your current NetWare-connected DOS/Windows or WFWG workstation to Windows 95, you should not have much of a problem.

To set up Windows 95 with the Novell client redirector software drivers, you will need to ensure that the NetWare drivers are all loaded first. Also, upgrading your existing drivers to the latest versions of LSL, IPXODI, NETBX, or VLMs is advisable. Given that the NetWare drivers are loaded before you upgrade or install Windows 95, the Windows 95 setup program will automatically detect the drivers and network configuration. This capability will greatly simplify the installation process. Even still, despite the automatic network client software detection, you will still have a little bit of work to do after the installation is complete.

Note that you can also run Windows 95 with the old version of NetWare client redirector or with Arcnet cards. However, we see no reason that you would want to do either. In fact, we advise against doing so, if at all possible. The old client redirector software for NetWare is often called the *monolithic version*. It can only talk to NetWare Bindery-based servers, and as such you could easily use the Microsoft Client for NetWare Networks and receive much better performance. As for using Arcnet cards, well . . .

GETTING STARTED WITH EXISTING NETBX OR VLM NET-WARE DRIVERS   Here's how to get started.

1. To get your NetWare client drivers running, do everything you did before with the earlier versions of Windows.

2. During the installation, the Network Configuration dialog box will be presented to you. Remove the Microsoft Client for NetWare Networks, which will be configured automatically because the system sees the NetWare network. However, if Windows 95 is already set up, you can perform the preceding and following functions through the Control Panel's Network program icon. (See Figure 4-53.)

3. Add a new Client component from the Network Component Type dialog box.

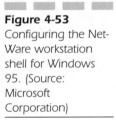

Figure 4-53
Configuring the NetWare workstation shell for Windows 95. (Source: Microsoft Corporation)

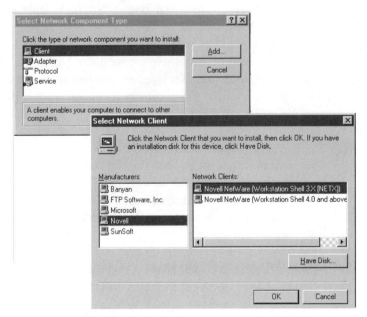

4. Select Novell from the Manufacturers list, and click on Workstation Shell 3.x for NETBX installations or Workstation Shell 4.x and Above for VLM installations. If you are installing the Workstation Shell 4.x and Above for VLM support, you will receive a message indicating that this shell must be installed by the Novell Workstation Installation Program. (See Figure 4-54.)

5. Continue through the setup as prompted if this is a new or upgraded installation, or click on OK to exit the Control Panel's Network program icon.

6. Restart your workstation. (See Figure 4-55.)

From here on in, you should be able to log on to NetWare network servers before you start Windows 95. All NetWare resources that you will access from Windows 95 should be mapped or redirected to before you run Windows 95. This can be accomplished from the NetWare login scripts.

COMMON PROBLEMS WITH NOVELL NETWARE WORKSTATION SHELLS 3.X AND 4.X   Once again, ensure you have the latest releases of the current workstation client redirector software that you are using. You can search for the latest client software from Novell's Internet Web site at **http://WWW.NOVELL.COM**.

Be prepared for the additional installation required after you configure the NetWare Workstation Shell 4.x and Above (VLM) on Windows 95.

If you cannot attach or log in to NetWare servers, verify that you are using the right frame type by looking into the NET.CFG file's ODI_Driver section. Verify this information against the NetWare server that you are trying to log in to.

If you cannot see a login drive after installing Windows 95, you will need to ensure that the **LASTDRIVE** statement in the Windows 95 Registry is set correctly.

Figure 4-54
Supporting NetWare Virtual Loadable Modules requires additional configuration outside Windows 95. (Source: Microsoft Corporation)

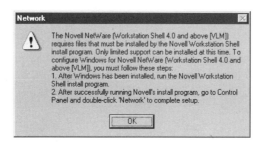

Figure 4-55
Novell NetWare
(Workstation Shell 4.0
and Above VLM) has
been partially in-
stalled. (Source:
Microsoft
Corporation)

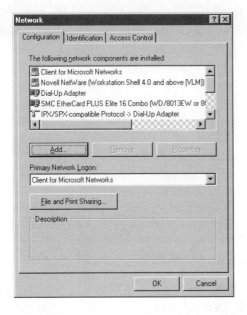

SOME REASONABLE EXPECTATIONS Realistically speaking, if you are currently using the NetWare Workstation Shell 3.x (NETBX) to connect to NetWare 3.x servers, you can probably replace it with the Microsoft Client for NetWare Networks and gain significant benefits in the areas of performance, configuration, and maintenance. However, if you are using NetWare Workstation Shell 4.x and Above (VLM) to connect to NetWare 4.x server using full NDS support, then you will need to keep the VLMs or consider moving to the NetWare Client 32 for Windows 95 drivers.

NOVELL'S NEW CLIENT NETWORK SOLUTION: CLIENT 32 FOR WINDOWS 95 The NetWare Client 32 for various versions of Windows is a fully revamped set of client driver redirector software in full 32-bit mode. As with the Microsoft Client for NetWare Networks, significant performance benefits are achieved by moving to the 32-bit drivers. However, with Novell's NetWare Client 32 for Windows 95, you also gain the advantage of being able to fully integrate Windows 95 with NetWare Directory Services—something the Client for NetWare Networks won't yet do. We introduced this issue earlier in this chapter. Although Microsoft may be able to design a better set of interfaces between the software running on the workstation and Windows 95, for obvious reasons Novell can probably design a better set of interfaces between the client redirector and the NetWare server.

The new redirector software provides a seamless integration of NetWare network resources through the Windows 95 Explorer and Desktop interfaces. The end result is the same as before, except that with Client 32 for Windows 95, you now can access more resources. It is designed on the Client 32 architecture, which is Novell's replacement or upgrade to the Workstation Shell 4.x and Above (VLM) implementation.

The following are some of the features of Client 32 for Windows 95:

- Uses VxD technology for loading by Windows 95
- Makes use of new NetWare Loadable Module technology
- Requires no conventional memory
- Uses Windows 95 Registry for configuration settings
- Provides full access to NetWare services through the Windows 95 Explorer and NetWork Neighborhood as well as through Novell's Provider interface, which provides the tightest integration with NDS
- Provides graphical user interface login and login script execution from within Windows 95
- Supports both NDIS and ODI drivers

The installation itself is as easy as Microsoft network client installations and is tied to the Windows 95 Network Setup program. Additionally, the installation can be done from a local disk (hard or floppy) or from a network server. A nice feature is that the installation dynamically configures for optimal settings at the workstation. Finally, it automatically detects the current hardware settings.

Probably one of the most important features is the addition of Novell's Windows 95 Provider interface. The Provider allows users to browse and access NDS services. Full NDS login script processing is supported. Both server- and client-side directory caching is provided to increase the performance for client/server network communications. Standard LIP and Packet Burst are also supported.

Many of the features built into NDS are also supported, such as when Client 32 for Windows 95 is implemented:

- Support for NetWare Applications Manager services
- Central administration of server and network applications
- Selection of available applications on a per user basis
- Automated application updates
- Tighter integration between applications and NDS

▦ SUPPORT for NetWare Administrator for NDS management from Windows 95 (This feature is important given it is the only client implementation.)

▦ Support for management of full NDS NetWare 4.x servers

▦ Graphical user interface for NetWare Administrator

▦ Automatic downloading of printer drivers for Windows 95 clients as needed

Additionally, the Client 32 for Windows 95 allows for remote control and configuration management, Windows 95 management agents, SNMP reporting via IPX or TCP/IP, and Plug-and-Play support. However, there is a price. Client 32 for Windows 95 does require the workstation to have at least 8M of random access memory.

Table 4-3 shows a comparison of the Windows 95 Client for NetWare Networks provided by Novell, Inc.

Table 4-3

Novell NetWare Client 32 for Windows 95 and Microsoft Client for NetWare Networks. (Source: Novell, Inc.)

Feature	Novell NetWare Client 32 for Windows 95	Microsoft Client for NetWare Networks
Installation Method		
Control Panel or Setup Wizard	a) via network control panel applet; b) migrates 16-bit VLM configuration to Windows 95; c) automatic client update (ACU) from server if newer version is is available; d) client deployed at the same time as Windows 95 (MSBATCH)	a) via network control panel applet only; b) no 16-bit VLM migration; c) no automatic update; d) seamless installation process not supported (for VLMs)
Login		
Graphical User Interface	Customizable by user or administrator; four advanced tabbed option sheets to mix and match	Not customizable
Login to multiple trees	Yes	No
Search and specify a NetWare server	Yes	Yes
Search and specify an NDS tree	Yes	Yes
Specify context	Yes	Yes

Table 4-3

Feature	Novell NetWare Client 32 for Windows 95	Microsoft Client for NetWare Networks
Specify login script at login	Yes	Yes
Specify login script at login	Yes	No
Drop-down lists at login	Last user names, server, NDS trees, and context	Server, NDS trees, and context
Specify login script variables at login	Yes	No
Clears other connections at login	Yes	No
Provider		
Displays NDS tree in Network Neighborhood, Explorer and other multi-tree-aware graphical interfaces	Yes	No, shows NDS only as a domain technology (Bindery Emulation Mode)
Supports the NetWare Application Manager (NAM)	Yes	No
Leverages NLM technology at the client	Yes	No
GUI management of network files directories and trustee rights	Yes	No
System policy support	Yes	Yes
User profile support in NDS environment	Yes	Yes
Auto Reconnect		
Fully configurable via a GUI interface	Yes	No
Reconnect to servers	Yes	Yes
Reconnect and authenticate to NDS tree	Yes	No
Reconnect drive mapping	Yes	Yes

Continues

Table 4-3

Continued.

Feature	Novell NetWare Client 32 for Windows 95	Microsoft Client for NetWare Networks
Reestablish open file states with server	Yes	No
Reestablish file lock states with server	Yes	No
Client Configuration		
Advanced parameter configuration	43 definable parameters	Only 1 definable parameter
Context-sensitive help for parameters	Yes	No
Dynamic parameters do not require a reboot to force changes to take effect	Around 40 definable parameters	1 definable parameter and requires reboot
NDS Support		
Login to multiple NDS trees	Yes	No
Supports extended NDS schema; view objects added to the NDS tree	Yes	Limited, does not give applications NDS schema extension
Manage/assign file access rights from the Windows 95 Network Neighborhood or Explorer	Yes	No
Supports application object extensions	Yes (via NetWare Application Manager)	No
General		
Client-side caching	Yes	Yes
Advanced NCP support (case 87)	Yes	No
Dial-up networking through NetWare Connect, RAS, third-party solutions	Yes	Yes
Network driver support	32-bit, 16-bit ODI, and NDIS 3.1	16-bit ODI, 16-bit NDIS, NDIS 3.1

Table 4-3

Feature	Novell NetWare Client 32 for Windows 95	Microsoft Client for NetWare Networks
32-bit NetWare Client API libraries	Yes	No
16-bit NetWare Client API libraries	Yes	Yes
Protocol Support		
IPX/SPX	Yes	Yes
TCP/IP	Yes	Yes
NetWare/IP 2.1 or above	Yes	No
Named Pipes	Yes	Yes
NetBIOS	Yes	Yes
SMB	Yes	Yes
NetBEUI	Yes	Yes
WINSOCK 1.1, IPX/SPX, TCP/IP	Yes	Yes
Fully supports Novell Packet Burst and Large Internet Packets (LIP)	Yes	No (but yes according to Microsoft)

As you can appreciate, Table 4-3 can be just a little biased toward Novell's solution. However, it is obvious by the list of features that, if you are using Windows 95 in a NetWare 4.x NDS environment, you will seriously want to consider the Client 32 for Windows 95 drivers from Novell. You would do so not because the Client 32 for Windows 95 will be any faster than Microsoft's 32-bit Client for NetWare Networks, but for the integration it provides with NDS and all the tools and applications built up around NDS.

INSTALLING CLIENT 32 FOR WINDOWS 95 You have a couple of choices as to how you can install the Client 32 for Windows 95. If you have the Novell IntranetWare CD-ROM, you can start the installation directly from the CD. This method is fast and easy. If you already have the NetWare 4.x but have not yet upgraded to IntranetWare, or if you simply want to run the Client 32 for Windows 95 with your existing NetWare 3.x network, hop on the Internet and download it from Novell's Internet Web site. This way, you get the latest version.

If you start the installation from the Novell IntranetWare CD-ROM, you can proceed as follows:

1. Insert the CD-ROM into your computer's CD-ROM drive, or access the CD-ROM over the network if you do not have a locally installed CD-ROM drive.

2. Make sure your Windows 95 Control Panel is closed; otherwise, the installation program will not complete. (This step is one of those "Why didn't you tell me before I started?")

3. Run the INSTALL.BAT command from the root of the CD-ROM.

4. Select English as the installation language unless you would prefer another language, of course. You should then see a screen similar to the one shown in Figure 4-56.

5. Press the spacebar four times as you carefully read the licensing agreement.

6. From the main installation menu, select the Client option.

7. Select the Client 32 for Windows 95 option as displayed on the following screen, as shown in Figure 4-57.

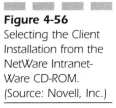

Figure 4-56
Selecting the Client Installation from the NetWare Intranet-Ware CD-ROM. (Source: Novell, Inc.)

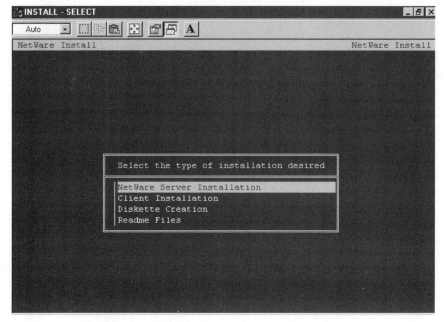

Figure 4-57
Select the Installing the NetWare Client 32 for Windows 95 option. (Source: Novell, Inc.)

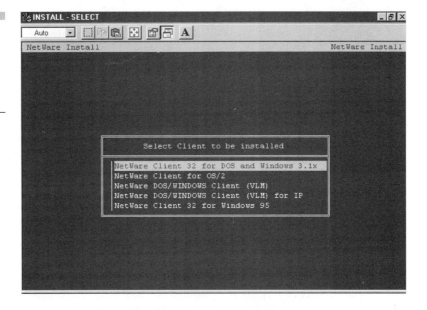

Figure 4-58
NetWare Client 32 for Windows 95 Installation Welcome screen. (Source: Novell, Inc.)

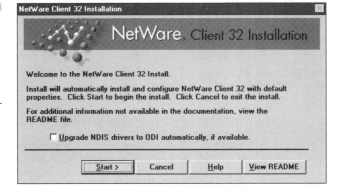

From here, the installation proceeds from the SETUP.EXE program. As the network administrator, you can download the Network Installation version of the Client 32 for Windows 95 and make it available on your network. Doing so would preclude you from having to run the INSTALL.BAT batch file from the IntranetWare CD-ROM. The Client 32 Installation program presents you with a Welcome screen to begin the installation process. The program, from this point on, guides you through a GUI setup and installation of the required files and Registry parameters. At this point, it is also asks you to decide whether you want to "upgrade" from NDIS drivers to ODI automatically during the installation process. (See Figure 4-58.)

If this is your first installation, an important piece of advice would be that you should at least browse through the Help and README files available from this menu. They are the main, if not only, installation instructions that you will get with NetWare Client 32 for Windows 95. The Help file in particular provides a host of valuable information. You should pay close attention to what information you are required to change on the various NetWare servers. As we pointed out earlier, you will need to support Long Name Space on the NetWare servers and that NetWare 3.x and NetWare 4.x do so in different ways. The Help file explains this process quite well and provides information on numerous other areas of the installation and configuration process. The README file includes up-to-date information not contained in the Help file—late breaking news, so to speak. Here again, you can learn a lot about the potential problems you may run into. So take a few moments to read through them both. In fact, you should open the Help file at this stage so that it is easily available during the installation itself.

As you progress through the installation, you will be prompted at various times for information and direction. However, these interruptions are minimal. The installation copies the required files to the hard drive. The first real point you are asked for input is with regards to the Recommended NetWare Client 32 Properties. At this stage, you need to have a few pieces of information at hand such as the names of your NetWare servers and NDS trees. But even if you don't, the installation will proceed satisfactorily if you use the defaults.

NETWARE CLIENT 32 FOR WINDOWS 95 PROPERTIES   If you choose to configure your NetWare Client 32 Properties at this stage, you will be prompted with a series of screens or forms wherein you will need to provide input. (See Figure 4-59.) The Properties forms here are the same ones that would be shown to you if you were to go into the Control Panel, Network program icon later, select Novell NetWare Client 32, and click on the Properties button. Lets walk through these configuration forms at this time.

PREFERRED SERVER   The first form requests that you enter your Preferred Server (if using NetWare 3.x servers), the Preferred Tree and Name Context (if using NetWare 4.x NDS servers), and your choice for the First Network Drive to be used as an assignable network drive. Figure 4-60 highlights how we have configured our initial installation.

LOGIN   The second form allows you to detail how the user login should proceed. A Display Connection Page can display the server or tree con-

Figure 4-59
Setting up your Net-
Ware Client 32 for
Windows 95 proper-
ties during installa-
tion is always a good
idea, although you
can do it later as
well. (Source:
Novell, Inc.)

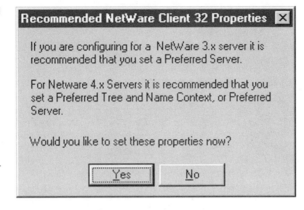

Figure 4-60
Configuring Client 32
Server/NDS Tree Pref-
erences. (Source:
Novell, Inc.)

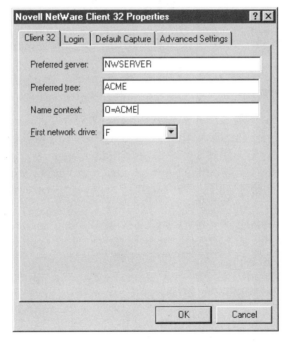

nection process as it is occurring. Although this information may be good
for the network administrator during the initial installation and testing,
it is probably not something you will want the end users to see. The type
of network login you will support is configured here. Will this client look
for an NDS Tree login or a Bindery-based login? As before, you can also
have the processing of the login script displayed on the screen; this feature is very helpful when you're trying to troubleshoot. One of the really
nice features available to you here is that you can specify the name of the
actual login script that you want to run. Although Microsoft supports this

Figure 4-61
Configuring Client 32
Login Preferences.
(Source: Novell, Inc.)

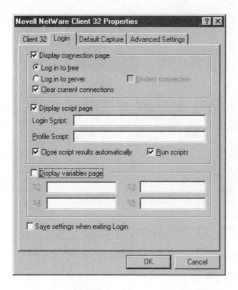

feature with the Windows NT Domain user accounts, it is not supported
by the Client for NetWare Networks. You can decide whether scripts will
be processed and if the settings will be saved upon exit. The Display Variables Page option allows you to pass up to four variables to the graphical
login utility. (See Figure 4-61.)

DEFAULT PRINTER CAPTURE   The Default Capture form allows you to specify printer redirection setting defaults. For example, you can specify the
number of copies that will be made of your print jobs, whether form feed
will be used (helpful with older DOS-based applications), whether you
want any banner page settings, as well as how the print job should be
treated when it arrives at the print queue. All these settings are the standard ones that were, and still are, supported with the `Capture` command.
However, now you don't need to use `Capture` to redirect output to printers because you will be able to drag and drop your print job directly on
the printer icon itself. This form will ensure that the correct printer settings are sent through. (See Figure 4-62.)

ADVANCED SETTINGS   The last form in the Properties screens is for Advanced Settings. Over 40 different settings are available, most of which
can be reconfigured dynamically on the fly without rebooting the workstation (nice feature). As you click on each setting, the current configuration is displayed. (See Figure 4-63.)

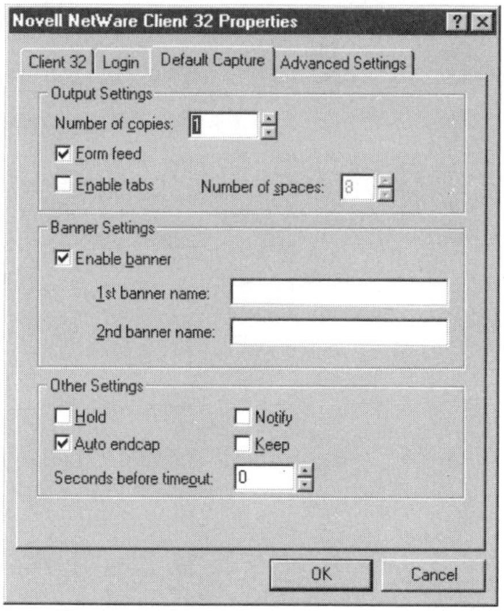

Figure 4-62

Configuring Client 32 Default Capture preferences. (Source: Novell, Inc.)

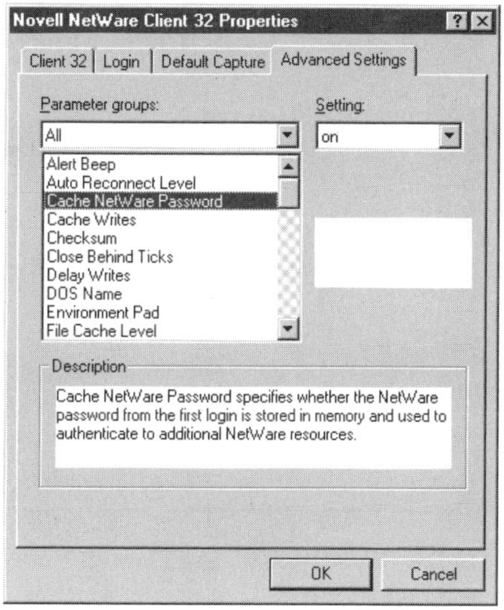

Figure 4-63

Configuring Client 32 advanced settings. (Source: Novell, Inc.)

Unfortunately, the screen has far too many settings for us to go into any detail here; however, Table 4-4 provides a list of the Advanced Settings Parameters.

Finally, after all the files have been copied and the configuration is completed, you will see a final NetWare Client 32 Installation screen, as shown in Figure 4-64, giving you three options:

Table 4-4

NetWare Client 32
Advanced Settings
List. (Source:
Novell, Inc.)

Alert Beep	Auto Reconnect Level
Cache NetWare Password	Cache Writes
Checksum	Close Behind Ticks
Delay Writes	DOS Name
Environment Pad	File Cache Level
Force First Network Drive	Handle Net Errors
Large Internet Packets	LIP Start Size
Lock Delay	Lock Retries
Log File	Log File Size
Long Machine Type	Link Support Layer Max Buffer Size
Max Cache Size	Max Cur Dir Length
Message Timeout	Minimum Time to Net
NCP* Max Timeout	Net Status Busy Timeout
Net Status Timeout	NetWare* Protocol
Network Printers	Opportunistic Locking
Packet Burst*	Packet Burst Read Window Size
Packet Burst Write Window Size	Print Header
Print Tail	Read Only Compatibility
Search Dirs First	Search Mode
Set Station Time	Short Machine Type
Show Dots	Signature Level
True Commit	Use Video BIOS

- Reboot the workstation
- Return to Windows 95 (although your changes will not yet have taken effect)
- Customize the current settings (Control Panel's Network program)

Should you choose the customize button, the installation program will exit and return you to the Control Panel's Network program where you can change the Novell NetWare Client 32 Properties. You will also notice that, in the Network configuration, the Primary Network Logon server entry has been changed to Novell NetWare Client 32, possibly from your

Figure 4-64
Finishing the Client 32 Setup. (Source: Novell, Inc.)

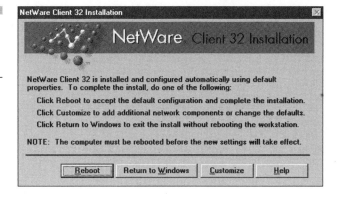

Figure 4-65
Viewing the changed network configuration with the new Novell NetWare Client 32 client and IPX 32-bit protocol. Notice that Novell Client 32 is the Primary Network Logon server. (Source: Microsoft Corporation)

previous Client for Microsoft Networks. If you want to maintain the Windows NT Domain as the Primary Network Logon server, you will need to change this option back.

In addition to the Novell client software, a new transport protocol has also been installed; it's Novell's IPX 32-bit Protocol for Novell NetWare Client 32. You may recall at the first GUI installation screen that we neglected (or chose not to) upgrade the NDIS drivers to ODI. Therefore, the installation program left the Microsoft IPX/SPX-compatible driver for the Client for Microsoft Networks to use instead of binding it to Novell's IPX implementation. (See Figure 4-65.)

CONFIGURING THE NETWARE LOGIN After you select the OK button, the new network settings will be saved, and you will be prompted to reboot the Windows 95 workstation. Rebooting is always a good idea. When Windows 95 reboots, a new GUI network logon screen will appear. (See Figure 4-66.) The GUI Novell NetWare Login screen has three option tabs for configuring, or rather changing, your initial login.

The first screen is for your user name and password. If everything else is already set, and you do not have to change anything else, then simply enter your user name and password, and click on OK. The second login option screen is for changing the preferred NDS tree or Bindery-based server that you want to initially connect to. If you have selected the NDS tree as your login point, you can also change the Context. Context is your position in the tree and is usually the place where your User object is located within the NDS tree. The third screen allows you to select the login script that will be run.

After you select the OK button, the Novell NetWare login script will begin to process. As we highlighted earlier, you have the option of display-

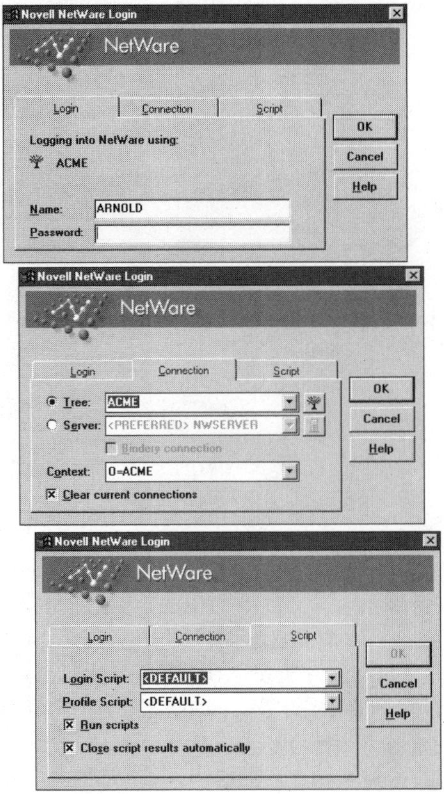

Figure 4-66
Entering your Net-Ware user name and password. (Source: Novell, Inc.)

Figure 4-67
Login script being
processed by In-
tranetWare Server.
(Source: Novell, Inc.)

ing the Login Results on-screen. The Login Results displayed include the connection information as well as the progress of any login scripts. In Figure 4-67, you can see that we have successfully attached to the NWSERVER within the NDS Organization container object ACME. The subsequent messages are from the actual NetWare user login script. Once again, you may not want to display the Login Results screen to the users, but it is a helpful login script debugging feature that any network administrator can certainly use.

After the NetWare NDS Tree and server attachments have been made, and the NetWare login scripts have been run, then the Microsoft connections come into play. However, this happens only when you have both the NetWare Client and the Microsoft Client client software configured for seamless, multiplatform integration (which is what we are trying to do in this book). The process of connecting to the Microsoft Windows NT Domain and running the login script is exactly the same as it was described earlier in this chapter. The Client for Microsoft Networks validates the user to the Windows NT Domain and runs the user's logon script (batch file). So you can see that with the NetWare Client 32 configured, the NetWare login script runs first, before the Windows NT Domain login script, unlike as was previously experienced. The flowchart in Figure 4-68 highlights the new login process.

WINDOWS 95 PROFILES AND POLICIES   The user's Windows NT Domain login script processes and then presents the user with a desktop, which brings us exactly to our next issue: What about the User Profiles and policy files?

Well, they are both equally supported by NetWare Client 32. However, we did notice one significant change when we migrated from the Microsoft

Figure 4-68
Flowchart showing new logon/login script processing after NetWare Client 32 Login Validation has been configured. (Courtesy of WWW. NETWORKOLOGIST. COM)

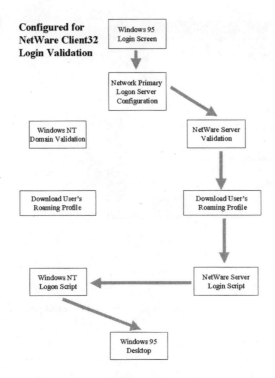

Configured for NetWare Client32 Login Validation

Windows 95 Login Screen

Network Primary Logon Server Configuration

Windows NT Domain Validation

NetWare Server Validation

Download User's Roaming Profile

Download User's Roaming Profile

Windows NT Logon Script

NetWare Server Login Script

Windows 95 Desktop

Client for NetWare Networks to the Novell NetWare Client 32. Under the Microsoft Client for NetWare Networks, the User Profile was stored in the NetWare user's unique MAIL subdirectory along with the LOGIN script file. However, when NetWare Client 32 was implemented, it tried to store the User Profile information in the NWSERVER\SYS:USERS\ USER_NAME directory (which we had not yet configured), which is similar to what the Microsoft Client for Microsoft Networks does on the Windows NT Domain side. Nonetheless, we simply created the directory the client software was looking for (it gave us an error message saying it could not create the Desktop folder in this directory), gave the NetWare user a trustee assignment to the directory, and voila, everything worked just has it had before.

Now, however, there is one big difference. When we go in to the Windows 95 Explorer, we can see all the NetWare NDS objects and network services. Although our example NDS tree is a simple one, it does illustrate the goal we had in mind—access to and management of the NDS objects. The integration is fairly good in that we can select NetWare file systems from Windows 95 and manage user trustee assignment through the regular Explorer Properties, just as we would any other file available to a Windows NT server's NTFS file system. In Figure 4-69, you can see all the previous file system items from Windows 95 Explorer to present, but now you can also see the ACME NDS Tree, ACME Organization container, and other NDS objects such as the file system volumes from the NetWare servers. If you look closely, you can also see where the User Profiles have been saved for the Arnold user account.

The final piece would be to run the NetWare Administrator and actually begin to manage the NDS tree and objects. The NetWare Administrator for Windows 95 needs to be installed after NetWare Client 32 is installed because it is not installed down to the Windows 95 desktop. However, this is not a major problem as it is available in the PUBLIC subdirectory of the NetWare server after you install it. It can be run simply by logging on to the NetWare server, locating the NetWare Administrator executable file in the PUBLIC directory, and double-clicking on it. From there, you can manage the entire NDS tree just as you probably used to do with Windows 3.x or WFWG. (See Figure 4-70.)

WINDOWS LOGON FIRST, THEN NETWARE LOGIN An interesting thing did occur when we decided to turn the tables around a bit. After the NetWare Client 32 for Windows 95 was installed, we decided to select the Client for Microsoft Networks as the Primary Network Logon server. Sure enough, after Windows 95 restarted, we were prompted with the usual Windows NT Domain logon screen from Windows 95. Entering

Figure 4-69
Windows 95 Explorer now has access to NDS objects. (Courtesy of WWW. NETWORKOLOGIST. COM)

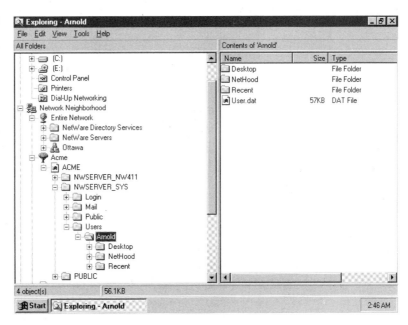

Figure 4-70
Managing NDS through the NetWare Administrator for Windows. (Source: Microsoft Corporation and Novell, Inc.)

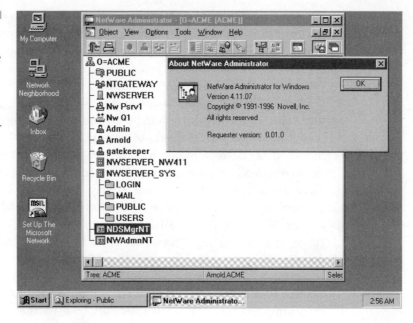

our user name and password was followed with the user logon script to be processed. Then we were faced with the Novell NetWare GUI Login screen, and we had to retype the user name and password. Either the Windows 95 logon screen information was not being passed to the NetWare login screen, or the NetWare login screen was not interested in received said information and subsequently wanted a manual login. The verdict is still out.

FINAL THOUGHTS ON THE WINDOWS CLIENT/NETWARE CLIENT QUESTION   Certainly, we like to keep things simple and to a minimum. So the thought of having to support two protocol stacks from two vendors at opposite ends of the playing field is certainly not very appealing, to say the least. However, we have made some observations that require some level of acceptance, regardless of our preferences. Some very simple observations have led us to this conclusion. For example, even if we support the Novell Client 32 for Windows 95 drivers, they have to be selected as the Primary Network Logon server in the Network configuration program of the Control Panel; otherwise the NetWare Administrator for NDS will not function properly. In other words, as soon as the Novell Client 32 for Windows 95 is made the primary protocol, everything with the Novell GUI administrator tools works fine. Now, we will be the first to acknowledge that there are probably some real technical issues behind this, but it proves a point: You can't have everything, and you have to make a decision as to which way you are going to lean with your client configurations.

As we stated earlier, if you are going to run Windows 95 in a NetWare 3.x environment, the Microsoft Client for NetWare Networks will probably do more than the job requires. However, if you are moving to the NetWare 4.x or IntranetWare environment with Windows 95 as the desktop platform, or you need to manage your NDS servers from Windows 95, then you will need to give serious consideration to the Novell Client 32 for Windows 95 drivers if you want tight integration with NetWare Directory Services.

WINDOWS 95 ACTING LIKE A NETWARE SERVER Although Windows 95 can provide great access to a NetWare server using either Microsoft's or Novell's client software, you will probably be surprised to know that it can also act as, or emulate, a NetWare 3.x file and print server of sorts. Using this feature, you can configure a Windows 95 computer to provide file and print sharing for both Microsoft- and NetWare-only configured clients. Acting as a central point of contract, the Windows 95 computer with NetWare-emulated file services can receive files from a NetWare client and store them for access by Microsoft clients connected to the same network.

Although this feature is not the focus of this book, it does provide a potential area of integration between NetWare clients and Windows NT Workstations where an administrator does not want to go through the cost of installing both Windows NT Server with File and Print Services for NetWare nor configure the NT Workstations to support NetWare protocols. Windows 95 could become the link. However, it is also important to point out that this kind of solution should only be considered for occasional file and print services sharing and should not be considered for serious file server duty. Figure 4-71 highlights this potential NetWare client and Windows NT Workstation integration solution.

After the Windows 95 workstation has been restarted, the existing NetWare clients can access the server as they would any other NetWare server. If they go to the Windows Explorer or even the MS-DOS prompt and run the **SLIST** (or **NLIST** for NetWare 4.x), they will be able to see the Windows 95 workstation listed as a NetWare server. (See Figure 4-72.) The Windows 95 File and Print Sharing Service for NetWare does require that you use Microsoft's Client for NetWare Networks, however.

We've now concluded our section on the possibilities for integrating Windows 95 into a NetWare and Windows NT server environment. You will be interested to know that much of what we have reviewed in the previous pages will be equally applicable to the next client subject: Windows NT.

Figure 4-71
Configuring Windows 95's File and Print Sharing Service for NetWare. (Source: Microsoft Corporation)

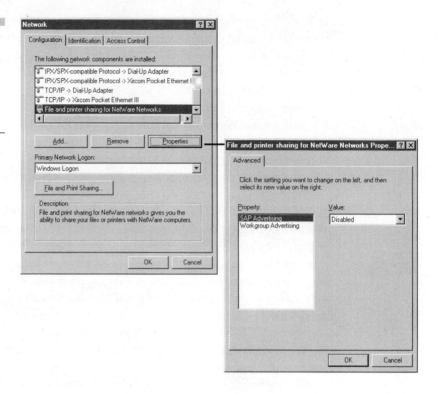

Figure 4-72
Displaying Windows 95 running File and Print Sharing Service for NetWare using the **SLIST** command. (Courtesy of WWW. NETWORKOLOGIST. COM)

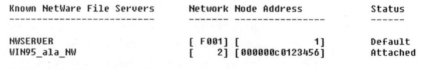

```
F:\>slist

Known NetWare File Servers        Network Node Address           Status
---------------------------       ------- ----------------       ------

NWSERVER                          [ F001] [              1]       Default
WIN95_ala_NW                      [    2] [000000c0123456]        Attached

Total of 2 file servers found
```

Windows NT Connectivity Options

Your organization requires some heavy-duty processing at the client desktop. You have evaluated all the Windows desktop operating systems and have settled on Windows NT Workstation. Everything looks good, but you have a mixed network server environment; you need to connect your Windows NT Workstations to NetWare servers as well as to the existing Windows NT Domain Controller servers. Let's look at your options.

Windows NT (New Technology) is a continual evolution of the Windows family of products. In fact, if we had presented the clients in chronological order, Windows NT would have been presented before Windows 95. However, that's another story. Because Windows NT turned out to be just too much operating system for most people at the time of its introduction, Microsoft introduced a "lighter" version with many of its features. Additionally, because no one was going with the Windows NT operating system, developers were not developing software for this new 32-bit platform. No software, no buyers. No buyers, no software. It's a vicious circle.

The intent of this lighter version was to get people to upgrade to a 32-bit version of an operating system so that software developers would start to write software for the 32-bit platform. Thus far, the strategy has succeeded nicely. So it will be no a surprise to find out that much of what is in Windows 95 is similar in nature to what is available in Windows NT—within limits of course. These limits are a result of the fact that Windows 95 is still based fundamentally on the MS-DOS operating system, whereas Windows NT is a whole new operating system. Table 4-5 shows a comparison of the features of Windows NT and Windows 95.

Table 4-5

Feature comparison of Windows NT and Windows 95. (Source: Microsoft Corpora-

Product Feature	Windows 95	Windows NT Workstation
System and Peripheral Requirements and Support		
Runs MS-DOS device drivers	Yes	No
Runs Win16 device drivers	Yes	No
Recommended RAM for running multiple applications	8+M	16+M
Typical disk space requirements	40	120M
Runs on PowerPC, MIPS R4x00 and DEC Alpha AXP-based RISC systems	No	Yes
Supports multiprocessor configurations for scaleable performance without changing operating system or applications	No	Yes
Application Support		
Win32 API for application development, OLE for linking data across applications	Yes	Yes

Continues

Table 4-5

Continued.

Product Feature	Windows 95	Windows NT Workstation
Preemptive multitasking for Win32 Applications	Yes	Yes
Runs Win16 applications	Yes	Yes
Multimedia APIs (DibEngine, DirectDraw, DirectSound, DirectInput, Reality Lab 3-D graphics libraries	Yes	Direct Draw and DirectSound. Others, 1997.
DCOM	No. Future Release	Yes
OpenGL graphics libraries for 3-D graphics	Yes, Service Pack 1	Yes
System Resources Capacity	Greatly Expanded	Unlimited
Runs MS-DOS applications	Yes	Most
Runs IBM Presentation Manager (through 1.3) and POSIX 1003.1 applications	No	Yes
Application and Data Protection		
Preemptive multitasking for Win16 applications	No	Yes
System completely protected from errant Win16 or Win32 applications	No	Yes
NTFS file system provides complete protection of files on a stand-alone system (files, folders, and applications can be made "invisible" to specific users)	No	Yes
Has automatic recovery from a system failure	No	Yes
Next-generation Windows	Yes	Yes
User Interface		
Plug-and-Play technology that lets you add hardware automatically and dynamically reconfigure the system	Yes	No. In 1997 release
Connectivity		
LAN connectivity and peer-to-peer networking, with all popular protocols including TCP/IP, IPX/SPX, DLC, and NetBEUI	Yes	Yes

Table 4-5

Product Feature	Windows 95	Windows NT Workstation
Open networking architecture provides a choice of clients, transports, drivers, and extensibility for support of third-party networking applications	Yes	Yes
Built-in Remote Access Services	Yes	Yes
Built-in Windows Messaging Client providing e-mail and fax	Yes	Fax support delivered post 4.0 release.
Built-in Microsoft Network (MSN) client software	Yes	Delivered separately post 4.0 release.
Manageability		
Open system management architecture provides infra-structure for third-party system management solutions	Yes	Yes
Supports existing and emerging system management standards (SNMP, DMI)	Yes	Yes
System policies to provide centralized control over desktop configuration	Yes	Yes
User profiles to provide consistent configuration for roving users or different users sharing a single system	Yes	Yes
Remote monitoring of system performance	Yes	Yes
System and Peripheral Support		
Fully exploits 386DX, 486, and Pentium platforms	Yes	486 and Pentium (no support for 386)

Windows NT Networking Architecture

The Windows NT networking architecture is just one of those areas that is very similar to what is in Windows 95. Therefore, we will spend only a brief amount of time on this area before moving off to the actual client connectivity solutions. Figure 4-73 reviews the Windows NT networking architecture.

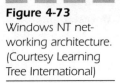

Figure 4-73
Windows NT networking architecture.
(Courtesy Learning
Tree International)

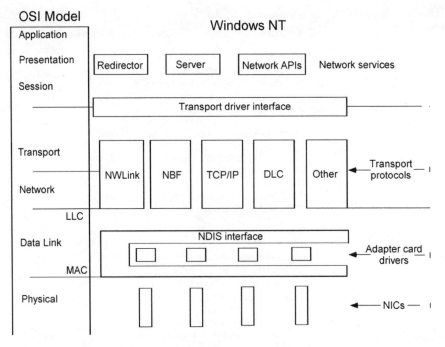

As you can see, Windows 95 and Windows NT use essentially the same networking architecture. What is different perhaps are the methods they use to deliver the goods. The Windows NT networking architecture supports the NDIS 3.x standard, the same transport protocols, and the same upper layer service protocols. It also supports file and print sharing services, *Uniform Naming Convention* (UNC) provider, and MultiProvider Router services. All the details regarding these network protocols were covered in Chapter 3 and equally well under the networking architecture sections of the Windows 95 section is this chapter.

The default network components for Windows NT are as follow:

- NetBIOS interface
- NWLink IPX/SPX-compatible transport protocol
- Workstation service—client redirector
- Server service—for sharing file and print services
- Computer browser—network service browser
- NDIS adapter drivers
- Remote Procedure Call (RPC)—name service provider

All the required network components are available. We saw in Chapter 3 that NWLink IPX/SPX was supported as a transport protocol. Now we need to look at how we can use that transport protocol, or one provided by Novell, to integrate Windows NT into a NetWare network environment. Now we need to look at what solutions either Microsoft or Novell offers us to integrate Windows NT into a multiplatform network environment yet still provide the end users with seamless access to network resources.

From a Windows NT or Microsoft networking standpoint, everything is there to provide easy integration and interoperability with other Microsoft networking clients and servers. We can, however, take two options or paths for integrating Windows NT workstations with NetWare servers: Microsoft's or Novell's. Microsoft's solution comes in the form of *Client Services for NetWare* (CSNW). This service is similar in nature and functionality to the Windows 95 Client for NetWare Networks client redirector software. Novell's solution is likewise similar to the one it provides for Windows 95 through the Client 32 networking architecture. Both services work very well and have individual advantages and disadvantages not unlike those found in the Windows 95 environment. In the ensuing sections of this chapter, we will look at placing Windows NT workstation in a Windows NT Domain and subsequently integrating it within a NetWare network environment.

Overview of the Windows NT Logon Process

Unlike Windows 95, Windows NT Workstation and Server both have local user account databases, and they require mandatory logon using valid user names and passwords. Whether the workstation is part of a network or running in stand-alone mode does not matter; a valid logon is still required. Of all the Microsoft desktop and server products, Windows NT is the only one in the series that requires mandatory logon. The local user database is called the *Security Accounts Manager* (SAM). As with Windows 95, all system configuration information is stored within a Registry. The SAM is also part of that Registry but can be accessed only by the User Manager for Domains (see earlier in this chapter).

In a stand-alone Windows NT workstation, a user's logon will be validated against the local SAM database. A local User Profile will be loaded if the user's account profile information has been configured to do so. If not, the local Windows NT workstation's Default User Profile will be loaded. The User Profile processes are similar to the Windows 95 ones, except that the profile information is configured somewhat differently and in a different format. (Windows 95 uses USER.DAT as the profile file name, whereas Windows NT uses NTUSER.DAT.) The end result is that, when logging on, the user gets a personal desktop provided that user always logs on at the same workstation.

In a networked environment in which the Windows NT workstation is part of (member) a Windows NT Domain, the user logon will normally be validated against the Windows NT Domain Controller servers. We say "normally" because, even though the workstation is part of the Windows NT Domain, a user could still log on using a local SAM account by changing the Domain selection in the Logon dialog box. However, in a regular corporate environment in which all the Windows NT workstations are part of a Domain directory structure, Domain user accounts will normally be used due to the benefits of centralized management.

To be part of the Windows NT Domain environment, the Windows NT workstation needs to have the Microsoft client software loaded as well as a valid network adapter. Both of these components are loaded (automatically in NTW 3.51 and selectable in NTW 4.0) during the initial installation. Effectively, Windows NT workstation, when connected to a network, is ready for Peer-to-Peer networking even if it is not part of a domain. In this case, the user logs on to Windows NT Workstation using a local user account and password. This user account is then passed to other Microsoft clients and servers through a method called *passthrough authentication*. If the remote system is also supporting User Level Access security, then the remote system will verify that an equivalent user account exists locally in its own user database. If not, it will look to see if the Guest account is Enabled. If not, the user can either specify a request to connect as a valid user on the remote system or is refused connection.

Although the discussion of how Windows NT processes logons and remote access may seem a somewhat distant topic from integration with NetWare servers and clients, nothing could be further from the truth. As we clearly demonstrated with Windows 95, the user name and password information is passed in the background to simply access remote resources. When Windows NT Workstation is part of a domain, the user logon is validated not by the local Windows NT workstation SAM database, but by the remote Windows NT Domain Controller SAM database. Subsequently, the Windows NT Domain Controller also gets into the discussion when ever further user validation or authentication is required by other servers—NetWare and Windows NT—because the Windows NT Domain user account is used for this validation.

In summary, the main parts to configure are the network adapter, selection of the transport protocol, and joining a Windows NT Domain as a member workstation. For the purposes of this discussion, we will assume that your workstation will be part of a domain for the sake of processing logon scripts from the Domain Controller. If your workstation is not part of a domain nor are you using Windows NT Workstation 4.0's implementation of CSNW (which allows for NetWare server script processing), you can have local Windows NT logon scripts process; however, you will be using only a connect or attach feature to access remote services. In this instance, it is as if you were performing Workgroup mode networking in which your local user name and password is sent to the remote service.

NetWare Connectivity

After the Windows NT Workstation is successfully connected to the Windows NT Domain environment, user login scripts are being processed, and User Profiles are being stored centrally on the server, then we can proceed through to the NetWare connection issues. Initially, we will look at the Microsoft client implementations for NetWare Bindery and NDS-based connectivity for Windows NT Workstation 3.51 and 4.0. Then we will move onto Novell's solutions. Comparisons will be made along the way, which we hope will assist you in determining which one will best address your particular requirements.

A bit of history is somewhat relevant. When Windows NT Workstation first hit the market, and even as late as NT Version 3.5, the Novell-developed drivers simply did not work very well at all. Regardless of what the technical obstacles were at the time, the fact was that Microsoft had waited some time for Novell to implement drivers and then simply decided to implement its own solution. The Microsoft CSNW client redirector software worked from the outset and continues to provide a very good solution today for NetWare access by Windows NT Workstations. However, the goalpost keeps moving, and with the advances in Novell NDS directory services technology, some serious consideration may need to be given if you are operating Windows NT in a full-blown NDS network environment. As with Windows 95, Novell's Client 32 for Windows NT is now a solid client redirector solution. So past problems with Novell's NetWare Client for Windows NT can be put aside.

Windows NT Workstation Is Tightly Integrated with Windows NT Domains

For completeness, allow us to state that you will need to perform a regular installation of Windows NT Workstation in an existing Windows NT Domain network environment. During the installation process, it is anticipated that you will have installed the Network Interface Card NDIS drivers and selected a relevant transport protocol for your network. If this is a pure Windows networking environment, it is unlikely that you have installed the NWLink IPX/SPX-compatible transport protocol, so we will save that part of the process for later in this section when we configure CSNW. The workstation's Server and Workstation services will be installed automatically. In fact, you cannot deselect them. These services will be bound (linked) to the NetBIOS protocol, which, in turn, will be bound to the transport protocol (probably NetBEUI or TCP/IP with the latter being the preference). The transport protocol will, in turn, be bound to the Network Interface Card. All these processes, acting in concert, will allow our workstation to access remote network resources or share its own resources over the network. Figure 4-74 highlights this protocol binding on a Windows NT 4.0 Workstation.

The next phase of the connectivity project is to have the workstation join the Windows NT Domain as a "member" workstation. This can be done initially at the Windows NT Domain server by the network administrator or by a user with sufficient administrative privileges at the Win-

Figure 4-74
Windows NT Workstation 4.0 and 3.51 protocol bindings in a Microsoft-only network environment. (Source: Microsoft Corporation)

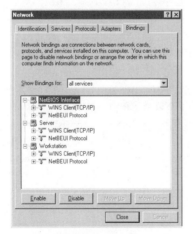

dows NT Workstation itself. For our purposes, we will look at the process of adding the workstation to a Windows NT Domain from the workstation's perspective. When this process is done from the server, we input only the name of the workstation that will join the domain, but we still need to go to the workstation and have it join the domain. When we do the job from the workstation, both efforts can be accomplished at the same time.

To have a workstation join a domain, take the following steps:

1. Open the Network program icon from the Control Panel. The Control Panel is in the Main Program Group in NT Version 3.51 and under the Settings folder in NT Version 4.0.

2. Select the Identification tab, and click on the Change button. You should now see the screen shown in Figure 4-75. Both NT Version 4.0 and 3.51 are similar, although the tabs are in different locations.

3. In the Member of: dialog box, click on the Domain radio button and enter the name of the domain.

4. Type the user name and password of an existing Windows NT Domain Administrator level account. Because we are performing this task from the workstation, we will need to add a current and valid Windows NT Domain Administrator (or equivalent) user account. Many people think that they are actually creating a User account in the Windows NT Domain at this point; nothing could be further from the truth, but it is still a source of confusion. At this stage, you are actually taking your Windows NT Workstation computer name and adding it as a member of the Windows NT Domain that you specified previously.

   In addition to adding our Windows NT Workstation to the domain as a member workstation, we are also changing our own service's configuration. The next time the workstation reboots, the Windows NT NETLOGON service will be started. You may remember that the NETLOGON share on the Windows NT Domain Controllers is attached to workstations that are seeking to have it validate their user accounts and to have access to user logon scripts.

5. Select the OK button, and reboot the workstation for the changes to take effect.

When the workstation reboots, you will have another option in the Logon dialog box. In this box, you will have one of two choices: log on using the local workstation's SAM user account database or point to the Domain Controller's SAM user account database for logon validation.

Figure 4-75
Joining a Windows
NT Domain—NT 4.0
and NT 3.51.
(Source: Microsoft
Corporation)

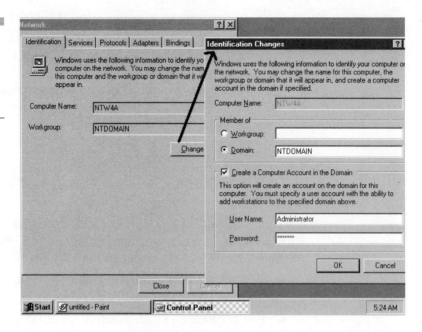

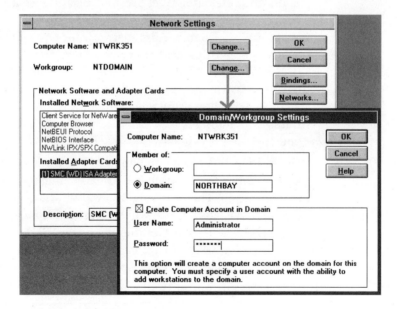

Logon Validation

From here on, the logon process is similar to that which occurs with Windows 95. The user types in a user name and password, which are passed to the Windows NT Domain Controller for validation. (See Figure 4-76.)

Figure 4-76

The logon window
of a Windows NT
Domain member
workstation.
(Source: Microsoft
Corporation)

Figure 4-77

Differences between
Windows 95 and
Windows NT User
Profile information
settings in the
Windows NT Domain
SAM database.
(Source: Microsoft
Corporation)

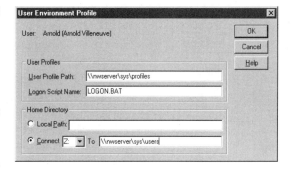

Once the user is approved, the logon process continues and looks for information in the user's profile information form. If a logon script entry has been made, then the logon script is searched for in the \%SYSTEM-ROOT%\SYSTEM32\REPL\IMPORT\SCRIPTS directory on the Windows NT Domain server that is authenticating the user's logon (either the PDC or any one of the BDCs). You may remember that this directory also is shared as the NETLOGON share.

Loading the User Profile

After the logon script is executed, then the logon script process continues and looks for a User Profile entry in the Profile information screen. However, this entry is made in a different location than it is for Windows 95. Figure 4-77 highlights the difference.

In Figure 4-77, you can see that an entry for the server to save the Windows 95 user's profile is made in the Home Directory dialog box, whereas the entry for a Windows NT Workstation user is made in the User Profile dialog box. This difference presents an interesting issue as well when you are trying to support users who log on from different workstation platforms (for example, Windows 95 and Windows NT) because the User Profiles are essentially not exchangeable. Nonetheless, profiles can be centrally stored even if they cannot be shared. The net effect is that the user ends up with a different main User Profile for Windows NT and Windows 95. (This point is not really relevant as far as integration between Windows NT and NetWare is concerned; it's just an interesting side note.)

The process we have just gone through is that the user logs on to the Windows ND Domain, the logon script is executed, and the personal profile is loaded. The processing of the logon script is for all intents and purposes the same as with Windows 95. The User Profile is stored in a different location under a different name. That's it. We now have a Windows NT Workstation configured as part of the Windows NT Domain, and we are ready to integrate it with the NetWare network environment. A quick peek through the Windows NT Windows Explorer will show that no NetWare resources are available as of yet. (See Figure 4-78.)

Microsoft's Client Services for NetWare (CSNW)

Client Services for NetWare is Microsoft's implementation of a NetWare client for Windows NT workstation. In a similar vein as with Windows 95, CSNW takes full advantage of the underlying Windows NT networking

Figure 4-78
Windows NT Windows Explorer in a Microsoft-only network environment. (Source: Microsoft Corporation)

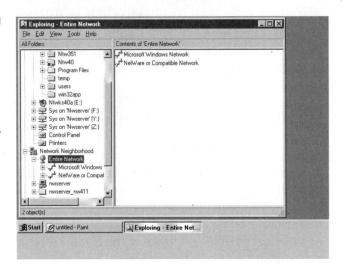

architecture and 32-bit processing capabilities of the operating system. It supports Microsoft's implementation of the IPX/SPX-compatible transport protocol and subsequent bindings to the NDIS driver stack. It allows users to access NetWare file servers. CSNW for Windows NT Workstation 3.51 supports access to NetWare 3.x Bindery-based and NetWare 4.x Bindery-emulated servers, whereas Windows NT Workstation 4.0 supports access to both NetWare 3.x Bindery-based and NetWare 4.x NDS-based servers. However, there are some limitations with NT Version 4.0 CSNW access to NDS administrative tools, which we will look at later. CSNW was originally called the *NetWare Workstation Compatible Service* (NWCS).

You should be aware that CSNW has some limitations when implemented on Windows NT Workstation 3.51. Probably one of the biggest limitation is its lack of support for processing NetWare login scripts. This shortcoming, however, has been corrected with CSNW for NT Version 4.0. Most of what you would need to do through a NetWare login script can probably be done through a Windows NT logon script anyway. Such tasks as attaching to a NetWare server, mapping drive letters to remote file systems, and redirecting printer output to NetWare print queues can also be done.

Here is summary of CSNW features:

- Allows users to access NetWare file and print servers
- Supports 16-bit NetWare applications such as SYSCON, CONSOLE, RCONSOLE, and others
- Supports NCP, Burst Mode, and LIP protocols
- Supports long file names on the NetWare server when the NetWare server is running the OS/2 (or LONG) name space

Implementing CSNW for Windows NT

Before installing CSNW, you must ensure that you have removed all existing Novell NetWare client redirector software. If you are working on an older installation of Windows NT workstation, it may have a copy of Novell's original client software called Novell's NetWare Client for Windows NT or even Microsoft's original implementation of CSNW, which was called NetWare Workstation Compatible Service. Existing drivers can be removed from the Network Settings dialog box of the Control Panel's Network program. After they are removed, restart your workstation for the changes to take effect. You are now ready to install the Client Services for

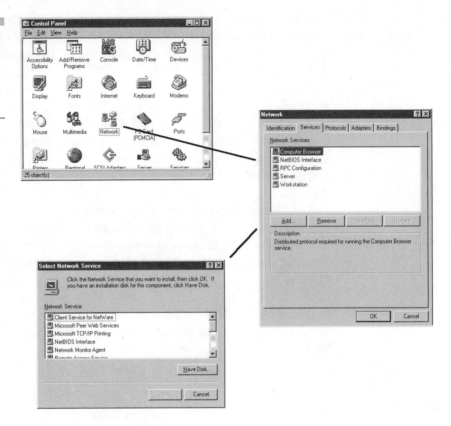

Figure 4-79
Installing Client
Services for NetWare
(CSNW). (Courtesy
of Learning Tree
International)

NetWare client redirector software on the Windows NT workstation. Remember, though, that CSNW on NT Version 3.51 supports only Bindery-based access to NetWare servers. However, the CSNW version with NT 4.0 supports access to IntranetWare 4.0 NDS but is not fully NDS compliant. (See Figure 4-79.)

Because you are changing the drivers associated with the Kernel Mode area of the Windows NT operating system, you will need to reboot. You reboot so that the newly configured/compiled operating system is loaded. After rebooting, you will be prompted to configure your preferred NetWare logon server. You can do so at that time or later through a new program item called CSNW that will be added to the Control Panel. You will see only the Select Preferred Server for NetWare screen the first time you log on at this workstation (or any other user logs on at this workstation). The Preferred Server for NetWare is a setting for each individual user, so although several different people log on at the same Windows NT Workstation, they can all have different preferred NetWare server connections. After you enter this information, you can later change it at the CSNW program from the Control Panel.

Changing Your CSNW Settings

You can do little to change the CSNW settings, or rather there are few of them to change. (See Figure 4-80.) You are essentially limited to changing your Preferred Server and setting Print Options. The Print Options provide three settings: Add Form Feed, Notify (user) When (job) Printed, and enable a Print Banner. Other than that, there is not much to it. You can access a really helpful Overview and Help file of the CSNW, which has some good tips for when you are trying to run 16-bit NetWare-aware applications and utilities; you should seriously consider reviewing (we will in a bit).

When Windows NT Workstation users log on, they will be attached to the NetWare server. The currently logged on Windows NT user names and passwords will be used to validate and attach the users to the NetWare server; therefore, it is important that the users have equivalent user accounts on the NetWare server. As such, the LOGIN.EXE utility will not be run, and no NetWare login script will be processed. The flowchart in Figure 4-81 highlights the logon process for a Windows NT CSNW-configured workstation.

Any requirement for drive mapping or printer capturing will have to be accomplished manually through the Windows NT User Profile settings. In the user's profile, we can retain settings for network connections and also have them reestablished at the time of logon at the Windows NT Workstation. When Windows NT starts up and users log on, it will load

Figure 4-80
Changing the CSNW settings through the Control Panel. (Source: Microsoft Corporation)

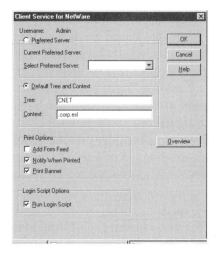

■■ ■■ ▮ ▮

Figure 4-81
Windows NT CSNW
logon flowchart.
(Courtesy of WWW.
NETWORKOLOGIST.
COM)

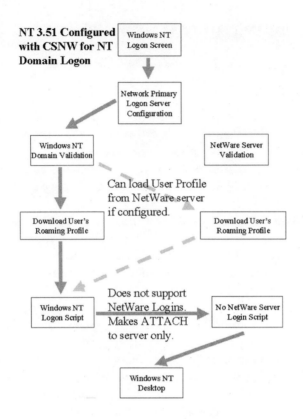

the users' individual profile settings and restore any network connections they had when they last logged off.

So what is the big deal about not having NetWare login scripts process then? Well, within a login script, you can have many specialized subroutines that perform functions based on users' group memberships, the types of machines on which they are logged on, time of day, and so on. Although these functions can probably be done after the users log on to the NetWare server, the NetWare login environment variables will not be available for **IF...THEN** processing within the batch file. This restriction may or may not be a big limitation at your site.

Although a NetWare login script cannot be processed, users' Windows NT profiles could be stored on a NetWare file server. This capability may be helpful in some organizations with a mixed Windows NT and NetWare server platform with various Windows client desktop platforms to store all the User Profiles in one central location for backup purposes, but where some of the Windows desktop platforms don't have access to the Windows NT servers. Figure 4-82 shows how we can change the users' Windows NT Domain account profile information to place the profile files on the NetWare server.

Figure 4-82
Storing Windows NT
Domain User Profiles
on a NetWare server.
(Source: Microsoft
Corporation)

The change is a rather easy one. Instead of pointing the profile file name and location to a Windows NT server, we simply redirect it to a NetWare server using a UNC format to point to the NetWare server name, volume, and directory.

Accessing NetWare Server Volumes and Directories

After CSNW has been installed, you can go through the File Manager to implement the NetWare services. Alternatively, you can start an MS-DOS command prompt and use either the Microsoft **NET** or NetWare **MAP** command. If you are connecting to a resource located on a server to which you have not yet attached, then your current Windows NT user name and password will be passed to the NetWare server, and you will be attached to that server. Your access to the NetWare services will be based on the NetWare account used to attach to that server. Within the File Manager, you can click on the Connect to Network drive button or select this option from the Disk menu. (See Figure 4-83.)

The Connect to Network drive button will present you with a browse list displaying which resources are currently "known" to be on the network. Now that CSNW has also been configured alongside the Microsoft client software, you will see an option in the Share Directories dialog box for Microsoft Windows Network and NetWare or Compatible Network. You will notice that one of the options is to Reconnect at Logon. This feature, which we mentioned earlier, allows you to reconnect to the selected NetWare network drive the next time you log on. You may also run into a situation in which the particular server you are trying to connect to is not yet listed or displayed in the Shared Directories selection area. In this event, you can simply type the UNC path to the NetWare server, volume, and subdirectory in the Path dialog box area. The UNC path format is as follows:

`\\SERVER_NAME\VOLUME\DIRECTORY`

Figure 4-83
Connecting to a Net-
Ware server file sys-
tem. (Courtesy of
Learning Tree Inter-
national)

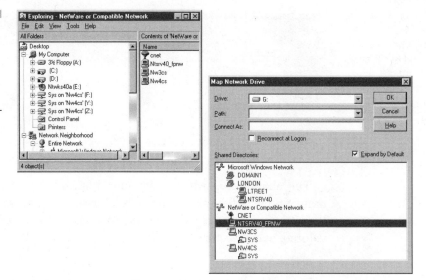

For example, to connect to the \USERS\ARNOLD subdirectory on the
SYS volume of the NWSERVER server, type the following UNC path:

```
\\NWSERVER\SYS\USERS\ARNOLD
```

Finally, you can specify a user name other than your currently logged-
on name in the Connect As: dialog box. This feature is helpful, for example, if you do not have a valid user account on the NetWare server you are
trying to connect to. However, if the Guest account is enabled on the Net-
Ware server, and no password is specified, you will be connected to that
server as the Guest user. If the Guest user account has a password associated with it, you will be prompted for the password.

Working with the MS-DOS-Compatible
Command Prompt to Access
Network Services

If you are working from the MS-DOS command prompt and trying to locate which NetWare services are available on the network, you can use
the Microsoft networking **NET** command to find them. To display a list of
NetWare file servers, type the following command at the command
prompt:

```
NET VIEW /NETWORK:NW
```

Furthermore, to display a list of file system volumes located on that server, type the following command at the command prompt:

```
NET VIEW \\SERVER_NAME /NETWORK:NW
```

After you locate it, you could use the **NET USE** or **MAP** commands to redirect a local drive letter to the remote NetWare server, as follows:

```
NET USE G: \\NWSERVER\SYS\USERS\ARNOLD
```

or

```
MAP G:=NWSERVER\SYS:USERS\ARNOLD
```

To see what your current drive settings are, you can use the **MAP** or **NET USE** command also within the command prompt.

We point out these commands not because we expect you to forgo your nice GUI File Manager interface, but because these commands can be helpful within batch files. You can even go as far as using the **NET** command to help you connect to a NetWare server as a different user—again a very helpful function from within a batch file. To perform this function, use the following command:

```
NET USE G: \\NWSERVER\SYS\USERS\DEFAULT   /USER:GUEST GUESTPW
```

The **/USER:GUEST GUESTPW** tells the **NET USE** command to present this user name and password to the remote NWSERVER NetWare server. Obviously, the user name and password are visible here to anyone who can read a batch file, so you will not want to use accounts with a lot of administrative capabilities for these types of functions. It is, however, a handy trick when you have batch processes running, and you want to upload files to a central server where the users processing the jobs do not have personal accounts nor need them.

Accessing NetWare Print Queues

The Print Manager is the main interface for establishing a connection to a NetWare print queue. (See Figure 4-84.) As with accessing NetWare file systems, several command-line options are also available from the command prompt.

You can then manage or redirect print jobs to the NetWare printer just as you would any other printer on the network. You can change the NetWare printer to be your default connected printer at the time of logon. You

Figure 4-84
Connecting to a Net-
Ware server print
queue. (Courtesy
of Learning Tree
International)

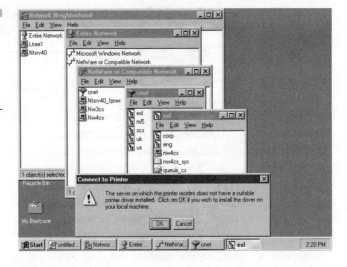

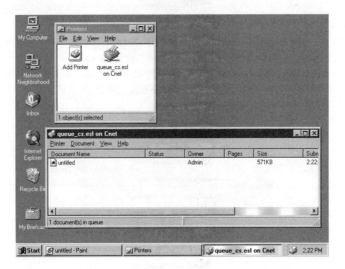

can also access or redirect output to the printer from the command
prompt as you would with the **CAPTURE** command. The following **NET USE**
and **CAPTURE** commands would produce the same results:

```
NET USE LPT1 \\NWSERVER\NWQUEUE
```

or

```
CAPTURE Q=NWQUEUE S=NWSERVER L=1
```

You can also copy print jobs directly to NetWare print queues without having any local printer port redirected. If you weren't using a redirected printer port using one of the preceding commands, and you still wanted to copy a file to the NetWare print queue, you could send it there directly with the following command:

```
COPY README.TBXT \\NWSERVER\NWQUEUE
```

The preceding print commands could also be used in conjunction with other commands in a batch file or Windows NT logon script.

Earlier in this section, we saw where you could change your print options through the CSNW program icon located in the Control Panel. You can change three options:

■ Add Form Feed
■ Notify When Printed
■ Print Banner

Support for NetWare-Aware Applications and Utilities

Although Windows NT Workstation has various 32-bit graphical network and user management utilities for managing Windows NT server resources, earlier versions of NetWare supplied only 16-bit nongraphical server management utilities. As such, it is important that Windows NT be able to support these utilities if you plan to manage your NetWare servers. With Windows NT Workstation CSNW installed, you can run some, but not all, the NetWare 16-bit command-line server management and resource sharing utilities from the command prompt. Some management functions can also be performed through the Windows NT management utilities, but they are limited to tasks such as moving files, maintaining print queues, connecting to servers, and viewing Bindery-based NetWare services. Windows NT can also support a number of NetWare-aware utilities and applications.

Table 4-6 provides a list of the supported NetWare utilities.

Don't Forget the Message Files

Note that if you try to run some of the utilities in Table 4-6, you will need to ensure that you also copy the appropriate message files to support

Table 4-6

Supported
NetWare utilities.
(Source: Microsoft
Corporation)

CHKVOL	COLORPAL	DSPACE	FLAG
FLAGDIR	FCONSOLE	FILER	GRANT
HELP	LISTDIR	MAP	NCOPY
NDIR	PCONSOLE	PSC	PSTAT
RCONSOLE	REMOVE	REVOKE	RIGHTS
SECURITY	SEND	SESSION	SETPASS
SETTS	SLIST	SYSCON	TLIST
USERLIST	VOLINFO	WHOAMI	

them; otherwise, they will not start. The main message file you need to ensure you have is the SYS$MSG.DAT file, which is located in the SYS:PUBLIC directory. If you want to run some of the preceding utilities outside the SYS:PUBLIC directory, then you should copy the SYS$MSG.DAT file to the directory from which you plan to run the utility or have SYS:PUBLIC as part of your environment path.

Running NetWare-Aware Applications

Not all the potential NetWare-aware applications run on Windows NT workstation. When a NetWare-aware application runs on a Windows NT workstation client, it needs to think it is running on a fully supported Net-Ware client, which is not the case when using Microsoft's CSNW. There-fore, you have to provide these applications with some of the files they are expecting to find. These files range from Terminate and Stay Resident (TSR) programs to special *.DLL files that are required when the application is run on DOS/Windows 3.x or WFWG.

As we saw earlier with Windows 95, some of those files include NET-WARE.DRV, NWIPXSPX.DLL, NWCALLS.DLL, and NWNETAPI.DLL. Also, one of the main requirements for many of these applications is that you are connected to a NetWare server. So if you have not already done so, configuring CSNW to be connected is probably a good idea. Table 4-7 provides a list of some of the NT-supported NetWare-aware applications. Additionally, you should place the files listed here in your \%SYSTEMROOT%\SYSTEM32 directory so that they can be located by Windows NT when a NetWare-aware application makes a call for them.

Table 4-7

Supported
NetWare-aware
applications.
(Source: Microsoft
Corporation)

Application	Version	Prerequisites
Attachmate Extra! MS-DOS for NetWare SAA Gateway	3.1	Batch Files
Attachmate Extra! MS-DOS for Attachmate 3270 Gateway	3.1	Batch Files
Attachmate Extra! Windows for NetWare SAA Gateway	3.5	TSR
Attachmate Extra! Windows for Attachmate 3270 Gateway	3.5	TSR
DCA IRMA LAN MS-DOS for NetWare SAA Gateway	2.1.0	None
Btrieve requester (BREQUEST.EXE)	6.10a	TSR
Gupta SQLBase for NetWare Systems	5.1.3	Btrieve support
Lotus Notes, SPX connectivity option	3.0	Must connect to NetWare server first
NetWare 3270 LAN Workstation for Windows	1.2	Runs only on Intel CPU platform

Monitoring CSNW Performance

After it is installed, you can actually monitor CSNW performance through the Windows NT Performance Monitor. This capability could prove helpful later when you are trying to compare performance between Microsoft and Novell client redirector software during your tests. To monitor the newly installed CSNW client software, start the Performance Monitor from the Administrative Tools Program Group and then follow these steps:

1. Start Performance Monitor.
2. Click on the + (plus) button, or select the Add menu item from the Edit menu.
3. Select the computer that you want to monitor using the UNC name or by browsing for it.
4. In the Object dialog box, select Client Services for NetWare.
5. Select all the counters that you would like to monitor by clicking on them and then clicking on the Add button.
6. After you have selected all your counters, click on the Done button. (See Figure 4-85.)

Figure 4-85
Monitoring CSNW
performance. (Cour-
tesy Learning Tree
International)

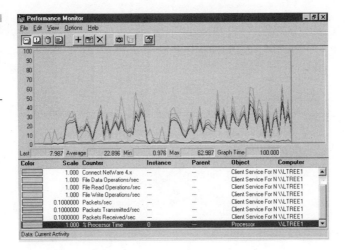

You should then begin to see a colorful graph across your screen high-lighting performance levels based on the network traffic you are transmitting or receiving. For fun, you can Hot Key to the File Manager, connect to a NetWare server, and start uploading or downloading large files to see some real activity on your Performance Monitor. Another good idea is to set up your Performance Monitor and then use a file transfer utility such as **NETBENCH** or **PERFORM3** to transfer data blocks between your workstation and the server. This test will give you a relatively good level against which to test other client redirector software implementations, such as Novell's.

General CSNW Troubleshooting Tips

Here are some general troubleshooting tips:

- CSNW does not support time synchronization with NetWare server time like DOS workstations do.

- If CSNW attach sessions on NetWare servers are not being released after the user has disconnected, you will need to install the Windows NT Service Pack 3. Alternatively, you can start an MS-DOS command prompt on the Windows NT Workstation and log off NetWare. This way, you can close the NetWare session.

- CSNW on Windows NT opens files slower when compared to access from other NetWare clients. This situation is potentially caused by an IPX router in between the Windows NT workstation and the NetWare server. The router reacts to the NCP Burst Mode

configuration information that CSNW sends it and, in turn, requests frequent resends.

▨ The **MAP** command is not fully supported. If you use the command

```
MAP F:=NWSERVER\SYS:\DATA\WP\CONFIG
```

and then go to the F: drive, you will be placed at the
NWSERVER\SYS: level of the volume instead of in the subdirectory you requested. To correct the situation, use the **MAP ROOT**
command instead.

▨ CSNW is slow to start programs when the preferred server cannot
be found because CSNW tries to locate the preferred NetWare
server each time you start an application. To avoid this problem,
set the Preferred Server setting in CSNW to **<NONE>** so that CSNW
does not look for one.

That's pretty much it for Windows NT Workstation 3.51 and Microsoft's
implementation of a NetWare client redirector called Client Services for
NetWare. Much like Windows 95's implementation of Microsoft Client for
NetWare Networks, CSNW works well on the operating system it was designed for. It provides adequate access to NetWare Bindery-based servers
with little to configure or maintain. It also supports most of the 16-bit
NetWare management utilities. The fact that it does not support NetWare
login scripts is a bit of an inconvenience, one that can be readily resolved
with a good batch file. So, if your NetWare servers are of the dated sort
(NetWare 3.x), and you don't need anything fancy, CSNW will more than
likely do everything you need.

This industry waits for no one, however. IntranetWare 4.11 with a more
advanced NDS rolls out across the land. Windows NT Workstation 4.0
equally gains ground as the new armor-strength desktop to replace many
of the old WFWG installations as new equipment is purchased or for those
people who have held off from moving to Windows 95. Windows NT Server
4.0 is also making significant inroads as a general-purpose application
server within many multiplatform network environments.

Let's look now at Windows NT Workstation 4.0 to see what improvements have been made to Client Services for NetWare.

Windows NT Workstation 4.0 and Client Services for NetWare

Without getting into a major discussion about the differences between
Windows NT Workstation 3.51 and 4.0, let us say that now you get the

Windows 95 interface, improved performance on the video side as part of the graphics subsystem has been moved down closer to the kernel, and 32-bit applications designed for Windows NT will run faster because, here again, part of the WIN32 subsystem has been moved down closer to the kernel as well. For a complete discussion of the differences between the two versions of the operating system, refer to Microsoft's Internet Web site for more information.

The installation process for Client Services for NetWare is essentially the same as it was with the previous version. Follow these steps:

1. Start the Network Program from the Control Panel.

2. Click on the Services tab (instead of the Add Software tab as in 3.51).

3. Select Client Services for NetWare and click on OK.

4. Indicate where the installation process can locate the CSNW files.

5. Close the Network program and restart the computer. (See Figure 4-86.)

When Windows NT Workstation first reboots, it will prompt you for NetWare-specific information regarding the login process. Here you will have an opportunity to specify whether you want to log on to a Preferred Server (most likely NetWare 3.x or NetWare 4.x with Bindery Emulation) or to a Default Tree and Context (for NetWare 4.x with NDS).

TIP: *When you enter your context information, make sure you specify the leading . (period); otherwise, NT won't find your context. Also at this point, you can specify whether you want your NetWare login script to process.*

Figure 4-86
Adding CSNW to Windows NT Workstation. (Source: Microsoft Corporation)

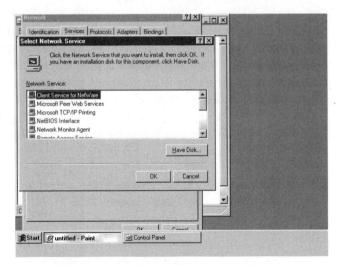

█████ ████ ████ ████

Figure 4-87
CSNW for NT Version
4.0 makes NT
NDS-aware. (Source:
Microsoft
Corporation)

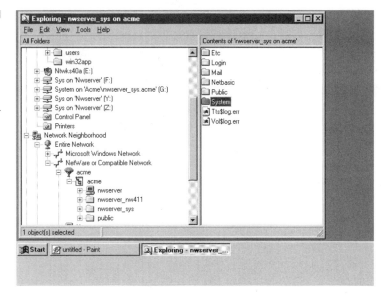

Before we begin, suffice it to say that Client Services for NetWare under Windows NT Workstation 4.0 is an improvement only on the previous version. In fact, one of the new features is support for NetWare Directory Services, which offers Windows NT users access to key NDS functions such as NDS authentication, property pages, and passwords. NDS support can be readily seen by opening the Windows Explorer after CSNW is installed and browsing the network neighborhood. (See Figure 4-87.)

After CSNW is installed, you can use a Network Access Order option on the Services tab of the Control Panel's Network program to specify in which order network resources are search. Therefore, if your network is predominantly NetWare oriented, you can specify that NetWare or Compatible Network resources should be searched first and then Microsoft ones. You can also easily change the order if your network is predominantly Microsoft-oriented.

Based on the preceding view of the Windows Explorer, you can see that we could easily map to a NetWare NDS-specified file system volume. A printer would be just as easy to access. You can also see that the Bindery Emulation version of the resources is also displayed (NWSERVER\SYS:), so providing access to NetWare 4.x NDS network resources would be relatively simple.

The configuration tools are different only in that they now use the Windows 95 interface's look and feel. Also, you have a few more options to configure in the CSNW screens of the CSNW configuration program found in

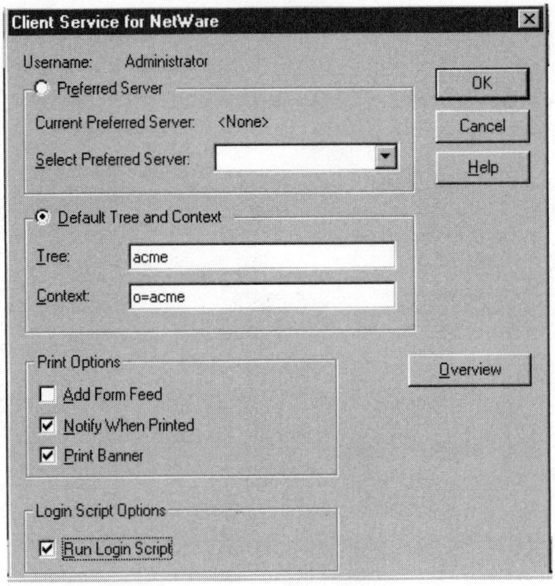

Figure 4-88
Configuring CSNW
options from the
Control Panel.
(Source: Microsoft
Corporation)

the Control Panel after CSNW is installed—particularly with regards to
NDS login capability. (See Figure 4-88.) You can now specify the NDS Tree
and Context for your login. Backward support (if you want to call it that)
is now available for standard Bindery-based NetWare logins. Another major feature is the ability to have NetWare login scripts process. You will
remember that this capability was something we could not do with Windows NT Workstation 3.51.

Another nice feature is the ability to change your NetWare password
right from the Windows NT Workstation security window. All you have to
do is press the famous Ctrl+Alt+Del key sequence and select the Change
Password button. From there, you can click on the Domain dialog box and
select NetWare or Compatible Network. (Unfortunately, we could not get
a screen shot of this one!) This feature is nice because you used to have
to be connected to the NetWare server(s) upon which your user account
existed, go to the PUBLIC subdirectorym and then run the **SETPASS** command. This feature make the process much easier. In all honesty, we have
to point out that NDS is really making the task simpler in that the Windows NT user is logging into the NDS tree, not an individual server.

Are Profiles and Policies Still Supported?

Yes, Windows NT Workstation 4.0 User Profiles and Policies are still supported in this multiplatform server environment. As we did with Windows

Figure 4-89
Logon flowchart for
NT 4.0 configured
with CSNW for NT
Domain Logon.
(Courtesy WWW.
NETWORKOLOGIST.
COM)

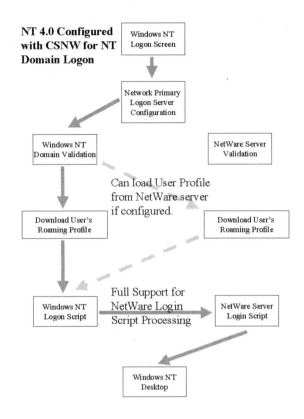

NT Workstation 3.51, we can decide to place our User Profile on either the Windows NT Domain server or the NetWare server. (See Figure 4-89.)

One problem we encountered is that Windows NT Workstation 4.0 will time out quickly when processing User Profiles that are stored on another server. The main reason for this problem is that authenticating against the other platform's server directory structure takes a bit more time. However, you will be happy to know that you can change a setting in the Registry for the workstations. You should be aware that you can use a Policy file to update all the Windows NT Workstations remotely from a central server and that it can be either a Windows NT or NetWare server. So Windows NT Workstation supports User Profiles and Policies equally well from either server platform. (See Figure 4-90.)

But why keep Windows NT Workstation User Profiles on a NetWare server? We already know they can be stored on a Windows NT Server, so why not place them there? Probably the only reason you might not do so is that you do not have a centralized Windows NT Domain SAM database and your users log in with NetWare user accounts. As such, they will require a place to put their centralized User Profiles so that they can have them when they wander around to other Windows NT workstations.

Other than the information provided in the preceding sections, we don't have much more to tell—except that the NetWare Administrator tools install okay but don't work with the Microsoft CSNW redirector drivers. You will need Novell's Client 32 to make that happen. We even tried to run the MS-DOS version of the NetWare Administrator and received the message shown in Figure 4-91.

You may remember that we did specify that we wanted to log in to the NetWare NDS Tree called ACME and that the Context was .ACME (O=ACME). The GUI version of the NetWare Administrator installed nicely, with no questions asked. However, when we ran it, we also received an error message, but of a different sort.

Although we were able to successfully access NetWare NDS-specified network resources, we were not yet able to manage them. Although having this capability is fine for users who need to access the resources, it does present a bit of a problem for those responsible for administering

Figure 4-90
Storing User Profiles on a NetWare server for Windows NT Workstation users. (Source: Microsoft Corporation.)

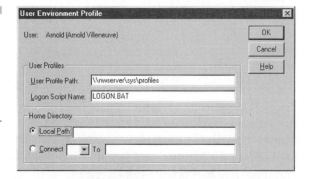

Figure 4-91
Running CSNW, the 16-bit non-GUI Net-Ware Administrator (NETADMIN) tells us we are not logged in to NDS. (Source: Microsoft Corporation)

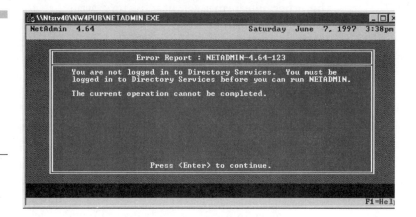

them. Therein lies the problem and the reason for moving onto the next section, where we will look at Novell's Client 32 for NT.

Novell NetWare Client Software for Windows NT Workstation

Currently, two versions of Novell client software for Windows NT Workstation are available: NetWare Client 32 for Windows NT and IntranetWare Client for Windows NT. The latter is simply a newer version with more tie-ins to the IntranetWare version of NetWare. Additionally, the IntranetWare version provides for a link between Windows NT Workstation and NDS. We'll look at the NetWare Client 32 for Windows NT and then investigate the IntranetWare Client for Windows NT next.

Novell's NetWare Client 32 for Windows NT

For this section of the book, we will concentrate on working with Windows NT Workstation 4.0 for the installation of Novell's NetWare Client 32 for Windows NT and IntranetWare client as the same redirector software is used. Therefore, most, if not all, of what we cover here will apply to both versions of Windows NT. This information covers the installation because you start it by clicking on a SETUPNW.EXE file, not by the usual method of going through the Control Panel's Network program.

Table 4-8 shows the comparison of NetWare Client 32 for Windows NT and Client Services for NetWare.

Table 4-8

Comparison of NetWare Client 32 for Windows NT and Client Service for NetWare. (Source: Novell, Inc.)

Features	Novell's Client 32 for NT 3.51 and 4.0	Microsoft's NT 4.0 with CSNW
Comparable features Remote Access Support	Yes	Yes
Unattended Install	Yes	Yes
Support for 32-bit IPX and SPX	Yes	Yes
Packet Burst	Yes	Yes
Multitree Login and View of Network	Yes	Yes

Continues

Table 4-8

Continued.

Features	Novell's Client 32 for NT 3.51 and 4.0	Microsoft's NT 4.0 with CSNW
Long File Name support	Yes	Yes
User Profile Storage External to Local Workstation	Yes	Yes
Source Routing Support	Yes	Yes
Simultaneous Login to NetWare and NT Domain	Yes	Yes
Coexist with Microsoft SMB Client (Peer-to-Peer Compatibility)	Yes	Yes
NetBEUI	Yes (coexists)	Yes
Utilize IP Address Leasing Through DHCP	Yes	Yes
SMP Aware Client	Yes	Yes
Advantages Of Novell's NetWare Client 32 for Windows NT		
Novell Application Launcher included	Yes	No
32-bit NetWare Administrator	Yes	No
Full Login Script Processing	Yes	No
NetWare /IP 2.2	Yes	No
GUI Login to NetWare	Yes	No (Passthrough only)
Advanced Background LIP Algorithm	Yes	No
View Access Rights from File Manager (Permission Provider)	Yes	No
Packet Signing	Yes	No
Extended Attribute Support	Yes	No
ODI 3.3 Assembly Driver Support	Yes	No
ODI 1.1 C Driver Support	Yes	No
Auto Client Update	Yes	No
Global DOS Support (VLM and NeTBX)	Yes	No
32-bit Native IPX/SPX API Support	Yes	No
Full 16-bit DOS/Windows IPX & SPX API Emulation	Yes	No
Automatic Password Synchronization	Yes	No
32-bit NetWare SDK Support	Yes	No

NetWare Client 32 for Windows NT 3.51 and 4.0 Installation

The installation process could not be easier. The NetWare Client 32 Drivers are available on the NetWare 4.11 CD-ROM. You can use the same process to start the installation as we did earlier in this chapter with the Client 32 for Windows 95. In fact, you will find the Windows NT version on the same installation screen. Just pick it instead of Windows 95. The files will decompress and begin to install to the client. You do not have to load them from within the Control Panel. All the required changes to the Network program-related Registry entries are made for you through the SETUPNW.EXE installation program.

The Novell logo appears, and you are prompted to perform the installation. The files are copied to your hard drive, Registry changes are made, and then you are asked to reboot (as opposed to restart) your computer. The simplicity of this process is overshadowed by the numerous changes that are taking place in the background.

Upon rebooting, you are presented with the NetWare Begin Login screen. The Novell NetWare Client Services GUI Login Utility has five option screens that are all similar to the one we reviewed with Windows 95. You can specify both your NetWare and Windows NT login information here, as well as whether logon/login scripts should be processed. From this screen, you can configure whether you should log on to a Windows NT Domain only or whether you should be logged on to both the Domain as well as a Preferred NetWare server or NDS Tree. However, this is the only place that you can specify that you want to log on only to Windows NT from the NetWare GUI utility because the option is not made available elsewhere. However, the assumption is that, if you are running the NetWare Client 32 for Windows NT, you will most likely log in to a NetWare server Bindery or NDS Tree.

To adjust your client settings, you can go to the Control Panel's Network program and select the Services tab. From there, you can open the Properties of the Novell NetWare Client Services Configuration forms. (See Figure 4-92.)

You have a number of options here. The Client tab allows you to specify which drive will be used as the first network drive, specify your preferred server or tree, and configure the system so that you can log in to multiple trees at the same time. The Login tab (shown in Figure 4-92) is probably the most important one because it allows you to further refine the client login configuration process. Although the Client form specifies where you log in, this form specifies what you will see and do when you

Figure 4-92
Configuring the Novell NetWare Client Services Configuration. (Source: Microsoft Corporation)

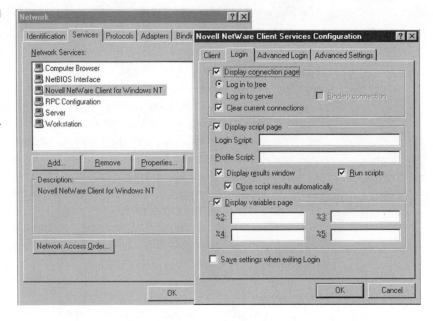

log in. You can enable or disable options determining whether you can run login scripts and display login progress and results windows in this form. You can also have the login scripts call certain external variables here. These variables can include test or graphics files.

The Advanced Login tab allows you to specify the use of policies and roaming user profiles. Corporate bitmaps for use as the Welcome screen can be presented here. The Advanced Settings are all similar to the ones we reviewed for the Client 32 for Windows 95 earlier in this chapter. The flowchart in Figure 4-93 highlights the new login process after Client 32 for Windows NT is installed. Notice that now the NetWare login scripts run first, before the Windows NT Domains scripts.

Another place you can look at or change configuration information is the NetWare (Common) folder that is installed with the client software. (See Figure 4-94.) The four configuration options here allow you to log in to other parts of the network from within your current session. This capability would be helpful if you were currently only logged on to Windows NT, for example, and wanted to access resources on the NetWare part of the network. The options for the NetWare Login GUI include specifying connections to other NDS Trees or preferred servers in the network, as well as your new NDS context. If you are not sure what your context is, you can search for it through the current or other NDS trees. This latter feature is nice in a large network environment.

Figure 4-93
Logon flowchart
showing new login
process with Client
32 for Windows NT.
(Courtesy WWW.
NETWORKOLOGIST.
COM)

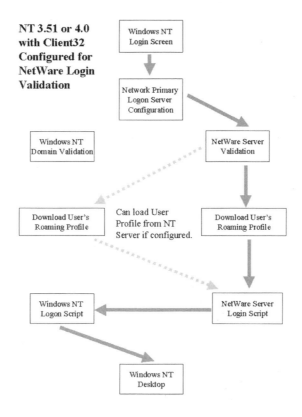

Figure 4-94
The NetWare (Common) folder utilities.
(Source: Microsoft
Corporation)

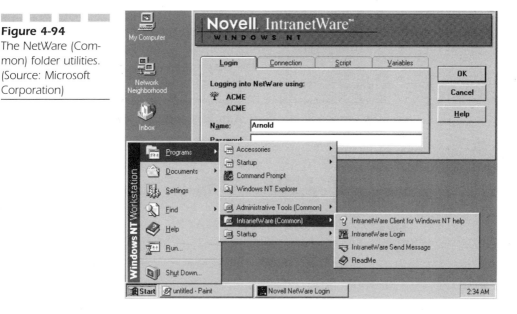

NetWare Administrator for Windows NT

We got logged into NDS! Now we need the NetWare Administrator for Windows NT. Well, one of the main reasons we would have gone this far in the process would be because we are working with a NetWare 4.x network, and we would like to be able to fully and completely manage our NDS tree from the relative safety of the Windows NT workstation. When you install the Client 32 software to Windows NT, the GUI version of the NetWare Administrator is also copied but is not installed. You can install it by locating the ADMSETUP.EXE program. This file can be found under the I386 folder within the Windows NT client driver directories. A newer version can also be downloaded from Novell's Internet site.

The installation itself is relatively easy. It asks you whether you want to install the NetWare Application Launcher and the NetWare Administrator at the same time. A list of servers is displayed so that you can pick which one you want to install it onto, and then the files are copied. A message follows to let you know that the installation has completed. The files themselves are copied onto the NetWare server into the SERVER_NAME\VOLUME:PUBLIC\WINNT subdirectory. One of the aspects of the installation that is not done is creating a folder within the Windows NT menuing system. This step is very easy and would certainly have made life a little easier. We reasoned that Novell left out this step because it wants you to use its NetWare Application Launcher instead (which is located in the PUBLIC directory and is called NALWIN32.EXE). (See Figure 4-95.)

After it is installed, though, you can easily manage your NetWare NDS tree objects through the NetWare Administrator. When we ran the full 32-bit version of the NetWare Administrator on NDS, we noticed a marked improvement in performance. All the standard NDS capabilities are available, and you are now ready to manage your tree. Figure 4-96 shows our successfully launched NetWare Administrator for Windows NT.

Figure 4-95
Running the NetWare Application Launcher for Windows NT. (Source: Microsoft Corporation and Novell, Inc.)

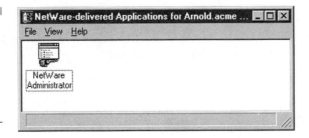

Figure 4-96
Running the Net-
Ware Administrator
for Windows NT.
(Source: Microsoft
Corporation and
Novell, Inc.)

Novell's IntranetWare Client for Windows NT

The IntranetWare client is the new and improved version of the NetWare Client 32 for Windows NT. The improvements lie in a continuation of tighter integration of Windows NT with NDS on the part of Novell. On the whole, Novell is integrating NDS more closely with the Internet, as is Microsoft with Internet Information Server. The installation is the same as in the preceding section, except that you need to download this big one (over 12Mbytes) from the Novell Internet site. (See Figure 4-97.) At the time of this writing, it is no yet available on the standard IntranetWare CD-ROMs. The best place to go for the current IntranetWare client software and administrative utilities is `http://www.novell.com/intranetware/ntint/`.

All the underlying networking architecture that Novell implemented with Client 32 is still the same. The NetWare Administrator and NetWare Application Launcher are also there. One new feature is the Workstation Manager Administration Module, which allows the Windows NT Workstation to be administered from within an NDS database.

The following are IntranetWare for Windows NT 3.51 and 4.0 Installation Utility features:

Figure 4-97

The IntranetWare Client for Windows NT Installation files after downloading and decompressing from Novell's Internet site. (Source: Microsoft Corporation and Novell, Inc.)

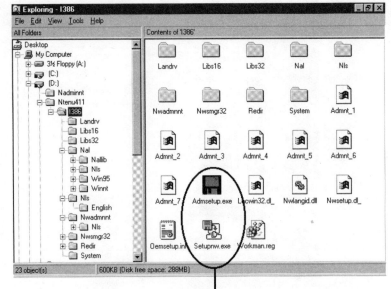

IntranetWare Client and Administrator Installation files for Windows NT 3.51 and 4.0 after download from Novell's Internet site. SETUPNW.EXE installs the IntranetWare Client redirector/provider. ADMSETUP.EXE installs the NetWare Administrator utilities up on the NetWare servers you select.

- You can install or update the current client software running on a Windows NT workstation.

- You can perform simultaneous unattended installations on multiple workstations across the network.

- Unattended installation is simplified by including client and configuration settings during the setup by setting parameters in a text file used during unattended installation.

- You can follow a simple graphical user interface installation with minimal questions asked.

- You can perform automatic client upgrades during login.

- Installation will automatically detect and replace Microsoft's Client for NetWare Networks because both Microsoft's and Novell's clients cannot be installed on the same workstation.

- Installation can be performed from disk, hard disk, server volume, or CD-ROM.

- Source routing can be removed if enabled when you install NetWare/IP*.

Installation Overview

The installation of IntranetWare Client for Windows NT itself is very simple. Run the SETUPNW.EXE program, click on a few buttons, and watch as the files are copied over to your Windows NT workstation. The installation is a lot like Client 32 for NetWare, only easier. For the local client installation, all the files required are copied locally. Reboot the workstation, and the installation is done. (See Figure 4-100.)

You can install the IntranetWare Client from the Windows NT Network Control Panel, but this method is somewhat more cumbersome. However, it does allow you to make changes to the configuration as you go. To install from the Windows NT Network Control Panel, follow these steps provided by Novell, Inc.:

1. Log in to the Windows NT workstation as an NT user who is a member of the Administrators group.

2. From the Start menu, choose Settings.

Figure 4-98
Starting the Intranet-Ware Client for Windows NT installation. (Source: Novell, Inc.)

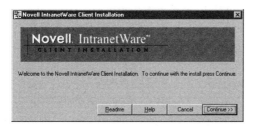

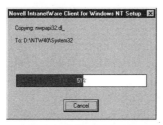

3. Choose Control Panel.

4. From the Control Panel, choose Network.

5. Choose the Services tab.

6. Choose Add.

7. Choose Have Disk.

8. Enter the path to the Novell IntranetWare Client for Windows NT files on the CD or network. For example, enter `D:\I386` or `C:\INTRANW\I386`.

8a. (Optional) Insert the IntranetWare CD into the CD-ROM drive and choose OK.

9. From the Select OEM Option dialog box, choose Novell Intranet-Ware Client for Windows NT and choose OK.

   The client software and driver are then installed on the workstation. After installation is complete, you will need to configure properties. You also need to install a Network Interface Card driver before you can make a successful connection. (See Figure 4-99.)

    This method enables you to use the Network control panel to install the IntranetWare Client as you would any other Windows NT service.

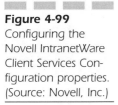

Figure 4-99
Configuring the Novell IntranetWare Client Services Configuration properties. (Source: Novell, Inc.)

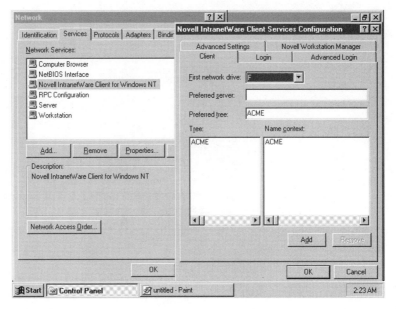

Unattended Installations May Reduce the Steps

The unattended installation option is ideal if you are installing Novell IntranetWare Client for Windows NT for the first time on many workstations. It can also be used for upgrading existing workstations. Unattended installation can be automated if you set configuration options by using the UNATTEND.TBXT file (if you run SETUPNW.EXE with the /u option). (For complete fairness, we must point out that Microsoft's client redirectors can also be installed in unattended mode.) An additional nice option is the ability to install both Windows NT and Novell IntranetWare Client at the same time. Installations can also be performed over the network.

Logging On

After the system has rebooted, you will be prompted with a new logon screen: the IntranetWare Login screen. This screen will allow you to configure both your NetWare and Windows NT login/logon information. NetWare Bindery or NDS Tree-based logins can be specified as well as Windows NT Local or Domain user accounts. Login/logon scripts are treated the same as was done with Client 32 for Windows NT Workstation, except that now you have a few more options for how you want the logins to proceed. Of course, the NetWare login script is executed first.

The installation process does create one menu item in the All Users profile folder called the IntranetWare (Common) folder. In it are placed a README and HELP file, as well as the IntranetWare GUI Login Utility and Messaging GUI Utility. The login utility can be used to connect you to additional servers and NDS trees, or to log you off any current network connections and reconnect you onto others. Figure 4-100 shows both the menu location and the IntranetWare GUI Login Utility.

The additional tabs on the login utility allow you to specify other connections and whether to clear all of your current connections. On the Script tab, you would identify which NetWare login scripts you want to execute. The Variables tab allows you to pass several variables to the login scripts themselves. You will no doubt notice that this screen looks very similar to the one from Client 32 for Windows NT Workstation.

Now that we have installed the new IntranetWare client, we need to install the NetWare Administrator so that we can manage the NDS tree objects and partitions.

Figure 4-100
The IntranetWare
GUI Login Utility.
(Source: Novell, Inc.)

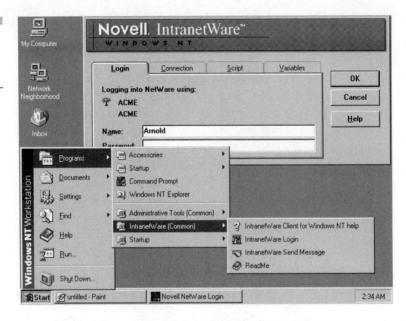

Installing Administration Utilities on the NetWare Server

The *NetWare Administrator NT* (NWADMNNT), *Novell Application Launcher* (NAL), and Workstation Manager Administration Module are bundled with the IntranetWare Client software so that you have everything you need to manage your NDS tree objects and partitions right away. (See Figure 4-101.) If you already have ManageWise for managing your network, you will be able to start to administer your Windows NT systems from the central network management point as well. The administration utilities require approximately 20Mbytes of hard disk space up on your NetWare server. Figure 4-102 shows where they were installed on the PUBLIC\WINNT folder of the NWSERVER NetWare server. We point out this fact because installing these tools does not create a menu item in yours or the All Users profiles for Windows NT—so they are not put on the menu.

To install the administration utilities (again, based on Novell's instructions), follow these steps:

1. Locate the ADMSETUP.EXE icon in the I386 directory on the Novell IntranetWare Client for Windows NT CD.

2. Double-click ADMSETUP.EXE.

Figure 4-101
Installing the Net-
Ware Administrator
Tools. (Source:
Novell, Inc.)

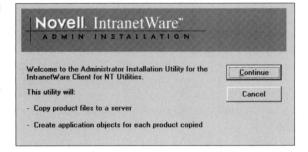

Figure 4-102
The secret location
of the NetWare
Administrator utility.
(Source: Microsoft
Corporation)

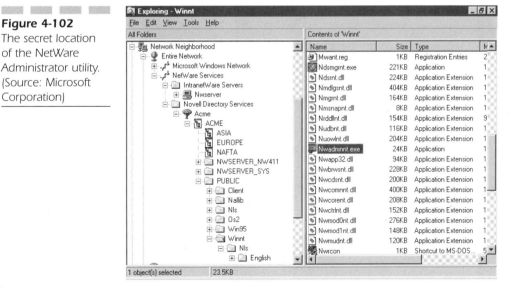

3. Choose Yes to accept the Novell Terms and Conditions.

   If you choose No, you will not be able to install the administration utilities.

4. Choose Continue after reading the Administrator Utility title screen.

   If you choose Cancel, you will not be able to complete the installation.

5. Choose the utilities you want to install by checking the check box next to the utility's name.

   You have two choices: Novell Application Launcher and NetWare Administrator.

6. Choose a server from the To Server list.

   You must have sufficient rights to write files to the server. You should choose a server to which you have Administrator rights.

7. Choose OK.

   A progress screen with two progress bars appears. The top bar shows which application is being installed. The bottom bar shows the percentage of files that have been installed. After the files are installed, the Installation Complete dialog box appears.

8. Choose Run NW Admin to start NetWare Administrator.

   or

   Choose Close to exit the installer without starting NetWare Administrator. (See Figure 4-103.)

One of the new features available is the Windows NT Integration Utility—previously code-named Tobasco (do you think Novell meant that this is hot stuff?). The utility allows you to integrate NDS and NT Domain user databases. Not only that, it allows you to resynchronize them as well. (See Figure 4-104.) It is a lot like the Synchronicity product. Refer to Chapter 6 for more information on this utility.

On the surface at least, the most noticeable difference is the change in the name from NetWare to IntranetWare on many of the menus and utilities. However, the changes are significant because Novell as laid the groundwork for integrating Windows NT systems and Security Accounts Manager databases into NDS. The Workstation Manager Administrator Module is just one step in this direction. The module for the IntranetWare client is only one piece of the puzzle, though, and you also require the Novell Administration for Windows NT Integration Utility as well as ManageWise to complete the picture.

Figure 4-103

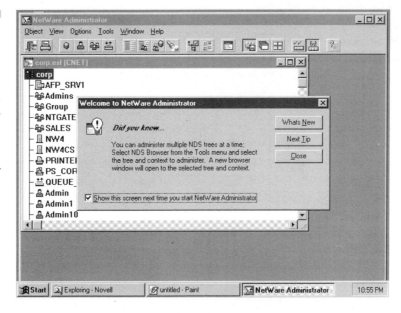

Figure 4-103
The new Intranet-
Ware NetWare
Administrator utility
looks a lot like the
old one, but don't be
fooled because many
new options are
under the hood.
(Source: Novell, Inc.)

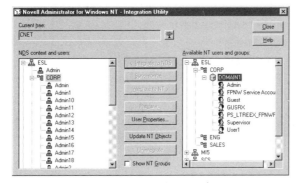

Figure 4-104
The new Novell
Administrator for
Windows NT - Inte-
gration Utility, which
allows management
of both NDS and NT
Domain user and
group accounts.
(Source: Novell, Inc.)

WINDOWS NT SERVER AS A CLIENT   Windows NT Server can also
be a client for NetWare servers. And as has been the theme so far throughout this chapter, there are two potential solutions: Microsoft's and Novell's. For Microsoft's NetWare connectivity solution, you need to look at
Gateway Service for NetWare, which is discussed in the next chapter. For
Novell's solution, see the previous few sections with regards to Client 32
and IntranetWare client.

The Gateway Service for NetWare enables Windows NT server to com-
municate with NetWare servers using the IPX/NCP protocol combination.
Therefore, GSNW is to the server what CSNW is to the Windows NT
Workstation. However, as you will see, there is an additional feature to

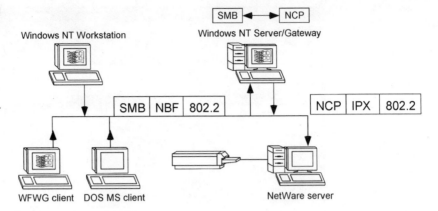

Figure 4-105
Accessing a NetWare
Server when you
don't support NCP.
(Courtesy of Learning
Tree International)

implementing GSNW, and it is a feature that Novell's client does not provide. GSNW can act as a translating gateway between Server Message Blocks and NetWare Core Protocols. (See Figure 4-105.)

So what has this got to do with network clients accessing network resources? Only one thing, and that is if your requirement to access NetWare servers is low for some of your network clients, you do not need to load any NetWare redirector for that client. You can simply configure the Windows NT Server to act as a gateway to the NetWare shared network resources and thereby provide transparent access to your NetWare resources. However, for every gain is usually an offsetting cost. In this case, you can have a few costs, so see Chapter 5 on Gateway Service for NetWare for more details.

Additional Connectivity Options

We have several other alternatives here where we can get Microsoft and Novell to come together on our network. The method is simple: Instead of getting either of them to talk to the other platform's main file and print sharing protocol, we get all of them to support a common denominator network resource sharing protocol. We have several potential choices for a common denominator protocol including Network File System and Apple File and Print Share. (See Figure 4-106.)

Are there any real disadvantages to this approach? Well, on the surface, not many—although one of them would be considered fairly important. Standard file and printer access is facilitated easily enough through this approach. Even communication server access can be provided. If you

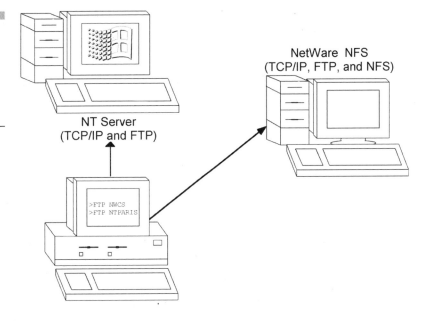

Figure 4-106
Using FTP and NFS as a common file and print sharing protocol. (Courtesy of Learning Tree International)

are using NFS, even the standard file and printer access GUI tools like File Manager and Explorer are available to locate and connect to these resources.

However, as we demonstrated earlier in this chapter, if you want to manage your server resources, you are going to need to run at least one NetWare-configured client somewhere on your network. You don't need a Microsoft-configured client because all the server management can be done at the server console.

This latter approach also has a huge upside. In the case of NFS, we can also provide a far greater number of network resources to our clients than with either SMB or NCP combined because many other server platforms such as UNIX, VMS, and others also support NFS. Enterprise networking in a multi, multiplatform environment, however, is the topic for another book. Check out a book called *Multivendor Networking* by A. Fortino and J. Gollick.

IF YOU CAN'T CHANGE THE CLIENT, CHANGE THE SERVER!
A final solution to this challenge of providing seamless network resource access to clients is to simply change the server. Instead of getting the Windows NT Workstations to support NCP, why not configure the NetWare server to support Server Message Blocks or the Windows NT Server to support NetWare Core Protocol. Both of these solutions are now possible, and we will look at them in the next chapter.

SUMMARY

You have now looked at many potential solutions for configuring your network clients (DOS/Windows 3.x, Windows for Workgroups, and Windows NT Workstation) to be able to seamlessly access both Windows NT Server and NetWare Server resources. You have seen that Microsoft provides a workable built-in NetWare client (Client Services for NetWare) that, for the most part, does a very good job of fulfilling the seamless access part without having to resort to third-party client redirector software. As we pointed out, Microsoft's solution works very well in a NetWare 3.x or NetWare 4.x environment when all you need to do is access the resources themselves. In fact, you can even manage the NetWare Bindery-based servers using Microsoft's client software. However, when you need to be able to actually manage your NetWare 4.x NDS resources from a Windows client using NetWare-provided administrative tools, then you will need to consider using Novell's client redirector software (Client 32 and IntranetWare Client). Which approach you take depends on your current network environment and future direction.

CHAPTER **5**

Server Integration

This chapter focuses on the server integration. It will help you plan your installation of the Gateway services for Net-Ware, which allow Windows NT server clients to access a NetWare server. We will also look at the installation of File and Print Services for NetWare, which allows Net-Ware clients to access Windows NT.

Chapter Objectives

■ Identify the server tools available for integrating a mixed server environment

■ Learn how to install *Gateway Services for NetWare* (GSNW)

■ Install Windows NT *File and Print Services for NetWare* (FPNW)

■ Understand how Samba for NetWare provides Microsoft clients access to a NetWare server

Server Integration Requirements

When you're introducing a Windows NT server to an existing NetWare environment, this need not necessarily mean performing a full conversion from NetWare to Windows NT. File and Print Services for NetWare can be used to disguise a Windows NT server so that it looks like a NetWare 3.x server. You don't need to modify the NetWare clients in any way. This solution is ideal for organizations who have a mixed environment or as an interim step to a full migration.

Consider an organization with 200 users who will migrate a NetWare server to Windows NT. It is unlikely that all 200 users can be converted to clients of a Windows NT server at one time. This process would involve changing the network drivers as well as their windows configuration. Chances are good that a percentage of the workstations would have some unique requirement that would delay the process. If the clients were running Windows NT or Windows 95 as a workstation operating system, this may not be an issue because both are capable of attaching to NetWare and Windows NT server simultaneously. Because these workstations are currently running Windows 3.x, we need a strategy that would allow us to migrate the clients over a number of days.

The first step would involve installing a Windows NT server and copying sample data from the NetWare server to the Windows NT server to test for application compatibility. A simple way to perform this task is to install *Gateway Services for NetWare* (GSNW) on the Windows NT server. Using GSNW, the server becomes a NetWare client and can log in to the server to copy the necessary files.

Sample workstations can be used to perform any necessary testing. Assuming all goes well, the next step is to move live data to the server and convert the clients.

You can use one of three approaches to overcome the challenge of converting a large number of users. The first approach to consider is first converting the clients so that they can connect to the Windows NT server. Gateway Services for NetWare can be used to provide access to the NetWare server where the data resides. For a short time, some users configured as NetWare clients will access the NetWare server directly, whereas others will gain access through the gateway, until eventually, all clients are converted. Be sure to consider the performance through the gateway. After all, users are converted, data can be moved to the Windows NT server, and the NetWare server can be shut down permanently.

A second approach would involve moving the data to the Windows NT server first. File and print access could be provided to the NetWare clients by installing NetWare File and Print Services on the Windows NT server. Using this approach, the NetWare server could be shut down almost immediately. Clients would not even need to know the server had been changed because the Windows NT server name could be changed to the same name previously used by the NetWare server. Clients could then be migrated one by one until FPNW is no longer required.

A third approach is what we like to call the "Big Hammer" approach in which everything will be changed at once, perhaps over a weekend. This approach, which is our least favorite, does have the risk of not completing the conversion by the time the users return to work. With all the approaches, you need to address a number of issues such as how will you recover any lost data that may have been backed up from the NetWare server? Is your new tape backup software for Windows NT capable of reading data that was backed up using a NetWare utility? Arcserve is one backup product that has both Windows NT and NetWare versions. The Windows NT version is capable of restoring from a backup made with the NetWare version.

Also, don't forget that Windows NT logon scripts must also be developed for the Windows NT server to provide the user environment that NetWare login scripts provided.

Of course, not all companies will be converting from NetWare to Windows NT. Short of a full conversion, a common requirement is for Windows NT clients to access existing NetWare servers. Consider this example: Users in the marketing department that has just installed Windows NT server require files from the NetWare servers in the finance department. Gateway Services for NetWare can be installed on the Windows NT server to provide a solution for occasional access. Gateway Services for NetWare allows the Windows NT server to translate any SMB requests to NCP, which NetWare servers understand.

Gateway Services for NetWare

Gateway Services for NetWare (GSNW) is a NetWare client utility for Windows NT server. It is supplied with the Windows NT server and can be installed from the Windows NT Control Panel.

GSNW allows Windows NT server to connect to a NetWare server and log on as a NetWare client. Any of the NetWare server's resources that the Windows NT server has access to can be treated as Windows NT server resources. The Windows NT server can share these resources to the network, providing Windows NT server clients with NetWare server access.

Because the NetWare server file and printer resources are provided to the network by the Windows NT server, access is controlled by Windows NT security. The NetWare account the Windows NT server uses to log on the NetWare server should be given maximum rights to the NetWare server's resources. User access is limited by the permissions assigned to the user's Windows NT account.

When a client requests a NetWare file from the Windows NT server, the Windows NT server requests the file from the NetWare server on behalf of the client. Because the Windows NT server relies on requests using *Server Message Blocks* (SMB), the Windows NT server must translate these requests to *NetWare Core Protocol* (NCP). See Chapter 3 for more details on the description of NCP versus SMB.

The main strength of GSNW is to simplify the client configuration by providing all network services using a common client interface and a single network protocol. As with any gateway, this solution has its limits. Performance through the gateway is slower than accessing the NetWare file server directly. Before implementing this solution in a production environment, you may want to evaluate performance and CPU utilization on the Windows NT server. For heavy use, installing the gateway on a Windows NT server dedicated to this task may be wise. This solution is not ideal for large numbers of users requiring frequent access to data on the NetWare server. It is best suited for servers that have a low volume and are seldom used due to the performance limitations.

Table 5-1 lists several considerations for using GSNW.

Figure 5-1 depicts a Windows NT client requesting a file from the Windows NT server using a Server Message Block (SMB) file open request. Because SMB is understood by Windows NT and not by NetWare, the Windows NT server must interpret the request and reissue it to the NetWare server using the NetWare Core Protocol (NCP).

The Windows NT client can use any network protocol supported by Windows NT—in this case, TCP/IP—to talk to the Windows NT server.

Table 5-1

Gateway
Considerations.
(Courtesy of
Learning Tree
International)

Advantages	Disadvantages
Requires only one NetWare server connection	Slow performance
Security administration is done through one NetWare user/group account	Very high CPU utilization on the Windows NT server
Additional level of security can be set up via NT shares	Does not support NetWare administration utilities (as you are not actually logged on to the NetWare server)

Figure 5-1

SMB to NCP
Translation via
Gateway Services.
(Courtesy of Learning
Tree International)

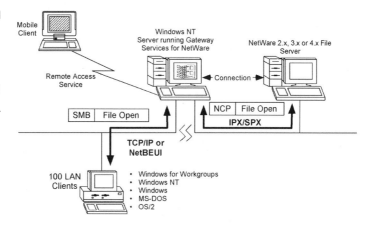

The Windows NT server has been configured to use the IPX protocol to talk to the Windows NT server. In the example, the Windows NT server has been configured with two network cards and is connected to two networks simultaneously. Although not necessary, this configuration is effective. It limits the IPX protocol to the network where the NetWare server resides, while continuing to allow access to the NetWare resources.

The Gateway Services for NetWare is composed of two components: File gateway services and Print gateway services. Both components are installed from the Network icon in the Windows NT Control Panel. After they are installed, each service must be configured separately. (See Figure 5-2.)

GSNW is provided with Windows NT server and performs two functions. It is the NetWare client for Windows NT server to access a NetWare server, as well as the gateway to allow clients of the Windows NT server to access NetWare servers. If the Windows NT server was being used as a client to access the NetWare server using the NetWare redirector from Novell, the Novell redirector must be removed.

▬ ▬ ▬ ▬

Figure 5-2
Gateway Services for
NetWare. (Source:
WWW.ITcoach.com)

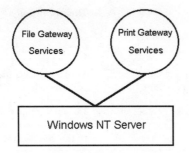

▬ ▬ ▬ ▬

Figure 5-3
Enabling Gateway
Services for NetWare
(GSNW). (Courtesy of
Learning Tree Inter-
national)

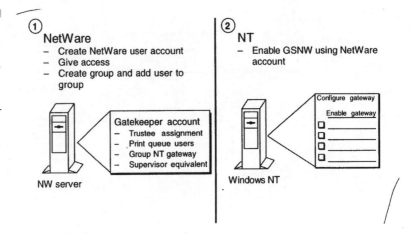

Installing Gateway Services for NetWare

Before you install the gateway on the Windows NT server, an account
must be created on the NetWare server to allow the Windows NT server
access to the NetWare server's files. Full NetWare access rights should be
granted to this new account because it must have sufficient access to any
NetWare files that users may require. Windows NT security will be used
to restrict user access. The most access any user has will be equal to the
permissions given to that user's Windows NT account.

▦ Create an account on the NetWare server for GSNW to use.

▦ On the Windows NT server, the Gateway Services must be configured to use the NetWare account. (See Figure 5-3.)

On the NetWare server, you must grant permissions to the account you
created for the gateway. (See Figure 5-4.)

Install GSNW on the Windows NT server by selecting the Network icon from the Windows NT Control Panel. The Control Panel can be found in the "main" group on the Windows NT server desktop. You must be logged on as the server Administrator to perform this task.

After the Network applet has been launched, you will be presented with a screen where you can view the existing network services. (See Figure 5-5.) The Gateway Services for NetWare service will be available from the Services tab. You must have access to the original installation files to proceed. These files are located on the Windows NT server CD in the \I386 directory if you are working with an Intel-based PC.

Figure 5-4
Setting NetWare permissions for the GSNW gateway account. (Courtesy of Learning Tree International)

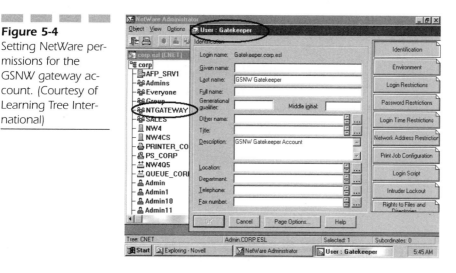

Figure 5-5
Windows NT Network applet. (Source: Microsoft Corporation)

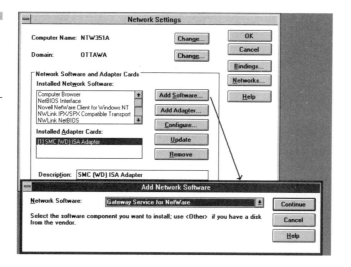

The Windows NT server must communicate with the NetWare Server using IPX, NetWare's native protocol. Microsoft bundles its own version of IPX named NWLINK. When GSNW is installed, it will automatically install any dependent services such as NWLINK. If any problems occur during installation, NWLINK can be installed manually using the same Network applet used to install GSNW.

During installation, you will be asked to configure the IPX/SPX protocol to match the configuration used by the NetWare server you will connect to. (See Figure 5-6.) By default, NWLINK automatically detects the Ethernet frame type. The internal network number must be unique in your network. This network number is reported to the network during service advertisement broadcasts. Refer to Chapter 3 for more information on network protocols.

For the changes to take effect, the server must be shut down and restarted.

You can modify the GSNW service at any time after installation by selecting the GSNW service icon that has been added to the Windows NT Control Panel.

After the server is restarted, you must log in as Administrator to configure the gateway. Because GSNW is now a NetWare client, you must supply the preferred server name of the NetWare server you will be connecting to.

Figure 5-6
Configuring NWLINK.
(Source: Microsoft
Corporation)

Enabling the File Gateway

To finish configuring GSNW, select the GSNW applet icon from the Windows NT server Control Panel. (See Figure 5-7.)

Gateway access to file services and print services can be configured separately. You will gain access to the gateway configuration by selecting the Gateway button. You must enable the gateway by selecting the check box and then entering the account name you will use to connect to the NetWare server. (See Figure 5-8.)

Figure 5-7
Configuring GSNW.
(Source: Microsoft
Corporation)

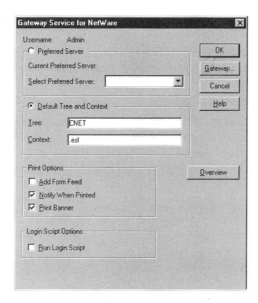

Figure 5-8
Configuring the
Gateway account.
(Source: Microsoft
Corporation)

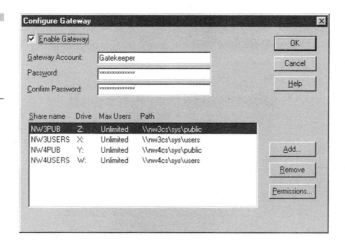

Unlike NetWare, the Windows NT resources must be shared to the network before they can be accessed. The share point is simply an alias for the physical location of the shared resources on the Windows NT server's hard drive. Access to the shared resources is accomplished using *Universal Naming Convention* (UNC) path names. The UNC path name is specified as `\\Servername\Sharename.` The `Servername` is the name of the Windows NT server where the resources are located, and the share name represents a logical name for a location on the server's hard disk.

As an example, for a DOS client to connect to a Windows NT share, it would use a local drive letter that is redirected to the server. To redirect the workstation's local drive H: to the Windows NT server share DATA, the command would be `NET USE H: \\SERVER1\DATA`. Windows clients can simply browse the network for shares or use the UNC commands from the command prompt. (See Figures 5-9 and 5-10.)

An example of a UNC path is `\\NTS_1\apps`, where `NTS_1` is the server name and Apps is the share name.

To make the NetWare server available to Windows NT clients, you must first connect to the NetWare server using the gateway account. You can then create a Windows NT share using GSNW. This step publishes a NetWare resource as Windows NT resources so clients can see and connect to them. Using GSNW, you will find an ADD button in the Configure Gateway dialog box; you can use it to create this share. You will be asked for the following three pieces of information:

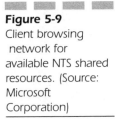

Figure 5-9
Client browsing
network for
available NTS shared
resources. (Source:
Microsoft
Corporation)

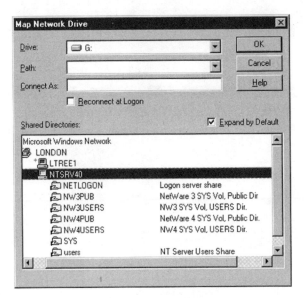

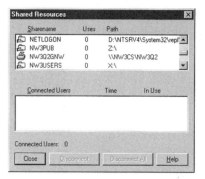

Figure 5-10
Windows NT server shared resources. (Source: Microsoft Corporation)

- Network path: The location of the NetWare server resource you want to share with Windows NT users. This path follows the Universal Naming Convention used by Microsoft. When the Windows NT server connects to the NetWare server, it does so by accessing the NetWare server using a UNC path such as `\\Net-Ware_server_name\volume_name\directory name`.

- Comment: This is a description of what the service is for or where it is located.

- Use drive: This is the drive letter the Windows NT server will redirect to the NetWare server. For example, if you were to use the Windows NT server as a workstation, drive C: would be your local drive and drive U: may be your connection to the NetWare server. This drive letter is the Windows NT server's drive and is redirected on the Windows NT server. The drive letter used has no effect on the clients. They must redirect their own drives to access any network resources.

GSNW also lets you limit the number of concurrent connections supported by each network share. This capability may be useful if you want to control the load on the gateway by limiting the number of users connected through the gateway at one time. (See Figure 5-11.)

After the share has been created, you must set the Windows NT security to limit who can access the files using this share. You can do so by selecting the share you created from the Configure Gateway dialog box and choosing the Permissions button. Here you will find an Access Through Share Permissions dialog box where you can add the selected Windows NT server users.

At this point, any valid Windows NT server users to whom you have granted access can now access files from the NetWare server by request-

Figure 5-11
Sharing the GSNW
connection.
(Source: Microsoft
Corporation)

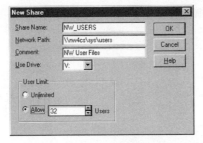

Figure 5-12
Browsing the Win-
dows NT server for
NetWare resources.
(Source: Microsoft
Corporation)

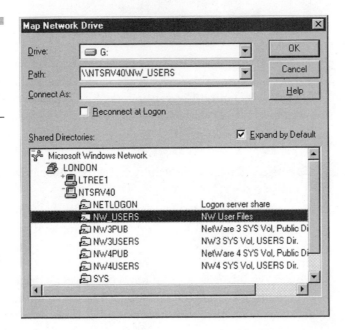

ing them from the gateway. The only indication users may have that these files are not actually located on the Windows NT server is that getting files from the NetWare server may take longer because access is through the gateway. (See Figure 5-12.)

Configuring the Print Service Gateway

Print services require that a logical printer be created on the Windows NT server. It is important during migration that the correct print drivers are available for Windows NT. Printers are added using the Print Wizard icon in the Control Panel. The printers must be connected to the print queue on the NetWare server. Because GSNW allows Windows NT server to become a client of NetWare, you will be able to browse for NetWare print queues in the Shared Printers box. (See Figure 5-13.)

After you connect the printer, it must be shared to the Windows NT server clients. You do so by choosing Properties from the printer menu and activating the Share this printer on the network option.

Clients can now browse the network to find any NetWare printers that are shared using GSNW. (See Figure 5-14.)

Troubleshooting the Gateway

Gateway services might not function properly for a number of reasons. Table 5-2 contains a checklist of some of them. Because GSNW is a service that runs on Windows NT server, you can verify that this service has been started correctly by clicking the Services icon in the Control Panel. Doing so gives you access to the list of server services so that you can verify their status as well as start and stop the services. Also, the Event viewer in the Network Administration Desktop Group allows you to view the server error log and the server application log. Services can fail for a variety of reasons including bad network cards or drivers.

Figure 5-13
Shared printer properties. (Source: Microsoft Corporation)

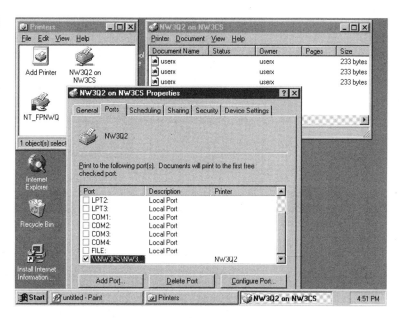

Figure 5-14
Browsing for
NetWare printers.
(Source: Microsoft
Corporation)

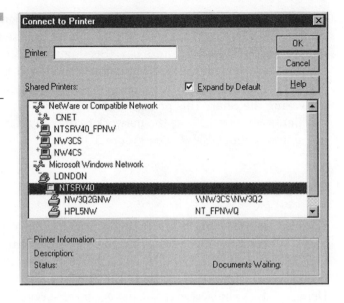

Table 5-2

Troubleshooting
Gateway Services
for NetWare
(GSNW). (Courtesy
of Learning Tree In-
ternational)

Problem Area	Problem Description	Recommended Action
Startup	Gateway Service doesn't start.	A subservice or protocol may not have started. Try to start the service manually.
	Gateway Service starts, but servers can't be found.	Network frame type may be set incorrectly. See the Network option in Control Panel.
	Gateway Service starts, but servers can't be found.	NetWare 4.x server must be running Bindery Emulation services.
	Gateway Service prompts for a password at each login.	The password for the NetWare server Gateway user account is different from the password for the Windows NT server Gateway user account.
	NetWare login scripts are not running.	GSNW does not support NetWare login scripts. Use Windows NT logon scripts.
Access Problems	Access to a NetWare file server is denied.	User name and password do not match for the NetWare server you are trying to access.
Application and Print Problems	NetWare print queues are not shown in Print Manager.	Missing rights to access print server print queues. Verify that you can see the NetWare file server on which the print queues reside.

Table 5-2

Continued.

Problem Area	Problem Description	Recommended Action
	NetWare-aware applications are not working correctly.	Ensure that application is supported under Windows NT.
	NetWare **MAP** utility fails with a memory allocation error,	Mapping table is getting too large for default environment for 16-bit applications. Increase the environment size to 4096 bytes in the CONFIG.NT file to `shell=%systemroot%\system32\command.com /e:4096`.
Other network problems	Duplicate computer names	Each computer on the network must have a unique name.
	Services or subsystems do not start.	Check service status. Try to start the services or subsystems manually.
	Interoperability with Windows for Workgroups	Ensure that workgroup and domain names are unique. Keep guest accounts enabled on domain controllers. Avoid duplicate user names in different domains.
	Using the last known good configuration	Can be used if you have problems starting Windows NT server and its services.
	Using emergency repair disk	Can be used if system files become corrupt and previous start configuration cannot be accessed.

▪ **If the gateway service starts, but the NetWare server cannot be contacted:** Ensure that all network cabling is intact, and perform any network tests including attempting a connection using a NetWare client. Keeping a bootable NetWare client disk is handy for this purpose. After establishing that the server is alive and well, try browsing for the server from File Manager on the Windows NT server. Also try mapping a drive from the command line. A common problem on NetWare networks is an incorrect frame type when using Ethernet networks. Verify that the Windows NT server is using the same network frame type as the NetWare server. This setting is available if you select the Network icon in the Control Panel. See Chapter 3 for more information on network protocols.

■ **If the service has started, but clients cannot access the resources:** Use the server's File Manager to browse for NetWare resources. It will help you confirm that the Windows NT server connection with the NetWare server is available and that the Gateway account has the proper NetWare rights. If the connection is all right, confirm that the Windows NT server has the appropriate access permissions.

■ **If NetWare 4.x servers cannot be located:** GSNW does not support NetWare 4.x natively. You need to configure the NetWare server to run in Bindery Emulation Mode. Bindery Emulation makes a NetWare 4.x server look like a NetWare 3.x server, which GSNW does support.

■ **If GSNW prompts for a password at each login:** The password for the NetWare server gateway account is different from the Windows NT Server account used to log on. If the passwords match, Windows NT will automatically pass the login information to the NetWare server.

■ **If the NetWare login scripts do not run when the client logs in:** GSNW does not support NetWare login scripts. Because clients connecting to NetWare through GSNW are Windows NT clients, a Windows NT logon script may be used instead.

FILE AND PRINT SERVICES FOR NETWARE Sometimes when a Windows NT server is introduced to a NetWare environment, the clients may be required to continue to run the NetWare client software. This requirement may be a temporary measure while a large scale migration is completed, or it may be that the Windows NT server resources will be accessed by another department running NetWare. Whatever the reason, Windows NT File and Print services for NetWare can solve the problem by making a Windows NT server look like a NetWare server. Windows NT servers running File and Print services can be accessed by both Microsoft clients and NetWare clients.

To a NetWare client, no distinguishable functional difference exists between a NetWare 3.12 server and a Windows NT server running File and Print Services for NetWare. To provide a user with access to File and Print Services, you must create a Windows NT account for the user, and the user's Windows NT account must be NetWare enabled. You don't need to maintain separate Windows NT and NetWare accounts for each user on the server. (See Figure 5-15.)

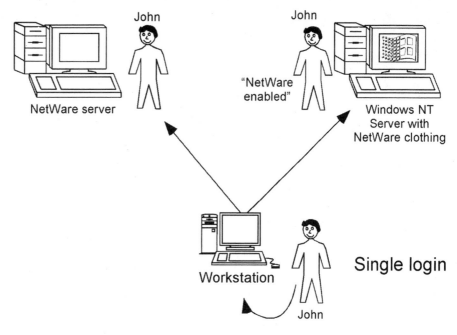

Figure 5-15
Logging in using a
NetWare client.
(Courtesy of Learning
Tree International)

Many of the functions of a NetWare server are supported using FPNW, and in fact, many of the NetWare management tools can be used to manage the FPNW server. For example, the NetWare management tool Syscon can be used. It will even display the NetWare server version as Windows NT 3.51. (See Table 5-3 for a complete list of functions supported.) When managing NetWare-enabled accounts on Windows NT, you can manage passwords, set station and time restrictions, disable accounts, manage grace logins, and set account lockout policies just as you can on a real NetWare server. Extensions are added to Windows NT User Manager, Windows NT Explorer, and Print Wizard, allowing you to manage everything from NetWare volumes to user connections.

Some features of NetWare are not supported by FPNW. They include features such as accounting and user disk volume restrictions, as well as NetWare 4.x services such as NDS. See Table 5-4 for a complete list.

FPNW PLANNING STEPS   Before beginning with the installation of FPNW, you should think about how it will be used in your environment and gather the necessary information that you may need about your existing NetWare servers. Treat the installation of FPNW as you would the installation of any NetWare server.

Table 5-3

Features supported by Windows NT server running FPNW.

Function Supported	NetWare	Windows NT
File access	NetWare client (NCP)	Windows NT client (SMB)
Printer access	NetWare Print Queue	Shared NT Print Queue
Printer management	Queue management using Novell's Pconsole	NT Print Manager
User management	Novell's SYSCON utility	NT User Manager for Domains
Secure Logins	NetWare LOGIN security	NT Domain Security
Packet Burst and Large Internet Packet (LIP) support	NetWare IPX support	
Long file name support	Compatible with OS/2 LFN	NTFS support

Table 5-4

Features not supported by Windows NT server running FPNW.

Workgroup managers

Accounting

User Disk Volume Restrictions (important!)

Inherited Rights Mask (IRM)

NetWare Loadable Modules (NLM)

Transaction Tracking System (TTS)

You need to first consider what the server will be used for and how it will provide these services. Will it provide file sharing, print services, or both? If it will be used for file sharing, is it important to note that Windows NT does not include the ability to limit the amount of disk space a user can consume? You may be relying on this feature if you already manage NetWare servers. If control over the amount of disk space available to each user is important to you, you may want to investigate third-party solutions for Windows NT. Quota Manager from New Technology Partners is one product that can provide this function.

When you're planning a migration project, try to cover as many bases as possible, and try to have a plan that allows the migration to be performed in stages. Always have a contingency plan in case you run into problems. The following is an example of how things can go wrong. We were told this story by a student. It seems that before beginning the next installation this company wanted to prepare a better plan. Because we have planned many successful migrations, we were able to help them.

The plan was to migrate 200 users from NetWare to Windows NT. All the users would be moved to the Windows NT server over a weekend. As a first step, the Windows NT server was configured in a test environment. This step is important because, although Windows NT can be installed very quickly, it can sometimes take days or even weeks to resolve hardware-compatibility problems. So tackling this step long before the server is actually needed is best.

The company had carefully planned the client migration and had pre-installed and configured the Windows NT server. Everything went well initially. User accounts were migrated, and data was moved to the new server without any major difficulty. Windows 3.1 client computers were reconfigured from NetWare to Microsoft clients. At this point, the first problems were encountered. Not all PCs had the same network cards, and the ones that did all had different hardware settings. New Network Interface Card drivers were downloaded, hardware settings were identified, and finally, Windows NT connectivity was tested. By the time all the workstation issues were resolved, logon scripts had been prepared and the server was ready to go. The old server, which was no longer needed, was converted to a workstation. It was now late Sunday night when someone realized that the network printers had not been configured and tested. Several print server boxes had been deployed throughout the organization to support these printers, and no one had considered how they would work with Windows NT!

Several of these types of devices are on the market. Hewlett-Packard's JetDirect cards are one example. They allow HP printers to be directly connected to the network. Other manufacturers sell black boxes that perform the same function—being connected between the printer and the network. These network printers can then service NetWare print queues. The problem is that many of the devices support one operating system or the other, but not both; this is especially true of older models.

The print servers in production in this company would work only with NetWare. Because the print servers would not work with Windows NT, and the migration was almost complete, the staff began to panic. By not having a plan, they frantically made some rash decisions late Sunday night and began reversing the process. Soon they were out of time, and they spent much of Monday dealing with unnecessary problems.

The solution to this company's problem was actually quite simple. The staff could have left the old NetWare server in place and used Gateway

Services for NetWare to provide printer access for their new Microsoft clients. Gateway Services would allow users to print to a shared Windows NT printer. The shared printer could actually be a print queue on the NetWare server made available by the Windows NT server.

Their second option was to load FPNW on the Windows NT server and service the print servers from the virtual NetWare server on Windows NT. FPNW basically looks like two servers on the network sharing the same physical devices. It is actually one server with two separate File and Print Services running. One can be seen by NetWare clients as a NetWare 3.12 server, and the other can be seen by Microsoft clients as a Windows NT server.

Both solutions would have solved their short-term problem of not having any printers for Monday morning. The long-term solution of replacing network print servers could be implemented over time. The mistakes made then were:

■ Not preparing a thorough plan taking into account all network devices

■ Attempting to perform a full migration over a very short time, not allowing for difficulties

■ Taking the NetWare server out of commission before at least one full day of production

You may find FPNW useful for sharing NetWare network print devices with both NetWare and Windows NT users. If you are migrating an existing NetWare environment to Windows NT, you may have overlooked some of the ancillary network components such as print servers and gateways. FPNW can be used as a NetWare server, allowing you to preserve your investment in HP JetDirect cards or other print server devices. The nice thing about this solution is that the same printers are available to your new Windows NT clients as well as the NetWare clients that are not yet migrated.

Before you install FPNW, you should review any existing NetWare installations to determine the Ethernet frame type in use. If the wrong frame type is selected, you will not be able to see the other servers. Also, some older print servers for NetWare tended to incorrectly advertise themselves and any other servers they knew about using any frame type they detected. Often this meant that servers were seen on more than one network, which caused IPX routing errors.

Internally, each NetWare server has an IPX network number. In essence, it is like a virtual network inside the server. We know from Chapter 3 that any IPX network number must be unique to the network it was assigned. The same goes for the internal network number that FPNW requires just like any other NetWare server. If duplicates exist, we will get routing errors and server conflicts. You should always enter a unique internal IPX network number on the FPNW server. If you do not, the server will use the IPX network number of the network it is connected to.

Creating the NetWare volume on a Windows NT server partition that uses the NTFS file system is important. Although Windows NT supports both FAT and NTFS, only NTFS provides file level security. Also, NTFS is a more robust file system. Selecting an NTFS partition will provide better fault tolerance and security for the data.

User accounts can be created by either migrating existing NetWare users to Windows NT or by creating new Windows NT accounts. Migration can be accomplished using the Migration tools for NetWare. Once the accounts exist on the Windows NT server, they must be NetWare enabled using the Windows NT User Manager.

Here are the FPNW planning steps:

- Identify services that FPNW will provide on your network.
- Determine how to support other NetWare-related services such as Gateways and print servers.
- Identify network topology and frame types in use.
- Select unique IPX network numbers for the FPNW service.
- Select the Windows NT NTFS volume into which you will install FPNW.
- Determine whether you will create new Windows NT NetWare-enabled accounts or migrate accounts from existing NetWare servers.
- Determine whether management of FPNW will be done from Windows NT or NetWare clients.

INSTALLING FPNW   FPNW is not included with Windows NT, so you will have had to purchase it as an add-on product from Microsoft for a nominal fee. To install FPNW, you must first log on to the server as Administrator or equivalent.

Install FPNW on the Windows NT server by selecting the Network icon from the Windows NT Control Panel. The Control Panel can be found on the Start menu. Select the Services tab. Click on the Have Disk button, and select the <OTHER> option from the pull-down menu to install FPNW from the FPNW disk. You can either choose to install FPNW and all its components, or just the administrative tools. You would choose to

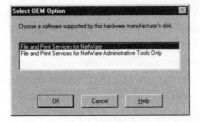

Figure 5-16
FPNW installation.
(Source: Microsoft
Corporation)

install just the administrative tools if FPNW were already installed and you wanted to remotely manage it from another PC. (See Figure 5-16.)

The FPNW installation requires you to enter information about the SYS volume used by FPNW, as well as the NetWare Supervisor account for the FPNW service. The SYS volume is actually just a Windows NT subdirectory to which all the NetWare system files will be copied. The Supervisor account is the Windows NT account you will use to manage FPNW. Remember that Windows NT account passwords are case sensitive. Because FPNW is a Windows NT service, it will need to create a service account to use to access Windows NT files when the server is started. This password should match the Supervisor's password. After the file copying process is complete, you can restart the server and verify that FPNW started successfully.

You have not fully configured FPNW at this point. You must log on and select the Control Panel Network applet. Configure the File and Print Services found in the Installed Network Software window by selecting it and clicking on the Configure button. From the main screen, you can tune the performance of FPNW relative to other Windows NT server services. Initially, you may set FPNW to perform at its peak and then later give back some resources to Windows NT after most of the clients have been migrated. (See Figure 5-17.)

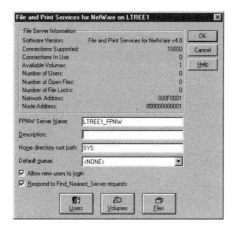

Figure 5-17
FPNW configuration.
(Source: Microsoft
Corporation)

By selecting the Advanced button, you can view and change the IPX/SPX protocol configuration for FPNW. Here you can specify the internal network number for the server. You can also choose an Ethernet frame type for the adapter cards and enable internal routing of IPX if required. FPNW will attempt to automatically detect the frame type used on your network; however, this must be verified. Also keep in mind that you may have multiple servers in your organization using different frame types. Ensure that the correct type was detected, or select the Manual Frame Type Detection option. Once again, refer to Chapter 3 for further information on frame types. Remember that the service must be stopped and restarted. You can either restart the server or simply stop the FPNW service by selecting the Services applet from the Control Panel. Doing so will give you a list of Windows NT services. You can stop the FPNW service at any time by selecting it from the list and clicking on the Stop button. You can also view the startup options by clicking on the Startup button. You will notice that the service account created earlier is listed here. (See Figure 5-18.)

To configure the FPNW print service to emulate a NetWare print server and print queue, you must first install and configure a Windows NT printer. A Windows NT printer is actually a logical device that connects to a physical printer, so in effect a Windows NT printer is a print queue. This Windows NT printer will act as the NetWare print queue. After the printer is installed and shared to the network, any NetWare client can use the NetWare **Capture** command to redirect a local printer port to the Windows NT printer.

FPNW can service a network print server such as a JetDirect card in an HP printer. To support these devices as a NetWare print server, you must install and configure a Windows NT printer. After the printer is

██ ██ ██ ██

Figure 5-18
FPNW service.
(Source: Microsoft
Corporation)

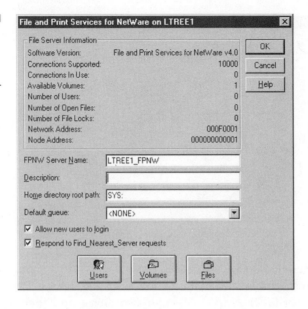

installed and configured, you can then create the FPNW print server to
service the printer. You will assign the printer to one of two default printer
ports created by FPNW and added to the printer properties in Print Manager. These ports are NetWare_PServer_0 and NetWare _Pserver_1. Many
of the newer print server devices are configurable for NetWare or Windows NT, in which case you can support them from Windows NT and still
provide access to these printers through FPNW.

To create an FPNW print server, you must run Server Manager. Server
Manager can be found in the Windows NT Administrative Tools group.
After you select the FPNW menu item, select Print Servers and add a
print server. You must provide a print server name for the new server you
are creating, as well as a description (Full Name) and a password. You can
then select the name of the NetWare server it will service. It will be your
FPNW NetWare server. (See Figure 5-19.)

You can then add printers to the new print server and select from the
list of available queues on the server. Once again, you will have to restart
the server or just the FPNW service.

MANAGING FPNW   When FPNW is installed on a Windows NT server,
an FPNW icon is placed in the Control Panel. This applet allows the Windows NT Administrator to determine how many NetWare users are connected to the Windows NT server as well as how the server behaves in a
NetWare environment. (See Figure 5-20.)

Figure 5-19
FPNW Print Service.
(Source: Microsoft
Corporation)

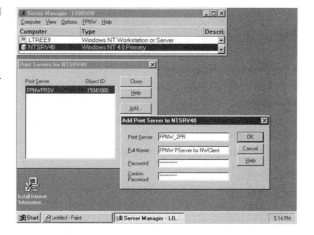

Figure 5-20
FPNW properties.
(Source: Microsoft
Corporation)

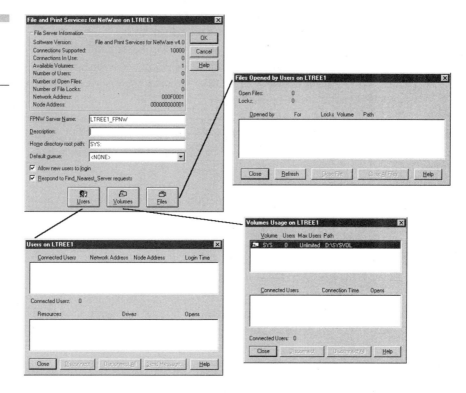

Many large NetWare sites experienced problems seeing all servers in a server list at one time. This problem is a result of a limit in the number of servers a single server list can maintain. The problem was solved with NetWare 2.15 by increasing the limit; however, Windows NT File and

Print Services for NetWare emulates NetWare 2.12. As such, Windows NT can reintroduce this problem. For this reason, you might consider turning off the Respond to Find_Nearest Server Requests setting on the FPNW server. It is equivalent to the Reply to get nearest server setting on NetWare servers. Let your existing NetWare servers respond to any NetWare client "get nearest server" requests. Of course, if FPNW is the only NetWare server, you would have to leave this setting turned on.

The FPNW server name is the name of the NetWare server service. This name can be changed independent of the Windows NT server name. The service will have to be restarted for any changes to take effect. The Home Directory Root path represents the top level, or root, of the NetWare SYS: volume where the users home directories will be located regardless of where they are actually stored on the Windows NT server's hard disk. For example, if the SYS: volume were located on C:\SYSVOL on the PARIS server, the Home Directory Root Path would be PARIS/SYS:USERS.

User connections are also managed from the FPNW properties. From here, you can view who is connected and for how long. You can identify the node address of the computer users have connected with as well as the address of the network they are connected to. You can identify any resources the users are currently accessing by selecting a user from the list and viewing the drives and resources in the resources window. Users can be disconnected if necessary. To ensure that the users have closed any files saved on the network, you can send a message to them first.

Enabling NetWare Accounts on the Windows NT Server

Both Windows NT and NetWare accounts can be managed using the same tools. To provide NetWare users with access to the Windows NT server, each user must be given a Windows NT account. This NT account must also be NetWare enabled. Any Windows NT groups can be used to provide access to server resources, but unlike user accounts, groups do not have to be NetWare enabled. To allow the FPNW server to be managed using NetWare utilities such as Syscon, a NetWare supervisor account is created automatically and is added to the Windows NT Administrators group.

Windows NT User Manager is modified when FPNW is installed. It will now include a check box to enable the Windows NT account as a NetWare account. (See Figure 5-21.)

If you will be adding many users to the server, you may prefer to create a batch file to process the user accounts. To create a Windows NT ac-

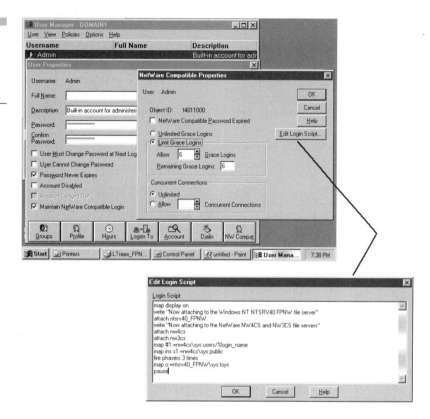

Figure 5-21
Windows NT User Manager. (Source: Microsoft Corporation)

count for user JOE and NetWare-enable this account, you can use the following command:

```
NET USER JOE    /ADD    /FPNW        Enable NetWare login

NET USER JOE    /ADD    /FPNW:no     Disable NetWare login
```

Windows NT directories must be shared to provide users with network access. For NetWare users, the shared directories must be given NetWare volume names. You can do so by using the Windows NT File Manager utility or Windows NT Server Manager. Multiple volume names can be assigned to the same Windows NT resource; in fact, a client that is configured as both a Windows NT and NetWare client can access the same resources using the NetWare volume name and the Windows NT share name. (See Figure 5-22.)

Network printers that are shared on a Windows NT server are automatically given the Windows NT share name as the NetWare Print queue name. (See Figure 5-23.) Management of print queues such as deleting

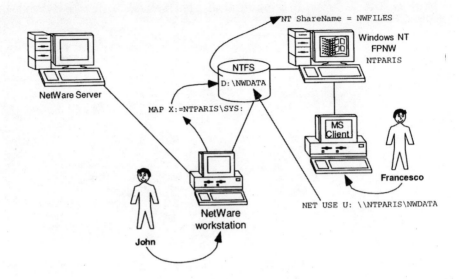

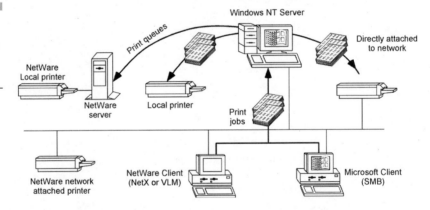

items or changing their order in the print queue must be performed using Windows NT Print Manager.

To manage the FPNW environment in a Windows NT domain, FPNW must also be loaded on the *Primary Domain Controller* (PDC). This step is necessary because, in a domain, all accounts are created in the Domain database on the PDC and then replicated to the *Backup Domain Controllers* (BDCs). You also need to create directories that hold NetWare login scripts. The directories are automatically created at the PDC by the FPNW service. The actual services that the users log in to can run on any BDC in the domain, and users can be created at the BDC. This is not an issue in a single server environment in which no PDC is present, and the server is not a member of a domain.

In a multidomain environment in which Windows NT trust relationships exist, Windows NT FPNW administrative utilities can be used as long as FPNW is installed in both the trusted domain where the user is logged in and the resource domain where the server resources reside. The Windows NT trust relationship will allow the user's account to be validated on the server where the resources are located.

Using a NetWare client, the NetWare administrative utilities cannot administer the FPNW server if the user is from a trusted domain. The Windows NT accounts associated with the FPNW server must be created in the same domain as the FPNW server.

The use of NetWare login scripts is supported using NetWare File and Print Services on the Windows NT server. This feature allows NetWare users whose accounts are moved from NetWare to Windows NT to continue accessing resources that have also been moved. The login script text file NET$LOG.DAT must be placed in the Windows NT server\sysvol\ public directory created by FPNW. Changes must be made to this file to reflect the name of the new server as well as the path to any resources the login script references. The login script is processed only for Windows NT accounts that have been NetWare enabled.

Making a NetWare Server Look Like Windows NT Using Samba

You are now familiar with making a Windows NT server look like a NetWare server. Microsoft's File and Print Services for NetWare (FPNW), as we now know, lets Novell clients connect to Windows NT using NetWare's NetWare Core Protocol (NCP). In other words, it supports native NetWare client connectivity.

Server integration, however, is not limited to NetWare users trying to access Windows NT. In an organization in which files must be shared among different groups, accessing NetWare files using a Microsoft client quite often is required. Samba is a similar solution to Microsoft's FPNW, but it's for NetWare. It can be loaded on a NetWare server to allow Microsoft clients to access the NetWare server.

Where Can I Get Samba?

Samba is a set of utilities that were originally designed for UNIX to allow SMB clients to access the UNIX host. SMB, if you recall, is the language Microsoft clients use to talk to Windows NT and LAN Manager servers. See Chapter 3 for more details on SMB. Samba has been recently ported to NetWare by Novell Consulting Services for use with NetWare 4.1. It is available free from the Novell Consulting Services Web site at `http://www.novell.com/corp/programs/ncs/`. Samba for NetWare is listed under "migration tools." Novell does not officially support Samba, so you are largely on your own; however, you can get help from some newsgroups and other resources dedicated to Samba. You can find more information from Novell Consulting Services at `http://www.novell.com/corp/programs/ncs/toolkit/migqt.html`.

An extremely useful Web site can be found at `http://www.gurdon.com/novell/netware4/samba/`. It is maintained by Gurdon E. Merchant, Jr. He has installation tips and instructions. The following information in the following section was drawn from this site.

Required NetWare NLMs

To make the NetWare server look like a Windows NT server, you must load a set of the Samba NLMs on the NetWare server. These NLMs include the following:

NBNS.nlm	Provides NETBIOS name service recognition
Samba.nlm	Acts as a NT Server emulator
Netbeui.nlm	Provides support for the NETBEUI protocol
NWglue.nlm	Ties it all together
TCPBEUI.nlm	Provides support for NETBIOS over TCP/IP

The following information was gathered from `http://www.gurdon.com/novell/netware4/samba/`. Permission to reprint information form this Web site was granted by Gurdon E. Merchant, Jr., who maintains the site.

Samba on NetWare Prerequisites

Your NetWare server must meet a few basic, minimum requirements before you can contemplate setting up Samba services on it:

- NetWare 4.1: Samba.nlm is only for NetWare 4.10 and higher.
- Bindery Emulation: The 4.1 server on which you will be loading samba.nlm must have its default context listed first in the Bindery context.

▓ domain.nlm: If you boot your NetWare 4.1 server with **load
domain.nlm** as the first non-comment line in your startup.ncf, you
have access to the rings in the Intel processor and a little protection from abends. (To fully benefit from domain.nlm, you need to
run the latest static and dynamic patches if necessary.)

▓ Latest Patches: Running the latest patches from Novell is very important. At a minimum, you should be running the 4.1 patches
from the archives libup8.exe, 41nds6.exe, 410pt3.exe, 41rtr3.exe,
landr5.exe, ps4x03.exe, pu4x03.exe, smsup4.exe, strtl4.exe, and
tcp41b.exe.

Use the modules and patches commands at the console to see what
you are running. You should also look into the other numerous
patches; however, the preceding list indicates the core patches
from Novell that you should be running.

▓ TCP/IP: You should be running IP on your NetWare server. In Microsoft terms, this is referred to as "NETBIOS over IP." If need be,
configure IP on your server with **load inetcfg.nlm**.

After you are done configuring your IP stack, reinitialize the system to
start the services. Use the ping.nlm to ping a machine not on the same
subnet to make sure everything works.

Detailed Installation Instructions for Downloading Samba

Step 1: Download All the Required Files

Gurdon has extracted five relevant files from the hundreds of files in Novell's Migration Toolkit and added a couple of *.ncf files that are useful.
Download NetWare Samba (about 150Kbytes) now, and install it according to the following directions.

Step 2: Download Samba Files for Installation in sys:system

Step 3: Download Samba Files for Installation in sys:samba

Step 4: Place the smb.cfg File in the sys:samba Directory

Step 5: Tweak the sys:etc\hosts File

Make sure that you have the loopback node and your server's IP address in your host's file. It should look something like this:

```
# Mappings of host names and host aliases to IP address.
#
127.0.0.1 loopback lb localhost # normal loopback address
a.b.c.d your_netware_server_name     # use YOUR IP ADDRESS
       for a.b.c.d
```

WARNING: *Several Novell files in sys:etc are whitespace sensitive. Always use a tab to separate non-comment entries. (That is, use tabs between the IP address and host name in sys:etc\hosts, not spaces.)*

Step 6: Tweak the sys:etc\services File

Whenever you're adding new IP services, updating the services file to reflect this fact is a good idea. Two entries are relevant to "NETBIOS over IP":

```
#
# Netbios/Samba Support
#
netbios-ns      137/tcp              # NETBIOS Name Service
netbios-dgm     138/udp              # NETBIOS Datagram Service
```

Step 7: Create a sys:samba Directory

Hard-coded into the Samba NLMs is a need for a sys:samba directory into which Samba places log files. Not having this directory means the Samba NLMs are quarantined when you load them (if you are running the latest patches and domain.nlm) or your server abends.

Step 8: Create a sys:samba\log Directory

This step is also mandatory. The Samba NLMs put some scratch files here.

Step 9: Create Empty Samba Log Files

With Windows Notepad (or whatever plain text editor you like), create two empty files called sys:samba\log.nmb and sys:samba\log.smb. Then enter `flag sys:samba\log.* sh rw` so that they are shareable and read/writable. By doing so, you will be able to view the log files while Samba is running.

Step 10: Tweak the sys:samba\lmhosts File

sys:samba\lmhosts is the SMB version of the hosts file. If the server is not using NetWare NFS 2.1 (configured as a DNS and NIS client), an lmhosts file can be used. Here's an example:

```
a.b.c.d       your_netware_server
a1.b1.c1.d1   your_nt_pdc
a2.b2.c2.d2   your_unix_samb_server
```

An lmhost file is similar to a hosts file; however, it can also be used to resolve NETBIOS names.

Samba.ncf or smbon.ncf/smboff.ncf? Novell's Samba distribution has a file called samba.ncf, which you place in the sys:system directory. It contains just two entries:

```
load nbns -G NTDOMAIN
load samba
```

At the very least, you need to edit this file and replace NTDOMAIN with the name of the Windows NT Domain whose browse list you want the server to appear in. The samba.ncf file is then run at the server console to load the Samba services.

Creating two files for every "service" is useful. A file named smbon.ncf can be used to turn on the service, and smboff.ncf can be used to turn off the service. Because unloading NLMs in the wrong order sometimes will cause an abend, this method makes the procedure much easier to remember.

The smbon.ncf and smboff.ncf files are shown on the following page.

Sample smbon.ncf:

```
# Save old Samba console messages in console.old.
# New ones go in console.smb
unload conlog
load conlog file=sys:\samba\console.smb
     save=sys:\samba\console.old
# Start Samba
load nwglue
load sys:system\nbns -H sys:samba\lmhosts -G NTDOMAIN
load sys:system\samba
# Turn off console logging.
unload conlog
```

Sample smboff.ncf:

```
unload samba
unload nbns
unload nwglue
```

Starting Samba

Before you load Samba, you need to take care of a few configuration details.

Step 1: Create Directory Map Objects in the NDS

If you want to configure Samba shares quickly, create Directory Map objects in the default Bindery context of the server on which you are going to load Samba services.

Step 2: Create Print Queue Aliases in the NDS

To share print queues with NDS objects, create NDS alias objects for the print queues as outlined in the documentation.

Step 3: Configure smb.cfg

If you want, you can also edit the sys:samba\smb.cfg file (which Novell has populated with examples and comments) instead of configuring NDS objects. You need to do so if you want comments to appear in the browse list.

Undocumented Parameters

The Samba NLMs have some undocumented parameters. Switches for the nbns.nlm include

Usage: `SYS:SYSTEM\NBNS.NLM [-n name] [-B bcast address] [-D]`
`[-p port] [-d debug level] [-1 log basename]`

Version 1.9.14p1

`-D`	Become a daemon
`-P`	Passive only; don't respond
`-R`	Reply only to queries; don't actively send claims
`-p port`	Listen on the specified port
`-d debuglevel`	Set the debuglevel
`-1 log basename`	Basename for log/debug files
`-n netbiosname`	The NETBIOS name to advertise for this host
`-B broadcast address`	The address to use for broadcasts
`-N netmask`	The netmask to use for subnet determination
`-L name`	Look up this NETBIOS name and then exit
`-S`	Serve queries via DNS if not on the same subnet
`-H hosts file`	Load a NETBIOS hosts file
`-G group name`	Add a group name to be part of
`-b`	Toggle browsing support (defaults to on)
`-M group name`	Search for a master browser for the given group
`-T interval`	Set the browse announcement interval in seconds
`-C comment`	Set the machine comment that appears in browse lists

If you want a log file to analyze, use the `-d 4` switch. On a test server, the log files grew to 25Mbytes in a couple of days, so use this switch with care.

On the Server Console

The following is a sample of what you will see on the server console after you have loaded Samba:

```
NWGLUE.NLM
   NWGlue - Support Library
        Version 1.01a   April 8, 1996
   (C) Copyright 1994-6 Novell, Inc.  All Rights Reserved.
NBNS.NLM
        NBNS - NetBIOS Name Service
     Version 9.14a   March 1, 1996
        (C) Copyright 1992-4 Andrew Tridgell
      Portions (C) Copyright 1995 Novell, Inc.  All Rights
           Reserved.
SAMBA.NLM
        Samba - SMB Server
     Version 9.15h   May 6, 1996
        (C) Copyright 1992-4 Andrew Tridgell
      Portions (C) Copyright 1995-6 Novell, Inc.  All
           Rights Reserved.
```

After Samba is loaded on your NetWare server, you should then be able to connect to the server using a Windows NT client.

NOTE: *Once again, thanks to Gurdon E. Merchant, Jr., for providing this information,*

SUMMARY

In this chapter, we identified the components that allow a Windows NT server to impersonate a NetWare server using File and Print Services for NetWare. Samba allows a NetWare 4.1 server to impersonate a Windows NT server. Gateway Services for NetWare provides Microsoft clients access to a NetWare server by converting SMB requests to NCP. All these solutions can be used to provide an easy integration of Windows NT and NetWare environments or as stepping stones to a full migration.

If your requirement is to introduce a Windows NT server as an application server in a NetWare environment, FPNW can be a useful tool when maintaining the server. If you simply want to allow two groups within your organization to share information when one group has NetWare and the other has Windows NT, again FPNW can be useful. Finally, if you are beginning a full-scale migration to Windows NT, FPNW can ease the transition by allowing you to leave the clients until later. The good news is the migration need not happen overnight.

CHAPTER

Directory Services Manager for NetWare

For most computer systems, the expense of initial purchase and installation is not nearly as significant as the cost of ongoing maintenance and support. It should not come as a surprise then that two technologies are more costly to support than one because the level or amount of expertise and labor could be double.

Having multiple network operating systems does not magically make the situation simpler. In essence, many of the same tasks must now be performed twice. These tasks include system backups, user account maintenance, and so on. If you are to introduce Windows NT into a NetWare environment, the best solution to user management is to find a common utility that will allow you to manage both systems.

Microsoft's Directory Services for NetWare allows NetWare servers to be managed as if they were resources in a Windows NT Domain. Novell is also introducing its own strategy code-named Tobasco to manage Windows NT servers. Tobasco allows Windows NT to use Novell's Directory Services by loading an NDS service on Windows NT. We will look at a similar third-party solution called Synchronicity for Windows NT from NetVision. Synchronicity allows Windows NT Domains to become part of the NetWare 4.x Directory Services. Windows NT Domain management is still used; however, Synchronicity synchronizes changes with the NetWare NDS. In this chapter, then, we will examine single management strategies based on Microsoft's *Directory Services for NetWare* (DSNW) and Synchronicity.

Chapter Objectives

- Managing NetWare servers as part of a Windows NT Domain
- Installing Directory Services for NetWare
- Migrating the NetWare User Directory Databases to Windows NT
- Propagating account changes back to NetWare Servers
- Troubleshooting Directory Services for NetWare
- Managing a Windows NT Domain as part of the NetWare Directory Services Tree

Managing NetWare Servers as Part of a Windows NT Domain

Figure 6-1 illustrates how to manage NetWare servers as part of a Windows NT Domain.

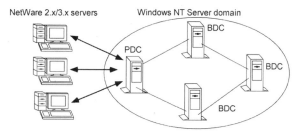

Figure 6-1
Managing NetWare
servers as part of a
Windows NT
Domain. (Courtesy of
Learning Tree
International)

*Centrally manage NetWare 2.x/3.x users and group
account information—maintain a single user account and
password and enable a single logon access to file, print,
and application resources*

Windows NT Directory Services Manager

Windows NT Directory Services Manager allows administrators to centrally manage Windows NT and NetWare user and group account information. Both NetWare 2.x and 3.x servers are supported; however, NetWare 4.x servers are not. If Bindery Emulation is used on NetWare 4 servers, they can be made to look like NetWare 3.x servers and supported by Windows NT Directory Services Manager.

The Windows NT Directory Services Manager service synchronizes changes between Windows NT and NetWare to allow NetWare to be managed as a Windows NT resource. This is accomplished by first copying the NetWare user and group information to the Windows NT server. Using Windows NT as the central management point, user account information can be modified as necessary using the Windows NT administrative tools. Any changes to the NetWare accounts are replicated back to the NetWare servers.

If your NetWare 3.x network has a user named Tom, then Tom would have an account on every NetWare server that he required access to. If your organization decides it will move to Windows NT, but existing NetWare servers will remain in place for some time, Tom now also needs an account on the Windows NT Domain. By using Directory Services for NetWare, any changes to Tom's account could be made once from a single point: the Windows NT server. Directory Services for NetWare would then propagate the changes to any NetWare server on which Tom has an account. Although both NetWare and Windows NT require separate ac-

Figure 6-2
Synchronizing user
accounts. (Courtesy
of ITcoach.com)

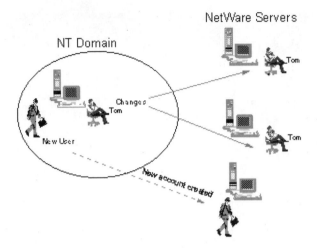

counts, Directory Services for NetWare can integrate the two management systems. (See Figure 6-2.)

The Windows NT Directory Services Manager service on the Windows NT server interacts with the NetWare server in a way that does not require any additional software to be installed on the NetWare server. After the decision has been made to manage NetWare servers in this manner, they should not be managed using NetWare management tools again because, after the initial user list is imported, synchronization occurs only one way, from Windows NT to NetWare.

Windows NT Directory Services Manager does not limit management to just making changes to existing NetWare accounts. If a new Windows NT account is created on Windows NT, that account can also be propagated to any authorized NetWare servers. Because all the NetWare accounts exist on the Windows NT Domain, if one of the NetWare servers crashes and must be rebuilt, the accounts can be propagated back to the NetWare server.

Benefits of Directory Services Manager for NetWare

Here are some benefits to using the Directory Services Manager for NetWare:

- Windows NT and NetWare users can be managed centrally.
- Existing clients can continue to access NetWare services.

- You have one set of user accounts to maintain.

- You have a point-and-click GUI for propagating user and group accounts from NetWare 2.x/3.x (and 4.x in Bindery Emulation Mode) to Windows NT Server Directory Services.

- End users can change their passwords once using **CHGPASS**, and the change is automatically propagated to all NetWare and Windows NT Server logon servers.

Directory Services Manager for NetWare Installation and Management

Directory Services Manager for NetWare installs from the Windows NT Control Panel Network applet. After it is installed, NetWare user accounts can be migrated to the Windows NT Domain, which requires a Windows NT server acting as a *Primary Domain Controller* (PDC).

You can install the Directory Services Manager for NetWare service on the Windows NT server or just the administrative tools for Directory Services Manager for NetWare on any Windows NT workstation or Windows NT Server version 3.51 or later. The administrative tools enable you to remotely administer Directory Services Manager on any domain or server on your network. You can also administer other domains on which you have a trust relationship.

You can install the Directory Services Manager for NetWare administrative tools from the Control Panel on the computer on which you are installing the software. Choose the Network icon in Control Panel and select the Add Software button. Directory Services Manager for NetWare is not included with Windows NT, so you must select <Other> from the bottom of the list of available software. You will be asked to insert the Directory Services Manager for NetWare CD-ROM. (See Figure 6-3.)

After it is installed, you must add a NetWare server to the domain. The status of each server can be determined by clicking on the Directory Services Manager for NetWare icon in the Control Panel, as shown in Figure 6-4.

You can choose to propagate individual users or entire NetWare groups to the domain. Table 6-1 identifies how the NetWare account restrictions are interpreted by Windows NT. If you have multiple NetWare servers,

Figure 6-3

Installing Directory
Services Manager for
NetWare. (Source:
Microsoft
Corporation)

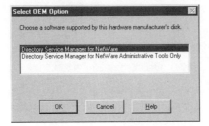

Figure 6-3

Installing Directory
Services Manager for
NetWare. (Source:
Microsoft
Corporation)

and the servers have groups with the same name, the groups are effectively merged in the domain.

Because NetWare servers store users' passwords in an encrypted format, Windows NT Server is unable to convert them. When NetWare users are propagated to a domain, the NetWare users' passwords are lost. Synchronization Manager provides the following options for managing user accounts as they are propagated:

- Gives each user a blank password
- Sets each user's password to be the same as user name
- Creates some other password to be assigned to all users
- Gives each user a different, randomly generated password
- Uses a mapping file, which specifies each user's new password

When you're importing NetWare users, you can control the process according to the type of user to be migrated. For example, the NetWare Supervisor can automatically be added to the Windows NT Administrators group if required. For each NetWare user, you can specify a new password or retain the old one. You can also exclude selected users from the migration. Selections can all be made using the Directory Services Manager applet in the Windows NT Server Control Panel.

Additional rules can be defined in a mapping file. A mapping file is simply an ASCII file listing group names, user names, and passwords. It is used to control how existing NetWare accounts are imported. It cannot be used to create new accounts. Any accounts not listed in the mapping file are ignored and not imported.

A mapping file can be created manually or by using Synchronization Manager, which is installed when the Directory Services Manager for NetWare is installed. Creating the file with Synchronization Manager is easier because it creates the proper format with headings. When you select the NetWare server to propagate, the NetWare users for that server are

Figure 6-4
Synchronizing the
NetWare user ac-
counts. (Source:
Microsoft
Corporation)

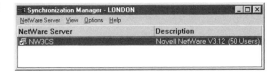

automatically placed in the mapping file. These entries can then be easily modified to reflect your account preferences.

As an example, imagine two users residing on two separate NetWare
servers with the same user accounts. User one on server one is Walter
McKinnon with the user ID WMCKINNON. User two on server two is
Wayne McKinnon with the same user ID WMCKINNON. Because both accounts cannot be migrated to the Windows NT server, at least one will
have to change. A mapping file can be defined containing a rule that
states how users from server one should be named. Changes could be
generic so that all users from server one receive the S1 prefix and the
users from server two receive the S2 prefix (S1_wmckinnon and S2_wm-
ckinnon). You may decide that you will change the user names to be more
specific. WMCKINNON might become MCKINNOW or WRMCKIN.

The entry in the mapping file would look like this:

```
[users]
WMCKINNON,        WRMCKINN,                PASSWORD
```

Before adding the NetWare server, you should review your plan and ensure that you have identified any situations that may cause the migration
to fail. Duplicate server names and duplicate user accounts must be addressed. Also, Windows NT does not allow user accounts to have the same
name as Windows NT groups. If NetWare user accounts are identical to
existing Windows NT accounts, the rights and permissions of the NetWare
user account will be granted to the existing Windows NT Server account,
unless you rename the NetWare user account using a mapping file.

Before you perform the migration, perform a trial migration and then
view the results log to ensure that you don't have any problems or con-
flicting names. The following is a checklist to review before beginning the
migration:

▨ Use NetWare utilities to back up the NetWare server's Bindery.

Table 6-1

NetWare to Windows NT Server account restrictions. (Courtesy of WWW.ITcoach. com)

NetWare Account Restriction	Windows NT Server Equivalent	Implemented
Account Expiration Date	Account Expiration Date	By individual user account; NetWare setting preserved.
Account Disabled	Account Disabled	By individual user account; NetWare setting preserved.
Limit Concurrent Connections	Limit Concurrent Connections	NetWare setting preserved.
Require Password	Permit Blank Password	As policy for all accounts; NetWare setting discarded.
Minimum Password Length	Minimum Password Length	As policy for all accounts; NetWare setting discarded.
Force Periodic Password Changes	Password Never Expires	By individual user account; NetWare setting preserved.
Days Between Forced Changes Password Expiration Date	Maximum Password Age	As policy for all accounts; NetWare setting discarded.
Require Unique Passwords	Password Uniqueness	As policy for all accounts; NetWare setting discarded
Allow User to Change Password	User Cannot Change Password	By individual user account; NetWare setting preserved.
Grace Logins	Grace Logins1	By individual user account; NetWare setting preserved.
Station Restrictions	Logon Workstations	By individual user account; NetWare setting preserved.
Time Restrictions	Logon Hours	By individual user account; NetWare setting preserved.
Intruder Detection/Lockout	Account Lockout	As policy for all accounts; NetWare setting discarded.
User Disk Volume Restrictions	None	Not transferred

■ Ensure that you don't have any duplicate NetWare and Windows NT server names.

■ If a user has different accounts on multiple NetWare servers being added to the domain, decide the user name you want the user to have on the domain, and transfer the other accounts to that user name using a mapping file.

■ Check the account policies of the domain, to make sure they are acceptable.

■ For compatibility with NetWare's password history, the domain's Password Uniqueness must be set to remember 8 or more. (See Figure 6-5.)

If the *File and Print Services for NetWare* (FPNW) product was previously installed on the primary domain controller, do the following:

■ You must reset the passwords of any user accounts that were Net-Ware enabled using FPNW before Directory Services Manager for NetWare was installed because Directory Services Manager for NetWare cannot read these users' existing passwords.

■ Perform a trial run and examine the report it produces to ensure that the effects are what you intend.

To perform a trial run, choose Add Server to Manage from the NetWare Server menu. You can then select the NetWare server to add from the Select NetWare Server list box, or type the name of the NetWare server in the NetWare Server box. You will be asked to type the user name and password to use to connect to the NetWare server. The user name you specify must have Supervisor privileges on the NetWare server.

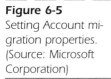

Figure 6-5
Setting Account migration properties. (Source: Microsoft Corporation)

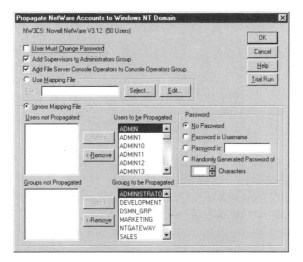

At this point, you can now specify how you want NetWare user accounts migrated to the domain. To do so, you must fill out the Propagate NetWare Accounts to Windows NT Domain dialog box. You can use the mapping file you created by selecting Use Mapping File, or you can type a new file name in the File box and choose Edit. This step creates a mapping file with the name you provide. You can also choose not to propagate some user and group accounts from the NetWare server to the Windows NT Server domain. If you do so, you will be prompted to delete those users or continue administering them on the NetWare server using NetWare administrative tools. You can also select not to propagate groups to the Windows NT Server domain. This will include all members of the groups you have specified.

You can now choose Trial Run, and then view the trial run results in Notepad by choosing Yes in the message box. After you view the results of a trial run, you can continue to propagate NetWare accounts to the Windows NT Domain, or you can choose Cancel to exit without adding the NetWare server to the domain.

Synchronizing Changes to the Windows NT Domain with NetWare Servers

Once Windows NT users and NetWare users are being managed from within a Windows NT Domain, any changes to the NetWare user accounts will have to be propagated back to the NetWare servers. Each user account is then required to be marked for propagation. To make the process easier to manage, you can place all required accounts in a Windows NT group, and the entire group can be propagated. This process can handle up to 2000 user accounts. (See Figure 6-6.)

Accounts to be propagated can be either existing NetWare accounts or accounts created in Windows NT Server and made NetWare enabled. When they are propagated to NetWare servers, their NetWare account restrictions must be set. Members of the Administrators group in the domain are given security equivalence to Supervisor on every NetWare server added to the domain.

Table 6-2 lists the Windows NT account restrictions and their equivalent NetWare settings. Notice that Windows NT restrictions that are not supported under NetWare are not propagated.

After the propagation has taken place, an account synchronization database is created on the Windows NT Domain's Primary Domain Controller. This database is responsible for tracking the users and groups be-

Figure 6-6
Selecting Windows
NT accounts to
propagate back to
NetWare. (Source:
Microsoft
Corporation)

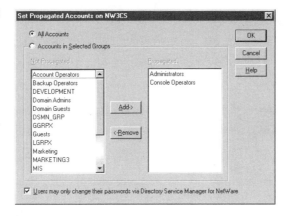

ing propagated to each server, as well as the status of all user and group accounts on each NetWare server. (See Figure 6-7.)

Rules for Managing NetWare Accounts Using Directory Services for NetWare

After the migration is complete and all accounts are being managed by DSNW, care should be taken not to manage these NetWare accounts using NetWare utilities such as SYSCON. If this were to happen, the synchronization process would become confused. Also, if password changes are to be made to NetWare accounts, the **CHGPASS** utility should be used. Directory Services Manager for NetWare provides the **CHGPASS** and **MSLOGIN** utilities.

The **CHGPASS** utility changes users' passwords, whereas the **MSLOGIN** utility is used to log in to a server and start a login script on the server. Just like the NetWare **LOGIN** command, **MSLOGIN** will log the users in to the specified file server and automatically log out of any servers to which the users were attached. If users passwords have expired, the users will see a message requesting them to use the **CHGPASS** command to change their passwords. Both utilities change the passwords on the Windows NT Server domain and all the NetWare servers to which the users' accounts are being propagated. Additionally, the users' passwords will also be changed on any NetWare server the users are currently attached to that is not participating in a domain.

Replacing all NetWare utilities with the equivalent Microsoft utilities provided with Directory Services Manager for NetWare is a good idea so

Table 6-2

Windows NT to NetWare account restrictions. (Courtesy of WWW. ITcoach.com)

Windows NT Account Restriction	NetWare Equivalent	How Propagated to NetWare
User Properties Dialog Box		
Username	Username	Propagated intact.
Full name	Full name	Propagated intact.
Description	None	Not propagated.
Password	Password	Propagated intact.
User Must Change Password at Next Logon	Password Expiration Date	When selected, the NetWare password expiration date is the current date.
User Cannot Change Password	Allow User to Change Password	Propagated intact.
Password Never Expires	Password Expiration Date	Propagated intact.
Account Disabled	Account Disabled	Propagated intact.
Account Locked Out	Intruder Detection/Lockout	Current setting not propagated.
Maintain NetWare Compatible Login	None	Must be selected for account to be propagated to NetWare servers.
Group Memberships		
Group memberships	Group memberships	Propagated intact.
Profile		
User Profile Path	None	Not propagated.
Logon Script Name	None	Not propagated.
Home Directory	Home Directory	Home Directory setting is ignored; NetWare Home Directory Relative Path is propagated.
Hours		
Logon Hours	Logon Hours	Propagated intact.
Log On To		
User May Log On to All Workstations	None	Not propagated. Governs logons from Microsoft client computers only.

Table 6-2

Continued.

Windows NT Account Restriction	NetWare Equivalent	How Propagated to NetWare
User May Log On From All NetWare Workstations	Station Restrictions	Propagated intact.
Account		
Account Expires	Account Expiration Date	Propagated intact.
Account Type	None	Not propagated.
NetWare Properties		
NetWare Account Password Expired	None	No effect when propagating from Windows NT Server to NetWare.
Grace Logins	Grace Logins	Propagated intact.
Concurrent Connections	Limit Concurrent Connections	Propagated intact.
Account Policies (Passwords)		
Maximum Password Age	Days Between Forced Changes	Propagated intact.
Minimum Password Age	None	Not propagated.
Minimum Password Length	Minimum Password Length	Propagated intact.
Password Uniqueness	Require Unique Passwords	Propagated intact, but effective only if set to 8 or greater.
Account Policies		
Account Lockout	Intruder Detection/ Lockout	Propagated intact.
Forcibly Disconnect When Logon Hours Expire	None	Not propagated.
Users Must Log On to Change Password	None	Not propagated.

that you can help ensure that your NetWare clients do not incorrectly change their passwords.

The utilities supplied with Directory Services Manager for NetWare include the following:

Figure 6-7
Synchronization database results. (Source: WWW.NETWORKOL-OGIST.COM)

Contents of the account synchronization database			
Account	PDC Version	NW1 Version	NW2 Version
Patricia	5	5	n/a
Joseph	10	9	8
Sales_Reps	2	2	2

CHGPASS.EXE

MSATTACH.EXE

MSMAP.EXE

MSLOGIN.EXE

These files are copied to the NetWare server's PUBLIC directory along with the library files RPC16C1.RPC, RPC16C6.RPC, and SECURITY.RPC. MSLOGIN.EXE and the .RPC files are also copied to the server's LOGIN directory. If users connect to servers not managed by Directory Services Manager for NetWare, you may want to copy the files manually to these servers so they will be available.

To prevent users from accidentally changing their passwords incorrectly, you can specify that the users can only change their passwords via Directory Services Manager for NetWare. If a problem does occur, the **CHGPASS** utility can be used to change the password again. This utility will synchronize the new password to all servers.

The following are rules for using Directory Services Manager for NetWare:

■ After migration, SYSCON should no longer be used.

■ To create new NetWare accounts, create a Windows NT account and make it "NetWare compatible."

■ Inform NetWare users of the DSNW **CHGPASS** utility. (You may also want to remove **SETPASS** from the public directory of your NetWare servers.)

■ Limit the number of NetWare servers in each domain to 32.

NOTE: *Directory Services Manager for NetWare is a User/Group account database tool only. It does not perform file migration!*

Troubleshooting Directory Services Manager for NetWare

If you experience problems with Directory Services Manager for NetWare, you should check a few things. First, ensure that the Windows NT Directory Services Manager for NetWare service was started correctly. You can use Server Manager to verify this fact. (See Figure 6-8.) You may also see an error in the Windows NT application log indicating that the service failed to start. The log can be viewed using the Windows NT Event Viewer. If the service did fail, the problem could be the result of the service account password being incorrect. (See Figure 6-9.)

So that you can troubleshoot Directory Services Manager for NetWare, understanding the error codes that may be generated is useful. The following list can be found in Microsoft Books on-line help file for Directory Services Manager for NetWare:

- `Account <account name> cannot be propagated to NetWare servers because the account name is invalid on NetWare servers.`

  One cause for this problem may be if the account name contains spaces. NetWare does not support spaces in account names. In particular, this problem may happen for many built-in Windows NT Server groups (such as PRINT OPERATORS). If you require this group to propagate to NetWare servers, you must change its name to a valid name. Otherwise, no administrator action is necessary.

- `The Sync Agent account will not propagate the account <account name> to the NetWare servers because it does not know the password of the account.`

  The account `account_name` was NetWare enabled before Directory Services Manager for NetWare was installed on the server. To cause this account to be propagated, reset the account password.

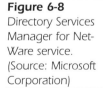

Figure 6-8
Directory Services Manager for NetWare service.
(Source: Microsoft Corporation)

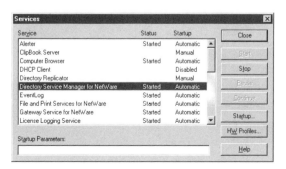

■ **The Sync Agent Service will stop because it can only run on the PDC of the domain.**

This error appears on the old Primary Domain Controller when a new Primary Domain Controller begins running in the domain.

■ **The Sync Agent Service failed to sync the server <servername> due to error 53.**

The server may be down, or this problem could be caused by timing issues during communications. The server will be synchronized when the next regular round of synchronizations is sent out. No administrator action is necessary, unless you see a long series of these errors for one server, in which case you should verify that the server is running.

■ **ERROR 58: The Sync Agent Service could not replicate the database to <server name\path> because of error 86.**

The password used to access this server to back up the account synchronization database has probably been changed. To correct the problem, in Synchronization Manager, choose Set Database Backup Options from the NetWare Server menu. Then remove and again add this backup path, specifying the current password for the account used to access the backup path.

■ **The Sync Agent Service could not replicate database to <server name> because of error 59.**

Directory Services Manager for NetWare could not access the server. This problem is probably momentary. No administrator action is necessary, unless you see a long series of these errors for one server, in which case you should verify that the server is running.

The Sync Agent Service could not replicate the database to <server name\path> because of error 67.

The specified path no longer exists on the server. In Synchronization Manager, choose Set Database Backup Options from the NetWare Server menu. Then remove this backup path.

Jet Error 1004: JET_wrnColumnNull

This error may indicate that the account synchronization database has become inconsistent because of a previous lack of disk space on the server. If these errors occur often, restore the account synchronization database using a version that was backed up before the disk space problem occurred.

A JET DATABASE ERROR -1102 HAS OCCURRED. JET_errWriteLock

A timing issue occurred with propagating an account change to NetWare servers. The account will be propagated in the next cycle, and no administrator action is necessary.

The Sync Agent Service failed to sync the NetWare server 386 due to error 1219 ERROR_SESSION_CREDENTIAL_CONFLICT. The credentials supplied conflict with an existing set of credentials.

This error sometimes occurs if you are using a NetWare server that is participating in a domain as a backup location for the Account Synchronization database. While the database is being backed up to the server, attempts to synchronize the server will fail. As soon as the backup is complete, synchronization attempts will again succeed. No administrator action is necessary.

1220 Error:

This error indicates that a NetWare server did not have any connections available. Directory Services Manager for NetWare logs this error until connections to the NetWare server are available again. No administrator action is necessary.

A jet database -1032 has occurred. JET_errFileAccessDenied

Check to see whether enough disk space is available on the computers containing the Synchronization Manager database backup paths.

■ **The Sync Agent Service failed to sync the NetWare server \<servername\> due to error 1317 ERROR_NO_SUCH_USER. The specified user does not exist.**

Check whether the WINNT_SYNC_AGENT account has been deleted from the NetWare server. This account must not be deleted from a NetWare server that has been added to a domain for management.

■ **1376: ERROR_NO_SUCH_ALIAS**

This error may indicate that the account synchronization database has become inconsistent because of a previous lack of disk space on the server. If these errors occur often, restore the account synchronization database using a version that was backed up before the disk space problem occurred.

■ **Jet Error: -1507 JET_errColumnNotFound**

This error indicates that Directory Services Manager for NetWare is trying to propagate to a server that no longer exists in the domain.

■ **Jet Error -1603 errors, JET_errNoCurrentRecord**

A process tried to add a user account to a group after the user account was deleted.

■ **Jet Error -1801: Jet_errDiskFull**

Check to see whether enough disk space is available on the computers containing the Synchronization Manager database backup paths.

■ **Jet Error -1808: JET_errDiskFull**

Free up disk space on the server.

■ **Jet Error -1811: Jet_errFileNotFound**

Check to see whether enough disk space is available on the computers containing the Synchronization Manager database backup paths.

Integrating Windows NT Servers with Novell Directory Services

We have examined how NetWare 3.x servers can be managed as part of a Windows NT Domain using Directory Services Manager for NetWare service and the Windows NT User Manager for Domains utility. With Synchronicity from NetVision, you can manage Windows NT servers as an NDS object that is part of a NetWare 4 directory tree. This capability allows all servers in your organization to be managed using the Novell NWAdmin utility.

To implement Synchronicity, you must load the *Synchronicity Global Event Service* (GES) on the NetWare server, and the Synchronization agent on one NT server or workstation with administrative privileges in each Windows NT Domain to be administered. For Windows NT servers that are not part of a domain, the Synchronization agent must be run on each server. The Global Event Service is a *NetWare Loadable Module* (NLM) while the synchronization agent is loaded on the Windows NT server as an NT service.

The Synchronicity GES NLM must be loaded on all NetWare servers in the NDS tree. All NetWare servers must be NetWare 4.1 servers with the NDS version 4.89c or later. Synchronicity is compatible with Windows NT 3.51 and later, including Windows NT 4.0. (See Figure 6-10.)

When you're configuring synchronization with NWAdmin, each Windows NT Domain can be configured to synchronize with a specific NetWare NDS organizational unit. As an example, if a company has Windows NT and NetWare servers installed for use within the engineering department, the Windows NT Engineering domain could be configured to synchronize only with the Engineering NDS organizational unit. If the domain is used by all departments in the company, it could be configured to synchronize with the entire NDS tree. (See Figure 6-11.)

When any changes are made to the directory tree, all Windows NT Domains running the synchronization agent will be notified. In this way, if a new user is created using the NetWare NWAdmin utility, Synchronic-

Figure 6-10
Location of Synchronicity components on the network. (Courtesy of www.ITcoach.com)

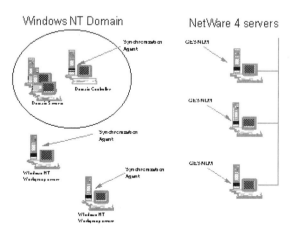

ity will automatically create the user in all Windows NT Domains except those that are not interested in the change. If Windows NT trust relationships exist, you may choose not to synchronize with all domains. Alternatively, you may decide to remove any trust relationships and allow Synchronicity to provide each domain with the required accounts. (See Figure 6-12.)

Figure 6-11
Domain synchronization with NDS.
(Courtesy of www. ITcoach.com)

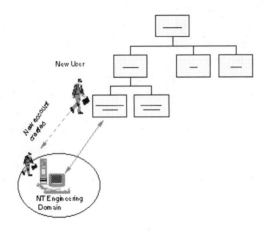

Figure 6-12
Synchronizing Windows NT Domains with Synchronicity. (Courtesy of WWW. NETWORKOLOGIST. COM)

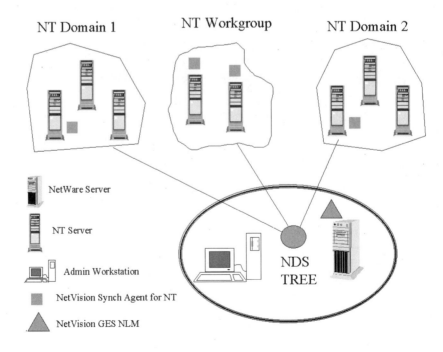

If users are to be added to Windows NT accounts only, NWAdmin can still be used. The appropriate Widows NT NDS object must be selected first. From there, a list of possible object types will be displayed, including Windows NT groups (both local or global and Windows NT users. The changes will then be sent to the appropriate Synchronization agent responsible for creating the actual Windows NT account. Because this object is an NT-only object, the changes are not synchronized with the rest of the NDS tree; however, a link can be created later.

SUMMARY

Directory Services Manager for NetWare is a useful utility primarily for organizations that will migrate fully to Windows NT at some point. During the transition period, which for some organizations will take years, Directory Services Manager for NetWare can be used effectively to manage "all" servers using a common set of tools.

By now, you may have made your decision that you will or will not perform a full migration to Windows NT. Directory Services Manager for NetWare is an effective tool where NetWare Bindery servers are being migrated or managed (Bindery servers being NetWare 3.x and older). NetWare 4.x servers are not supported.

If you are truly looking for a good central management approach, you should also consider a migration to NetWare 4 because NetWare's Directory Services (NDS) has advantages over Windows NT Domain architecture, as discussed in Chapter 1. Using the Synchronicity product to manage Windows NT servers from within NetWare's NDS, you gain the advantages of NDS to manage both Novell and Windows NT servers using a hierarchical approach to server management, which NDS offers.

Novell has introduced NDS support for Windows NT; this support will allow you to choose NDS instead of domain management. If you choose this approach, you must consider the impact this decision may have on Windows NT services that require domain security. Such services include Microsoft Exchange. Synchronicity simply synchronizes changes between the two environments while allowing each system to maintain its native management model.

Microsoft has also announced that Windows NT 5.0 will include its own Directory Services, which will be similar to Novell's NDS in that it will be x.500 based and provide an LDAP interface. Finally, Banyan offers its Street Talk Directory Services as an add-on service for Windows NT server. Street Talk has been the main strength of the Banyan Vines network operating system for many years.

For access to Directory Services from any vendor, Microsoft has released *Active Directory Services Interface* (ADSI). ADSI is a set of open interfaces that can be used to present a single view for accessing and managing network resources. Administrators and developers can use ADSI services to manage resources in a Directory Service from any network environment. It can be an LDAP-based, NDS-based, or Windows NT Directory Services when it arrives.

Migration

The main focus of this chapter will be on migrating Net-Ware server information to Windows NT servers using the Migration Tool for NetWare. Migration planning stages and steps will be discussed. Case studies will be used to demonstrate the various migration options and scenarios that can be taken. In-depth study will be made of how NetWare user and group accounts and NetWare file system security information are migrated to Windows NT. A trial migration and review of trial migration logs files will be included, highlighting areas where problems are generally encountered with possible solutions. Finally, a live migration will be demonstrated.

During the course of integrating Windows NT Domain servers into an existing NetWare server environment, however, user and file system information may be required to migrate from Windows NT to NetWare. Such an action can facilitate single login and attach capability to a multiserver, multiplatform network environment by having the same user account information on both server platforms. In the latter part of the chapter, we will explore what options are available to accomplish this task.

Chapter Objectives

- Determining the scope of the migration project
- Stages of the migration
- Types of migrations
- Comparing Windows NT and NetWare User and System Information
- Comparing user accounts
- Comparing administrative accounts
- Comparing system settings
- Comparing file and directory security
- NetWare to Windows NT: Introduction to the Migration Tool for NetWare
- Overview of the Migration Tool for NetWare
- Transferring user, group, security, and file system information
- Running the Migration Tool for NetWare
- Configuration options
- Trial migrations
- Migration log files
- Performing the live migration
- Windows NT to NetWare: Introduction to Migration Toolkit
- Overview of the Novell Consulting Group's Migration Toolkit
- Migration Toolkit processes and requirements
- Migration phases
- Migrated information
- Performing the migration

Determining the Scope of the Migration Project

Before you begin head long into the migration itself, being aware of the various phases of the project is a very good idea. (See Figure 7-1.) In doing so,

Figure 7-1
How big is your
migration mountain?
(Courtesy WWW.
NETWORKOLOGIST.
COM))

you will start to develop a better idea for the size and scale of the project you are about to commence. The migration project has eight basic phases.

Stages of a Server Migration

1. Objective of the Migration

By this time, you should have worked through the business requirements, business cases, potential alternatives, and agreed upon a solution. Now you are ready to do the actual migration part of the bigger project. The migration objective statement would be something similar to the following:

> The purpose of this migration is to relocate Department A users, groups, applications, and data files from Server platform X to Server platform Y. System security will be established by the destination server and not brought over from the current system. However, current user level file access security will be translated (converted) to the new server's format. The migration will take place the long weekend of August 1st.

2. Current System Analysis

Implementing new systems can place very different loads on a network and its resources. Different applications require different network bandwidth. The best example available to demonstrate this situation is a case in which one company migrated from DOS-based applications stored on a server to Windows-based applications stored on the server. The company migrated the 150 DOS-based clients to Windows over the weekend. Everything worked fine during the two or three workstation post migration tests: the applications ran and the print jobs printed. However, Monday morning when the 150 users logged on and started working, network utilization increased to unacceptable levels, and people started to lose connections to the server. The solution was to create three separate segments by placing three Network Interface Cards in the server. However, initial analysis of the current system's handling capacity would have prevented the "Monday Morning Network Blues."

Many organizations have a periodic systems analysis performed on their network and applications. If your organization does not, take the time to perform a short one over the space of a week while the other migration planning work is beginning. Calculate as best possible the network, server, disk, and printer capacity of the current network resources. Then estimate (yes, estimate) as best possible what the impact of the migration to a new environment is likely to be. You can develop a better estimate by creating a test lab and then extrapolating the information for the size of your network.

3. Identification of Affected Network Components

At this stage, we need to identify exactly what areas of the network will be affected by the migration. These areas include the network resources in general, which were described previously. However, you need to get into more detail. If a physical printer is being migrated to the new server platform, you will also need to identify print driver installation, print server and print queue locations, as well as configure the applications or desktop operating systems that are going to access the printer. The latter aspect can be the bigger task. Likely areas to be affected include servers, workstations, applications, protocol implementations, and internetworking devices such as routers, bridges, and gateways.

4. Proposed System Design

Now that you have identified all the potential areas affected by the migration, you can begin to develop a new system. You need to ask some questions like "Will the equipment be located in the same place and just the software components change?" or "How will we redesign the internetwork to handle the increased demand for network bandwidth?" or "What will the new server's directory structure look like?" or "How will we access data backed up on the old server?" People tend to always overlook this last question, so at this stage, getting as many people involved in the process as possible is best.

5. Migration Strategy

To a large degree, the proposed system's design will help identify the migration strategy. Here, we are referring to the specifics of the migration itself. What is the source server, and what is the destination? Will it be one to many (servers) or many to one (server)? What users and groups are being moved and to where? What files are being moved and to where? Identifying all these elements will allow you to create your time line and sequence of events.

6. Test Migration and Refinement to Process

If done properly, a migration of the type we are discussing in this book can be done without ever affecting the current servers. As such, extensive testing of the migration strategy can be done. To accomplish this task, however, you need to upgrade to new server and leave the old ones intact. This is a great backdoor policy to try to enforce. It does cost a bit more, but let's face it, if you are moving to a new server platform, you will most likely be upgrading your servers anyway.

Probably the greatest downfall that the personal computer is associated with is its lack of planning, testing, and implementation procedures. In the mainframe environment, migrations can take significant amounts of time. Personal computer's are small, so we tend to treat them that way. However, the data they hold is quite large in the scale of its impact on an organization. Testing the migration is an absolute requirement in the project if you are to accomplish the project successfully.

During the test migration, you will need to become familiar with the migration log files so that you can find and refine the migration settings and options you have selected. Be sure to save your settings files, and document the changes each one has so that you know which one to go back to when you have one that works.

During this stage, you will identify all the software drivers, components, hardware, and whatever else you will need for the migration. Although software drivers can generally be added around the clock from vendor Internet sites, getting new hardware is difficult when the distributor is closed. You will bring several people together for the migration, and you will be interrupting business continuity, so make sure you dot your i's and cross your t's.

Finally, develop a list of post migration tests that will need to be conducted to verify that the migration has worked. These tests will be very important after the initial information has been migrated.

NOTE: *You will no doubt notice that, out of the eight phases, we gave more space to testing than all the over seven. This indication alone should tell you how important the testing phase is. You bypass this phase at your peril. Nothing ever works exactly like the vendor claims 100 percent of the time, so testing helps to prepare you for problems you may encounter later.*

7. Live Migration

The big day has arrived—not quite as big as the summer holidays but with more significance on career moves than anything else. It is probably Friday night of a long three-day weekend. Before you reached this stage, the people in the affected areas were all repeatedly advised that the system will not be available. Some will still try to access it, so make sure you isolate all the affected servers on their own networks to eliminate the potential of someone logging on and stopping the process 14 hours into the job.

Before you do anything else, back up your file server twice and test your backup tapes. And remember, as far as career-advancing moves go, the following statement should be well heeded: "The only thing worse than not having a backup is having a backup that does not work" So test your backup to ensure that you can restore from it. Also, during these backups, ensure that you use detailed log levels so that if files are missing later, you can determine whether they were backed up in the first place.

Keep a log book of the migration process. Print and save all log files as they are created. Some of them get deleted afterward, and others remain to be reviewed, so don't take a chance. Yes, keeping a log book takes longer, but the information can be invaluable.

Although there you might be tempted to start the migration process, hit the road for a while and then come back; just don't do it now! Someone should be present at all times during the migration process. If something happens, your recovery time is increased already. Remember, time is a limited resource, and it is amazing how fast Sunday night arrives.

Finally, you should look into Chapter 8 for a list of well-defined forms that will help you solidify your testing phase and implementation phases.

Here are the migration strategy steps:

1. Select all servers taking part in the migration.
2. Ensure that all users are logged off the system.
3. Back up all servers involved in the migration with their respective backup systems.
4. Clean the server's user and group directory structures.
5. Clean the server's file system (using virus scans and so on).
6. Select users and groups to transfer.
7. Select files and directories to transfer.
8. Run a trial migration.
9. Review error log files and correct problems.
10. Run the migration.
11. Change user environment for access to the new migrated network (if needed).

8. Post Migration Testing and Maintenance

The job is done. Run your battery of post migration tests to ensure that applications are accessible and users are able to log in or log on. You should have someone test each and every aspect of the migrated areas. Log on to each workstation to ensure proper network access (fixing problems is a lot easier when users are not around). Test each application using a regular user account. Send print jobs to every printer. The more testing you can do over the weekend part of the migration, the fewer problems you are likely to have to deal with Monday or Tuesday morning.

Types of Migrations

From a broader perspective, there are essentially two types of migrations: simple and complex. By *simple*, we are referring to a one-to-one server migration: everything from one server is migrated to another server. Everything else gets complicated (complex). A one-to-one server migration is fairly straightforward, especially if you are migrating everything over to the other server. With this kind of migration, you simply need to select the users, groups, and files to be migrated, as well as specify which system and user security settings will take precedence. (See Figure 7-2.)

More complex migrations involve more careful analysis because usually more servers are involved, as a greater potential for duplication exists between each source and destination server taking place in the migration. Figure 7-3 shows an example of a many-to-one migration.

Figure 7-2
A one-to-one server migration. (Courtesy of Learning Tree International)

- ## One NetWare server to one NT server

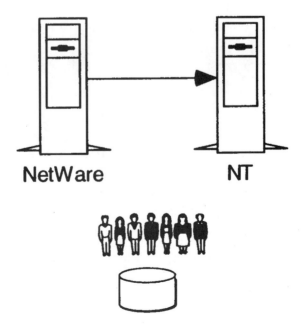

NetWare　　　　NT

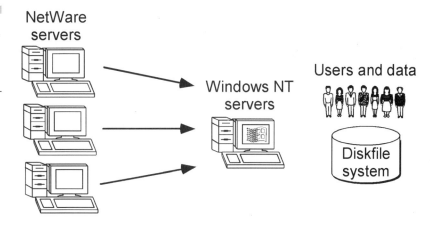

Figure 7-3
A many-to-one server
migration. (Courtesy
of Learning Tree
International)

Consolidate several NetWare servers into a single
Windows NT Server

Finally, the migration tools provided by Novell and Microsoft allow you to migrate information from one server and split it to many servers, creating a one-to-many migration. In this scenario, the user and file information on one server is migrated to several other servers, usually with user information going to one central server, and the files are spread across one or several other resource servers. (See Figure 7-4.)

Obviously, as the migration scenario gets more complex, you will need to allocate sufficient resources to deal with the greater requirement. More people, more time, more planning, and more testing will all be needed to elevate your chances of success. We will look at some additional scenarios as we move into using the actual migration tools.

Comparing Windows NT and NetWare User and System Information

Why is comparing NetWare and Windows NT Domain user and group accounts important? Probably the main reason is so that when we migrate accounts from one system to the other, we want to ensure that some of the current settings are available on the new system. If they are not, we need to know what the equivalents are and how we can provide similar functionality. It is also important that we understand the differences between the types of administrative accounts because these accounts can

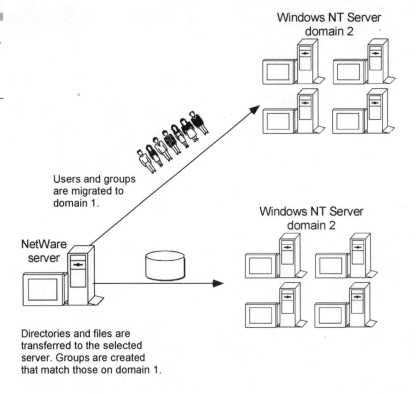

Windows NT Server
domain 2

Windows NT Server
domain 2

Users and groups
are migrated to
domain 1.

NetWare
server

Directories and files are
transferred to the selected
server. Groups are created
that match those on domain 1.

be transferred and assume equivalent status on the new system. This capability may or may not be desired, depending on the type of administrative account.

Comparing System Settings: Account Restrictions

By system settings or account restrictions, we are referring to settings
that are defined for all users on the system. These settings include Minimum Password Length, Maximum Password Age, Account Lockout, Lockout Duration, and so on. In Windows NT, these settings must be made for
all users within a domain. In NetWare 3.x, they can be set for all users on
a server, or they can be set for users individually. The answer as to which
is better is debatable—all settings the same across all servers for all users
or having to set the settings on individual servers for each group of users.
In NetWare 4.x, the rules are wide open and through NDS can be set and
changed at various levels of the tree or on a per container basis.

For the purposes of migration, however, the following main user and group account restrictions are of relevance. This comparison applies mainly to NetWare 3.x and Windows NT 3.51 and 4.0.

ACCOUNT RESTRICTIONS:

- Expiration Date: Both NetWare and Windows NT networks support user account expiration dates. At the end of this particular day, the account can no longer be used.

- Account Disabled: You can disable individual user accounts or have them become disabled automatically through the Intruder Detection process. Both NetWare and Windows NT support this capability.

- Limit Concurrent Connections: NetWare supports limiting the number of concurrent network connections (logins) that a user can have at any one time. Windows NT, on the other hand, supports only workstation access restrictions in that you can specify from which workstation names (NetBIOS names) the user can log on.

PASSWORD RESTRICTIONS:

- Require Password: This restriction specifies whether passwords are required on user accounts. Both platforms support this capability.

- Minimum Password Length: This restriction specifies the minimum number of characters that are required for a user's password. Windows NT defaults to a minimum of six characters, whereas NetWare's is five characters.

- Force Periodic Password Changes: This restriction specifies the number of days a password can be used before the users are required to change to a new one. The Windows NT default is 42 days, whereas NetWare's is 40 days.

- Require Unique Passwords: This restriction specifies the number of different passwords users are required to use before the system will allow them to reuse old passwords. The Windows NT default is five, whereas NetWare requires eight different passwords before reuse and they cannot be changed.

- Allow User to Change Password: Basically, this restriction defines whether users are allowed to change their own passwords. Both NetWare and Windows NT, by default, allow users to perform this function.

- Grace Logins: When users' passwords have expired, the Grace logins define how many times the users can still log in before they are forced to change their passwords or be refused access. Windows NT does not support this function.

- Station Restrictions: This function limits the number of workstations from which users can log in. NetWare uses network numbers (IPX) and node addresses (network interface MAC addresses) to specify from which workstations users can log in. Windows NT supports a similar feature by limiting from which workstations users can log in based on the Windows workstation NetBIOS name.

- Time Restrictions: Time restrictions define what hours the users are allowed or disallowed access to the network servers. Both Windows NT and NetWare support time restrictions. However, in Windows NT, time restrictions are set in blocks of one hour from start of the hour to end of the hour (for example, 7:00 a.m. to 8:00 a.m.). NetWare, on the other hand, allows time restrictions to be set in half-hour increments.

- Intruder Detection/Lockout: When implemented, this restriction specifies a predefined number of unsuccessful login/logon attempts that will lock out users' accounts. The amount of time accounts are locked out can also be set. This function disables the account from being used for network access for a time. Both Windows NT and NetWare support this function. Windows NT has an additional option of locking the account indefinitely until the Administrator unlocks it.

- User Disk Volume Restrictions: This function restricts the amount of disk space users are allowed to use on the server. Windows NT does not support this function.

Effect of Restrictions During a Migration

During a migration from NetWare 3.x to Windows NT, for example, the Supervisor options will or can be transferred to Windows NT Domain policies. However, a one-to-one match does not occur, and transferred restrictions are matched to those of Windows NT. The restrictions that cannot be matched are not transferred. Table 7-1 demonstrates how account restrictions are transferred in this example.

Table 7-1

Transferring
account
restrictions.
(Courtesy of WWW.
NETWORKOLOGIST.
COM)

NetWare Account Expiration Date	Expiration Date	User Account
Account Disabled	Account Disabled	User Account
Limit Concurrent Connections	None	Not Transferred
Require Password	Permit Blank Password	System Account Policy
Minimum Password Length	Minimum Password Length	System Account Policy
Force Periodic Password Changes	Password Never Expires	User Account
Days Between Forced Changes	Maximum Password Age	System Account Policy
Grace Logins	None	Not Transferred
Allow User to Change Password	User Cannot Change Password	User Account
Require Unique Passwords	Password Uniqueness	System Account Policy
Station Restrictions	None	Not Transferred
Time Restrictions	Logon Hours	User Account
Intruder Detection/Lockout	Account Lockout	System Account Policy
User Disk Volume Restrictions	None	Not Transferred

Windows NT Domain

In addition to restrictions found in each platform, because of the high
level of security available to Windows NT workstations, several other restrictions can be set. However, they have no relevance in a migration.
These additional restrictions come in the form of Rights and Abilities.
Rights and Abilities are similar in that they give a user or group the capability to perform a function (for example, shut down the system). They
are categorized as Rights and Abilities mainly as a way of distinguishing
them because Rights can be changed (granted or revoked) individually,
whereas you get an Ability by being a member of a predefined group. (See
"Comparing Administrative Accounts" later in this chapter.) Abilities are
hard-coded into the system and cannot be changed on an individual basis. However, Rights and Abilities themselves are not transferred or mi-

grated between platforms. For NetWare users to have similar capabilities on the Windows NT side, they must be made members of an appropriate administrative group or be given individual Rights. Figure 7-5 shows Windows NT account restrictions in the User Manager for Domains.

The Account Policy selection allows you to set the various password and account lockout settings for all users in the domain. (See Figure 7-6.)

The User Rights Policy allows administrators to grant or revoke individual rights for users. Rights include items such as Shut Down the Sys-

Figure 7-5
The account restrictions are set through the Policies menu item of the User Manager for Domains. (Source: Microsoft Corporation)

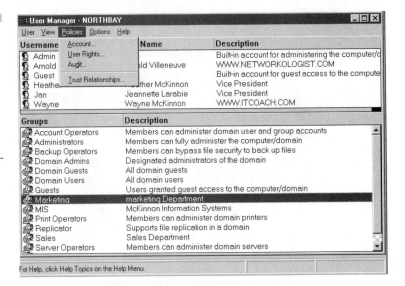

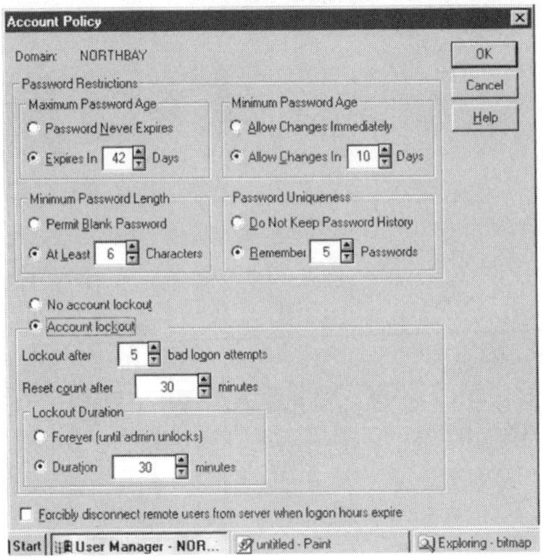

Figure 7-6
Account policies are used to establish better security in Windows NT Domains. (Source: Microsoft Corporation)

tem, Log on Locally, Access the Computer From the Network, and others. Rights are usually specific to the workstation but also apply to the server. They are not relevant to a migration because they are not supported by a NetWare server. (See Figure 7-7.)

Finally, an Audit Policy can be established on Windows NT. It tracks a number of different items in two areas: Success and Failure to perform a function. The functions include logon/logoff, file and object access, and others. Here again, auditing is not a function that is migrated, although both systems support the auditing function. (See Figure 7-8.)

NetWare 3.x

The main user and group administration tool in NetWare 3.x is SYSCON, a nongraphical user interface-based SYStem CONfiguration utility. (See Figure 7-9.) SYSCON is used to administer the user and group accounts, serverwide system login scripts, default account restrictions, and server start-up settings.

We will be looking at User and Group settings later in this chapter. For now, however, let's look at the account restriction areas that can be set on

Figure 7-7
The account restrictions are set through the Policies menu item of the User Manager for Domains. (Source: Microsoft Corporation)

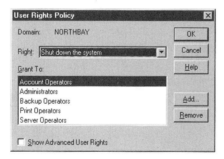

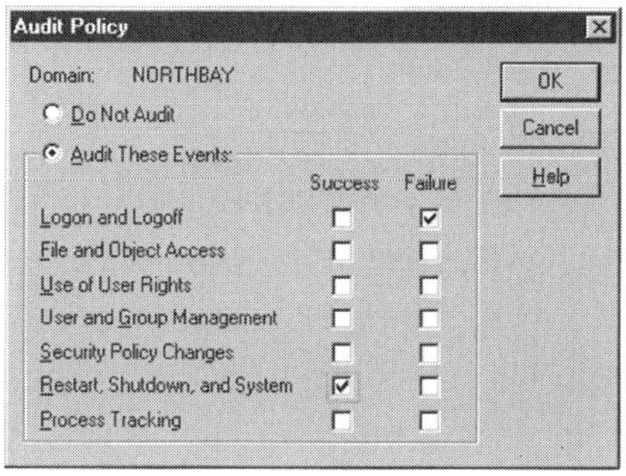

Figure 7-8
Auditing of certain areas can be maintained in Windows NT. (Source: Microsoft Corporation)

Figure 7-9
The SYStem CONfigu-
ration utility main
menu. (Source: Nov-
ell, Inc.)

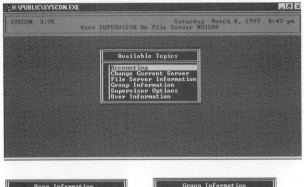

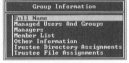

a NetWare 3.x server so that we can compare them to what we have just seen in the Windows NT environment. Figure 7-10 shows the bulk of the account restrictions that can be set. Unlike Windows NT, these restrictions do not apply to all users but are used as the basis for newly created user accounts. Each new user account will use these default settings in the account. Thereafter, the supervisor can change the settings on an individual basis. This information can be transferred to Windows NT to become the default Account Policy settings.

The Edit System AUTOEXEC file is specific to the NetWare server. It details how the server should start up. Windows NT accomplishes this task through Registry settings. This information is not transferred or migrated, so we won't dwell on it here.

File Console Operators for NetWare are set through the Supervisor Options screen as demonstrated in Figure 7-11. This is not an account restriction and is done under group membership on the Windows NT side. For NetWare, however, this task is accomplished here. The Intruder Detection/Lockout status is an account restriction similar to what we saw earlier in the Account Policy section of Windows NT. This information can be transferred from NetWare to Windows NT during a migration.

The next Supervisor option is for the server System Login Script. This script is applied to all users when they logon. However, it is not applicable to Windows NT nor a migration, so we won't focus on it. Likewise, the View

Figure 7-10
Setting the default
account balance and
restrictions. (Source:
Novell, Inc.)

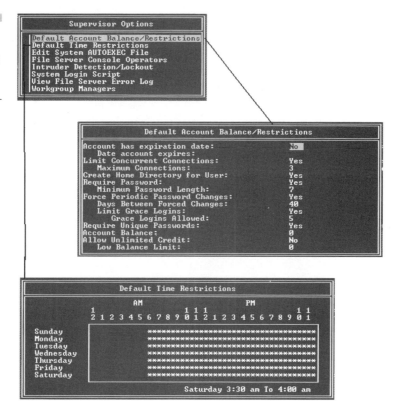

Figure 7-11
Intruder
Detection/Lockout
configuration in
NetWare 3.x
SYSCON. (Source:
Novell, Inc.)

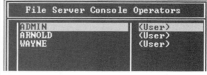

File Server Error Log shows NetWare server-specific errors. It may be of use, however, when migrating from Windows NT to NetWare. The last option is for setting Workgroup Managers, and this function can be performed through the user configuration menus, so we will look at it later.

NetWare 4.x

In NetWare 4.x, the default settings are essentially the same as in NetWare 3.x. However, because NDS is such a distributed database resting on many servers where separate administrators can be responsible for individual containers, defaults are not really set in one place. Instead, an administrator of a certain container may, in fact, create a User_Template account for which all the settings for new user accounts will be made. The administrator will then use this account to create new user accounts. In NetWare 3.x, systemwide settings were specific to one server. Now they can be individually configured down to the container level (for example, login scripts) and are not server specific.

Because these settings are similar to the ones available in NetWare 3.x, we will not review the login screens here. For more information on available settings, see the preceding figures showing the NetWare 3.x User Settings screens.

Comparing Administrative Accounts

As you may have noticed so far in this chapter, User and Group account management for NetWare 3.x Bindery seems to be surpassed in flexibility and options by Windows NT Domains (although, we know people who would argue this point). Likewise, this is true in our opinion with Windows NT Domains being surpassed by NetWare 4.x NDS in similar ways. This flow is also true when it comes to Administrative accounts.

Table 7-2 shows a comparison between NetWare 3.x and Windows NT Domains administrative accounts.

These account relationships can also be important during a migration. For example, during a migration from NetWare 3.x to Windows NT, the Supervisor account can be added to the Administrators group. This is done through a Transfer Administrative Privileges option in the Windows NT Migration Tool for NetWare. Other than during a migration, however, the accounts have no bearing on your ability to access the other platform. For example, being

Table 7-2

NetWare 3.x and
Windows NT
Domains
Administrative
account
comparison.

NetWare 3.x	Windows NT 4.0 Domain
Supervisor	Administrator
Supervisor Equivalent	Administrators Group
Workgroup/User Account Manager	Account Operators Group
File Server Console Operator	Server Operators Group
Print Server/Queue Operator	Print Operators Group
None (function performed by Supervisor)	Backup Operator

an Administrator of a Windows NT Domain does not give you any access or privileges to the NetWare servers unless you have a duplicate account on that server with Security Equivalence to the Supervisor. (Note: The account does not have to be a duplicate; just having one simplifies access.)

Workgroup Managers, User Account Managers, and Account Operators are close matches for what they allow network administrators to do: delegate the management of user accounts without making someone an Administrator or Supervisor. On Windows NT, user account administration is centralized, so account administration does not need to be assigned for specific servers.

File Server Console Operators and the Server Operator Group are also close; however, the Server Operator Group in Windows NT gives the assigned users a lot more power over what they can do to the server. As with user account management, the Windows NT administrator can delegate server management without having to give the individual full Administrative privileges to the entire domain and the servers in it. For example, Server Operators have the right to back up and restore files and directories on the server, lock and unlock file server consoles, and even enable or disable shared directory volumes. NetWare Console Operators, on the other hand, are fairly restricted to what they can do, and those privileges are usually limited to the file server console itself.

Print Server/Queue Operator Groups in NetWare provide the same capabilities given to the Windows NT Print Operators Group: the ability to manage print services. Both are equally as powerful in their scope of managing printer service.

Finally, Windows NT provides for a Backup Operators Group, which is not found in NetWare 3.x. This function in NetWare 3.x is carried out by the Supervisor. The Backup Operators can back up domain servers and workstations. In particular, they can access what are called *Administrative shares*. These shares are set up on the workstation and servers by default to share all the drives (both floppy, hard, and CD-ROM-based) but without advertising them in the browse list. Administrative shares can also be created by placing a dollar sign ($) after the share name.

What About NetWare 4.x NDS?

We specifically did not try to draw comparisons between Windows NT Domain and NetWare 4.x NDS administrative accounts because NDS does not create any by default. However, this is far from a limitation. NDS is so flexible that you can create any type or level of administrative account that you might require for a specific function within your organization. So, from that perspective, you could duplicate any of the similar administrative functions that both NOSs support: Windows NT by default, but created in NDS.

Will These Capabilities Change in the Future?

The only thing constant is change. And given the continued competition between Novell and Microsoft in the "server wars," significant changes are likely to level the playing field once again. The promised introduction of Windows NT Version 5 will bring forth a hierarchical directory structure similar to what is available now in Microsoft Exchange (electronic mail server for Windows NT).

Comparing User Accounts

NetWare and Windows NT user and group accounts contain the same basic information and perform the same basic functions. However, as the two network operating systems continue to evolve, a greater number of differences appears to be taking place in the type and level of information that they provide. The following figures show account information that is stored by each operating system with a brief explanation of the information stored therein.

Windows NT Domain User and Group Accounts

Figure 7-12 shows Windows NT Domain User and Group Account information screens. Windows NT Workstation accounts are similar but maintain less information than is kept in a domain. Because we will be concentrating our migration on domain level information, the Figure 7-12 will represent User and Group account information fields available in the domain.

The User Manager for Domains is the utility used to manage Domain user and group accounts. In Figure 7-12, the users are listed on the top part of the screen, and the groups are listed at the bottom.

A Windows NT Domain database contains two types of users and two types of groups: both local and global user and group account types. Without getting into too much detail (we will leave that information for a book dedicated to Windows NT), the global user accounts are used by regular users of the network. These users usually work at one workstation, but because their accounts are "global" in nature and stored on a central server(s), they can also use these accounts to log on at other workstations. Global groups are the group types that will be used to create groupings of global users. This is done to simplify administration, file permissions, and system security settings.

Figure 7-12

Windows NT User Manager for Domains. (Source: Microsoft Corporation)

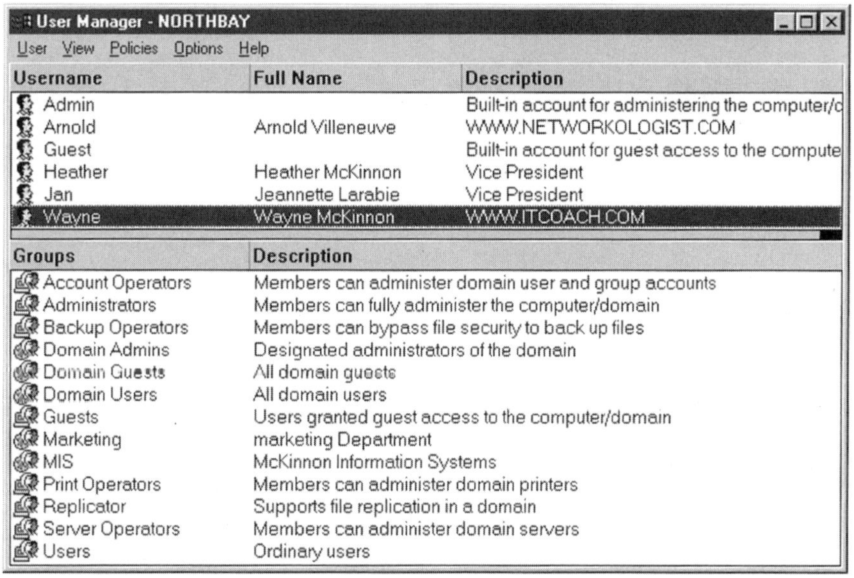

Local users and groups have scope only on the Primary and Backup Domain Controllers. These accounts are normally used to manage domain controllers but occasionally to provide access to domain resources by users who are not part of the domain in question. For our part, during a migration, we will most likely be migrating global users and groups. However, we still can migrate the local user and group accounts as well.

The following few pages will deal with the User Manager for Domain figures I mentioned earlier. We will highlight all the user options and then move to the group options.

User Settings

When you double-click on a user, the User Properties screen is displayed. (See Figure 7-13.) It allows you to set a number of fields of information that are particularly relevant during a migration. This screen also contains buttons that allow you to configure settings for this user such as Group Members, User Profile (and Home Directory) details, Hours of Access, from where the user can log on, account type, and whether the user can use the Remote Access Server. Many of these settings fall under some of the account restrictions we saw earlier and are therefore relevant during a migration. Others, such as Account Type and Dial In, have no relevance to a migration.

Figure 7-13
The User Properties form allows you to configure user-specific information such as group membership and profile settings. (Source: Microsoft Corporation)

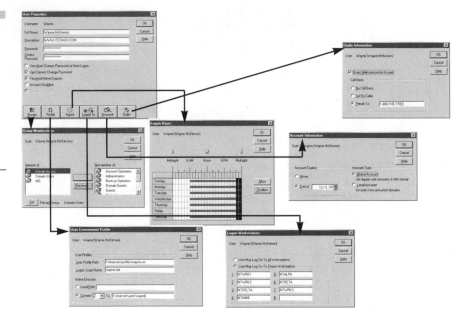

Figure 7-14
Creating a new
Windows NT Domain
global group and
making users
members of the
group. (Source:
Microsoft
Corporation)

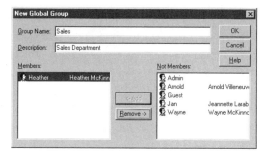

Figure 7-14
Creating a new
Windows NT Domain
global group and
making users
members of the
group. (Source:
Microsoft
Corporation)

Group Settings

Groups can be created on Windows NT to simplify management and administration. File system permissions and system rights can be assigned to groups. (See Figure 7-14.)

NetWare 3.x Bindery-Based User and Group Accounts

The following figures will highlight the settings and options available to NetWare 3.x Bindery-based servers. As we stated earlier, SYSCON is the main utility for editing user, group, and server system settings for NetWare 3.x servers. We will concentrate on the User Information and Group Information menu selections in this section. The information in this areas—in addition to the Supervisor Option Account Balance Restrictions—is transferred during any migration to Windows NT. (See Figure 7-15.)

User Settings

After clicking on User Information, you would pick a user or click on Insert to create a new one. Then the User Information screen would be presented. You can then configure or set a number of options for the user account including Individual Account Restrictions, Change the Password, Full Name, and others. (See Figure 7-16.)

Here we see the individual account restrictions for users' accounts, where the users can change their passwords, their full names, what

Figure 7-15
User and group information selections under SYSCON.
(Source: Novell, Inc.)

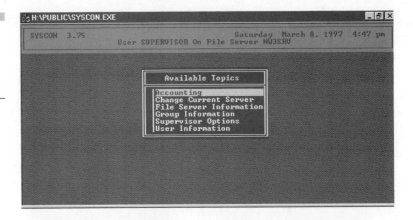

Figure 7-16
Changing the user's account restrictions, password, full name, group membership, and verifying the account's intruder lockout status.
(Source: Novell, Inc.)

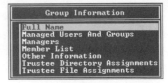

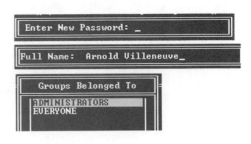

groups they belong to, and what is the status of the Intruder Lockout for their accounts (which is also the place where the Supervisor would unlock it if necessary). (See Figure 7-17.)

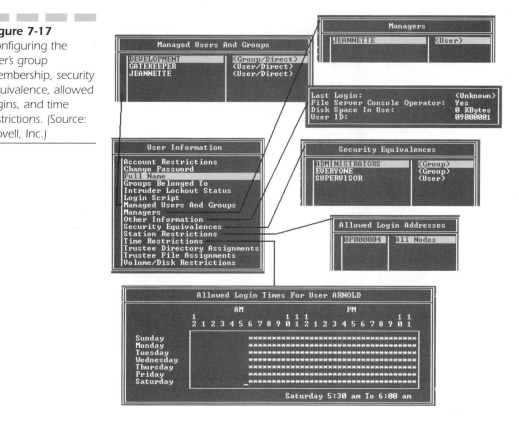

Figure 7-17
Configuring the
user's group
membership, security
equivalence, allowed
logins, and time
restrictions. (Source:
Novell, Inc.)

Continuing with the User Information menu settings, we move through the following items. Login Script (which is not shown) shows the users' personal login scripts. Most network administrators prefer to use a system login script as opposed to managing hundreds, if not thousands, of individual login scripts. Also, from a purely migration perspective, Net-Ware login scripts are relevant on Windows NT only if File and Print Services for NetWare is also running. NetWare login scripts are not converted to Windows NT logon scripts. Managed Users and Groups allows NetWare administrators to allow one user to manage the User Information of another user or group. This feature is similar to Account Operator in Windows NT. Subsequently, the Managers screen shows what users and groups can actually manage the user in question. The Other Information field can be a very important one when migrating NetWare accounts to Windows NT; it goes along with the Login Script menu item because users' login scripts are stored in a subdirectory of the SYS:MAIL directory, and that subdirectory uses the User ID values displayed here.

Security equivalence details who this user is equivalent to in terms of capabilities on the network. In Figure 7-17, the user is equivalent to the

Figure 7-18
Giving the user
access to the file
system through
trustee assignments
and disk space
restrictions. (Source:
Novell, Inc.)

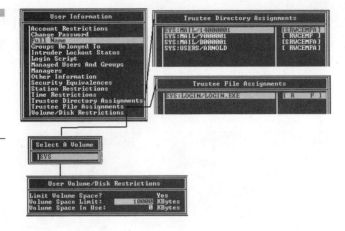

NetWare Supervisor. The user would lose this function during a migration. The Allowed Login Addresses details from which networks and workstations the user is allowed to log in. Finally, the Time Restrictions screen is displayed showing what times the user is allowed to log in to the server. (See Figure 7-18.)

The final part of the User Information selections allow you to define what parts of the server's volumes, directories, and files users will have access to. Additionally, you can even restrict how much space they have access to on the disk. Windows NT file system restrictions are set through File Manager or Windows NT Explorer, whereas with NetWare 3.x they are generally set through SYSCON. FILER is a NetWare file system management utility that also allows you to make trustee assignments.

As you can see, much of the user information available to Windows NT Domains is also available in NetWare (and UNIX, VMS, Vines, and so on).

Group Settings

Figure 7-19 shows the available group settings.

Other than the trustee assignments, the Group settings for NetWare and Windows NT are very similar. The group itself is not really the important element here; the important part is how you use it to manage your system. However, like users, groups are a very important part of a migration in either direction because they are one of the elements transferred.

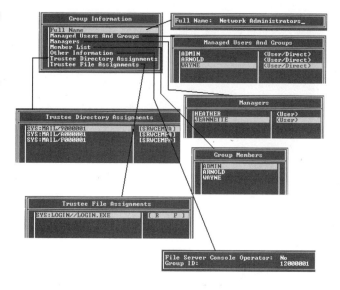

Figure 7-19

Configuring groups in NetWare 3.x. (Source: Novell, Inc.)

NetWare 4.x

NetWare 4.x NDS has all the information that NetWare 3.x has with regards to Account Restrictions and User and Group Settings. It also has a whole lot more, many of which are not relevant to a migration between either platform. Also, over 30 screens are associated with user and group information—more if you include all the potential subscreens. So, for simplicity's sake (and because our editor would not let us include them all), we have included the screens with the main parts of information that we would be concerned with during any migration. They were taken from the NetWare Administrator, the GUI system configuration manager for NetWare 4.x and IntranetWare. A non-GUI version called NETADMIN is also available for the real die-hard fans (for the same people who still use EDLIN).

Figure 7-20 displays our access to NDS through the NetWare Administrator. It details a typical user's account information. The current screen or page for "User-Drew" is the Identification page containing Login Name, Given Name, Last Name, and other general information about who the user is. Notice how NDS maintains a significant amount of additional information over NetWare 3.x and Windows NT Domains. However, this information is of little value to us during a migration because only the main fields are actually migrated (Login Name, User Name, Description, Time Restrictions, and so on). Many of the other buttons such as Password Restrictions, Network Address Restrictions, Print Job Configuration, and

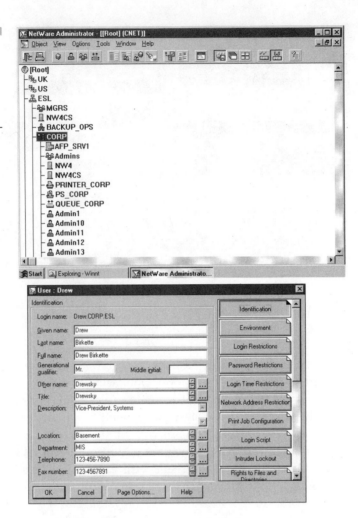

Figure 7-20
NetWare
Administrator and
the main User
Properties page.
(Source: Novell, Inc.)

Intruder Lockout are either supported under a central Windows NT Domain Account Policy applied to all user accounts or are not supported directly during a migration.

Fewer fields are available for Group information, and here at least, NDS is closer in information content to the other NOS versions discussed. (See Figure 7-21.) The See Also pages in both the User and Group areas are simply for additional information to tell who or what is related to this user or group. The Applications page works with the NetWare Application Launcher program to provide users with easy access to application programs. The Client Configuration page is used by the NT Integration Utility of NetWare Administrator for Windows NT Workstation users. Two of the last three items are not relevant to a migration in either direction.

Figure 7-21
NetWare
Administrator and
the main Group
Properties page.
(Source: Novell, Inc.)

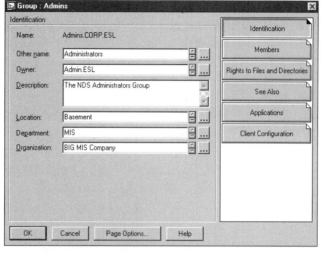

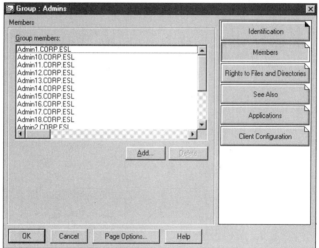

As stated, NDS provides you with all the user information found in NetWare 3.x and Windows NT Domains, and a whole lot more. Unfortunately, none of the additional information that is additional to NetWare 3.x is of use during a migration.

Comparing File and Directory Security

Both NetWare servers and Windows NT secure files and directories. Although the terms they use to describe the setting of security on files and directories may be different, as are their methods for implementing it, the end result is still the same: file system security that grants or restricts access to files and directories based on user and group level security. The only difference between the two, perhaps, is that Windows NT security can be applied to both the workstation and the server, whereas NetWare's has scope only on the server.

Table 7-3 compares the rights in NetWare with the permissions in Windows NT.

NOTE: *The NetWare Create and File Scan rights are* not *directly supported in Windows NT.*

Table 7-3

Comparing NetWare Rights with Windows NT Permissions. (Courtesy of WWW. NETWORKOLOGIST. COM)

NetWare Right	Windows NT Permission
Directory	**Directory**
Supervisory	Full Control (ALL)
Read (R)	Read (RX)
Write (W)	Write (W)
Create (C)	Write (W)
Erase (E)	Delete (D)
Modify (M)	Delete (D)
File Scan (F)	Read (R)
Access Control (A)	Change Permission (PO)
File	**File**
Supervisory	Full Control (ALL)
Read (R)	Read (RX)
Access Control	Change Permission (PO)
Create (C)	Write (W)
Erase (E)	Delete (D)
Modify (M)	Delete (D)
Write (W)	Write (W)

NetWare File System Security (in a Very Small Nutshell)

To give a user or group access to files or directories in NetWare, you usually select the user or group in question and then give that user or group the required right. This is done in NetWare 3.x through the SYSCON utility or in NetWare 4.x through NWADMIN or NETADMIN (although you can accomplish the same task using FILER and starting from the directory or file in question first). (See Figures 7-22 and 7-23.)

Figure 7-22
NetWare 3.x being used to make new trustee assignments to a Directory and File. (Source: Novell, Inc.)

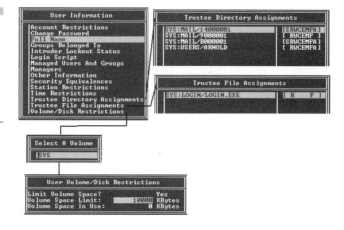

Figure 7-23
NetWare 4.x NetWare Administrator being used to make new trustee assignments to a directory. (Source: Novell, Inc.)

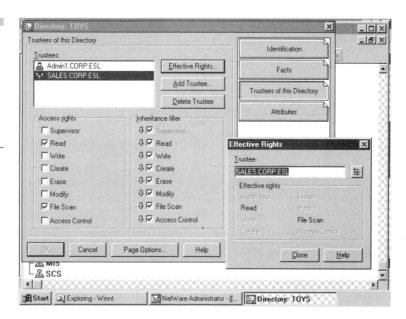

NetWare uses "rights" to protect files. Rights are assigned to users to grant them a certain access to a file. Users' rights to a directory are given through trustee assignments. Trustee assignments do not flow down the directory, nor are they copied to lower levels of the directory tree. Inheritance is used to simplify the granting of rights so that an individual trustee assignment does not have to be made for all users and groups at all levels of the file system. However, the fact that users have been given a set of rights to a file or directory does not guarantee that the users will, in fact, have access to the subdirectories and its contents below the directory for which the trustee assignment was given. That happens because Inherited Rights can be filtered out as users progress further down the file system from the place where they last received trustee assignments. When rights are filtered out, the end result is referred to as the users' *effective rights*. Simply stated, effective rights define the users' actual access to a directory and its contents.

In summary, not all NetWare directories and files have an actual set of trustee assignments associated with them, but rather rely on the concept of Inheritance of Rights from higher parts of the file system to determine users' effective rights to a given directory or file.

NetWare 3.x and NetWare 4.x have some slight yet very important differences with respect to file system security. The main difference is that in NetWare 3.x, the Supervisor has full rights to all server volumes, whereas in NetWare 4.x the initial Admin (a.k.a. Supervisor) can be restricted from accessing or managing parts of the file system.

Windows NT Security (in Another Nutshell)

To provide access to the file system in Windows NT, you select the directory or file and then add users to the Access Control List. Once the users are added, you grant the users or groups the permission you want them to have. (See Figure 7-24.)

In contrast to NetWare's approach, Windows NT directories and files all have permissions associated with them unless explicitly removed, in which case no one would have access to the directory or file. To accomplish the assignment of permissions with each and every directory and file, Windows NT uses a concept called *Inheritance*, but it is different from NetWare's definition. Here, whenever a directory is created, it receives an exact duplicate of the parent directory's permission set, regardless of who creates the subdirectory (provided, of course, that person has permission to do so). Inheritance is also applied when a file is created in a subdirectory. Each directory has two sets of permissions

■■■ ■■■ ■■■ ■■■

Figure 7-24
Using Windows
Explorer to make
entries into the
Access Control List.
(Source: Microsoft
Corporation)

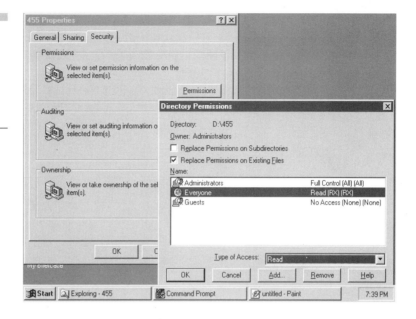

associated with it: Directory and File Inheritance. The first permission determines users' access to the actual directory (or management of). The second permission is used to assign permissions newly created within or copied into the directory.

Finally, Windows NT does not automatically provide the administrator with automatic access to all user created directories and files on a server. Windows NT applies the concept of Ownership and Discretionary Access Control (DAC) to further protect the file system. DAC basically states that the owner of a file (resource) has discretion over who can access the file and as such can even restrict the administrator from accessing it. However, administrators always have one final trump card: the ability to take ownership of a file or directory whereby they can grant themselves access to the resource. At least, the user can audit or check to see who the current owner is because one thing the administrator cannot do is make you the owner of the file again.

NetWare and Windows NT File System Attributes

Both NetWare and Windows NT support file system attributes. However, both also support different types of attributes. Windows NT file system attributes are similar to DOS attributes. (See Figure 7-25.)

NetWare supports all the standard DOS attributes and a significant number of other attributes that are specific to the NetWare file system. (See Table 7-4.) We will explore file system attributes more during the migration processes in the following section.

In summary, we have now looked at the most crucial elements of a migration:

Figure 7-25
Windows NT Explorer showing the Attributes properties of a file. (Source: Microsoft Corporation)

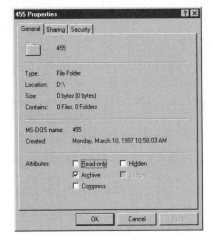

Table 7-4

NetWare File and Directory Attribute List. (Source: Novell, Inc.)

Read Only (Ro)	Read Write (Rw)
Delete Inhibit (D)	Rename Inhibit (R)
Archive Needed (A)	System (Sy)
Hidden (H)	Execute Only (X) *
Read Audit (Ra) *	Write Audit (Wa) *
File Compress *	Immediate Compress *
Can't Compress *	Don't Compress *
Index FAX Entries * (I)	Shareable * (Sh)
Transaction Tracking Enabled * (T)	Purge * (P)
Copy Inhibit * (C)	Don't Migrate *
File Migrated *	

The asterisk (*) denotes that these attributes are not supported during a migration from NetWare to Windows NT.

- Account Restrictions
- Administrative Level Accounts
- Users Accounts
- Groups Accounts
- File Systems

In the following sections of this chapter, we will explore the migration utilities provided by both NetWare and Windows NT to facilitate a migration. We will start with the Migration Tool for NetWare from Microsoft, which facilitates NetWare to Windows NT migration. We will then provide an overview of Novell's Migration Toolkit, which facilitates LAN Manager, LAN Server, and Windows NT Server migration to NetWare.

NetWare to Windows NT: Introduction to the Migration Tool for NetWare

Microsoft's Migration Toolkit for NetWare is the utility that transfers users, groups, and files and directories along with their security settings to Windows NT servers from NetWare servers. The elements discussed in the preceding sections cover the details of what are potential migration candidates.

The Migration Tool can do the following:

- Transfer certain user account information
- Manage how user and group login names are transferred
- Specify passwords for migrated user accounts (as passwords themselves cannot be migrated due to encryption)
- Transfer account restrictions and administrative rights in a specified manner
- Select which directories and files are transferred
- Transfer existing file system security settings

Also see Figure 7-26 to see more migration options.

REQUIREMENTS FOR RUNNING THE MIGRATION TOOL FOR NETWARE To run the Migration Tool for NetWare, you will require at least one Windows NT server. The Migration Tool can be run from either the server to which you are migrating or from another Windows NT server. The latter approach offloads some of the processing from the server

Figure 7-26
Migration options for
the Migration Tool
for NetWare.
(Courtesy of Learning
Tree International)

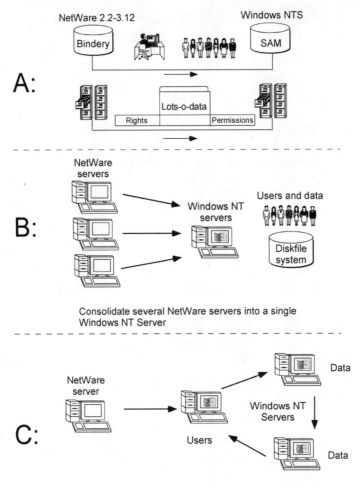

to be migrated to. Before you install the Migration Tool, you will need to ensure that you have already configured several other items.

The NetWare servers being migrated from should be either NetWare 3.x Bindery-based or are NetWare 4.x running with Bindery Emulation mode (only the NDS containers that are in Bindery Emulation Mode are transferred). The Windows NT servers being migrated to can be either Primary Domain Controllers, Backup Domain Controllers, or member servers (servers without SAM database copies, which are usually called *applications servers*). User account and file system information can both be migrated to a Primary Domain Controller, whereas only file system information can be migrated to a Backup Domain Controller or member server.

PREREQUISITE SOFTWARE AND ADMINISTRATIVE ACCOUNTS

The following is a list of prerequisite software and administrative accounts:

- Ideally, the Windows NT file system should be NTFS formatted. This is required if you want to transfer file system rights from NetWare to Windows NT permissions.

- The NetWare Link IPX/SPX Compatible Transport protocol must be loaded on the computer that is running the Migration Tool.

- The NetWare client software for Windows NT server, Gateway Service for NetWare, must be installed on the computer that is running the Migration Tool.

- You must be the administrator or member of the Administrators group to run NWCONV.EXE.

- You must have Supervisor rights on the NetWare server that is being migrated. (See Figure 7-27.)

RUNNING THE MIGRATION TOOL FOR NETWARE The flowchart in Figure 7-28 will provide you with an understanding of all the options you have as you progress through the Migration Tool.

Figure 7-27
NWLink IPX/SPX, GSNW, and the Migration Tool facilitating a migration of NetWare users and files to two Windows NT servers. (Courtesy: Learning Tree International)

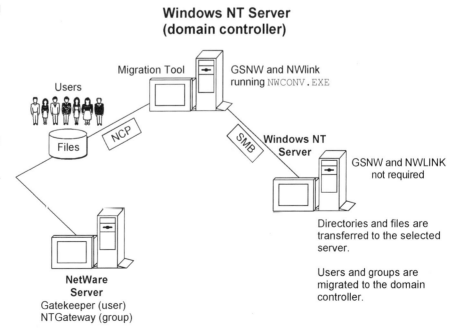

Figure 7-28
Migration Tool for
NetWare decision
flowchart. (Courtesy
of Learning Tree
International)

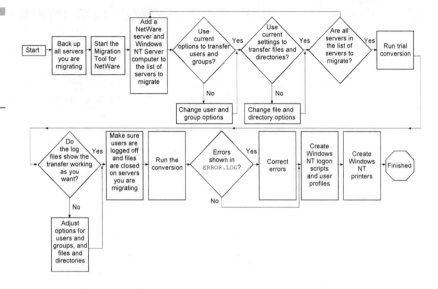

Figure 7-29
The Migration Tool
for NetWare.
(Source: Microsoft
Corporation)

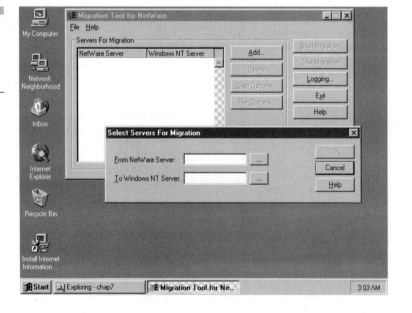

As we pointed out, you should back up all the affected servers before starting any migration process. When the Migration Tool for NetWare is first started, it displays the Select Servers for Migration dialog box allowing you to enter NetWare and Windows NT server names that will be participating in the migration. (See Figure 7-29.) From here, you will add all the servers you want migrated, both source (NetWare) and destination (Windows NT).

By clicking on the Ellipses button [. . .], you can select the servers you want to migrate. When you select the From NetWare Server and To Windows NT Server Ellipses buttons, you will be presented with the screens shown in Figure 7-30 to make your selection. In the following example, we have begun our migration by selecting a NetWare 3.x (NW3SRV) server and a Windows NT 4.0 (NTSRV40) server.

You will need to pick servers in pairs on a one-to-one ratio. In other words, you need to select one NetWare server and one Windows NT server. After you select a pair of servers, you can then set your user, group, and file system migration options for the one pair. You can also select several pairs of servers and then set options; however, you will have to repeat the process for each pair. If you pick one pair of servers first and set the options, however, all other servers that you pick will use these new options as the default. The latter approach is certainly easier but works only if you are using the same option settings for all servers in the migration. Our selection of servers is now displayed in the Migration Tool for NetWare - Servers For Migration dialog box. (See Figure 7-31.)

Figure 7-30
Selecting a NetWare and Windows NT server for migration. (Source: Microsoft Corporation)

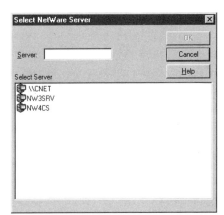

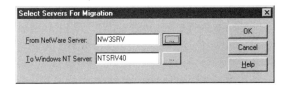

Next, we will select an additional pair of servers for our migration. This server, however, will be a NetWare 4.x NDS-based server. From the Migration Tool for NetWare dialog box, select the Add button and use the same process as before to pick your servers. In our sample migration, we are going to migrate two NetWare servers to the same Windows NT Domain server. In Figure 7-32, we have selected our NetWare server and reselected our Windows NT Domain server.

Figure 7-31
Displaying our current migration servers. (Source: Microsoft Corporation)

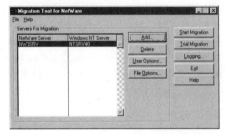

Figure 7-32
Selecting the NetWare 4.x server and Windows NT Domain server. (Source: Microsoft Corporation)

A SPECIAL NOTE ABOUT MIGRATING NETWARE 4.X NDS INFORMATION TO WINDOWS NT In the Select NetWare Server dialog box, you can see that three servers are listed: \\CNET, NW3SRV, and NW4CS. The \\CNET is actually our NetWare 4.x NDS tree name. However, because of the way the Migration Tool reads NetWare's Service Advertising Protocol information being broadcast over the network, it is actually interpreting the CNET tree broadcasts as being from a server.

Hence, it adds the name to the list. If you tried to select it, you would receive an error message. The second server listed is our NetWare 3.x Bindery-based server, and the other server listed is our NetWare 4.x NDS-based server. Although the entire contents (user, groups, and file system) of the NetWare 3.x Bindery can be transferred to the Windows NT server, only the contents (user, group, and file system) of Bindery-emulated containers can be transferred. Figure 7-33 highlights what information will be transferred from the NetWare 4.x server during our upcoming migration. To migrate information from several NDS containers, you would have to set all the desired containers to Bindery Emulation Mode. The file systems you want would also have to appear as objects in a Bindery-emulated container for information to be migrated. Furthermore, when more than one container is in Bindery Emulation Mode, and user or group objects have same object name but reside in different containers, the object from the first Bindery-emulated container will be transferred, and the one in the second container will be ignored.

Now that we have selected our servers, we are ready to proceed with configuring our migration options for users and file systems.

TRANSFERRING USER, GROUP, SECURITY, AND FILE SYSTEM INFORMATION By clicking on the User Options button from the Migration Tool for NetWare dialog box, you will be presented with the first configuration screen. At this stage, you need to decide whether you want

Figure 7-33
NDS Bindery Emulation in a NetWare 4.x server. (Source: Novell, Inc.)

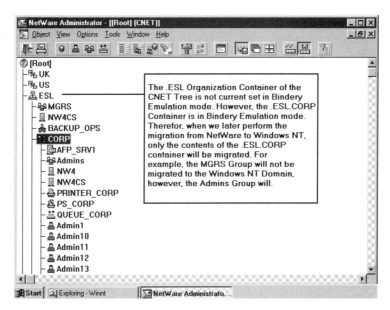

Figure 7-34
User and group
options transfer
decision flowchart.
(Source: Microsoft
Corporation)

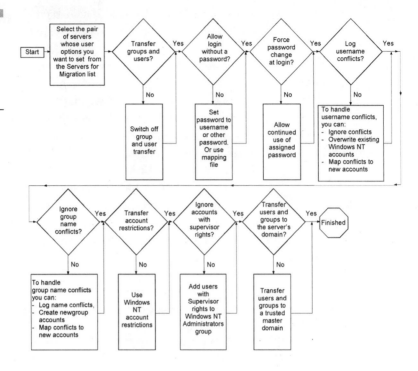

to transfer User and Group information at all. You can disable this option by deselecting the Transfer Users and Groups check box. If you deselect this option, all the other options will be grayed out. (See Figure 7-34.)

The next decision to make is whether you will use a mapping file to map how NetWare users and groups are mapped to Windows NT users and groups. We will look at mapping files in more detail after we cover the basic user transfer options.

NOTE ON MIGRATIONS AND TRUSTED DOMAINS You use the Advanced >> configuration button if you have Windows NT Domain Trusted Environments. When it is implemented, the NetWare user accounts will be transferred to a trusted domain of your selection. This option is usually done when you are working with Master/Resource Domain Models. In this model, all the organization's user and group accounts are stored on the master domain. The resource domains trust the users of the master domain to access their resources (directly by logging on at the workstations or by going through the network). In a migration of this sort, the Migration Tool for NetWare is being run on a Windows NT server in the resource domain. The files and directories from the

NetWare server are probably being transferred to a resource domain server, but the NetWare user accounts are being transferred to the Master Domain Primary Domain Controller server.

Although the user name transfers to the master domain are fairly straightforward, groups become a little bit more challenging given that there are two types: global and local. In this scenario, the NetWare groups are transferred to the master domain server as global groups. The same NetWare groups are also transferred as local groups to the resource domain servers indicated in the Servers for Migration list (of the Migration Tool for NetWare main screen). These local groups, in turn, contain the global groups that were defined in the master domain. This process, although we admit that it sounds more complex than it really is, facilitates that access of resource domain servers by users who have been defined in the master domain.

THE USER AND GROUP OPTION TAB SELECTION FORMS   The User and Group Options screen provides four tab-selected dialog box forms on which you can configure your user and group transfer options. The Passwords tab form allows you to determine how passwords will be created on the Windows NT server for the user accounts that are transferred. Remember that NetWare passwords are encrypted on the NetWare server and therefore cannot be read for direct transfer to the Windows NT Domain *Security Accounts Manager* (SAM) database. We can basically decide that the newly created Windows NT accounts should have "no password," use the "username as a password," or establish a common password for all accounts. Additionally, we can automatically configure the new user accounts so that the first time the users log on, they will be prompted for passwords. (See Figure 7-35.)

TIP: *Our preferred approach for the password settings option is to use the Password is: option for all users. This way, you will set the same password for all users transferred. Then you can send an individual e-mail message to all users telling them what their personal passwords are and that they are not to share their passwords with anyone. They will then be prompted to change their passwords at the time of first login. Users are becoming more security conscious in general and will not share their passwords with anyone. The other alternative is to use a mapping file to provide users with individual passwords, but this approach can be an onerous task for large migrations.*

The next User and Group Options tab form is for setting the manner in which user names are transferred. Here, as with group names, we are

Figure 7-35
Setting user and
group password
transfer options.
(Source: Microsoft
Corporation)

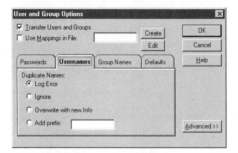

Figure 7-36
Setting user and
group user name
transfer options.
(Source: Microsoft
Corporation)

particularly concerned about discovering duplicate user names so that we
can make changes before a live migration. The available options for dealing with duplicate names include simply logging an error message,
ignoring the duplicate names altogether, overwriting the existing Windows NT user account with the information from the NetWare account,
or adding a prefix (leading characters) to the newly created account when
a duplicate is discovered first. (See Figure 7-36.)

The Group Names tab form allows you to configure how the migration process will respond to duplicate group names. The options are the
same as with the User Names tab except that this tab has no provision
to overwrite existing Windows NT groups. Probably the main reason for
this is that Windows NT has some administrative level accounts that
must not be changed or have new members inadvertently added to. (See
Figure 7-37.)

The last User and Group Options tab specifies how NetWare account
restrictions are transferred (if at all) as well as whether the NetWare
Supervisor account should be added to the Windows NT Local Administrators Group. The option to Migrate NetWare Specific Account Information is new to Windows NT 4.0 and is used when the Windows NT server
being migrated to also supports File and Print Services for NetWare. (See
Figure 7-38.)

Figure 7-37
Setting user and group names transfer options. (Source: Microsoft Corporation)

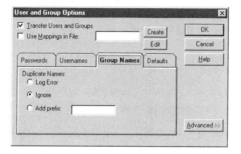

Figure 7-38
Setting user and group defaults transfer options. (Source: Microsoft Corporation)

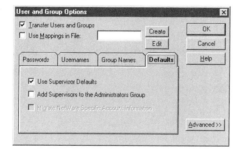

When you select to transfer the NetWare Supervisor Option-Default Account Restrictions, the following information is imported to the equivalent Windows NT Domain Account Policy settings:

- Require Password: Determines whether user account passwords are required.

- Minimum Password Length: Specifies the minimum allowable number of characters required for a password. The NetWare 3.x default is five, whereas the Windows NT default is six.

- Require Password Change: Specifies the number of days for which passwords are valid before the users are required to change them. The NetWare 3.x default is 40, whereas the Windows NT default is 42.

- Password Reuse: Determines the number of different passwords that users must use before they can reuse old passwords. The NetWare 3.x default is fixed at eight; although the Windows NT default is five, it can be set between one and eight.

- Intruder Lockout: Determines how many unsuccessful login/logon attempts are allowed before the account is locked or disabled. The NetWare default is seven, whereas the Windows NT default is five.

SUMMARY OF MIGRATION TOOL FOR NETWARE USER AND GROUP OPTIONS TABS DEFAULT SETTINGS The following are default settings for the Migration Tool for NetWare User and Group Options tabs:

- Transfer all user and group accounts to Windows NT Server except when a name conflict occurs.
- Duplicate NetWare user or group accounts are not transferred, and an error is logged.
- Transferred accounts have no password.
- NetWare account restrictions for password and intruder lockout are transferred.
- Groups and users with Supervisor, Workgroup Manager, and User Manager rights are transferred but without Windows NT administrative privileges.

USING A MAPPING FILE You can use a mapping file to facilitate the transfer of user and group names; however, as we stated previously, this task can be cumbersome for large migrations involving many user and group accounts. In the User and Group Options dialog box, click on the Use Mappings File check box, and then click on the Create button. You will then be presented with the Create Mapping File configuration screen, which is shown in Figure 7-39.

The process of creating the mapping file is straightforward. The Migration Tool for NetWare reads the NetWare Bindery and then creates a text file of the name you specify. The contents of the mapping file include all the users and groups from the NetWare Bindery (or NDS Bindery-emulated container). Before you create the actual mapping file, you need to specify that you want to include user and group names and specify how the file will work with passwords. The password options are the same as those on the User and Group Options Password Tab form.

Figure 7-39
Creating a mapping file. (Source: Microsoft Corporation)

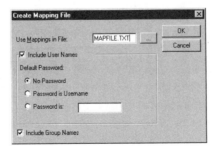

Figure 7-40
User and group
options mapping file
for our NetWare 3.x
Server NW3SRV.
(Source: Microsoft
Corporation)

Figure 7-40
User and group
options mapping file
for our NetWare 3.x
Server NW3SRV.
(Source: Microsoft
Corporation)

```
Nw3map.map - Notepad
File   Edit   Search   Help
;+----------------------------------------------------------
;| NWConv Mapping for: NW3SRV
;| Version: 1.1
;|
;| Format Is:
;|     OldName, NewName, Password
;|
;+----------------------------------------------------------
[USERS]
ARNOLD, ARNOLDNW3, ARNOLD
GATEKEEPER, GATEKEEPER, GATEKEEPER
HEATHER, HEATHERNW3, HEATHER
JEANNETTE, JEANNETTE, JEANNETTE
RYAN, RYAN, RYAN
SABRINA, SABRINA, SABRINA
SAMANTHA, SAMANTHA, SAMANTHA
SHELBY, SHELBY, SHELBY
WAYNE, WAYNENW3, WAYNE

[GROUPS]
ADMINISTRATORS, ADMINISTRATORS
DEVELOPMENTNW3, DEVELOPMENT
MARKETINGNW3, MARKETING
NTGATEWAY, NTGATEWAY
SALESNW3, SALES
```

Figure 7-41
User and group op-
tions mapping file for
our NetWare 4.x
Server NW4CS.
(Source: Microsoft
Corporation)

```
Nw4map.map - Notepad
File   Edit   Search   Help
;+----------------------------------------------------------
;| NWConv Mapping for: NW4CS
;| Version: 1.1
;|
;| Format Is:
;|     OldName, NewName, Password
;|
;+----------------------------------------------------------
[USERS]
ADMIN1, ADMIN1, ADMIN1
ADMIN10, ADMIN10, ADMIN10
ADMIN11, ADMIN11, ADMIN11
ADMIN12, ADMIN12, ADMIN12
ADMIN2, ADMIN2, ADMIN2
ADMIN3, ADMIN3, ADMIN3
ADMIN4, ADMIN4, ADMIN4
ADMIN5, ADMIN5, ADMIN5
ADMIN6, ADMIN6, ADMIN6
ADMIN7, ADMIN7, ADMIN7
ADMIN8, ADMIN8, ADMIN8
ADMIN9, ADMIN9, ADMIN9
ARNOLD, ARNOLDNW4, ARNOLD
DREW, DREWNW4, DREW

[GROUPS]
ADMINS, ADMINS
```

After you configure these options, the NetWare Bindery information will
be read and the mapping text file created. (See Figures 7-40 and 7-41.)

The following shows the user and group options mapping file for our
NetWare 3.x Server NW3SRV:

```
;+--------------------------------------------------------------+
;| NWConv Mapping for: NW3SRV                                   |
;| Version: 1.1                                                 |
;|                                                              |
;| Format Is:                                                   |
;|     OldName, NewName, Password                               |
;|                                                              |
;+--------------------------------------------------------------+
[USERS]
ARNOLD, ARNOLD, ARNOLD
GATEKEEPER, GATEKEEPER, GATEKEEPER
HEATHER, HEATHER, HEATHER
JEANNETTE, JEANNETTE, JEANNETTE
RYAN, RYAN, RYAN
SABRINA, SABRINA, SABRINA
SAMANTHA, SAMANTHA, SAMANTHA
SHELBY, SHELBY, SHELBY
WAYNE, WAYNE, WAYNE

[GROUPS]
ADMINISTRATORS, ADMINISTRATORS
DEVELOPMENT, DEVELOPMENT
MARKETING, MARKETING
NTGATEWAY, NTGATEWAY
SALES, SALES
```

The following shows the user and group options mapping file for our NetWare 4.x Server NW4CS:

```
;+--------------------------------------------------------------+
;| NWConv Mapping for: NW4CS                                    |
;| Version: 1.1                                                 |
;|                                                              |
;| Format Is:                                                   |
;|     OldName, NewName, Password                               |
;|                                                              |
;+--------------------------------------------------------------+
[USERS]
ADMIN1, ADMIN1, ADMIN1
ADMIN10, ADMIN10, ADMIN10
ADMIN11, ADMIN11, ADMIN11
ADMIN12, ADMIN12, ADMIN12
ADMIN2, ADMIN2, ADMIN2
ADMIN3, ADMIN3, ADMIN3
ADMIN4, ADMIN4, ADMIN4
ADMIN5, ADMIN5, ADMIN5
ADMIN6, ADMIN6, ADMIN6
ADMIN7, ADMIN7, ADMIN7
ADMIN8, ADMIN8, ADMIN8
ADMIN9, ADMIN9, ADMIN9
ARNOLD, ARNOLD, ARNOLD
DREW, DREW, DREW
```

[GROUPS]
ADMINS, ADMINS

The NetWare 4.x mapping file is interesting because it proves that only Bindery-emulated container contents get migrated. You may recall that earlier, under our special note for migrating NetWare 4.x servers, we displayed an NDS container called .ESL.CORP. There we stated that the ADMINS group from that container would be transferred, but that the MGRS group from the non-Bindery-emulated container above would not be. The mapping file just created further highlights this issue.

Although the mapping file has been imported, we will not know whether any duplicates exist with the Windows NT Server until we run a trial migration. By looking at the two preceding mapping files, we that there will, in fact, be a conflict between the ARNOLD account because it exists on both NetWare servers currently. It may also exist on the Windows NT server. If it does, an error will be registered during the trial migration. Looking back at our Windows NT Domain server briefly, we can see that, in fact, there is an ARNOLD account (every server should have one ;-) and that we can expect an error message later. (See Figure 7-42.)

You would therefore think that the mapping file is most useful after you have performed a trial migration. However, this is not the case. Let's follow the process through. We'll create a mapping file and then run a trial migration. The Trial Migration Error Log file tells us that an ARNOLD account already exists on the Windows NT Domain server. The natural tendency would be to go to the mapping file and change the NewName field and rerun the migration program. However, this approach does not work as you would sus-

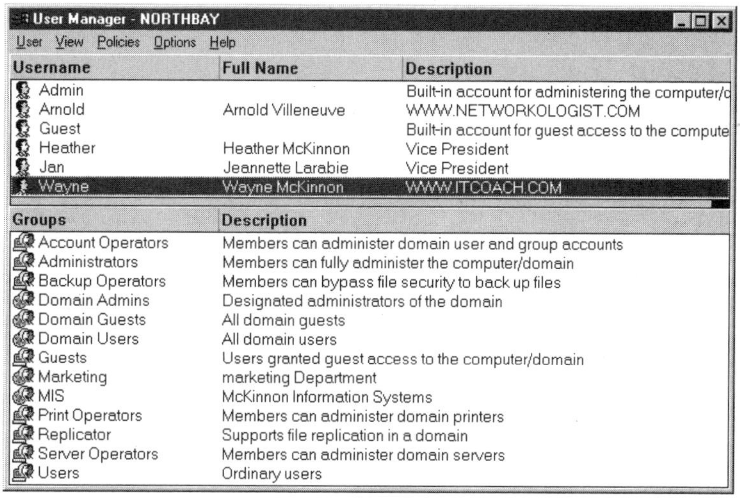

Figure 7-42
Windows NT Domain User and Group SAM Database. (Source: Microsoft Corporation)

pect. When the migration is run, the process compares the OldName (which is from the NetWare server) with the existing name on the Windows NT server. If a duplicate exists, you might think that the NewName is used to create a new Windows NT user account, but it does not function in this manner. Instead, an error is logged and no new account is created.

When editing the mapping file, you should be aware that you cannot use certain characters. They are as follow:

" / \ [ ] : ; | = , + ? < >

The maximum password length is 14 characters. Also, remember that Windows NT passwords are case sensitive. The maximum user name length is 20 characters, and user names are not case sensitive.

TRANSFERRING FILES AND DIRECTORIES   Before you begin to transfer files and directories, you should be made aware that you can turn off the transfer of files altogether. To do so, simply clear the Transfer Files check box within the File Options button of the Migration Tool for NetWare. (See Figure 7-43.)

During a migration of file information, we are interested only in transferring user applications and data. We are not interested in transferring NetWare NOS applications such as NetWare Loadable Modules or NetWare system files (*.LAN, *.NAM, *.DSK, and so on) because they cannot

Figure 7-43
User and group options transfer decision flowchart. (Source: Microsoft Corporation)

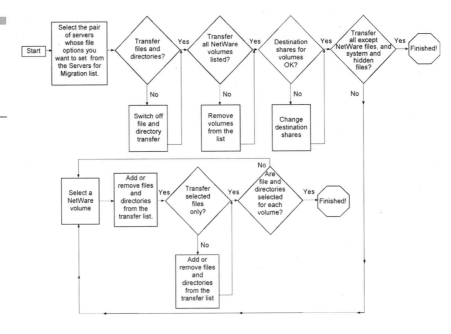

be used by Windows NT. So, essentially, we are not interested in transferring all the NetWare operating system-related files. The Migration Tool for NetWare takes this fact into account and ensures that the following areas of the file system are not transferred:

- Hidden files
- System files
- The \LOGIN, \SYSTEM, \MAIL, and \ETC directories

The important aspect of any migration from NetWare to Windows NT is that NetWare rights are transferred only to a Windows NT NTFS formatted file system. The error message shown in Figure 7-44 will be displayed if you try to migrate to a FAT formatted file system.

To determine what the default files transfer selections are, you can click on the File Options button of the Migration Tool for NetWare screen. This action will initially select all files and directories except for those that are considered to be NetWare system-related files. From the File To Transfer screen, you can select which directories and files you want to transfer. In the Figure 7-45, notice that although the entire [x] \\NW3SRV\SYS\ volume has been selected, the \ETC, \LOGIN, \MAIL, \and SYSTEM directories have been omitted. Figures 7-45 and 7-46 display the SYS volumes of the two NetWare servers (one 3.x and

Figure 7-44
You cannot preserve NetWare equivalent rights if you migrate files to a Windows NT FAT file system. (Source: Microsoft Corporation)

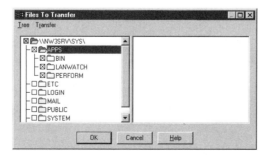

Figure 7-45
Files to transfer from a NetWare 3.x server. (Source: Microsoft Corporation)

Figure 7-46
Files to transfer from
a NetWare 4.x server.
(Source: Microsoft
Corporation)

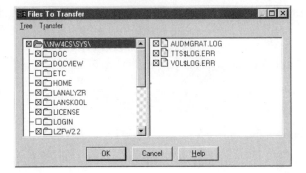

one 4.x) that we are about to transfer. The directories and files with the [x] check box on the left are the ones that will be transferred.

In Figures 7-45 and 7-46, we have selected the APPS directory of the NetWare 3.x server, and we will select only the TOYS directory of the Net-Ware 4.x server. (Although the figure shows that several more directories are currently selected, we will reduce this number to only the TOYS directory for the actual transfer.)

Another way to have a clear and detailed picture of what files will be transferred is to run a trial migration. Although the files are not actually transferred, the log files generated by the trial migration will provide details about the impending transfer. We will review log files in more detail shortly, but the log file you want to review after a trial migration to view file transfer information is called LOGFILE.LOG.

During the actual migration, the Migration Tool will look for a file share on the Windows NT server that matches the NetWare volume name. If one is not available, then the Migration Tool will create one for the actual transfer. However, before the Migration Tool creates a share, it will look on the NTFS volumes for one with sufficient disk space to place the NetWare volume. If an NTFS volume with enough disk space cannot be located, then the Migration Tool will search available FAT formatted file systems and create a share on one if found. You must be aware of this fact because files transferred from NetWare to a Windows NT FAT file system preserve equivalent NetWare rights. Finally, you can modify the default destination for the new Windows NT share volume through the Modify button within the Files Options screen. (See Figure 7-47.)

TRANSFERRING NETWARE RIGHTS Before we proceed any further, now is probably a good time to establish the current file security settings for the directories and files we are about to transfer. We stated previously that we were going to transfer the APPS directory and its contents from the NetWare 3.x server. The following list details the current Net-

Figure 7-47
Modifying the file
transfer destination
on the Windows NT
server. (Source:
Microsoft
Corporation)

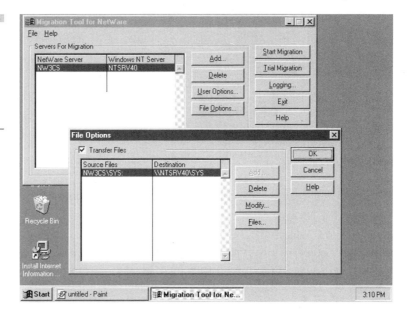

Figure 7-47
Modifying the file
transfer destination
on the Windows NT
server. (Source:
Microsoft
Corporation)

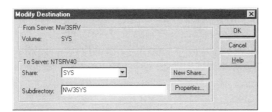

Ware security settings for the files and directories we are about to transfer. In it, you can observe that various groups have trustee assignments
to the directories. Later in this section, we will look at the Windows NT
Permissions to see how well the file security equivalency issue transfers
from NetWare to Windows NT. (Also see Figure 7-48.)

```
NW3SRV\SYS:APPS
No user trustees.
Group trustees:
   SALES                                                      [SRWCEMFA]

NW3SRV\SYS:APPS\BIN
No user trustees.
Group trustees:
   DEVELOPMENT                                                [ RWCEMF ]
   MARKETING                                                  [ R    F ]
   SALES                                                      [ R    F ]

NW3SRV\SYS:APPS\LANWATCH
```

```
No user trustees.
Group trustees:
   DEVELOPMENT                                              [ R       F ]
   MARKETING                                                [ R       F ]
   SALES                                                    [ R       F ]


NW3SRV\SYS:APPS\PERFORM
No user trustees.
Group trustees:
   DEVELOPMENT                                              [ RWCE F ]
   MARKETING                                                [ R       F ]
   SALES                                                    [ R       F ]
```

MIGRATING NETWARE LOGIN SCRIPTS   File and Print Services
for NetWare supports NetWare login scripts. Therefore, if you are performing a migration from a NetWare server to a Windows NT server that
will be running FPNW, you may want to migrate NetWare login scripts.
There is no button to select. All you have to do is ensure that you select
the NetWare server's MAIL directory. Login scripts are contained in the
user's personal subdirectory within the MAIL directory. You must
remember that, although you can transfer NetWare login scripts to Windows NT, those login scripts are only good FPNW users and *not* Windows
NT users. If you are migrating away form NetWare redirector-based
clients altogether, you will need to create Windows NT profiles and logon
scripts to replace the functions previously available within login scripts.

**OVERRIDING THE NO-TRANSFER OF HIDDEN AND SYSTEM
FILES**   We stated earlier that, by default, Hidden and System files were

Figure 7-48
Current NetWare 3.x
rights to the APPS
directory and
subdirectories.
(Source: Microsoft
Corporation)

```
NW3SRV\SYS:APPS
No user trustees.
Group trustees:
  SALES                        [SRWCEMFA]

NW3SRV\SYS:APPS\BIN
No user trustees.
Group trustees:
  DEVELOPMENT                  [ RWCEMF ]
  MARKETING                    [ R  F ]
  SALES                        [ R  F ]

NW3SRV\SYS:APPS\LANWATCH
No user trustees.
Group trustees:
  DEVELOPMENT                  [ R  F ]
  MARKETING                    [ R  F ]
  SALES                        [ R  F ]

NW3SRV\SYS:APPS\PERFORM
No user trustees.
Group trustees:
  DEVELOPMENT                  [ RWCE F ]
  MARKETING                    [ R  F ]
  SALES                        [ R  F ]
```

not transferred. Hidden and System files have (H) and (S) file attributes. You can override this option by selecting the Hidden Files and System Files check box options from the Files To Transfer screen.

SAVING AND RESTORING MIGRATION TOOL FOR NETWARE CONFIGURATIONS You have reached the stage when you are ready to run a trial migration. However, you may have made many special changes to the User and File transfer options, and saving them in a format that you can restore at some later point would only be prudent. This feature is also helpful for running different migration configurations during trials to test the results of certain configuration combinations.

To save the current server list and user and file options configuration, simply choose Save Configuration from the File menu at the top-left corner of the Migration Tool for NetWare dialog screen. You will then be prompted to provide a name under which to save the file. These files end with a .CFG extension and are in a format readable only by the Migration Tool for NetWare. To restore a configuration file, reverse the process.

TRIAL MIGRATIONS Running a trial migration is a very important stage in the migration process. You should actually run several trial migrations before you run the live migration. Performing a trial migration will generate important log files detailing the migration process without actually performing any of the transfers. This way, you can review important log files and make adjustments to your current migration configuration before you take that final leap. You should also remember to save the various configurations so that you can test them and review the log files to determine the optimum settings. Even if you are performing a large migration, we suggest strongly that you enable the Popup On Errors for the first few times you run the trial migration because this function will give you a good indication of how much work you are in for before you can perform an actual migration. Verbose logging of both user and file transfer will also be helpful. (See Figure 7-49.)

TURNING ON THE MIGRATION LOGGING OPTIONS You should change the default logging options to select all three because the files created will be valuable when you are trying to research migration problems later. (See Figure 7-50.)

RUNNING THE TRIAL By now, you have selected all your servers, you have configured your user and file transfer options, and you have saved your current configuration to a file. You are therefore ready to run a trial

Figure 7-49
Starting the trial migration. (Source: Microsoft Corporation)

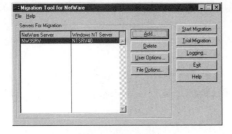

Figure 7-50
Turning on the migration logging options. (Source: Microsoft Corporation)

Figure 7-51
The trial migration tests conversion of NetWare 4.x users to Windows NT. (Source: Microsoft Corporation)

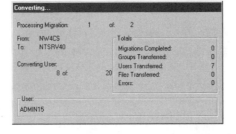

migration. The next step is easy. Simply click on the Trial Migration button from the Migration Tool for NetWare screen.

The Trial Migration process will then notify you that it will not actually transfer files or affect any of the source or destination file systems. It will then begin to process the User and Group accounts on the servers that you have selected for migration. (See Figure 7-51.)

If you have selected the Popup On Errors check box in the Logging form of the main Migration Tool for NetWare screen, you will most likely receive at least one or two error messages relating to duplicate user or group names. When the error popup window appears, you are provided with an opportunity to correct the problem before proceeding with the migration process. (See Figure 7-52.)

After the transfer has completed, you will see a Transfer Completed message box. The message box will indicate to you how many migrations were completed (based on the number of pairs of servers you selected), how many groups and users were transferred, how many potential files will be transferred during a live migration, and how many errors were encountered during the migration itself. (See Figure 7-53.)

After the trial migration is completed, you can review the log files that have been generated to refine the process before your eventual live migration.

MIGRATION LOG FILES During either a trial or live migration, three log files are created: LOGFILE.LOG, SUMMARY.LOG, and ERROR.LOG. (See Figure 7-54.)

LOGFILE.LOG includes information on the following:

- Transfer options
- Supervisor defaults
- Group information

Figure 7-52
Popup Error Message for Duplicate Name. (Source: Microsoft Corporation)

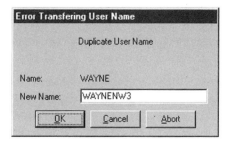

Figure 7-53
Summary of trial migration transfer. (Source: Microsoft Corporation)

Figure 7-54
Location of the Three Migration Log Files. (Source: Microsoft Corporation)

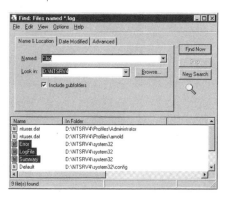

■ User information

■ File information

SUMMARY.LOG includes information on the following:

■ Names of migrated servers

■ Total running time for the migration process (which is always shorter for the trial migration because the files are not actually transferred)

■ Total number of users transferred per server

■ Total number of groups transferred per server

■ Total number of files transferred per server

■ Total number of name conflicts

■ Total number of errors

ERROR.LOG includes information on the following:

■ User and group names of accounts that were not transferred successfully

■ Network errors, such as an inability to access a server

■ System errors for lack of disk space or insufficient transfer rights

The migration log files are saved in the \%systemroot%\SYSTEM32 directory. (Note: %systemroot% is the directory from which Windows NT is currently running.) The log files can be immediately viewed from the Transfer Completed migration summary window. The Log View screen, which is shown in Figure 7-55, then appears.

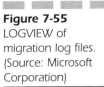

Figure 7-55
LOGVIEW of migration log files. (Source: Microsoft Corporation)

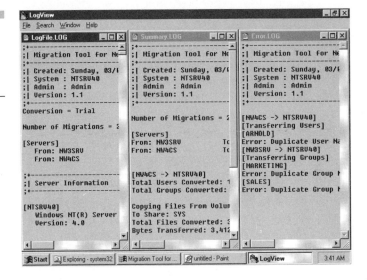

From the LOGVIEW application, you can review each log file for potential problems with the current migration user and file transfer option selections. The following are the full printouts of the migration text files that were created during our trial migration.

LOGFILE.LOG

```
;+----------------------------------------------------------------+
;| Migration Tool for NetWare Log File                            |
;+----------------------------------------------------------------+
;| Created: Sunday, 03/09/1997 (03:39:19)                         |
;| System : NTSRV40                                               |
;| Admin  : Admin                                                 |
;| Version: 1.1                                                   |
;+----------------------------------------------------------------+
Conversion = Trial

Number of Migrations = 2

[Servers]
    From: NW3SRV          To: NTSRV40
    From: NW4CS           To: NTSRV40


;+----------------------------------------------------------------+
;| Server Information                                             |
;+----------------------------------------------------------------+

[NTSRV40]
   Windows NT(R) Server
   Version: 4.0

   [Drives]
      C: [ FAT]
         Free Space: 136,335,360
      D: [NTFS]
         Free Space: 351,374,336
      E: [CDFS] NTWKSCHK351
         Free Space: 0

   [Shares]
      NETLOGON
         Path: D:\NTSRV4\System32\repl\import\scripts

[NW3SRV]
   NetWare(R) Server
   Version: 3.12

   [Shares]
      SYS

[NW4CS]
   NetWare(R) Server
```

Continues

Continued.

```
      Version: 4.11

      [Shares]
         SYS


;+------------------------------------------------------------+
;| Setting User Defaults from Supervisor Defaults             |
;+------------------------------------------------------------+
[Original Defaults: NTSRV40]
   Minimum Password Length: 6
   Maximum Password Age: 42 days
   Force Logoff: -1

[Supervisor Defaults: NW3SRV]
   Account expires: (Never)
   Restrictions:
      Anyone who knows password can change it
      Unique passwords required: Yes
   # days to Password Expiration: 40
   Initial Grace Logins: 5
   Minimum Password Length: 7
   Maximum Number of Connections: 3
   Default Current Account Balance: 0
   Default Credit Limit: 0
   Max Disk Blocks: (Unlimited)

[New Defaults: NTSRV40]
   Minimum Password Length: 6
   Maximum Password Age: 40 days
   Force Logoff: 5


;+------------------------------------------------------------+
;| From: NW4CS                                                |
;| To:   NTSRV40                                              |
;+------------------------------------------------------------+
;| Converted: Sunday, 03/09/1997 (03:39:20)                   |
;+------------------------------------------------------------+

[Transfer Options]
   Convert Users and Groups: Yes

   User Transfer Options:
      Use mapping file: No
      Passwords: 1 - Use NULL
         User must change password: Yes
      Duplicate Names: Log Error

      Duplicate Groups: Ignore

      Use supervisor defaults: Yes
      Add Supervisors to the Administrators Group: No
```

Continued.

```
[File Options]
   Convert Files: Yes

[New Shares]
   SYS
      Path: d:\SYS

[Users]
   Number of Users = 20

   Users to Transfer
   +-----------------------------------------------------------+
    ADMIN1
    ADMIN10
    ADMIN11
    ADMIN12
    ADMIN13
    ADMIN14
    ADMIN15
    ADMIN16
    ADMIN17
    ADMIN18
    ADMIN2
    ADMIN3
    ADMIN4
    ADMIN5
    ADMIN6
    ADMIN7
    ADMIN8
    ADMIN9
    ARNOLD                                          (Duplicate)
    DREW

   [ADMIN1]                                         (Added)
   Original Account Info:
      Name:
      Account disabled: No
      Account expires: (Never)
      Password expires: (Never)
      Grace Logins: (Unlimited)
      Initial Grace Logins: (Unlimited)
      Minimum Password Length: 0
      # days to Password Expiration: (Never)
      Maximum Number of Connections: (Unlimited)
      Restrictions:
         Anyone who knows password can change it
         Unique passwords required: No
      Number of login failures: 0
      Max Disk Blocks: (Unlimited)

   Login Times:
```

Continues

Continued.

```
Midnight                    AM                      Noon
  PM
12 1   2   3   4   5   6   7   8   9   10 11 12 1   2   3   4   5
  6   7   8   9   10 11
+------------------------------------------------------------+
Sun ** ** ** ** ** ** ** ** ** ** ** ** ** ** ** **
    ** ** ** ** ** ** ** **
Mon ** ** ** ** ** ** ** ** ** ** ** ** ** ** ** **
    ** ** ** ** ** ** ** **
Tue ** ** ** ** ** ** ** ** ** ** ** ** ** ** ** **
    ** ** ** ** ** ** ** **
Wed ** ** ** ** ** ** ** ** ** ** ** ** ** ** ** **
    ** ** ** ** ** ** ** **
Thu ** ** ** ** ** ** ** ** ** ** ** ** ** ** ** **
    ** ** ** ** ** ** ** **
Fri ** ** ** ** ** ** ** ** ** ** ** ** ** ** ** **
    ** ** ** ** ** ** ** **
Sat ** ** ** ** ** ** ** ** ** ** ** ** ** ** ** **
    ** ** ** ** ** ** ** **


New Account Info:
   Name:
   Password:
   Privilege: User
   Home Dir:
   Comment:
   Flags:
      Execute login script: Yes
      Account disabled: No
      Deleting prohibited: No
      Home dir required: No
      Password required: Yes
      User can change password: Yes
   Script path:
   Full Name:
   Logon Server:

Logon Hours:
 Midnight                    AM                      Noon
   PM
      12 1   2   3   4   5   6   7   8   9   10 11 12 1   2   3   4
    5   6   7   8   9   10 11
    +------------------------------------------------------------+
Sun ** ** ** ** ** ** ** ** ** ** ** ** ** ** ** ** **
    ** ** ** ** ** ** ** **
Mon ** ** ** ** ** ** ** ** ** ** ** ** ** ** ** ** **
    ** ** ** ** ** ** **
Tue ** ** ** ** ** ** ** ** ** ** ** ** ** ** ** ** **
    ** ** ** ** ** ** **
Wed ** ** ** ** ** ** ** ** ** ** ** ** ** ** ** ** **
    ** ** ** ** ** ** **
Thu ** ** ** ** ** ** ** ** ** ** ** ** ** ** ** ** **
```

Continued.

```
      ** ** ** ** ** ** **
Fri ** ** ** ** ** ** ** ** ** ** ** ** ** ** ** ** ** **
      ** ** ** ** ** ** **
Sat ** ** ** ** ** ** ** ** ** ** ** ** ** ** ** ** ** **
      ** ** ** ** ** ** **


[ADMIN10]                                           (Added)
Original Account Info:
   Name:
   Account disabled: No
   Account expires: (Never)
   Password expires: (Never)
   Grace Logins: (Unlimited)
   Initial Grace Logins: (Unlimited)
   Minimum Password Length: 0
   # days to Password Expiration: (Never)
   Maximum Number of Connections: (Unlimited)
   Restrictions:
       Anyone who knows password can change it
       Unique passwords required: No
   Number of login failures: 0
   Max Disk Blocks: (Unlimited)

Login Times:
 Midnight                    AM                    Noon
   PM
      12 1   2   3   4   5   6   7   8   9   10 11 12 1   2   3   4
      5   6   7   8   9   10 11
      +------------------------------------------------------+
Sun ** ** ** ** ** ** ** ** ** ** ** ** ** ** ** ** ** **
      ** ** ** ** ** ** **
Mon ** ** ** ** ** ** ** ** ** ** ** ** ** ** ** ** ** **
      ** ** ** ** ** ** **
Tue ** ** ** ** ** ** ** ** ** ** ** ** ** ** ** ** ** **
      ** ** ** ** ** ** **
Wed ** ** ** ** ** ** ** ** ** ** ** ** ** ** ** ** ** **
      ** ** ** ** ** ** **
Thu ** ** ** ** ** ** ** ** ** ** ** ** ** ** ** ** ** **
      ** ** ** ** ** ** **
Fri ** ** ** ** ** ** ** ** ** ** ** ** ** ** ** ** ** **
      ** ** ** ** ** ** **
Sat ** ** ** ** ** ** ** ** ** ** ** ** ** ** ** ** ** **
      ** ** ** ** ** ** **


New Account Info:
   Name:
   Password:
   Privilege: User
   Home Dir:
```

Continues

Continued. _____

```
       Comment:
       Flags:
           Execute login script: Yes
           Account disabled: No
           Deleting prohibited: No
           Home dir required: No
           Password required: Yes
           User can change password: Yes
       Script path:
       Full Name:
       Logon Server:

   Logon Hours:
     Midnight                   AM                      Noon
       PM
         12  1   2   3   4   5   6   7   8   9  10  11  12  1   2   3   4
         5   6   7   8   9  10  11
         +----------------------------------------------------------+
   Sun  **  **  **  **  **  **  **  **  **  **  **  **  **  **  **  **  **
        **  **  **  **  **  **  **
   Mon  **  **  **  **  **  **  **  **  **  **  **  **  **  **  **  **  **
        **  **  **  **  **  **  **
   Tue  **  **  **  **  **  **  **  **  **  **  **  **  **  **  **  **  **
        **  **  **  **  **  **  **
   Wed  **  **  **  **  **  **  **  **  **  **  **  **  **  **  **  **  **
        **  **  **  **  **  **  **
   Thu  **  **  **  **  **  **  **  **  **  **  **  **  **  **  **  **  **
        **  **  **  **  **  **  **
   Fri  **  **  **  **  **  **  **  **  **  **  **  **  **  **  **  **  **
        **  **  **  **  **  **  **
   Sat  **  **  **  **  **  **  **  **  **  **  **  **  **  **  **  **  **
        **  **  **  **  **  **  **
```

NOTE: *User Accounts ADMIN11 through ADMIN15 have been skipped here as they they are simply duplicates of the last two accounts.*

```
   [ARNOLD]                                          (Duplicate)

   [DREW]                                            (Added)
   Original Account Info:
       Name:        Drew Birks
       Account disabled: No
       Account expires: (Never)
```

```
     Password expires: (Never)
     Grace Logins: (Unlimited)
     Initial Grace Logins: (Unlimited)
     Minimum Password Length: 0
     # days to Password Expiration: (Never)
     Maximum Number of Connections: (Unlimited)
     Restrictions:
         Anyone who knows password can change it
         Unique passwords required: No
     Number of login failures: 0
     Max Disk Blocks: (Unlimited)

 Login Times:
   Midnight                      AM                        Noon
     PM
       12 1  2  3  4  5  6  7  8  9  10 11 12 1  2  3  4
       5  6  7  8  9  10 11
     +------------------------------------------------------------+
 Sun ** ** ** ** ** ** ** ** ** ** ** ** ** ** ** ** **
     ** ** ** ** ** ** **
 Mon ** ** ** ** ** ** ** ** ** ** ** ** ** ** ** ** **
     ** ** ** ** ** ** **
 Tue ** ** ** ** ** ** ** ** ** ** ** ** ** ** ** ** **
     ** ** ** ** ** ** **
 Wed ** ** ** ** ** ** ** ** ** ** ** ** ** ** ** ** **
     ** ** ** ** ** ** **
 Thu ** ** ** ** ** ** ** ** ** ** ** ** ** ** ** ** **
     ** ** ** ** ** ** **
 Fri ** ** ** ** ** ** ** ** ** ** ** ** ** ** ** ** **
     ** ** ** ** ** ** **
 Sat ** ** ** ** ** ** ** ** ** ** ** ** ** ** ** ** **
     ** ** ** ** ** ** **


 New Account Info:
   Name: Drew Birks
   Password:
   Privilege: User
   Home Dir:
   Comment:
   Flags:
       Execute login script: Yes
       Account disabled: No
       Deleting prohibited: No
       Home dir required: No
       Password required: Yes
       User can change password: Yes
   Script path:
   Full Name: Drew Birks
   Logon Server:

 Logon Hours:
```

Continues

Continued.

```
     Midnight                    AM                      Noon
       PM
         12  1   2   3   4   5   6   7   8   9   10  11  12  1   2   3   4
       5   6   7   8   9   10  11
       +------------------------------------------------------------+
Sun  ** ** ** ** ** ** ** ** ** ** ** ** ** ** ** ** **
     ** ** ** ** ** ** **
Mon  ** ** ** ** ** ** ** ** ** ** ** ** ** ** ** ** **
     ** ** ** ** ** ** **
Tue  ** ** ** ** ** ** ** ** ** ** ** ** ** ** ** ** **
     ** ** ** ** ** ** **
Wed  ** ** ** ** ** ** ** ** ** ** ** ** ** ** ** ** **
     ** ** ** ** ** ** **
Thu  ** ** ** ** ** ** ** ** ** ** ** ** ** ** ** ** **
     ** ** ** ** ** ** **
Fri  ** ** ** ** ** ** ** ** ** ** ** ** ** ** ** ** **
     ** ** ** ** ** ** **
Sat  ** ** ** ** ** ** ** ** ** ** ** ** ** ** ** ** **
     ** ** ** ** ** ** **




[Groups]
   Number Groups = 1
   ADMINS                                              (Added)

   [ADMINS]
      ADMIN1
      ADMIN10
      ADMIN11
      ADMIN12
      ADMIN13
      ADMIN14
      ADMIN15
      ADMIN16
      ADMIN17
      ADMIN18
      ADMIN2
      ADMIN3
      ADMIN4
      ADMIN5
      ADMIN6
      ADMIN7
      ADMIN8
      ADMIN9


[Security Equivalences]
   [ADMIN1]
      ADMINS
```

Continued.

```
[ADMIN10]
    ADMINS

[ADMIN11]
    ADMINS

[ADMIN12]
    ADMINS

[ADMIN13]
    ADMINS

[ADMIN14]
    ADMINS

[ADMIN15]
    ADMINS

[ADMIN16]
    ADMINS

[ADMIN17]
    ADMINS

[ADMIN18]
    ADMINS

[ADMIN2]
    ADMINS

[ADMIN3]
    ADMINS

[ADMIN4]
    ADMINS

[ADMIN5]
    ADMINS

[ADMIN6]
    ADMINS

[ADMIN7]
    ADMINS

[ADMIN8]
    ADMINS

[ADMIN9]
    ADMINS
```

Continues

Continued.

```
;+-----------------------------------------------------------------+
;| Files are shown in the following format:                        |
;|    [Files]                                                       |
;|           1,234,567 [RAHS] TEST.TXT                             |
;|                     | ||||  |                                   |
;|                     | ||||  +- Name of the File                 |
;|                     | ||||                                      |
;|                     | |||+- System                             |
;|                     | ||+-- Hidden                             |
;|                     | |+--- Archived                           |
;|                     | +---- Read Only                          |
;|                     |                                           |
;|                     +----- File size (in Bytes)                 |
;|                                                                 |
;| The Access Rights are shown in the following format:            |
;|    [Access Rights]                                              |
;|       [SRWCEMFA] TestUser                                       |
;|        ||||||||  |                                              |
;|        ||||||||  +- User or Group the Rights apply to           |
;|        ||||||||                                                 |
;|        |||||||+- Access Control                                 |
;|        ||||||+-- File Scan                                      |
;|        |||||+-- Modify                                          |
;|        ||||+--- Erase                                           |
;|        |||+--- Create                                           |
;|        ||+---- Write                                            |
;|        |+--- Read                                               |
;|        +---- Supervisory                                        |
;+-----------------------------------------------------------------+
[Files]

    Copying Files From Volume: SYS
    To Share: SYS

       Source Directory: \\NW4CS\SYS
       Dest Directory  : \\NTSRV40\d$\SYS\
        [ R        ] EVERYONE                    -> Domain Users
    Read (RX)
     [Files]

       Source Directory: \\NW4CS\SYS\TOYS
       Dest Directory  : \\NTSRV40\d$\SYS\TOYS
        [Files]
              622,754 [ A ] BAY.BMP
               64,896 [ A ] CHEETAH.PIC
               64,896 [ A ] CLNTSWM.PIC
               64,896 [ A ] EAGLE.PIC
               40,383 [ A ] EHSA64.GIF
               30,548 [ A ] EXAMPLE3.GIF
               64,896 [ A ] FALL.PIC
               43,100 [ A ] FLAG.EXE
               64,896 [ A ] FLAG.PIC
```

Continued.

```
            22,262  [ A ]  FLASH.EXE
            49,152  [ A ]  GIRL.GIF
            72,920  [ A ]  HEATH16.BMP
           146,680  [ A ]  HEATHER.BMP
           155,964  [ A ]  HORSE16Z.BMP
           787,510  [ A ]  HORSE768.BMP
           310,842  [ A ]  HORSES8Z.BMP
            52,224  [ A ]  KYM256.GIF
           155,971  [ A ]  LTI.HLP
            66,046  [ A ]  LTREE.BMP
               520  [ A ]  MAIN.DAT
               309  [ A ]  MAIN.MNU
               990  [ A ]  MAIN.SRC
            31,744  [ A ]  MOUSE.GIF
               334  [ A ]  MYMENU.MNU
            10,769  [ A ]  SAMPLE.GIF
           153,718  [ A ]  TREELOGO.BMP
            43,648  [ A ]  VGIF.EXE
            90,144  [ A ]  WINGIF.EXE
            32,219  [ A ]  WINGIF.HLP
            62,042  [ A ]  WSEARCH.HLP
           104,989  [ A ]  XSPACE.HLP
;+------------------------------------------------------------+
;|  From:  NW3SRV                                             |
;|  To:    NTSRV40                                           |
;+------------------------------------------------------------+
;|  Converted: Sunday, 03/09/1997 (03:39:34)                 |
;+------------------------------------------------------------+

[Transfer Options]
   Convert Users and Groups: Yes

   User Transfer Options:
      Use mapping file: No
      Passwords: 2 - Password is username
         User must change password: Yes
      Duplicate Names: Log Error

      Duplicate Groups: Log Error

      Use supervisor defaults: Yes
      Add Supervisors to the Administrators Group: Yes


[File Options]
   Convert Files: Yes

[Users]
   Number of Users = 9

   Users to Transfer
```

Continues

Continued.

```
;+------------------------------------------------------------+
  ARNOLD -> ARNOLD#2
  GATEKEEPER
  HEATHER -> HEATHER#2
  JEANNETTE
  RYAN
  SABRINA
  SAMANTHA
  SHELBY
  WAYNE -> WAYNE#2

  [ARNOLD -> ARNOLD#2]                                (Added)
  Original Account Info:
     Name:          Arnold Villeneuve
     Account disabled: No
     Account expires: 12/31/1997
     Password expires: 04/17/1997
Grace Logins: 5
     Initial Grace Logins: 5
     Minimum Password Length: 7
     # days to Password Expiration: 40
     Maximum Number of Connections: 3
     Restrictions:
        Anyone who knows password can change it
        Unique passwords required: Yes
     Number of login failures: 0
     Max Disk Blocks: (Unlimited)


  Login Times:
   Midnight                  AM                   Noon
    PM
      12 1  2  3  4  5  6  7  8  9  10 11 12 1  2  3  4
      5  6  7  8  9  10 11
      +------------------------------------------------+
  Sun                    ** ** ** ** ** ** ** ** ** **
    ** ** ** ** ** ** ** **
  Mon                    ** ** ** ** ** ** ** ** ** **
    ** ** ** ** ** ** ** **
  Tue                    ** ** ** ** ** ** ** ** ** **
    ** ** ** ** ** ** ** **
  Wed                    ** ** ** ** ** ** ** ** ** **
    ** ** ** ** ** ** ** **
  Thu                    ** ** ** ** ** ** ** ** ** **
    ** ** ** ** ** ** ** **
  Fri                    ** ** ** ** ** ** ** ** ** **
    ** ** ** ** ** ** ** **
  Sat                    ** ** ** ** ** ** ** ** ** **
    ** ** ** ** ** ** ** **


  New Account Info:
     Name: Arnold Villeneuve
     Password: ARNOLD#2
```

Continued.

```
      Privilege: User
      Home Dir:
      Comment:
      Flags:
          Execute login script: Yes
          Account disabled: No
          Deleting prohibited: No
          Home dir required: No
          Password required: Yes
          User can change password: Yes
      Script path:
      Full Name: Arnold Villeneuve
      Logon Server:

Logon Hours:
  Midnight                     AM                    Noon
    PM
      12 1  2  3  4  5  6  7  8  9  10 11 12 1  2  3  4
      5  6  7  8  9  10 11
      +-------------------------------------------------+
Sun                       ** ** ** ** ** ** ** ** ** **
  ** ** ** ** ** ** ** **
Mon                       ** ** ** ** ** ** ** ** ** **
  ** ** ** ** ** ** ** **
Tue                       ** ** ** ** ** ** ** ** ** **
  ** ** ** ** ** ** ** **
Wed                       ** ** ** ** ** ** ** ** ** **
  ** ** ** ** ** ** ** **
Thu                       ** ** ** ** ** ** ** ** ** **
  ** ** ** ** ** ** ** **
Fri                       ** ** ** ** ** ** ** ** ** **
  ** ** ** ** ** ** ** **
Sat                       ** ** ** ** ** ** ** ** ** **
  ** ** ** ** ** ** ** **



[GATEKEEPER]                                        (Added)
Original Account Info:
   Name:
   Account disabled: No
   Account expires: (Never)
   Password expires: (Never)
   Grace Logins: (Unlimited)
   Initial Grace Logins: (Unlimited)
   Minimum Password Length: 0
   # days to Password Expiration: (Never)
   Maximum Number of Connections: (Unlimited)
   Restrictions:
      Anyone who knows password can change it
      Unique passwords required: No
```

Continues

Continued.

```
    Number of login failures: 0
    Max Disk Blocks: (Unlimited)

Login Times:
 Midnight                    AM                      Noon
   PM
    12 1  2  3  4  5  6  7  8  9  10 11 12 1  2  3  4
    5  6  7  8  9  10 11
    +-------------------------------------------------------+
Sun ** ** ** ** ** ** ** ** ** ** ** ** ** ** ** ** **
    ** ** ** ** ** ** **
Mon ** ** ** ** ** ** ** ** ** ** ** ** ** ** ** ** **
    ** ** ** ** ** ** **
Tue ** ** ** ** ** ** ** ** ** ** ** ** ** ** ** ** **
    ** ** ** ** ** ** **
Wed ** ** ** ** ** ** ** ** ** ** ** ** ** ** ** ** **
    ** ** ** ** ** ** **
Thu ** ** ** ** ** ** ** ** ** ** ** ** ** ** ** ** **
    ** ** ** ** ** ** **
Fri ** ** ** ** ** ** ** ** ** ** ** ** ** ** ** ** **
    ** ** ** ** ** ** **
Sat ** ** ** ** ** ** ** ** ** ** ** ** ** ** ** ** **
    ** ** ** ** ** ** **

New Account Info:
   Name:
   Password: GATEKEEPER
   Privilege: User
   Home Dir:
   Comment:
   Flags:
      Execute login script: Yes
      Account disabled: No
      Deleting prohibited: No
      Home dir required: No
      Password required: Yes
      User can change password: Yes
   Script path:
   Full Name:
   Logon Server:

Logon Hours:
 Midnight                    AM                      Noon
   PM
    12 1  2  3  4  5  6  7  8  9  10 11 12 1  2  3  4
    5  6  7  8  9  10 11
    +-------------------------------------------------------+
Sun ** ** ** ** ** ** ** ** ** ** ** ** ** ** ** ** **
    ** ** ** ** ** ** **
Mon ** ** ** ** ** ** ** ** ** ** ** ** ** ** ** ** **
    ** ** ** ** ** ** **
Tue ** ** ** ** ** ** ** ** ** ** ** ** ** ** ** ** **
```

Continued.

```
         ** ** ** ** ** ** **
Wed ** ** ** ** ** ** ** ** ** ** ** ** ** ** ** ** **
    ** ** ** ** ** ** **
Thu ** ** ** ** ** ** ** ** ** ** ** ** ** ** ** ** **
    ** ** ** ** ** ** **
Fri ** ** ** ** ** ** ** ** ** ** ** ** ** ** ** ** **
    ** ** ** ** ** ** **
Sat ** ** ** ** ** ** ** ** ** ** ** ** ** ** ** ** **
    ** ** ** ** ** ** **


[HEATHER -> HEATHER#2]                            (Added)
Original Account Info:
   Name:
   Account disabled: No
   Account expires: (Never)
   Password expires: (Never)
   Grace Logins: (Unlimited)
   Initial Grace Logins: (Unlimited)
   Minimum Password Length: 0
   # days to Password Expiration: (Never)
   Maximum Number of Connections: (Unlimited)
   Restrictions:
       Anyone who knows password can change it
       Unique passwords required: No
   Number of login failures: 0
   Max Disk Blocks: (Unlimited)

Login Times:
 Midnight                 AM              Noon
   PM
    12 1  2  3  4  5  6  7  8  9  10 11 12 1  2  3  4
    5  6  7  8  9  10 11
    +---------------------------------------------------+
Sun ** ** ** ** ** ** ** ** ** ** ** ** ** ** ** ** **
    ** ** ** ** ** ** **
Mon ** ** ** ** ** ** ** ** ** ** ** ** ** ** ** ** **
    ** ** ** ** ** ** **
Tue ** ** ** ** ** ** ** ** ** ** ** ** ** ** ** ** **
    ** ** ** ** ** ** **
Wed ** ** ** ** ** ** ** ** ** ** ** ** ** ** ** ** **
    ** ** ** ** ** ** **
Thu ** ** ** ** ** ** ** ** ** ** ** ** ** ** ** ** **
    ** ** ** ** ** ** **
Fri ** ** ** ** ** ** ** ** ** ** ** ** ** ** ** ** **
    ** ** ** ** ** ** **
Sat ** ** ** ** ** ** ** ** ** ** ** ** ** ** ** ** **
    ** ** ** ** ** ** **

New Account Info:
```

Continues

Continued.

```
    Name:
    Password: HEATHER#2
    Privilege: User
    Home Dir:
    Comment:
    Flags:
        Execute login script: Yes
        Account disabled: No
        Deleting prohibited: No
        Home dir required: No
        Password required: Yes
        User can change password: Yes
    Script path:
    Full Name:
    Logon Server:

Logon Hours:
 Midnight                  AM                      Noon
   PM
     12 1  2  3  4  5  6  7  8  9 10 11 12 1  2  3  4
      5  6  7  8  9 10 11
     +----------------------------------------------------+
Sun  ** ** ** ** ** ** ** ** ** ** ** ** ** ** ** ** **
     ** ** ** ** ** ** **
Mon  ** ** ** ** ** ** ** ** ** ** ** ** ** ** ** ** **
     ** ** ** ** ** ** **
Tue  ** ** ** ** ** ** ** ** ** ** ** ** ** ** ** ** **
     ** ** ** ** ** ** **
Wed  ** ** ** ** ** ** ** ** ** ** ** ** ** ** ** ** **
     ** ** ** ** ** ** **
Thu  ** ** ** ** ** ** ** ** ** ** ** ** ** ** ** ** **
     ** ** ** ** ** ** **
Fri  ** ** ** ** ** ** ** ** ** ** ** ** ** ** ** ** **
     ** ** ** ** ** ** **
Sat  ** ** ** ** ** ** ** ** ** ** ** ** ** ** ** ** **
     ** ** ** ** ** ** **


[JEANNETTE]                                       (Added)
Original Account Info:
   Name:
   Account disabled: No
   Account expires: (Never)
   Password expires: (Never)
   Grace Logins: (Unlimited)
   Initial Grace Logins: (Unlimited)
   Minimum Password Length: 0
   # days to Password Expiration: (Never)
   Maximum Number of Connections: (Unlimited)
   Restrictions:
       Anyone who knows password can change it
       Unique passwords required: No
```

Continued.

```
    Number of login failures: 0
    Max Disk Blocks: (Unlimited)

Login Times:
 Midnight                    AM                        Noon
  PM
    12 1  2  3  4  5  6  7  8  9  10 11 12 1  2  3  4
    5  6  7  8  9  10 11
    +-------------------------------------------------------+
Sun ** ** ** ** ** ** ** ** ** ** ** ** ** ** ** ** **
    ** ** ** ** ** ** **
Mon ** ** ** ** ** ** ** ** ** ** ** ** ** ** ** ** **
    ** ** ** ** ** ** **
Tue ** ** ** ** ** ** ** ** ** ** ** ** ** ** ** ** **
    ** ** ** ** ** ** **
Wed ** ** ** ** ** ** ** ** ** ** ** ** ** ** ** ** **
    ** ** ** ** ** ** **
Thu ** ** ** ** ** ** ** ** ** ** ** ** ** ** ** ** **
    ** ** ** ** ** ** **
Fri ** ** ** ** ** ** ** ** ** ** ** ** ** ** ** ** **
    ** ** ** ** ** ** **
Sat ** ** ** ** ** ** ** ** ** ** ** ** ** ** ** ** **
    ** ** ** ** ** ** **

New Account Info:
   Name:
   Password: JEANNETTE
   Privilege: User
   Home Dir:
   Comment:
   Flags:
       Execute login script: Yes
       Account disabled: No
       Deleting prohibited: No
       Home dir required: No
       Password required: Yes
       User can change password: Yes
   Script path:
   Full Name:
   Logon Server:

Logon Hours:
 Midnight                    AM                        Noon
  PM
    12 1  2  3  4  5  6  7  8  9  10 11 12 1  2  3  4
    5  6  7  8  9  10 11
    +-------------------------------------------------------+
Sun ** ** ** ** ** ** ** ** ** ** ** ** ** ** ** ** **
    ** ** ** ** ** ** **
Mon ** ** ** ** ** ** ** ** ** ** ** ** ** ** ** ** **
    ** ** ** ** ** ** **
```

Continues

Continued.

```
Tue ** ** ** ** ** ** ** ** ** ** ** ** ** ** ** **
    ** ** ** ** ** ** **
Wed ** ** ** ** ** ** ** ** ** ** ** ** ** ** ** **
    ** ** ** ** ** ** **
Thu ** ** ** ** ** ** ** ** ** ** ** ** ** ** ** **
    ** ** ** ** ** ** **
Fri ** ** ** ** ** ** ** ** ** ** ** ** ** ** ** **
    ** ** ** ** ** ** **
Sat ** ** ** ** ** ** ** ** ** ** ** ** ** ** ** **
    ** ** ** ** ** ** **
```

NOTE: *Rest of user accounts have been skipped as they present the same information.*

```
[Groups]
    Number Groups = 5
    ADMINISTRATORS                                  (Added)
    DEVELOPMENT                                     (Added)
    MARKETING                                       (Duplicate)
    NTGATEWAY                                       (Added)
    SALES                                           (Duplicate)

    [ADMINISTRATORS]
        Domain Admins
        ARNOLD#2
        WAYNE#2

    [DEVELOPMENT]
        SAMANTHA
        SHELBY

    [MARKETING]
        RYAN
        SABRINA

    [NTGATEWAY]
        GATEKEEPER

    [SALES]
        HEATHER#2
        JEANNETTE


[Security Equivalences]
```

Continued.

```
        [ARNOLD#2]
            ADMINISTRATORS
            Domain Admins

        [GATEKEEPER]
            NTGATEWAY

        [HEATHER#2]
            SALES

        [JEANNETTE]
            SALES

        [RYAN]
            MARKETING

        [SABRINA]
            MARKETING

        [SAMANTHA]
            DEVELOPMENT

        [SHELBY]
            DEVELOPMENT

        [WAYNE#2]
            ADMINISTRATORS


[Print Operators]
        Domain Admins
        ARNOLD#2
        WAYNE#2
;+-------------------------------------------------------------+
;| Files are shown in the following format:                    |
;|     [Files]                                                 |
;|              1,234,567 [RAHS] TEST.TXT                      |
;|                          ||||  |                            |
;|                          ||||  +- Name of the File          |
;|                          ||||                               |
;|                          |||+- System                       |
;|                          ||+-- Hidden                       |
;|                          |+--- Archived                     |
;|                          +---- Read Only                    |
;|                                                             |
;|                        +---- File size (in Bytes)           |
;|                                                             |
;| The Access Rights are shown in the following format:        |
;|     [Access Rights]                                         |
;|         [SRWCEMFA] TestUser                                 |
;|          ||||||||  |                                        |
```

Continues

Continued.

```
; |              ||||||||        +- User or Group the Rights apply to  |
; |              ||||||||                                              |
; |              |||||||+— Access Control                             |
; |              ||||||+—- File Scan                                  |
; |              |||||+—- Modify                                      |
; |      ||||+— Erase                                                  |
; |         |||+— Create                                              |
; |         ||+—- Write                                               |
; |         |+—- Read                                                 |
; |         +—— Supervisory                                           |
;+-------------------------------------------------------------+
```

[Files]

    Copying Files From Volume: SYS
    To Share: SYS

        Source Directory: \\NW3SRV\SYS
        Dest Directory : \\NTSRV40\d$\SYS\
            [R   ] EVERYONE   -> Domain Users
    Read (RX)
        [Files]

        Source Directory: \\NW3SRV\SYS\APPS
        Dest Directory : \\NTSRV40\d$\SYS\APPS
        [Access Rights]
            [SRWCEMFA] SALES   -> SALES
    Full Control (All)

        Source Directory: \\NW3SRV\SYS\APPS\BIN
        Dest Directory : \\NTSRV40\d$\SYS\APPS\BIN
        [Access Rights]
            [RWCEMF] DEVELOPMENT   -> DEVELOPMENT
    Change (RWXD)
            [R   F] MARKETING   -> MARKETING
    Read (RX)
            [R   F] SALES   -> SALES
    Read (RX)
        [Files]
                    18,860 [A] 2FILE.EXE
                    23,364 [A] 2FLOPPY.EXE
                        49 [A] ADDSCSI.BAT
                    30,142 [A] ARC.EXE
                       627 [A] ATTR.COM
                    36,027 [A] AWK.EXE
                    42,400 [A] BOOT.COM
                    51,303 [A] CALIBRAT.EXE
                    14,888 [A] CALIBRAT.HLP
                     7,168 [A] CED.COM
                       186 [A] CLOCK.COM
                    24,038 [A] COPYQM.COM
                    29,002 [A] COPYQM.DOC
```
```

Continued.

```
        65,185  [ A  ]  COPYQM.EXE
        12,961  [ A  ]  D.EXE
       235,480  [ A  ]  DE.EXE
       131,884  [ A  ]  DISKEDIT.EXE
        85,628  [ A  ]  DISKEDIT.HLP
         8,611  [ A  ]  DISKMON.HLP
        54,239  [ A  ]  DISKTOOL.EXE
        10,129  [ A  ]  DISKTOOL.HLP
        34,731  [ A  ]  DM.EXE
         7,772  [ A  ]  DMDRVR.BIN
            28  [ A  ]  DRV.BAT
        28,516  [ A  ]  DS.EXE
        14,131  [ A  ]  DUPDISK.EXE
         4,806  [ A  ]  DUPDISK.HLP
           117  [ A  ]  DWS.BAT
           142  [ A  ]  DWSN.BAT
        21,819  [ A  ]  E.EXE
```

NOTE: *Files have been removed to shorten the list.*

```
         1,096  [ A  ]  WINQC.BAT
             9  [ A  ]  WSETUP.BAT
           111  [ A  ]  WZIP.BAT
        14,716  [ A  ]  XARC.COM
        29,378  [ A  ]  XZIP.EXE
        42,166  [ A  ]  ZIP.EXE
        27,319  [ A  ]  ZIP2EXE.EXE
         7,687  [ A  ]  ZIPFIX.EXE

 Source Directory: \\NW3SRV\SYS\APPS\LANWATCH
 Dest Directory  : \\NTSRV40\d$\SYS\APPS\LANWATCH
 [Access Rights]
     [ R     F ] DEVELOPMENT              -> DEVELOPMENT
 Read (RX)
     [ R     F ] MARKETING                -> MARKETING
 Read (RX)
     [ R     F ] SALES                    -> SALES
 Read (RX)
 [Files]
       541,658  [ A  ]  LANWATCH.EXE

 Source Directory: \\NW3SRV\SYS\APPS\PERFORM
 Dest Directory  : \\NTSRV40\d$\SYS\APPS\PERFORM
 [Access Rights]
     [ RWCE F ] DEVELOPMENT               -> DEVELOPMENT
 Change (RWXD)
```

Continues

Continued.

```
          [ R      F ]  MARKETING                    -> MARKETING
     Read (RX)
          [ R      F ]  SALES                         -> SALES
     Read (RX)
     [Files]
                    87,090 [ A  ]  PERFORM.EXE


Conversion Finished: Sunday, 03/09/1997 (03:40:38)
```

SUMMARY.LOG

```
;+----------------------------------------------------------------+
;| Migration Tool for NetWare Summary Log File                    |
;+-----------------------+                                        |
;| Created: Sunday, 03/09/1997 (03:39:19)                         |
;| System : NTSRV40                                               |
;| Admin  : Admin                                                 |
;| Version: 1.1                                                   |
;+----------------------------------------------------------------+


Number of Migrations = 2

[Servers]
From: NW3SRV            To: NTSRV40
From: NW4CS             To: NTSRV40


[NW4CS -> NTSRV40]
Total Users Converted: 19
Total Groups Converted: 1

Copying Files From Volume: SYS
To Share: SYS
Total Files Converted: 31
Bytes Transferred: 3,412,262

[NW3SRV -> NTSRV40]
Total Users Converted: 9
Total Groups Converted: 3

Copying Files From Volume: SYS
To Share: SYS
Total Files Converted: 130
Bytes Transferred: 4,686,101


Conversion Finished: Sunday, 03/09/1997 (03:40:38)
```

ERROR.LOG

```
;+----------------------------------------------------------------+
;| Migration Tool for NetWare Error Log File                      |
;+----------------------------------------------------------------+
;| Created: Sunday, 03/09/1997 (03:39:19)                         |
;| System : NTSRV40                                               |
;| Admin  : Admin                                                 |
;| Version: 1.1                                                   |
;+----------------------------------------------------------------+

[NW4CS -> NTSRV40]
[Transferring Users]
[ARNOLD]
Error: Duplicate User Name
[NW3SRV -> NTSRV40]
[Transferring Groups]
[MARKETING]
Error: Duplicate Group Name
[SALES]
Error: Duplicate Group Name
```

As you can see, the migration log files present a great deal of detailed information that can be helpful to resolving migration conflicts. At this stage, you should review the migration logs for potential duplicate user and groups names. It is most likely that you are transferring to a new area of the Windows NT file system, so having duplicate file names is unlikely, unless you are transferring two servers to the same Windows NT file system share.

The easiest way to correct problems is to return to the original server and change the offending user or group account name. After you are finished, you are then ready to proceed with a live migration. However, just to be safe, you should rerun another trial migration with the same migration settings to ensure you have located and resolved all the errors.

PERFORMING THE LIVE MIGRATION The big day has arrived. You have run several trial migrations, reviewed your log files, and resolved any errors. You are now ready to proceed with the final migration process. Before you run a migration, you should do a final verification of the following items:

▨ Ensure that you have sufficient disk space on the destination servers to transfer files.

▨ Check to be sure that destination volumes support the NTFS file system.

■ Ensure directory and file names do not conflict.

If you have resolved the user and name conflicts, the migration should proceed without much of a problem. To start the migration process, simply click on the Start Migration button of the Migration Tool for NetWare screen. After the user and group account information has been transferred to the Windows NT Primary Domain Controller, regular synchronization to Backup Domain Controllers of these accounts will take place. As the actual migration takes place, you will be presented with a status screen displaying the progress of the migration. (See Figure 7-56.)

After the migration is finished, save and review the log files carefully to ensure that all information has been transferred as you had designed. Your migrated users should now be able to log on to Windows NT using Microsoft network clients and access their files.

VERIFYING TRANSFERRED FILE RIGHTS   After the files have been transferred, you should go into the file permissions settings of either File Manager or NT Windows Explorer and verify that the NetWare trustee assignments were, in fact, transferred to equivalent Windows NT Permission settings. Remember that we looked at the NetWare Rights trustee assignments before we did the initial transfer. Here they are again so that we can compare them to the Windows NT permissions that were made as a result of the transfer. In between each NetWare directory rights listing, the resulting Windows NT permissions will be displayed for comparison. (See Figures 7-57 through 7-62.)

POST MIGRATION ISSUES   After the user and group accounts and file system information have been transferred to Windows NT, you will need to configure the user's access to the new Windows NT network resources. Although you may have migrated their NetWare login scripts, they will be of use to you only if you are also using File and Print Services for NetWare on your Windows NT server. Chances are, however, that you

Figure 7-56
Processing the migration. (Source: Microsoft Corporation)

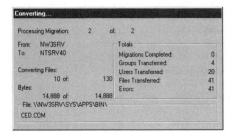

Figure 7-57
NetWare Rights
trustee assignments
on
NW3SRV\SYS:APPS
prior to the
migration. (Source:
Novell, Inc.)

```
NW3SRV\SYS:APPS
No user trustees.
Group trustees:
  SALES                                                    [SRWCEMFA]
```

Figure 7-58
Windows Explorer
post migration
permission settings
for NW3 APPS
directory. (Source:
Microsoft
Corporation)

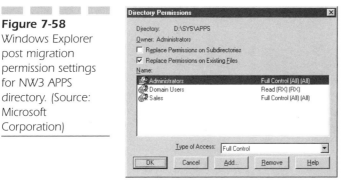

Figure 7-59
NetWare Rights
trustee assignments
on NW3SRV\SYS:
APPS\BIN prior to the
migration. (Source:
Novell, Inc

```
NW3SRV\SYS:APPS\BIN
No user trustees.
Group trustees:
  DEVELOPMENT                                          [ RWCEMF ]
  MARKETING                                            [ R     F ]
                              SALES                     [ R     F ]
```

Figure 7-60
Windows Explorer
post migration per-
mission settings for
NW3SRV\SYS:
APPS\BIN directory.
(Source: Microsoft
Corporation Inc.)

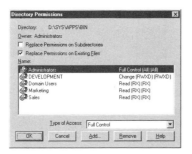

▀▀ ▀▀ ▀▀ ▀▀
Figure 7-61
NetWare Rights
trustee assignments
on NW3SRV\SYS:
APPS\LANWATCH
prior to the
migration. (Source:
Novell, Inc.)

```
NW3SRV\SYS:APPS\LANWATCH
No user trustees.
Group trustees:
  DEVELOPMENT                          [ R    F ]
  MARKETING                            [ R    F ]
  SALES                                [ R    F ]
```

will want to provide the migrated users with a new network access logon process and desktop environment. To do so, you will need to create Windows NT logon scripts to replace the NetWare login scripts. You may also want to configure User Profiles.

To create new Windows NT logon scripts, you will need to evaluate what applications and data directories the users require access to now that they have been migrated. The logon scripts for the new users will, in all likelihood resemble the existing users logon scripts if you have any. If you don't, you will need to create a script that maps network drives to remote files systems, captures printer output, and performs a range of other potential functions that can be performed within a logon script.

- Map Local Drives to Remote Network File Systems: This result can be accomplished through User Profiles with "Reconnect at Logon" or the "net use" command in a login script batch file

- Redirect Local Printer Output to a Network Printer: This result can be accomplished through User Profiles with the Print Manager or the **net use** command in a login script batch file.

- Launch Programs after Login: This result can be achieved through User Profiles by including the program icon in the Startup Program Group or Startup Menu folder.

CREATING LOGON SCRIPTS   Creating logon scripts is a two-step process:

1. Make the logon script entry in the user's Profile form of the User Manager for Domains.

2. Create the actual batch file (.BAT for DOS/WFWG/95/NT clients and .CMD for OS/2 clients) and store the batch file in the \%SYSTEMROOT%\SYSTEM32\IMPORT\SCRIPTS directory.

Figure 7-62

Windows Explorer post migration permission settings for NW3SRV\SYS: APPS\LANWATCH directory. (Source: Microsoft Corporation)

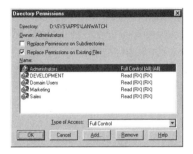

Additionally, due to the fact that any Windows NT Domain Controller (Primary and Backup) can validate a user's logon, you will need to ensure that the user's logon script is replicated over to the other servers. You can do so by using the Directory Replication Service.

User Profiles provide users with a way of maintaining their Windows environment settings. Under WFWG, this feat was accomplished through .INI file settings. And because WFWG was not based on individual users, the .INI files applied to anyone who sat down at the computer. However, with Windows 95 and Windows NT, the users are requested or required to provide user names prior to accessing the computer. The user names are then used to establish User Profile directories and profile files for those users. Desktop colors, network drive and printer connections, open programs, and Windows utility settings (for example, File Manager or Windows Explorer) are all saved in the User Profiles.

We saw earlier (in the Chapter 4 in particular) that the User Profile location pointer is configured in the User Manager for Domains. Unlike the user login scripts, profiles cannot be replicated to other domain controllers and must be stored on one server. Yes, if that server is unavailable, then so are the users' profiles. Also, you do not have to manually create User Profiles like you do with the login scripts. The first time users log on to the network, if User Profile pointers are defined in their user accounts and no profile are available, then the user profiles will be created from the authenticating Domain Controller's Default User Profile.

WINDOWS NT TO NETWARE: INTRODUCTION TO MIGRATION TOOLKIT A constant theme we have tried to touch upon throughout this book is that a majority of corporations are dealing with the "integration" side of network platforms rather than full and complete "migrations" from one platform to another. To facilitate the integration process and provide a single end user login/logon across the both NOS platforms, you will potentially need to get the Windows NT user accounts over to the NetWare server. Having duplicate accounts on both servers will allow the user to log on to a Windows computer and connect to the Windows NT and NetWare servers without having to reenter additional user name and password information. This, however, does not resolve the issue of synchronizing user databases between Windows NT and NetWare (that was the topic of Chapter 6).

OVERVIEW OF THE NOVELL CONSULTING GROUP'S MIGRATION TOOLKIT
The Migration Toolkit from the Novell Consulting Group provides a collection of utilities that allow the network administrator to easily migrate existing LAN Server, LAN Manager, and Windows NT Server (LS/LM/NT) Domain-based server information over to a NetWare 4.x NDS server. The utilities are offered "as is" and are not standard Novell-supported products. The utilities offer a method of migrating the information from the domain server in a nondestructive manner. In other words, the migration process only reads and transfers information from the original domain server and does not change it in any way. Some utilities provide client migrations as well, so you can migrate your clients to the NetWare client redirector/provider software. (See Figure 7-63.)

MIGRATION TOOLKIT PROCESSES AND REQUIREMENTS The migration process involves the following:

- User and group domain object migration
- File system migration
- Share emulation server support (optional)
- Client migration

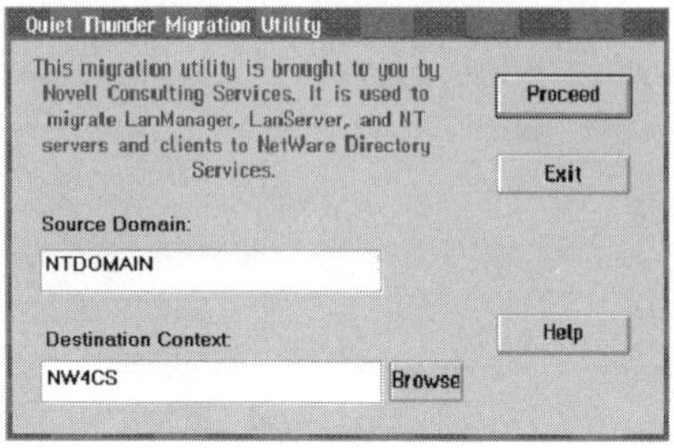

Figure 7-63
The Quite Thunder Migration Toolkit from Novell allows you to migrate LAN Server, LAN Manager, and Windows NT Server Domains to NetWare 4.x. (Source: Novell Consulting Group, Novell, Inc.)

The migration process can take several hours to complete when you're working with large domains. The Novell Consulting Group stated that for an average domain with 1000 users using a 486/66 as the NetWare server, the migration will take about 12 seconds per object totaling about 3.5 hours to complete. Faster hardware would obviously reduce this time. The Novell Consulting Group also estimated that file transfers on a typical 10 Mbs Ethernet network will proceed at about 500Mbytes per hour on a network segment reserved for the migration.

MIGRATION TOOLKIT HARDWARE REQUIREMENTS   The following are the Migration Toolkit hardware requirements:

- A NetWare 4.x server with NDS and Long File Name support on the NetWare volumes to be migrated to.
- An LS/LM/NT domain server from which to transfer information. Current supported domain server versions include

   LAN Manager versions 2.0 or 2.2

   LAN Server versions 2.x, 3.x, 4.0

   Windows NT Server version 3.5 or 3.51 (although we see no reason why 4.0 should not be supported either)
- An OS/2 Warp workstation from which to perform the migration. (You will need to install the NetWare OS/2 Requester.)

THE MIGRATION TOOLKIT SOFTWARE REQUIREMENTS   The Migration Toolkit comes with a number of software applications that are used to support the migration process. They are as follow:

- LMIGRATE.EXE: Used to migrate domain user and group objects to the NetWare server. It is run once for each Primary Domain Controller in the migration process.
- WINMIG.EXE and OS2MIG.EXE: Used to migrate existing Windows and OS/2 clients to the NetWare client redirecter/requester software. Although the OS/2 client is required for the Migration Toolkit migration itself, implementing Novell's client at the desktop will depend on your overall integration and migration strategy. (See Chapter 4 for more information on the topic of client support.) These applications include the NetWare OS/2 Requester, NetWare NT Client Requester, and NetWare Client 32 drivers.
- SAMBA.NLM: The functional equivalent of Microsoft's File and Print Services for NetWare. SAMBA.NLM allows a NetWare server

to support Server Message Block-based file and print services. The Samba service is not required for the migration itself but can be used to allow LS/LM/NT SMB-based clients to access files and printers on the NetWare server without loading the NetWare client software.

■ NTAGENT.EXE: Used on the Windows NT server for the LMI-GRATE.EXE software to obtain NT Domain local groups and Access Control Lists (permissions) associated with directories and files.

MIGRATION PHASES For the NetWare 4.x server, you will need to ensure that all the standard server setup is performed, an NDS tree has been designed, and that sufficient disk space is available to perform the migration.

The only precaution noted for the domain servers is with regards to Windows NT Server. In this instance, you must ensure that Windows NT server is configured to support LAN Manager-type requests. You can do so through the Network Control Panel.

The Novell Consulting Group recommends the following general procedures for performing the migration:

1. Back up the current LS/LM/NT servers several times, and verify that your backups are good.

2. Log out all users except the one who will perform the migration (logged on at the OS/2 Warp workstation).

3. Ensure that all user and application files are closed before the migration process begins.

4. Clean up any directories or files prior to the migration, and try to consolidate as many of them as possible to one migration area to increase migration speed.

5. Reduce your migration size and time by not migrating unnecessary files such as *.TMP, *.BAK, or *.LST.

6. Set the maximum subdirectory tree depth on the NetWare server to the required depth based on your migration because NetWare uses a default of 25. (This number can be changed in the NetWare server's STARTUP.NCF file.)

7. Remove unnecessary user and group accounts from the domain servers prior to migration.

MIGRATED INFORMATION The LMIGRATE program will migrate the following information from a LS/LM/NT server into the NetWare NDS database (also see Figure 7-64):

Figure 7-64
Selecting migration
source and destina-
tion options. (Source:
Novell Consulting
Group, Novell, Inc.)

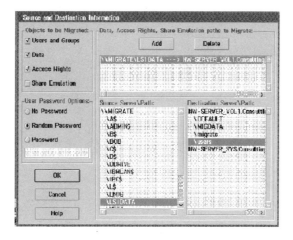

- User information:

  User login name

  User description

  Login restrictions such as account expiration, password, and time restrictions

  Network Address Restrictions (if supported)

  USER_TEMPLATE and USER_OVERRIDE: Used to add information to NDS during the migration that is not available or supported from the domain user accounts—for example, Phone Number, Fax Number, Title, Department, Grace Logins, and Home Directories

  You should note that when a Domain user account being migrated already exists in the NetWare NDS tree, the information is combined and merged into the existing NetWare NDS account.

- Group Information:

  Group name

  Group description

  Group Membership

- File and Directory Information:

  Directory structure including any Long File Name support

  File data

  Extended attributes

  Directory and file permissions

You should note that no precopy verification is done to ensure that the files being migrated do not already exist. If they do, they will simply be overwritten. Therefore, always migrating to a new directory on the NetWare server is probably a good idea.

INFORMATION THAT IS NOT MIGRATED   The following information is not migrated in this process:

- User Profiles
- Print services
- Mail services
- Passwords (although you can generate passwords randomly during the migration for the new accounts, have no passwords, or use one password for all migrated accounts)

PERFORMING THE ACTUAL MIGRATION   When you are ready to perform the actual migration, the Novell Consulting group recommends that you use the following steps:

1. Plan the NDS directory tree structure into which you are migrating the domain objects.
2. Understand how to use the utilities in the toolkit.
3. Configure your hardware.
4. Install the NetWare 4.x destination server.
5. Install the Novell OS/2 Requester on the workstation from which you plan to perform the migration.
6. Maintain relevant migration planning documentation detailing elements to be migrated.
7. Implement any NetWare-related software that you require.
8. Create the USER_TEMPLATE and USER_OVERRIDE templates to facilitate migration information not supported or migrated from the domain.
9. Add Long File Name support on the NetWare server.
10. Log off all users.
11. Run the LMIGRATE.EXE utility on the OS/2 workstation.

FOR MORE INFORMATION   For more information on this migration utility from the Novell Consulting Group, refer to the following Novell Web page:

`http://NetWare.Novell.com/corp/programs/NCS/toolkit/miggt.htm`

(Note: Novell Inc. may have changed this URL since this printing.)

In summary, the Migration Toolkit provides you with everything you need to migrate LAN Manager, LAN Server, and Windows NT Server Domain user and file system information to a NetWare NDS directory.

SUMMARY

In this chapter, we focused on migrating NetWare server information to Windows NT servers using the Migration Tool for NetWare. The migration planning stages and steps were discussed. In-depth study was done regarding the transfer of NetWare user and group accounts, as well as NetWare file system security information. The processes involved in performing a trial migration, reviewing migration log files, and a finishing with a live migration were reviewed.

We also undertook a review of the Novell Migration Toolkit utilities, which allow a migration of LAN Server, LAN Manager, and Windows NT Server Domain user and file system information to a NetWare server.

Based on the information presented in this chapter, you should now be aware that you can migrate user and file system information from either platform to the other. This knowledge should facilitate your integrating and migration project.

CHAPTER **8**

Migration Project Planning Overview

The main focus of this chapter will be an overview of some of the issues associated with project management. Many good books have been written on project management, so we won't try to make you an expert in one chapter. Many technical people are simply not good planners. We are great doers and carry out technology implementation at breakneck speeds. But projects of this type take serious consideration and need to be well thought out if they are to be implemented successfully. Therefore, the goal of this chapter is to introduce you to some of the project planning issues you may want to look into further.

Chapter Objectives

- Migration and what it means
- Migration planning stages
- Migration planning checklists

Migration and What It Means

We end this book with the beginning. By this, we mean that you should really be starting here by doing some of the things suggested in this last chapter before you begin to implement all the wonderful technology that you learned about in preceding chapters. The success of any project depends on how clear you are about what you are trying to accomplish and then how you go about accomplishing these tasks. Clarity of the project goals and objectives comes from putting the plan in writing so that you can get feedback on assumptions and expectations, both your own and others.

Webster's Dictionary refers to migration as moving "from one country, place, or locality to another." Certainly, then, moving from Windows NT to NetWare or from NetWare to Windows NT would be considered a migration. Many people think of a migration as a one-way ticket from place A to place B. However, nothing could be further from the truth in our context. Although it is certainly true that in the current market many people (at least the media anyway) are thinking of "migrating" their networks to Windows NT Server from a variety of existing network operating systems including NetWare, many others are simply trying to cope with integrating the two of them together for some level of coexistence. And there, at least in our opinion, lies the true benefit of the migration process that both vendors provide. Of course, Microsoft and Novell would both like you to migrate completely to their network products. In some cases, you might be able to do so; in others you may not.

When we first started looking at developing a course on this topic for Learning Tree International and had plans to write a subsequent book, everyone wanted the initial focus to be on migrating from NetWare to Windows NT entirely. However, we did some research on the Internet and CompuServe to poll network administrators about their plans in early 1996 and found that over 90 percent of them were more concerned about integration of the two network operating systems than they were with doing a complete migration from one to the other. Besides, if they were going to migrate, they had to perform some level of integration first! Although many of them were going to migrate to Windows NT, they were also equally honest about having to support both platforms because of the large investment in existing NetWare network products that were built into their organization's business processes.

The general industry press in the meantime seemed to be persistent with their buzz and hype about the death of Novell and Microsoft's Windows NT Server's impending takeover of the market. Both vendors countered each other's marketing briefs and bulletins with more of the same. Meanwhile, an industry survey of value-added resellers and systems integrators by *VAR Business* (in February 1997) says that more than 60 percent of them believe NetWare provides still a bigger opportunity for them to sell network solutions. Finally, an article in *Information Week* (July 15, 1996) details how "early NT adopters are taking a second look at Novell's NetWare offerings" due to limitations in Windows NT's Domain structure. Microsoft counters that Windows NT Server 5.0 will have full directory synchronization and hierarchy shortly. And the game goes on!

The technical complexities of the vendor solutions are fought out in the front pages of the press. (Courtesy of WWW. NETWORKOLOGIST. COM)

But what does all this information mean to you, the network administrator, when your job is to provide a single user logon/login to your multiplatform network, you have anywhere from several hundred to many thousands of users, and you have gigabytes of server files that you need to move to another platform? Given the current size of the NetWare market and the rapid increase in Windows NT's penetration to this market, this information probably means that you'll need to get information from NetWare to Windows NT. You may equally need to get existing information from a Windows NT server onto the NetWare platform as the two systems are merged (like when two government departments with differing systems are merged or reorganized). So the coin may be turned either way. Besides a lot of work, you need some tools to help you. For that reason, in preparing for this chapter, we researched the possibilities of migrating in either direction and are happy to say that both vendors provide the tools to help you accomplish this task.

So what does migration mean in our context? From our perspective, migration means getting information from one server platform to the other. It also encompasses many other elements that support this objective. In this book, we are mainly dealing with migrating server platforms that require an understanding of networking protocols and the finding integration and migration tools available to assist us in our tasks. However, many other factors to be considered are also important but not the focus of this book. These factors include what server hardware platform to use

(Intel versus Risc), Ethernet, Token Ring, or FDDI, switched hubs or not, and many others. You need to explore these issues as well.

For our purposes, however, a migration includes the following types of information:

Common migration elements. (Courtesy of WWW. NETWORKOLOGIST. COM)

■ User and Group account information

■ System security policies or rules

■ Volumes, files, and directories/folders

■ File system security

Let's look at each one of these types of information in more detail.

User and Group Account Information

NetWare and Windows NT users and groups. (Courtesy of WWW. NETWORKOLOGIST. COM)

Windows NT and NetWare user accounts contain the same basic account information: user name, password, user's full name, and so on. This information is essentially the same for all network operating systems. Some information, however, may be specific to each user; this information may be configured differently than that of the standard system settings defined for new users. In some areas, NetWare and Windows NT Domain user and group information does not line up, and we need to decide how to migrate (if we can) this information. Additionally, we need to consider differences in the Administrative level accounts.

System Security Policies or Rules

Making sure the system is safe. (Courtesy of WWW. NETWORKOLOGIST. COM)

System security policies or rules are settings that apply to the users' ability to log in to the server at a given time of day or how many times they can log on or log in with the wrong password before intruder detection kicks in, whether the users can change their own passwords, and others. However, these settings are made for the system as a whole and are applied to all users unless their own individual settings override the system settings. NetWare and Windows NT have different levels or types of system settings (who would have thought!), and once again, not all of them line up nicely.

Some place to store your files. (Courtesy of WWW. NETWORKOLOGIST. COM)

Volumes, Files, and Directories/Folders

Although the underlying file system is not the same (NetWare uses the NetWare file system, whereas Windows NT uses NTFS), the end result is still the same: a place to store files. The migration process needs simply to copy these files between the two servers by identifying the source and destination.

File System Security

Keeping the file system safe. (Courtesy of WWW. NETWORKOLOGIST. COM)

The statement in the preceding section with regards to simply copying files between the two server platforms, however, would be an oversimplification. File system security needs to be considered. Are we going to use the security already present on the source server and try to migrate similar security restrictions to the destination server side? Or are we going to apply the destination's server security when the files are copied?

Migration does not entail getting the information back over to the original platform after it is subsequently changed on the other. That is the responsibility of directory synchronization, which was addressed in a previous chapter.

Migration Planning

Create a list of your objectives and plan. (Courtesy of WWW. NETWORKOLOGIST. COM)

As with any MIS project, some level of planning is in order. We need to identify all the responsible people, critical objectives (goals) or desired outcome, affected areas, project milestones, and the time line. In the following sections, we will go through the details of working with the actual migration tools themselves. However, we have included in the appendixes of the book, as well as in electronic format on the CD-ROM, two excellent documents detailing project planning issues about the migration from either platform's viewpoint. These documents—one by the people at Valinor Inc. for Microsoft Corporation and the other by the people at Novell's Consulting Group—are both excellent documents detailing a wide range of issues that you will need to consider as you prepare for your migratory journey.

Plan Your Work and Work Your Plan

"Plan Your Work and Work Your Plan" is sound advice for any project, but even more important when you consider that many people are depending on you to do the right thing. So where do you start? The following is a list of issues to consider:

- Picking the team
- Determining corporate technology processing requirements: present and planned
- Evaluating potential solutions
- Defining the solution
- Specifying the details
- Creating a time line
- Implementing the project
- Performing a follow-up project review

Components of a Migration Plan

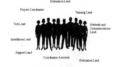

Picking the right team members is crucial to the project's success. (Courtesy of WWW. NETWORKOLOGIST. COM)

We may be in an industry in which technology permeates everything we do. At the end of the day, though, we are still people, and good people are required to deal with technology changes of this magnitude and scale. You will need to create a dream team. However, we still understand that the team might have only one member: you. In either case, someone will need to wear the hat dealing with each area of the project; some teams members may wear several hats. According to the good people at Valinor Inc., some of the roles defined for specific team players include the following:

- Project Coordinator
- Project Coordinator Assistant
- Project Evaluation Lead
- Project Test Lead
- Project Training Lead
- Project Support Lead
- Project Evaluation Tech 1
- Project Test Tech 1
- Project Network and Communications Tech 1

- Installation Team Lead
- Installation Tech 1-3

These project roles can also be categorized into subteams to assign certain task groupings. Subteams should have cross-functional members from different parts of the project to ensure that everyone in the group has input into the impact changes may have on their parts of the project. Project subteams include the following:

- Planning Team
- Evaluation Team
- Deployment Team
- Training Team
- Support Team

Now, you might be sitting there thinking "What huge company do these authors work for that they have so many people in MIS?" Again, you need to scale the project to your particular organization. However, regardless of the size of the project, all the preceding roles will come into play whether one person or several dozen people are involved. You will still have to plan the project requirements and evaluate and test solutions; then someone will have to implement the project. Because new technology is involved, you might have to train both MIS staff and end users if any changes are required from their perspective (although we will certainly try to minimize them). So, creating teams is really only a matter of whether 1 person or 20 are working on the teams.

Corporate Technology Processing Requirements: Present and Planned

You will need to identify the current limitations with your corporate technology infrastructure that you are trying to address. You will also need to identify what the organization's future requirements are likely to be where technology is concerned. This task it not as daunting as it sounds.

Consider an easy example. Say your company's customer database now has 10,000 customers on file. You would need to talk to the sales department to find out how many customers it is estimating to increase over the next two years, three years, and five years. If each current customer record on file is approximately 100 kilobytes, then you will need to multiply the estimated increased customer total by this size. Now that does not mean you have to rush out today and buy the disk drives, but you do need to ensure that the server platform and subsequent hardware will be able to expand as your company does. This same theory can be applied to all areas of technology whether it is network traffic, the amount of random access memory required for the server, client connection licenses, and so on. The process is not very hard; it just takes some thought and work. Many tools are out there to help you, so make use of them. For example, both Novell and Microsoft have Internet pages that will help you calculate server memory requirements based on number of potential users, number of server-based applications, and disk drive space.

Evaluating Alternatives

Checking out the alternatives can take time, but it is the only way to find the right solution. (Courtesy of WWW. NETWORKOLOGIST. COM)

I once worked for a man, Len Hendershott, who taught me an important lesson about selecting a solution for business requirements: You must have something to benchmark the alternatives against; otherwise, you will never be able to make sound decisions. Instead you will be swayed by factors such as personal feelings, salesperson persuasion, marketing hype, or price alone (which is not always the defining factor when you are looking for a quality solution).

Mr. Hendershott was originally responsible for planning the upgrade of a Digital VAX system that eventually lead to the migration to a PC LAN-based operating system by the organization. To properly evaluate his alternatives, he created a set of objectives to which each vendor was to submit a response addressing each objective. Those who did not follow the proposal format were eliminated from the potential vendor list. Within the company, Mr. Hendershott allocated each objective a score with which he would use to evaluate the vendors' proposals. Table 8-1 illustrates this exercise: Comparative Scoring of Proposed Alternatives: High score is best!

Many decisions are also based on the people behind the solution. (Courtesy of WWW. NETWORKOLOGIST. COM)

Selecting the Solution

Table 8-1 should help point out some obvious factors such as who potentially is supplying the best solution. It helps take out all the warm and fuzzies you may have had about one salesperson, while actually pointing to a solution that a salesperson you did not warm up to is presenting. The exercise takes the emotion out of the purchase and allows you to proceed with the selection on a more informed basis.

Table 8-1

Using comparative scoring to help evaluate alternatives. (Courtesy of Len Hendershott)

Weighting	Objective	Vendor A	Vendor B	Vendor C
8	Cost	7.6	3.7	8.0
2	Software Compatibility	2.0	1.0	0.5
1	Training Requirement	1.0	0.5	0.5
3	Equipment Power	3.0	2.5	1.0
2	Simplicity	1.5	0.5	0.0
2	Flexibility	1.0	1.8	2.0
1	Accessibility	1.0	0.8	0.8
1	Continuity	0.2	1.0	0.8
2	Completeness	2.0	1.5	1.0
1	Reputation	0.8	1.0	0.5
2	Upgradability	2.0	2.0	0.0
25	**Total**	**22.1**	**16.3**	**15.0**

Specifying the Details

Migration Plan

Putting in the details. (Courtesy of WWW. NETWORKOLOGIST. COM)

Part of the solution in the preceding exercise was to define some of the specifics as to what had to be done in the project. However, now you need to get down to the details: which servers, what software, which groups of users, what will be tested, how will it be tested, and so on. At this stage, you need to get right down to the nitty-gritty where no stone is left unturned. By identifying all the affected areas, you will then be able to assign people to look after each one and give them the "responsibility" for the task completion. However, if you do assign the task to other people, you also need to ensure that they have the "authority" to carry out the task. They also need to understand that they are "accountable" for the successful completion of the task or will have to face the consequences in the event of its failure. (As an aside, we are always amazed to see how much work gets done when someone is responsible and accountable for the successful completion of a task. These responsible parties will very quickly let you know if they do not have the authority to complete a task at each moment someone or something stands in their way!)

Creating a Time Line

After you have defined all the aspects and tasks of the migration project in more detail, you are then ready to assign them to a schedule. (See Figure 8-1.) By walking through the actual tasks, you will be able to identify the critical paths for the project—what needs to happen before, in synch, or after each individual task. When these factors are put on the schedule, you can associate the people with each task for which they are responsible and produce individual and team activity plans. Then, as tasks are completed, you can update your plan. Because you are keeping the work progress up to date, you can quickly identify areas that are behind or ahead of schedule in the migration. Another benefit of keeping the project documentation up to date is that you can quickly produce management reports and keep everyone associated with the project up to date.

Figure 8-1
Milestones and time lines are critical for judging the progress of the project. (Courtesy of WWW. NETWORKOLOGIST. COM)

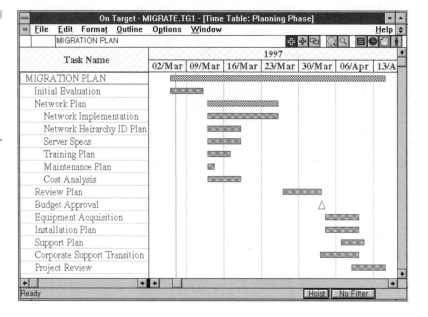

Implementing the Migration Project

All the planning is done; now we have to sit down and get the work done. (Courtesy of WWW. NETWORKOLOGIST. COM)

Now we are starting to get to what is really the heart of this book: Migration. Now we really start to migrate information from one server platform to another. (See Figure 8-13.) The migration entails a number of factors that should have been identified as tasks earlier in the process. These factors are based on the following questions:

"Which servers will be affected by the migration?"

"What file system components will be moved and to where?"

"Will user security settings be moved or established by the new server?"

"What department users and groups will be moved or otherwise affected?"

Now we have to start going through the process of working with the tools provided to perform the actual plan. This task will also involve a certain amount of testing prior to the actual migration itself so that we can elevate our chances of success. Always make sure you have a back door. And we don't mean a back door through which you can exit when the project fails! We mean a method of reversing whatever you do through restores of information and systems. We all know and agree that technical problems happen. Hardware fails or software does not function as specified or indicated in a certain configuration. Although you can minimize the potential of this problem occurring, you cannot possibly calculate every downfall. So be prepared to backtrack on occasion.

Follow-up Project Review

Review and evaluate original project assumptions with everyone involved. (Courtesy of WWW. NETWORKOLOGIST. COM)

You should actually be doing a whole series of mini-reviews as you progress through the migration itself. However, now is the time to go back over your project assumptions with all the project members and evaluate the success of the project and to plan your next one.

Migration Planning Checklists

We have adopted the following checklists and forms from several other sources including both Microsoft Corporation and Novell, Inc., in addition to others. A lion's share of credit for the concepts for the original checklists and forms that follow deservedly goes to the great people at the Novell Consulting Group, as does a lot of credit for the project migration planning concepts to the good people at Valinor Inc.

Our intent is to provide you with a series of helpful migration checklists and forms to better assist you with planning and implementing your project. The following plans have also been included in electronic format, and we recommend highly that you make use of them to assist you in implementing a very successful migration.

Here's a list of the migration worksheets:

- Hardware Platform Capacity Planning Worksheet: Server & Disk (see Figure 8-2)

- Hardware Platform Capacity Planning Worksheet: RAM Requirements (see Figure 8-3)

- Software Requirement Planning Worksheet: RAM Requirements (see Figure 8-4)

- Server Based Application Software (see Figure 8-5)

- Final Pre-Migration Checklist (see Figure 8-6)

- Test Migration Plan (see Figure 8-7)

- Client Redirector Migration Worksheet (see Figure 8-8)

- Full Migration Plan (see Figure 8-9)

- Post-Migration Manual Procedures (see Figure 8-10)

(These forms are based on forms originally developed by Novell, Inc. for migrating from Windows NT to IntraNetWare.)

Hardware Platform Capacity Planning Worksheet

Server Platform: _ INTEL   _ RISC   _ ALPHA   _PPC   _OTHER

Server Disk Space Requirements

Disk Space	Minimum	Actual/Preferred	Cost
DOS/FAT Partition if Required		MB	
NTFS or NetWare Partitions			
System Drive / Volume		MB	
Application Drive / Volume		MB	
User Data Drive / Volume		MB	
_____ Drive / Volume		MB	
_____ Drive / Volume		MB	
_____ Drive / Volume		MB	
_____ Drive / Volume		MB	
_____ Drive / Volume		MB	

Client/Server Apps Requirements:

Name:	MB	
Name:	MB	
Name:	MB	
Name:	MB	
Name:	MB	
Name:	MB	
Name:	MB	
Name:	MB	

Disk Capacity Sub-Total:

CD ROM Drive:

Total Number of Units:

Backup Tape Drive: MB

Tape Capacity Sub-Total:

Figure 8-3
Hardware Platform
Capacity Planning
Worksheet: RAM
Requirements.

Hardware Platform Capacity Planning Worksheet

Server Additional RAM Requirements: Check only those that apply.

Client/Server Applications	**Minimum**	**Actual/Preferred**

Migration Software Requirements:

Check all that apply.

NT Migration Tool for NetWare

NW Migration Toolkit

    Each Client migrating

    _____ KB Multiplied by _____ Clients

Integration Tools: Check all that apply:

Additional protocol stacks

NW SAMBA or NT FPNW

NT GSNW (N/A for NW)

NW NT Integration Tool or NT DSNW

Name:

Name:

                            RAM Subtotal

Total Additional Disk Space Required:_____

Total Additional RAM Required:_____

Figure 8-4
Software Require-
ment Planning
Worksheet: RAM
Requirements.

Software Requirement Planning Worksheet

Check off which of the following software may be used in the migration:

Windows NT	IntranetWare
NWCONV.EXE	LMIGRATE.EXE
IPX/SPX Compatible Transport Protocol	WINMIG.EXE
GSNW Client Service	OS2MIG.EXE
CSNW Client Service	SAMBA.NLM
	NetWare OS/2 Requester
	NetWare Client 32 for Windows NT
	IntranetWare Client
	NetWare Administrator - NT Integration Tool

Comments:

_____

_____

_____

_____

_____

_____

_____

_____

_____

_____

_____

_____

Figure 8-5
Server-Based Application Software

Server Based Application Software

| Application | Current | Proposed | Tested | | Status | |
			Pass	Failed	On Hand or Ordered	To Be Ordered
E-mail						
Backup						
Word Processing						
Spreadsheets						
Databases						
LAN Security						
Other						

Comments:

_____

_____

_____

_____

_____

_____

_____

_____

_____

_____

_____

_____

Figure 8-6

Final Pre-Migration
Checklist.

Final Pre-Migration Check List

Knowledge & Training

____ Current O/S Knowledge

____ Current O/S Documentation

____ File System Structure
Plan Completed

____ Directory/Domain Structure
Design

____ Technical Certification

____ NOS Documentation

Planning & Preparation

____ Directory/Domain Structure Services Tree designed

____ Destination server installed & configured

____ File system structure initiated or server prepared to receive new one

____ All required software tools, utility packages, and documentation on hand

____ All versions of required software and drivers on hand or ordered

____ All versions of required software and drivers tested and verified

____ Emulation server services started as required (SAMBA or FPNW) (Worksheet
filled out if required)

____ Naming Standard implemented

____ Full system backup performed (multiple copies recommended and tested)

____ Test migration population identified

____ Full migration plan developed

Other Checks and Tasks

_____

_____

_____

Testing & Verification

____ Test migration performed and verified

____ Full migration performed and verified

____ Post-migration procedures performed and verified

Certification

Migration Performed, Tested & Approved _____ Date:_____

Figure 8-7
Test Migration Plan.

Test Migration Plan

Use this worksheet for your test migration. Make note of any items that do not migrate or of any other problems you encounter.

Test Source Directory/Domain/Bindery Server Name:_____

Destination Server Type:		
	NetWare 3.x	_____
	NetWare 4.x	_____
	IntranetWare	_____
	Banyan Vines	_____
	LAN Manager	_____
	NT Server	_____
	LAN Server	_____

	Pass	**Fail**	**Notes**
Migrate:			
Directory Objects			
Domain Objects			
Bindery Objects			
Verify:			
Directory Objects			
Domain Objects			
Bindery Objects			
Migrate:			
Application Files			
Data Files			
Migrate Client Redirector			
Test Client Applications			
Verify All Applications			

Comments:_____

Note: Verify that all information has migrated correctly. If some items did not migrate or fail verification testing, be sure to make complete notes. These notes will help you tie up loose ends before you begin full migration.

Figure 8-8
Client Redirector
Migration Worksheet.

Client Redirector Migration Worksheet

Client Name:_____

Client OS Type: _____ DOS _____ OS/2 _____ Windows 3.x _____ WFWG

_____ Windows 95 _____ Windows NT

This client is #_____ in the migration order.

	Pass	**Fail**	**Notes**
Select Client Redirector			
Migrate Client			
Test Client Applications			
Name:			
Name:			
Name:			
Verify all Applications			
Name:			
Name:			
Name:			
Name:			

Additional Notes:_____

_____

_____

_____

_____

Figure 8-9
Full Migration Plan.

Full Migration Plan

Copy this worksheet once for each Directory/Domain/Bindery and server you plan to migrate (other than those that were included in the test migration). Fill out the information as it applies to the individual Directory/Domain/Bindery. Arrange the plans in the order you plan to migrate the systems. Use the Notes section to list attributes not migrated, information that was lost or fails verification, etc.

Directory/Domain/Bindery Name:_____   **Server Type:**

NetWare 3.x	_____
NetWare 4.x	_____
IntranetWare	_____
Banyan Vines:	_____
LAN Manager	_____
NT Server	_____
LAN Server	_____

This Directory/Domain/Bindery is #_____ in the migration order.

	Pass	**Fail**	**Notes**
Migrate:			
Directory Objects			
Domain Objects			
Bindery Objects			
Verify:			
Directory Objects			
Domain Objects			
Bindery Objects			
Migrate:			
Application Files			
Data Files			
Migrate Client Redirector			
Test Client Applications			
Verify all Applications			

Comments:_____

Note: Verify that all information has migrated correctly. If some items did not migrate or fail verification testing, be sure to make complete notes. These notes will help you tie up loose ends after your full migration is complete.

Figure 8-10
Post-Migration
Manual Procedures.

Post-Migration Manual Procedures

Use this worksheet to note any procedures you must perform by hand after the full migration is completed.

Configuration Information: (e.g. Additional Administration User, Groups, etc.)

_____

_____

Attributes, Properties, etc., for manual migration:

Attribute, Property, Object, Value, etc.	Pass	Fail	Notes

New, Custom, or In-House Applications to Load & Test:

Application	Pass	Fail	Notes

Reintegrate Test Migration Directory/Domain/Bindery? _____ Yes _____ No

Additional Notes:_____

_____

_____

_____

_____

SUMMARY

In this chapter, we provided an overview of some of the issues associated with project management. As stated, we did not try to make you an expert in the art of project planning. However, we did try to bring to your attention many of the project planning-related functions that you should be bringing to your migration. Obviously, the size and scope of the project will dictate the size and scope of your plan, so you will need to adjust it accordingly. Don't be guilty of overplanning! Eventually, you just have to do the job.

Both Wayne McKinnon and I wish you the best of success in your migration project, whichever direction it takes!

Appendix A

Terminology Guide: The Novell to Microsoft Dictionary

About This Guide

This appendix was prepared by Valinor Inc. Valinor Inc. is a national, full-service, privately owned system integrator. Using Microsoft BackOffice and Microsoft Office, Valinor is structured to integrate, develop, train, and transfer knowledge across a broad spectrum of technologies and products in both mixed-vendor and Microsoft-only environments. Valinor offers a high density of industry technical certifications and has offices and training facilities in Clifton, NJ; New York, NY; Manchester, NH (Corporate Headquarters); Atlanta, GA; Bellevue, WA; and Waltham, MA and people in Raleigh, NC. For more information, call (603) 668-1776 or access the Web site at `http://www.valinor.com`.

Introduction

The purpose of this appendix is to correlate familiar terms and acronyms from the Novell world to equivalent products, features, technologies, or services from Microsoft. This appendix is designed for Certified NetWare Engineers (CNEs) and other Novell-literate managers. Terms included are both client-level and server products, tools, applications, and concepts.

The Terminology Map is arranged alphabetically based on the Novell term. You will find three columns:

1. The Novell term and a brief description
2. The comparable Microsoft term (if a reasonable match exists) and a brief description
3. How they differ

Also included in the list are Microsoft terms for which no Novell matches exist. The technology will be focused around NetWare and the Microsoft Windows NT operating system, but not exclusively. LAN Manager for OS/2 will be referenced only where appropriate.

Document Conventions

Acronyms are spelled out the first time they appear (except for extremely common ones, such as *DOS*). All key words and acronyms that are defined or used elsewhere in the table will appear in **boldface**. Commands look like this: `Attach`.

N: Novell Term: Novell Description
M: Microsoft Term: Microsoft Description
D: Differences
Rules separate the sets of descriptions.

N: AppWare: Client-side application development tool consisting of two major components: AppWare Foundation and AppWare Bus. The AppWare Foundation is a set of libraries that make it easier to create portable applications by providing developers with a single, unified API. The resulting code can then be compiled for the specific operating system or GUI required. The AppWare Bus provides large-grained, interchangeable software modules that corporate and vertical developers can use and reuse to quickly construct new network applications without having to write new code.

M: No direct equivalent for AppWare Foundation. Both Visual C++ and Visual Basic have some similarity to AppWare Bus.

D: Visual Basic and Visual C++ are high-level, object-oriented programming languages that provide developers with a wide assortment of prewritten modifiable software modules that can be quickly connected to allow developers to rapidly develop graphical applications for both DOS and the Windows family. Client software created with AppWare can communicate only with servers running NetWare NLMs, whereas Visual Basic and Visual C++ can communicate with server-based applications via network APIs, including Windows Sockets, IPX Sockets, NetBIOS, Named Pipes, and RPCs. Visual C++ and Visual Basic do not provide application portability; they are designed strictly for the MS Windows environment and can fully exploit the power of the Windows APIs.

N: `Attach`: Command that establishes a connection to a server other than the one currently logged in to. Users may log in to server with same or different user ID.

M: No direct match. N/A

D: Explicitly attaching to a specific server prior to establishing a session with a Microsoft network server is not necessary. Loading the MS network client does not automatically attach to a server as does loading the NetWare shell **NETX**.

N: Bindery: A NetWare 2.x and 3.x database residing on each server that keeps records of users, groups, workgroups, printers, services, and other user-definable objects (via an exposed API).

M: Security Accounts Manager (SAM): Resides on Windows NT and Windows NT Advanced Server systems and contains the database of all users and groups.

D: SAMs are replicated to all servers participating in a **domain**. The SAM is only one component of the Windows NT security model. Two other major components—the Local Security Authority (**LSA**) and the Security Reference Monitor (**SRM**)—use the SAM to provide logon and object security.

N: Brainshare: Annual technical conference sponsored by Novell.

M: TechEd: Annual technical conference sponsored by Microsoft.

N: C2 Security: Novell NetWare 4.01 was designed to this U.S. Department of Defense security specification, whereas versions 2.X to 3.X were not.

M: C2 Security: Windows NT Workstation and Windows NT Server were designed to meet these security requirements.

D: Close match.

N: Capture: Redirects workstation print output to a network print queue or file.

M: Net use lpt$N$: User command to redirect print output from local printer port to a network print queue.

D: Capture allows setting of numerous parameters.

N: Certified NetWare Engineer (CNE): An individual who has demonstrated competency to install and support Novell products by passing a series of standard tests.

M: Microsoft Certified Systems Engineer (MCSE): An individual who has demonstrated competency to install and support Microsoft systems and workgroup products by passing a series of standard tests.

D: Microsoft also has the category Certified Product Specialist, which is focused on supporting applications (including MS Mail).

N: Certified NetWare Instructor (CNI): A trainer authorized by Novell to deliver courses via an authorized training center. Intensive training and testing as well as periodic update training are required to achieve and maintain this status.

D: Microsoft Certified Trainer: A trainer authorized by Microsoft to deliver courses via an Authorized Technical Education Center. Intensive training and testing as well as periodic update training are required to achieve and maintain this status.

N: Directory Services, NetWare (NDS): Distributed, replicated NetWare 4.x database with names and access information for almost every object on the network.

M: Enterprise-wide Domains: Windows NT Authentication system that provides single logon to entire enterprise. Users are able to browse for resources distributed throughout the network.

D: NDS uses a hierarchical model. Domains can be set up in hierarchical, peer, or mixed configurations.

N: Endcap: Returns print output to local port (stops redirection)
M: Net use lptN: /d: Returns print output to local port.
D: None.

N: Enterprise Certified NetWare Engineer (ECNE): A CNE who has additional experience, course work, and testing in a broader range of NetWare products focusing on enterprisewide connectivity.

M: No directly comparable Microsoft certification category. N/A.

D: There are course offerings and tests in Microsoft enterprise technologies, but there is not currently a classification for having taken and passed these courses.

N: Fake Root: A server's directory, not necessarily its root, which appears to a workstation user as the root of a local drive. Often used in conjunction with **Search Drives**.

M: Redirected drive or a **Network Use:** A server directory that appears to the workstation user as the root of a drive. Can be added to the PATH environment variable.

D: All local drives redirected to MS servers appear as fake roots.

N: Global Message Handling Service (MHS): Messaging architecture consisting of server software, gateway software, and the **Standard Messaging Format (SMF) API**. Many ISVs have written e-mail, scheduling, and workflow applications that utilize MHS for message handling.

M: Microsoft Enterprise Messaging: Currently, a set of user mail programs, gateways, and published APIs that can all access the standard MS Mail Server database structure. Products are evolving to a client/server architecture.

D: Microsoft's focus is currently on the client software and gateways. ISVs are being encouraged to write mail server applications. Integration of mail with Windows applications is very strong. Novell's focus is on the server software and gateways. Most sites use third-party client mail software.

N: Hot Fix: When the **Read-after-Write** function identifies defective areas of a server's disk, the system lists them in a table so they will not be used in the future. Data is then written to a location known as a **Hot Fix Redirection Area.**

M: Sparing bad disk sectors: When a disk is formatted, bad sectors are spared from service. If a sector subsequently fails and Windows NT fault tolerance services are configured, the bad sector will be spared at either the device or file system level. If sparing occurs at the device level, a good copy of data will be written to a different location on the disk that experienced the failure.

D: Both provide similar results.

N: Independent Manufacturer Support Program: NetWare program that allows hardware vendors to test NetWare products on their various hardware configurations for compatibility. Any hardware configuration that successfully meets the test criteria is listed in Novell's technical bulletins and compatibility database.

M: Hardware Compatibility List: In cooperation with its IHVs, Microsoft makes a major effort to test new networking products on various hardware platforms. Hardware vendors must test each product vigorously and must be approved before they appear on the compatibility list.

D: Close match.

N: Internal Routing: An NLM that provides routing capability on a NetWare 3.1x or greater file server. NetWare internal routers can route IPX, IP, and AppleTalk. Includes **Routing Information Protocol (RIP)** for both IPX and IP.

M: TCP/IP routing: Basic IP routing using static routes. RIP is not supported.

D: Third parties have announced plans to develop router software to run on the Windows NT operating system.

N: IP 1.1, NetWare: Product family enabling NetWare servers and clients to communicate over a TCP/IP stack instead of IPX.

M: TCP/IP for DOS, Windows, and Windows NT: IP protocol suite delivered with all MS Networking products. Enables servers and clients to communicate over an IP Stack.

D: NetWare IP is a recent addition to Novell and is provided as an add-on purchase. Microsoft includes TCP/IP with its network operating systems.

N: IP Tunneling: Encapsulation of IPX/SPX packets within UDP/IP for transport across existing IP network enabling connection with remote NetWare Servers.

M: N/A (Windows NT and LAN Manager support TCP/IP natively): Windows NT does not provide encapsulation of traffic within IP packets.

D: See **NetWare IP**.

N: IPX Internetwork Packet Exchange: Network layer protocol providing transportation of data between computers on a Novell network. IPX is a very fast and small connectionless datagram protocol. Often run in conjunction with **SPX.**

M: NWLink: Microsoft's **NDIS**-compliant version of IPX/SPX supplied by Microsoft, included with Windows NT and Windows NT Advanced Server.

D: Interoperable.

N: LAN WorkPlace: A software product family for MS-DOS, Windows, OS/2, and Macintosh clients enabling participation in a TCP/IP environment. Included are various levels of terminal emulation and file transfer capabilities depending on client version.

M: Microsoft TCP/IP: A software product family for MS-DOS, Windows, OS/2, and Windows NT-based clients and servers enabling participation in a TCP/IP environment. Terminal emulation and file transfer are included with Windows NT, and are available separately for the others.

D: Differences are primarily in product bundling and pricing. Microsoft TCP/IP protocols are included with the entire family of Windows operating systems.

N: Lastdrive: Drive letters above this CONFIG.SYS parameter are used for network connections. The drive letter immediately following is automatically mapped to the login directory of a server to provide access to the user login program.

M: Lastdrive: Indicates highest drive letter that can be redirected to a network share.

D: NetWare network drives are typically mapped after LASTDRIVE, whereas Microsoft network drives must be connected to letters preceding LASTDRIVE. NetWare can map drive letters preceding LASTDRIVE to network directories.

N: Managers and Operators: Users with additional rights so as to be able to assist with the operation and maintenance of various network systems such as printers or user accounts. Categories are Workgroup Manager

User Account Manager

Print Server Operator

Print Queue Operator

File Server Console Operator

M: Operator Groups: Users who are members of special groups that enable them to assist with the operation and maintenance of various network systems such as printers or user accounts. Groups are

Account Operators

Backup Operators

Print Operators

Server Operators

D: Similar functionality.

N: Map: Command used to connect to a directory on a server.

M: Net use: Command used to connect to a shared directory on a server.

D: See **Share name** below. The **Net** command has numerous options in addition to the **USE** switch. The **Net use** command is equivalent to **Map Root**. **Map** provides an option, **Search**, which has the effect of adding the mapped drive to the path.

N: MHS Remote: NetWare Remote MHS provides a remote messaging architecture fully compatible with network MHS. Functions via asynchronous modems and network cards.

M: Microsoft Mail Remote: Microsoft Remote Mail provides DOS and Windows users with e-mail and mail-enabled functions through asynchronous modems. All MAPI functions are available to Mail Remote users.

D: Microsoft does not currently support the Schedule+ API (SAPI) over Remote Mail connections.

N: MHS: Gateways: SNADS, SMTP, X.400: SNADS, SMTP, and X.400 NLM-based gateways for the Global MHS messaging system. Each product allows for messages to be sent to systems of their respective formats.

M: MS Mail Gateway(s) to X.400, SNADS, SMTP: Additional add-ons to Microsoft Mail that allow MS Mail clients to communicate with different common mail formats.

D: Close match.

N: MONITOR: NetWare console monitor utility. Tracks and displays numerous server performance statistics and configuration parameters in text form.

M: Performance Monitor: Windows NT utility program that tracks and displays numerous performance statistics in both graphical and textual form.

D: MONITOR gives protocol statistics, memory allocation, up-time statistics, and more. Performance Monitor supports alarms, multiple parameters, and even multiple servers simultaneously.

N: NetBIOS (for NetWare): Network interface layer required by some client programs written to the IBM NetBIOS interface specification. This layer runs "on top" of **IPX/SPX** and is not required for file and print services.

M: NetBEUI (NetBIOS Extended User Interface) and NBT (NetBIOS over TCP/IP): NetBIOS interface either built into the protocol stack as is the case with NetBEUI or as an add-on software module, NBT.

D: NetBIOS is currently an integral piece of the Microsoft Network Architecture. File and Print Services rely on NetBIOS support. NetBIOS support is built right in to the NetBEUI protocol. In NetWare, NetBIOS is used only for supporting third-party applications that require it.

N: NetWare 2.x, 3.12, 4.01, and 4.01 for OS/2: Novell's family of **network operating systems (NOS**s). These products allow users to share files and printing resources. Most Novell add-on products are built to enhance the basic file and print services that NetWare NOS products provide.

M: Microsoft Windows for Workgroups 3.11, Microsoft LAN Manager 2.2B, Microsoft Windows NT Workstation, and Microsoft Windows NT Server: Microsoft's family of network operating systems. These products allow users to share files and printing resources. All the Microsoft network operating systems are designed for compatibility with previous operating system versions.

D: With the exception of LAN Manager, Microsoft's NOSs are both operating systems and network operating systems. Each also can provide peer services. All client and server applications run in *user space* and can communicate via network interprocess communication (IPC) protocols. NetWare 3.x and above support server-based programs called *NLMs* that run in *kernel space*, which imposes some additional problems and constraints in exchange for high performance.

N: NetWare Admin: Formerly *Supervisor*, Admin is the user account with complete access to all file and printer devices. Also the Admin account is used to administer a NetWare network including defining users, security, logon scripts, and access control.

M: Administrator: Administrator is the Windows NT user account (Admin in LAN Manager) with complete access to all file and printer devices. The Administrator account is also used to administer the network, including defining users, security, logon scripts, and access control permissions.

D: Both accounts perform the same basic functions. In both cases, additional groups can be created with access equivalent to the Admin account.

N: NetWare Asynchronous Communication Services (NACS) and NetWare Access Server (NAS): A combination of hardware and software components that enable users to access and share modem pools, minicomputer ports, and X.25 services for both dial-in network access and dial-out asynchronous communications.

M: Remote Access Service (RAS): Windows NT Advanced Server RAS allows up to 256 dial-up users to access Windows NT networks via modem pools, X.25, or Integrated Services Digital Network (ISDN) lines. After they are connected, users have access to the same resources as if they were directly connected to the network.

D: RAS supports 32 more connections. No Integrated Services Digital Network (ISDN) services have been incorporated into the NACS product. Unlike NACS, RAS does not support dial-out asynchronous communications, nor are Macintosh clients supported for dial-in access.

N: NetWare Btrieve: Server-based record management system. Provides high-performance, secure data management functions. Has two components: the Server Manager and the Btrieve requester.

M: Btrieve: Btrieve has been tested successfully as a third-party add-on product for Microsoft networks. Applications written to Btrieve specifications provide high-performance, secure data management functions.

D: Btrieve is not yet available for Windows NT Workstation and NT Server.

N: NetWare Core Protocol (NCP): Structured rules defining how workstations request services from the server and how servers interpret and respond to those requests. Requests are typically for file, print, or account manipulation.

M: Server Message Blocks (SMB): Structured rules defining how workstations request services from the server and how servers interpret and respond to those requests. Requests are typically for file, print, or account manipulation.

D: SMB protocol is written to use the NetBIOS interface, whereas NCP writes directly to protocol-based sockets.

N: NetWare Directory Services (NDS): Provides an integrated view of your entire network, provides a single login and password for users and administrators, and gives a single graphical interface for your administrative tasks.

M: Trusted Domains: Provides single login for users and centralized management.

N: NetWare Distributed Management Services (NDMS): A suite of integrated products giving the flexibility to customize a network and system management solution. It is designed to cut the costs and complexity of managing multivendor networks.

M: Systems Management Server (SMS): SMS includes desktop inventory management.

N: NetWare for Macintosh: File, print, and routing services that provide services to Apple Macintosh computers.

M: Services for Macintosh: Provides an AppleTalk network protocol stack and integrates LocalTalk-, EtherTalk-, or TokenTalk-equipped Macs into a Windows NT Server network. Mac clients are fully integrated with security and name services.

D: Services for the Macintosh is tightly integrated with the Windows NT Server domain security, so any server can authenticate a Mac client.

N: NetWare for SNA: A set of NLMs that allow a NetWare 3.x server to become a gateway to SNA-based networks.

M: SNA Server: A 32-bit NT-based gateway application that allows any TCP/IP-, IPX-, or NetBEUI-based network to connect to SNA-based networks.

D: SNA Server can service NetWare clients as well as MS network clients.

N: NetWare for UNIX: Provides NetWare services on general-purpose operating systems. NetWare for UNIX can run multiuser applications and simultaneously function as a NetWare server. It allows users to extend access from their business-critical applications running on UNIX.

M: LAN Manager for UNIX (LMU): An implementation of Microsoft Windows networking for servers that run UNIX variants. LMU allows Microsoft clients to access data stored on UNIX hosts. LMU is based on SMB, a set of protocols developed by Microsoft that are now an X/Open standard. It allows users to extend access from their business-critical applications running on UNIX.

D: Close match.

N: NetWare Global MHS: Set of NLMs provides robust store-and-forward capabilities which support e-mail, calendar and scheduling, and fax services. This e-mail platform supports a multitude of gateway formats such as X.400 and MHS.

M: Messaging API (MAPI); Microsoft Mail for PC networks: Robust store-and-forward e-mail messaging system. Supports e-mail, calendaring, fax, and a multitude of gateways including X.400, MHS, MCI, Internet, PROFS, SNADS, and more. Developers can utilize MAPI to message-enable applications.

D: Microsoft bundles a complete e-mail client and workgroup server with the Windows family, MHS requires third-party mail to run on top of MHS. Global MHS includes an MS Mail driver to allow MS Mail to run on top of Global MHS.

N: NetWare Licensing Services (NetWare LS): Allows independent software vendors to build licensing and metering features into their applications, and enables administrators to monitor the usage statistics of all the applications of the network to better choose from different licensing options.

M: Systems Management Server (SMS): Allows you to monitor all the versions running the desktops and servers.

N: NetWare Lite for DOS and Windows: Simple, inexpensive peer-to-peer network operating system allowing as few as two PCs to share information, applications, and other PC resources. Designed for small workgroups, it is completely compatible with MS Windows 3.0 and 3.1.

M: Microsoft Windows for Work groups 3.11: Easy-to-use peer-to-peer network operating system allowing as few as two PCs to share information, applications, and other PC resources including fax boards and printers. Fully compatible with the rest of the MS networking operating system family.

D: MS Windows for Workgroups has built-in fax support and is compatible with NetWare, whereas NetWare Lite does not interoperate with NetWare 2.2, 3.1x, or 4.x.

N: NetWare Loadable Module (NLM): A server-based software module that can be dynamically loaded on or unloaded from the server without having to restart the server.

M: Application: Not a direct equivalent. All Windows NT-based server applications are written to one of several common APIs, including **DOS, Win16, Win32, OS/2,** or **POSIX.** These server applications can also be written to communicate with network client applications via an assortment of network IPC APIs.

D: Applications for Windows NT run in protected subsystems in user space and do not have to be specially written for the operating system

(**OS**). By nature, they are dynamically loaded and unloaded. **NLM**s must be specially designed and compiled so that they can run in kernel space.

N: NetWare Management Agent (NMA): Runs on NetWare 3.1x and NetWare 4.x. Acts as a universal interface between NetWare Services Manager and the managed resources of a NetWare 3.1X server. Its two primary functions are to allow server resources to register as manageable objects and to provide a set of functions to support the management and monitoring of objects.

M: Remote Administration: Microsoft incorporates Remote Administration into Windows NT Server. This feature allows the administering of remote servers by selecting the server in that domain. After users establish Admin privileges on that domain, they can manage any server located on that domain. Also see **Domains.**

D: NMA is an add-on product for NetWare, whereas Microsoft incorporates remote administration into its network operating system.

N: NetWare Name Services: When added to a NetWare network, this service enables users to access resources on multiple servers with a single login. For network Admins, it simplifies the task of maintaining consistent user environments.

M: Domains: Domains are incorporated into the Microsoft LAN operating system products. They allow users to access resources on multiple servers with a single login. For Administrators, they simplify the task of maintaining consistent user environments.

D: NetWare Name Services is an additional add-on, whereas Domains have been incorporated into Microsoft networks since LAN Manager. Windows NT Advanced Server extends this concept with *Trusted Domains* to allow single-login access into a multidomain environment.

N: NetWare NFS: Transparently integrates UNIX systems with NetWare. UNIX users can use NetWare NFS to share files and print to NetWare and UNIX printers using the Line Printer Daemon (LPD) print service.

M: NFS: Available as a third-party add-on, runs on top of Microsoft Windows NT TCP/IP.

D: N/A.

N: NetWare Support Encyclopedia (NSE): Technical CD containing solutions to problems, bug fixes, and technical bulletins. Updated and released 12 times per year.

M: Microsoft TechNet CD: Technical CD containing solutions to problems, bug fixes, and technical bulletins. Updated and distributed 12 times per year.

D: Close match.

N: NetWare Users' Conference (NETUCON): NetWare user conference designed to keep NetWare customers abreast of current and new products, also to provide demonstrations of products by giving hands-on examples.

M: Microsoft Network Users Group: Microsoft Network User Group designed to keep Microsoft customers abreast of current and new products, also to provide demonstrations of products by giving hands-on examples of future and current software and networking applications.

D: Close match.

N: NetWare Users International (NUI): Independent NetWare charter that directs its membership to promote the exchange of information among users of NetWare-related products worldwide.

M: None.

N: Novell Authorized Education Center: Educational partners with Novell that provide the channel through which Novell leverages its training expertise.

M: Microsoft Authorized Technical Education Center: Microsoft partners that have been authorized and certified by Microsoft to provide Microsoft-developed training courses on Microsoft systems products.

D: Close match.

N: Novell Authorized Reseller Program: Authorized, Gold, Platinum and UNIX Master levels: An organization that meets the sales and technical staff requirements to sell and support NetWare networking products. Based on the quantity of technical staffing, organizations receive a Gold or Platinum status. UNIX Master is given to a company or organization that has met the UNIX requirements. Novell provides sales leads to organizations that are under this program.

M: Microsoft Solution Providers: Partner and Member levels: An organization that meets more stringent sales and technical staff requirements than plain resellers, these organizations are usually developers, VARs, or system integrators with the skills needed to build complex solutions involving Microsoft system products.

D: Microsoft's program is focused more at value-added services, whereas Novell's is focused more at software sales.

N: Novell Authorized Service Center (NASC): Company or organization that has met the staffing criteria, including CNE and ECNE certification. NASCs will be given leads directly form Novell. Novell does not have a direct service center within its corporate structure.

M: Microsoft Authorized Support Center

N: Novell Consulting Services (NCS): Systems and software consultants are available on a contract basis to help meet specific design needs. These services are available in the United States and, with some limitations, worldwide.

M: Microsoft Consulting Services (MCS): Consultants are Microsoft system architects with experience and expertise in Microsoft technology, methodologies, and tools; they are designated to help organizations through complex and strategic problems. In conjunction with third-party vendors (Solution Providers), Microsoft offers customers a number of services customized to their unique environments.

D: Microsoft extends its consulting service by leveraging the skills of its Solution Provider channel.

N: ODI (Open Data-Link Interface): Specification defining how network protocol drivers and adapters communicate. Permits multiple protocols to share single or multiple **NICs**. Software layer between NIC and higher-level protocols is known as the Link Support Layer (**LSL**).

M: NDIS Network Driver Interface Specification: Specification defining how network protocol drivers and adapters communicate. Permits multiple protocols to share single or multiple **NICs**. Network Adapter drivers are known as Media Access Control (**MAC**) drivers. Software layer between NIC and higher-level protocols is known as the Protocol Manager.

D: MS has developed protected mode versions of NetBEUI, IPX/SPX, and TCP/IP for Windows for Workgroups 3.11 that reduce DOS memory consumption. All ODI drivers run in real mode.

N: PCONSOLE: Creates, assigns, modifies, deletes, and monitors print queues, print servers, and printers. Sends, modifies, pauses, resumes, and deletes print jobs. Quickly installs basic print services.

M: Print Manager: Windows NT program that provides both configuration, monitoring, and management of printers and print queues.

D: Close match.

N: Personal NetWare: Peer-to-peer network operating system enabling users to share their directories, printers, and CD-ROMs. Uses **ODI** drivers and **Virtual Loadable Modules** (**VLMs**). Supports Windows 3.1.

M: Windows for Workgroups and Windows for Workgroup MS-DOS Add-on: Peer-to-peer network operating system enabling users to share directories, printers, and CD-ROMs. Uses either **NDIS** drivers, **ODI** drivers, or a combination of both.

D: Security models are different. Personal NetWare servers use a scaled-back user-level security scheme in which access is controlled on a directory basis. Windows for Workgroups uses share-level security. Windows for Workgroups integrates well with NetWare environments. It supports simultaneous connection to both NetWare and Microsoft servers. Personal NetWare does not integrate into a Microsoft network.

N: Pserver: Print Server. Both an **NLM** running on 3.x and 4.x servers and an executable (*.EXE) running on a dedicated DOS workstation.

M: Print Manager: Print Manager incorporates utilities necessary for creating queues, defining printers, and establishing their association.

D: NetWare requires PCONSOLE, SPOOL, PSC, PRINTDEF, and PRINTCON to complete setup of printing environment, whereas Windows NT requires only Print Manager. Pserver supports servicing queues from multiple servers.

N: RCONSOLE: Remote Console utility used to manage NetWare servers from NetWare clients. Administrators can load and unload modules, execute all console commands, and copy files to the file server's NetWare directories or DOS partition.

M: No direct equivalent: User Manager for Domains, Server Manager for Domains, and Print Manager all provide portions of the capability to remotely manage Windows NT Workstations and Windows NT Servers. However, some configuration functions must be executed on the console of the server in question.

D: RCONSOLE remotely executes commands on the server, whereas the Windows NT management utilities use interprocess communications.

N: Requestor: DOS, OS/2, and NT: ODI and monolithic requestors for MS-DOS and Windows, OS/2, and Windows NT run on client PCs and allow each client to connect to NetWare file servers across a network.

M: Client redirectors: NDIS-based client redirectors are available for MS-DOS, Windows, Windows for Workgroups 3.11, MS OS/2 1.3, IBM OS/2 2.1, Windows NT Workstation, and Windows NT Server. Allows each client to connect to Microsoft file servers across a network.

D: The Microsoft redirectors can also be configured to allow connectivity to both NetWare and Microsoft servers.

N: Rights Security: The combination of **trustee** assignments and **inherited rights mask**. The intersection of these two access control mechanisms determine the actual access rights, known as **effective rights**, a user or group has to a particular directory or file. The eight settings are

Supervisory

Read

Write

Create

Erase

Modify

File Scan

Access Control

The effect of these settings depends on whether they are applied to a directory or a file.

M: File/Directory Security: Applies to files and directories on NTFS partitions only (FAT, HPFS, and also NTFS partitions can be protected against network access using Share Security). The eight settings are

Read

Write

Execute

Delete

Change Permissions

Take Ownership

Full Control (All)

No Access

The effect of these settings depend on whether they are applied to a directory or a file.

D: In Windows NTFS security, "No Access" overrides all other permissions. All files and directories have an owner, which initially (by default) is the creator. Owners have complete control over their files and directories, and even Administrators cannot access restricted files or directories unless they first take ownership. In the Windows NT security model, ownership can only be taken, not given.

N: Search Drive: Search drives are equivalent to the DOS PATH command. Specifies which server directories a program will search to execute an application.

M: PATH: The PATH environment variable specifies which directories a program will search to execute an application; can include both local and network drives.

D: Close match.

N: Sequenced Packet Exchange (SPX): A Novell communication protocol that monitors network transmission to ensure successful delivery. SPX is derived from Novell's IPX using the Xerox Sequenced Packet Protocol. SPX enhances the IPX protocol by supervising the data sent out across the network.

M: NWLink: Microsoft's **NDIS**-compliant version of IPX/SPX supplied by Microsoft, included with Windows NT workstation and Windows NT Server.

D: Interoperable over a network.

N: Service Advertising Protocol: A protocol service providing nodes such as file servers, print servers, and gateway servers to advertise services and addresses. Clients use SAP to determine what network resources are available.

M: Browser Service: Service that broadcasts shared files, directories, and printers categorized first by domain/workgroup and then by server name.

D: Because Microsoft network usually includes peer services, the browser is not dependent on a central server. One of the peers on the network will always take over the Browser service if an existing browser server is shut down.

N: SQL Server for NetWare, Sybase: SQL-based relational database designed for distributed networked environments. Supports TCP/IP and SPX/IPX protocols. Allows interoperability with all platforms running Sybase.

M: Microsoft SQL Server 4.2 and SQL Server NT: SQL-based relational database designed for distributed networked environments. Supports TCP/IP, IPX/SPX, and NetBEUI protocols. Allows interoperability with all platforms running Sybase.

D: NetWare servers usually are single-purpose database servers because of their NLM architecture. Because an RDBMS looks just like any other application to the operating system, Microsoft servers can provide file and print services, run multiple applications at once, and still be stable.

N: Storage Management Services (SMS): Provides reliable backup/restore capabilities for enhanced data and storage solutions for all versions of NetWare.

M: Backup is part of Windows NT Server.

N: Supervisor: Highest level of server authority. Automatically created when server is installed. Cannot be deleted.

M: Administrator: Highest level of server authority. Automatically created when server is installed. Cannot be deleted.

D: "Supervisor" has total access to all files and directories. "Administrator" does not automatically have rights to files created by users but can obtain rights by first taking ownership and then granting itself desired rights.

N: Supervisor /Admin.: "Supervisor and Admin" for NetWare 4.01 is the user account with complete access to all file and printer devices. This account is also used to administer the NetWare network, including defining users, security, logon scripts, and access control rights.

M: Admin/Administrator: "Administrator" is the user account with complete access to all file and printer devices. The Administrator account is also used to administer a Microsoft network including defining users, security, logon scripts, and access control permissions.

D: Close match.

N: Supervisor Equivalence: Account property that makes users have same resource rights and authority as Supervisor.

M: Administrators Group Membership: Members of the local group "Administrators" have same the rights and authority as Administrator.

D: Close match.

N: SYSCON: Administrative utility for managing user accounts, groups, and auditing. DOS-based menu-driven format. SYSCON also manages accounting features of NetWare.

M: User Manager for Domains: Windows NT Advanced Server graphical administrative utility for managing user accounts, groups, and security policies.

D: User Manager for Domains also sets up **Domain Trust** relationships that enable access to a multidomain environment with a single logon. Microsoft networks do not include usage accounting functions.

N: System Fault Tolerance (SFT): Duplicating data on multiple storage devices so that if one storage device fails, the data is available from another device. Various options are available, with the highest level called SFT III. (Complete server duplexing.)

M: Fault Tolerance: Windows NT Advanced Server and LAN Manager both support disk mirroring, disk duplexing, and disk striping with parity.

D: Microsoft has no equivalent to SFT III. Microsoft bundles fault tolerance with Windows NT Advanced Server and LAN Manager, whereas Novell packages and charges for SFT as a separate product.

N: Trustee rights: A user or group's access permission assignments for directories and files. A user with rights to a specific directory or file is said to be a trustee of that resource.

M: File Security: One of two methods of controlling user rights to directories and files.

D: Requires the Windows NT File System (**NTFS**). Users can be assigned rights on a per directory or per file basis. Share Permissions is the other method and can work in conjunction with Windows NT File Security (See **Share Security**). The network **SUPERVISOR** has all rights to all directories and files. This is also the case for the LAN Manager account **Admin**. In Windows NT, the account ADMINISTRATORs can be denied access to resources but can regain access by taking ownership and then granting themselves desired access rights. The ADMINISTRATORs cannot return ownership to the original owner. This serves as an audit trail for the original owner.

N: UnixWare: Provides NetWare services on top of a System V Release 4 UNIX operating system. UnixWare can run multiuser applications and simultaneously function as a NetWare server.

M: LAN Manager for UNIX (LMU): An OEM implementation of LAN Manager for servers that run UNIX variants. LMU allows Microsoft clients to access data stored on UNIX hosts. LMU is based on SMB, a set of protocols developed by Microsoft that are now an X/Open standard.

D: Close match. Windows NT Advanced Server provides much of the same capabilities and characteristics as UnixWare, and can support POSIX applications.

N: Value Added Process (VAP): VAPS are implemented in the NetWare 2.x product line. They are enhancements to the basic operating system. VAPS can be loaded and unloaded as needed. One VAP that ships with NetWare 2.x is the print server.

M: Services: Services are additional utilities that enhance the functionality of Microsoft file servers. These additional services can be started or stopped. An example of a Microsoft service is the Browser service.

D: All Microsoft services run in protected user space just like an application.

N: Virtual Loadable Modules (VLMs): Net Requestor architecture used by NetWare 4.01 DOS clients and required to connect to 4.01 servers. Allows all network components to be linked into virtual memory, thus freeing up low memory for applications. VLMs may be used to access NetWare 2.x and 3.x servers as well.

M: Virtual Device Drivers: Network Drivers designed to run in virtual mode (also known as a *VxD*). They allow network drivers and protocols which communicate through the Windows interface to be linked in to virtual memory. VLMs are not designed specifically for Windows. They allow DOS drivers to be linked into virtual memory and can be used for DOS-only network applications.

D: The VxD is a virtual driver architecture for Windows that can be used for other types of drivers besides network drivers. To upgrade from NetWare 3.x to 4.01, the older clients must be replaced with 4.01 client utilizing VLMs. All MS NOSs are backward compatible with older client redirectors.

N: Volume: The "root" of the NetWare server directory structure. A Volume refers to a physical amount of disk space that can be part or all of a non-DOS partition on the server. Multiple Volumes can be on a single disk. Volumes can span multiple disks.

M: Partition: The "root" of the MS server directory structure. A physical amount of disk space. Can be part or all of a server's disk. Multiple partitions can be on a single disk.

D: Users mapped to directories within a NetWare Volume can walk back up the tree to the root of the volume itself. The root of an MS partition is accessible over the network only if the root directory is shared and the user connects directly to it.

N: Volume-Disk Restrictions: Limit to amount of disk space user can have on a specific Volume.

M: User Storage Limit: In LAN Manager, an upper limit for space used by a home directory can be specified. In Windows NT, no such setting exists.

D: The limit in NetWare produces the same effect as running out of space on a local drive does. On LAN Manager, the limit issues an alert message but does not prevent the user from consuming more space.

Microsoft Terms with No Direct Novell Equivalent

M: Event Viewer: A Windows NT graphical utility that logs and displays all important system, security, and application events.

D: Users can view event logs on any other Windows NT-based server on the network if they have permission.

M: Local Logon: Ability to log on at the server itself and run programs. Windows NT permissions control who has LOCAL LOGON authority. NT Security is still enforced for files located in NTFS formatted partitions.

D: The NetWare server can run on top of UNIX and OS/2 2.x, but in these cases access to the overall system is controlled by the host OS, not the Novell OS. On an Intel and DOS-based dedicated NetWare server, the user does not log on at the server.

M: Registry: Windows NT hierarchical database of configuration parameters for the entire operating system and 32-bit applications.

D: Because Windows NT is a multiuser OS, the Registry also stores individual settings and parameters for each user.

M: Share name: Directories on servers must first be shared prior to users connecting to them over the network. Nonshared directories can still be accessed if they are subdirectories of an already-shared directory.

D: This is an essential security function on a peer network.

M: Share security: A simple, easy-to-use security scheme for Windows for Workgroups or for enterprise resources with uniform access rights requirements. Access rights are associated with the Share name and password pair used to connect to the directory. Rights are uniform down through the directory tree within the Share. Share security controls access only over a network connection. It does not apply to a user logged on locally.

M: SMPSymmetrical Multi-Processor: Windows NT supports for two or more processors in a single server. Load (threads) is automatically balanced between processors.

D: No Novell equivalent, although Novell has announced that it intends to support Asymmetric Multi Processing in a future release of NetWare.

NetWare Terms Without Microsoft Equivalents

N: FleX/IP: Designed for environments in which NetWare, UNIX, and TCP/IP systems need to communicate. It provides a cost-effective way for UNIX and NetWare users to share printers and files (via **ftp**), regardless of their native computing environments. Also enables UNIX network supervisors to manage NetWare servers from the X Windows environment.

N: Transaction Tracking System: Protects database applications from corruption by backing out incomplete transactions that result from a failure in a network component. In NetWare, it also protects the Bindery and the queuing database file from corruption.

N: NetWare Link State Protocol (NLSP): A Novell routing protocol that tracks the status of other routers and links. This protocol adapts more quickly to network topology changes than do distance-vector protocols.

N: Storage Management Systems: Resides on a NetWare server and provides a reliable and efficient method of creating backup and restore applications for NetWare servers. Additionally, backup and restore operations can be created to specifically meet customer expectations.

N: OracleWare: NLM-based Oracle 7 RDBMS built specifically for NetWare 3.1x and 4.x environments.

D: Oracle has announced a version of Oracle 7 compatible with Windows NT to ship in 1994.

N: Packet Burst Protocol: Burst mode is designed to transmit multipacket messages efficiently over a network, which can result in faster data transmission between workstations and servers. Is enabled by loading the PBURST.NLM.

N: Network Navigator Electronic Software Distribution: Makes the process of installing or updating software, including new applications, data, client operating systems, and network operation systems, completely transparent to users. Uses the MS Windows GUI interface.

N: NetWare UNIX Client (NUC): Software that allows a UnixWare system to behave as a client to NetWare servers.

N: NetWare FTAM from Firefox: Permits a wide variety of OSI FTAM clients to access the NetWare file systems and enables DOS workstation users to attach to OSI networks and communicate with FTAM host on the network. Is fully compliant with the U.S. Government OSI Protocols (GOSIP).

Appendix B

A Brief Description of the NT Deployment document

The Microsoft Windows NT Server Deployment Guide: NetWare Integration document has graciously been provided for you from both Microsoft Corporation and Valinor Inc. Like this book, the purpose of the guide is to provide you with detailed information regarding the integration and migration of NetWare and Windows NT. You will find the complete document contained on the CD-ROM included with this book.

The following is a Table of Contents for the Windows NT Server Deployment Guide:

PHASE 1. INTRODUCTION
Project Overview
  Mission Statement
  Define Prioritized Project Goals
  Create Business Plan
  Identify Project Team Players
  Identify the Subteam Members
  Milestone I: Review Preparation and Approve Planning Phase

PHASE 2. DEFINE THE PROJECT
  Review of Current Environment
  Define Project Objectives
  Define Project Standards
  Milestone II: Review Project Definition and Approve
  Planning Phase

PHASE 3. EVALUATION AND PRELIMINARY TESTING
  Overview
  Network Plan
  Design Process
  Update the Business Plan
  Installation Plan
  Training Plan

This excellent document was prepared by Valinor Inc., and is a must read for anyone preparing a migration from NetWare to Windows NT. The full document is available on the CD-ROM disk with permission from Valinor Inc., and Microsoft Corporation. Valinor Inc. is a national, full-service, privately-owned system integrator. They can be reached at 603-688-1776 or at their Web site at `http://www.valinor.com`.

Appendix C

Hello and welcome to the NetWare to Windows NT: Integration and Migration CD-ROM disk. We hope you find many of the utilities and documents on this CD of great value in your quest to achieve a unified, integrated network platform; I know we did.

The following is a list of the directory contents you will find herein. Please note that while the documents can be easily read from the CD-ROM disk directly, some of the utilities will need to be copied from the CD-ROM disk to your server or workstation before they can be run. However, any of the client drivers present can be installed directly from the CD-ROM disk itself.

Good luck and good information hunting!

Wayne McKinnon and Arnold Villeneuve

Directory/Contents

ROOT of CD-ROM DISK: Several batch files are placed on the Root of the CD-ROM disk to assist the starting of Banalyzer, which is a Protocol Reference Database working demo with detailed information on over 100 networking related communication protocols.

!BANAL: Banalyzer is a Protocol Reference Database working demo with detailed information on over 100 networking related communication protocols. It also contains a complete glossary of terms and definitions. Additionally, there is a lot of helpful troubleshooting tips and recommendations to assist you in building a more solid network.

NTDEPLOY: This directory contains an excellent document on deploying NT throughout your organization with some particular emphasis on migrating your NetWare servers. The files contained herein are the electronic version of the ones printed in the Appendix.

SAMBA: This directory contains all the required files to turn your NetWare 4.1 server into a Server Message Block server. Doing so means that your Microsoft clients can communicate with the NetWare server without having to load the NetWare NCP client software. Great tool to facilitate integration between the two platforms.

SMB: This directory contains one of the best documents we have come across explaining exactly what Server Message Blocks are. This is a must read. Thanks to the author for his reprint permissions. Please check out his WEB page and providing him with some feedback as I am sure he would like to hear from you.

OSITEACH: While somewhat old, this OSI tutorial is an excellent introduction to the concepts the OSI model pushes.

NETVISN: This directory contains live demonstrations of the NetVision product called Synchronicity. It is an excellent set of tools for integrating your NetWare NDS and Windows NT Domains user and group databases. There is also several documents regarding the User Manual and Troubleshooting of Synchronicity.

NWFAQ: A NetWare Frequently Asked Questions application. Run from within Windows.

NTFAQ: Although starting to get dated, this document is an excellent overview of a lot of the issues you may encounter installing and maintaining Windows NT. Much of the information is still very relevant.

NWDOCS: This directory contains several documents from Novell regarding NetWare and Windows NT integration.

NTDOCS: This directory contains several documents from Microsoft regarding Windows NT and NetWare integration.

RFC: This document contains a fairly complete set of Request For Comments documents available from the Internet (although a lot faster to lookup here).

WORDVIEW: This directory contains the Microsoft Wordview program which you can use to view many of the documents on this CD-ROM disk.

INDEX

D

X

ABOUT THE AUTHORS

Arnold Villeneuve assists current and aspiring "networkologists" in establishing their own technology consulting practices. He has developed the *Network Consulting Guide Handbook* which shows you how to build your own business with as few as ten clients. E-mail him for more information on this exciting opportunity.

FAX   (613) 830-9580

E-mail   **Infomen@Compuserve.com**

Web site   **http://www.Networkologist.com**

Infomentat Inc.
PO Box 62034
Convent Glen Mall, Orleans, ON
Canada K1C 7H8

Wayne McKinnon coaches managers who require a better understanding of technology. He regularly leads seminars and speaks to business owners about the effective use of technology.

FAX   (613) 825-4895

E-mail   HYPERLINK mail to: **Wayne@ITcoach.com**

Web site   **http://www.ITcoach.com**

ITcoach.com
23 Masonbrook Street
Nepean, ON
Canada K2J 4C5

CONTACTING US

Since NetWare has such a large installed base, and with Windows NT gaining in popularity, the need to integrate Windows NT and NetWare will continue for many years to come. Existing products to ease the migration or integration of the two operating systems will continue to evolve and perhaps new products will be developed.

We would be pleased to hear of any new products you may come across, challenges you have overcome, or suggestions for the next edition of this book.

SOFTWARE AND INFORMATION LICENSE

The software and information on this diskette (collectively referred to as the "Product") are the property of The McGraw-Hill Companies, Inc. ("McGraw-Hill") and are protected by both United States copyright law and international copyright treaty provision. You must treat this Product just like a book, except that you may copy it into a computer to be used and you may make archival copies of the Products for the sole purpose of backing up our software and protecting your investment from loss.

By saying "just like a book," McGraw-Hill means, for example, that the Product may be used by any number of people and may be freely moved from one computer location to another, so long as there is no possibility of the Product (or any part of the Product) being used at one location or on one computer while it is being used at another. Just a book cannot be read by two different people in two different places at the same time, neither can the Product be used by two different people in two different places at the same time (unless, of course, McGraw-Hill's rights are being violated).

McGraw-Hill reserves the right to alter or modify the contents of the Product at any time.

This agreement is effective until terminated. The Agreement will terminate automatically without notice if you fail to comply with any provisions of this Agreement. In the event of termination by reason of your breach, you will destroy or erase all copies of the Product installed on any computer system or made for backup purposes and shall expunge the Product from your data storage facilities.

LIMITED WARRANTY

McGraw-Hill warrants the physical diskette(s) enclosed herein to be free of defects in materials and workmanship for a period of sixty days from the purchase date. If McGraw-Hill receives written notification within the warranty period of defects in materials or workmanship, and such notification is determined by McGraw-Hill to be correct, McGraw-Hill will replace the defective diskette(s). Send request to:

Customer Service
McGraw-Hill
Gahanna Industrial Park
860 Taylor Station Road
Blacklick, OH 43004-9615

The entire and exclusive liability and remedy for breach of this Limited Warranty shall be limited to replacement of defective diskette(s) and shall not include or extend any claim for or right to cover any other damages, including but not limited to, loss of profit, data, or use of the software, or special, incidental, or consequential damages or other similar claims, even if McGraw-Hill has been specifically advised as to the possibility of such damages. In no event will McGraw-Hill's liability for any damages to you or any other person ever exceed the lower of suggested list price or actual price paid for the license to use the Product, regardless of any form of the claim.

THE McGRAW-HILL COMPANIES, INC. SPECIFICALLY DISCLAIMS ALL OTHER WARRANTIES, EXPRESS OR IMPLIED, INCLUDING BUT NOT LIMITED TO, ANY IMPLIED WARRANTY OF MERCHANTABILITY OR FITNESS FOR A PARTICULAR PURPOSE. Specifically, McGraw-Hill makes no representation or warranty that the Product is fit for any particular purpose and any implied warranty of merchantability is limited to the sixty day duration of the Limited Warranty covering the physical diskette(s) only (and not the software or information) and is otherwise expressly and specifically disclaimed.

This Limited Warranty gives you specific legal rights; you may have others which may vary from state to state. Some states do not allow the exclusion of incidental or consequential damages, or the limitation on how long an implied warranty lasts, so some of the above may not apply to you.

This Agreement constitutes the entire agreement between the parties relating to use of the Product. The terms of any purchase order shall have no effect on the terms of this Agreement. Failure of McGraw-Hill to insist at any time on strict compliance with this Agreement shall not constitute a waiver of any rights under this Agreement. This Agreement shall be construed and governed in accordance with the laws of New York. If any provision of this Agreement is held to be contrary to law, that provision will be enforced to the maximum extent permissible and the remaining provisions will remain in force and effect.